Innovative Business Practices

Innovative Business Practices:
Prevailing a Turbulent Era

Edited by

Demetris Vrontis and Alkis Thrassou

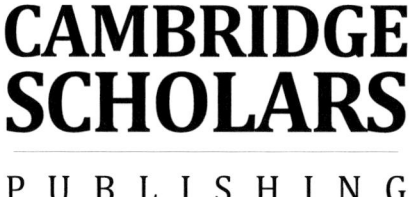

Innovative Business Practices: Prevailing a Turbulent Era,
Edited by Demetris Vrontis and Alkis Thrassou

This book first published 2013

Cambridge Scholars Publishing

12 Back Chapman Street, Newcastle upon Tyne, NE6 2XX, UK

British Library Cataloguing in Publication Data
A catalogue record for this book is available from the British Library

Copyright © 2013 by Demetris Vrontis and Alkis Thrassou and contributors

All rights for this book reserved. No part of this book may be reproduced, stored in a retrieval system, or transmitted, in any form or by any means, electronic, mechanical, photocopying, recording or otherwise, without the prior permission of the copyright owner.

ISBN (10): 1-4438-4604-X, ISBN (13): 978-1-4438-4604-2

TABLE OF CONTENTS

Chapter One 1
Knowledge Hybridization: An Innovative Business Practice to Overcome the Limits of the Top-Down Transfers within a Multinational Corporation
Hela Chebbi, Dorra Yahiaoui, Demetris Vrontis and Alkis Thrassou

Chapter Two 17
Rethinking Talent Management in Organizations:
Towards a Boundary-less Model
Carrie Foster, Neil Moore and Peter Stokes

Chapter Three 42
Solidarity as a "Commons" to be Promoted: Organisation of Collective Action for a More Responsible Management
Bernard Paranque

Chapter Four 65
Mindset and Behaviour Effect on Firm Performance
Stefano Bresciani, Demetris Vrontis and Alkis Thrassou

Chapter Five 87
Strategic Decision-Making during Uncertainty: Implications for SMEs
Constantinos Theodoridis and Constantinos V. Priporas

Chapter Six 112
A Redefinition of the Path of Indian Banking through Information Technology
Saroj Kumar Datta and Sukanya Kundu

Chapter Seven 143
Value-based Management for Small- and Medium-sized Enterprises:
Findings of an Empirical Study on its Diffusion and Obstacles
to its Implementation
Bernd Britzelmaier, Anastasia Paul and Carola Normann

Chapter Eight 168
Open Innovation System and New Forms of Investment:
Venture Capital's Role in Innovation
Matteo Rossi, Alkis Thrassou and Demetris Vrontis

Chapter Nine 195
Policy Strategies for Innovation in Switzerland
Ruth Rios-Morales, John C. Crotts and Max Schweizer

Chapter Ten 211
The Nature of Company Image Management and the Use
of Brand Personality in the Social Network Environment:
Shifts toward Consumer Control
Kip Becker and Helena Nobre

Chapter Eleven 232
Ethical Business Practice and CSR in Times of Economic Turbulence
Angelo Nicolaides

Chapter Twelve 263
A Conceptual Framework towards Succession Effectiveness in Family
Wineries: An Innovative Means for Wine Sector Development in Cyprus
Thoukis Georgiou and Demetris Vrontis

Chapter Thirteen 292
The Internationalization of Fashion Retail in Today's Modulating
Environment
Gabriella Mandara and Christopher M. Moore

Chapter Fourteen 317
Gender and Cultural Idiosyncrasies of Perceived Entrepreneurial
Personality Traits: An Empirical Study in Greece
Evangelos Tsoukatos

Chapter Fifteen 342
Mobile Marketing: A New Direct Marketing Promotional Channel
Monaliz Amirkhanpour and Demetris Vrontis

Chapter Sixteen 371
Global Sustainable Tourism Criteria: An International Perspective
on Restaurant Sustainability Model Development
Ian Jenkins and Robert S. Bristow

Contributors 392

CHAPTER ONE

KNOWLEDGE HYBRIDIZATION: AN INNOVATIVE BUSINESS PRACTICE TO OVERCOME THE LIMITS OF THE TOP-DOWN TRANSFERS WITHIN A MULTINATIONAL CORPORATION

HELA CHEBBI, DORRA YAHIAOUI, DEMETRIS VRONTIS AND ALKIS THRASSOU

Introduction

This chapter proposes a theoretical analysis framework to highlight the challenge of the knowledge transfer between headquarter and subsidiaries and how the intra-organisational hybridization could overcome the limits of the top-down transfer. By highlighting the added value of local subsidiaries, this chapter focuses on the features of the knowledge hybridization as a new managerial practice tendency. Two main questions will be answered: What are the limits of the top-down transfer in Multinational Corporations? And how could companies integrate the knowledge hybridization as an innovative practice to develop their activities? These multinational corporations require to be studied in isolation to other firms whose size, structure and style often allow for flexibilities and adaptive qualities impossible to be replicated or even imitated (Thrassou and Vrontis, 2008; Bresciani et al., 2012).

Due to the globalisation of economic activity and the resulting increase in foreign direct investment, a growing number of companies are managing entities in several foreign countries. In order to create synergy, develop the competitive advantage of the parent company, build a sense of community, or simply for the sake of convenience, multinational companies (MNCs) often transfer the management practices in operation within the parent company to foreign subsidiaries (Smith and Elger, 2000). Even if MNCs adopt a divided structure, "type M" or network, the same practices are generally applied. Therefore, these practices rooted in MNCs become real organizational routines and create sometimes difficulties within the foreign subsidiaries. The awareness therefore, of the challenges inherent in this situation, prompt the Headquarter to rethink its operations and develop new practices such as the hybridization of its knowledge; which could lead to innovative products and services more suitable to the different local contexts of its subsidiaries. Hybridization as a new practice and as an organizational innovation is a combination of sharing knowledge held by the parent with that of its subsidiaries (Chebbi et al., 2011).

This chapter highlights firstly the challenge of the knowledge transfer within MNCs and secondly the features and added value of hybridization. Finally, it focuses on hybridization in MNCs as an organizational innovation.

Knowledge and Creative Innovation

To think about the uphill phases of the innovation process, we have to study the generation, selection and assessment of ideas. Thus, creativity and the transition to innovation can take on a truly strategic character for all innovating firms, with knowledge in the epicentre. Some authors have attempted to integrate creativity into the process of innovation.

Getz (2002) suggests that research and development (R&D) activity is removed from the reality of the market. This is why it should be included in what he called "the execution of the idea". Creativity can even be considered as the first step toward "intrapreneurship" (Carrier, 1997) by making innovation more dynamic. Another important work has been presented by Flynn et al. (2003), who propose an integrator model called "the Innovation Funnel". This model integrates a sub-creativity and a sub-innovation process. The authors distinguish two main funnels: the first one concerns the creative process (environment analysis, identification of opportunities and ideas generation); the second transforms creative ideas into real innovations (objectives, teams and resources). In their model, the authors focused mainly on creativity, while proposing a tool, based on creativity techniques (like brainstorming for example).

Although all these quoted authors have the privilege of introducing the first integrative reflections on creativity in the innovation process, this research underlines the lack of operationalisation of the ideas' transformation steps. According to Stoycheva and Lubart (2001), this transient phase is strategic because it can be included within a "pre-conception" logic: selecting projects, reducing risks and time to market (TTM). This research's extensive review has encountered only one work (Hatchuel and Weil, 2003) that really covers this phenomenon. They, while studying the innovation strategies within "Sekurit Saint Gobain", showed that each enterprise must think about new creative tracks, without cutting down on planned objectives. Thus, they developed the R-I-D (Research-Innovation-Development) model. Embedded in collective action theory, this model marks the passage of the reflections dealing with innovation to those studying the innovating organizations. Their so-named "I" function consists of managing the "*fields of innovation, which are conductive to new programs of product developments and new questions for research*". It creates value and manages the process of the emergence and structuring of new knowledge.

According to Hatchuel and Weil (2003), this knowledge-based strategic dimension appears on three levels:

- *Piloting by concepts* - Innovation activity is characterized by a "prudential" logic. It aims to explore the strategic space in order to generate new ideas with potential value;
- *Joint learning* - The learning takes place at the internal level and with customers;
- *The conception of strategy* - The strategy is based on the previous two kinds of piloting.

Additionally, knowledge surfaces again as a key component in larger companies' exploration activity, calling for various kinds of knowledge: design of services, marketing, information systems and networks, technology, etc. Chebbi et al., (2012) found that the ideas of new business concepts to explore are formulated by their owners in the setting of an exploration file: a procedure that guarantees better homogeneity and internal coordination. In this setting, for each concept under study, the actors are invited to exchange their thoughts about the aspects summarized in table 1.

Type of exchanged Knowledge	Features
Knowledge linked to services and customer uses	Evolution of customer uses, uncertainty, divergences / convergences
The group's strategy	The adequacy of the potential offering within the group's services portfolio, the ecosystem
Technological knowledge	Risks, problems, infrastructure and technical network
The cost structure	Profits, uses, costs
The customers' knowledge	Tests and technical experiments, customer perceptions
Knowledge linked to materials	Technical specifications to consider, design, universality, potential industrial partners, integration of the service
Business needs	Pricing, media and sales plan

Table1. The content of explorations (Chebbi et al. (2012)

As shown, exploring and analyzing innovative concepts require a continuous knowledge exchange among the actors, which facilitates the transition of a creative idea to a real, market-accepted innovation.

Knowledge transfer within Multinational Corporations

The phenomenon of intra-organizational knowledge transfer within MNCs is a fundamental subject of research (Kotabe et al., 2007). To achieve a successful transfer, improve capability of the receiving unit and enhance the innovatory performance, MNCs should use replication and adaptation (Williams, 2007). However, learning and experimentation, based on these two activities, depend on whether flows are vertical (between Headquarters and subsidiaries) or horizontal (between subsidiaries).

The top-down knowledge transfer was often used from Headquarters to subsidiaries (Inkpen, Dinur, 1998; Szulanski, 1996). In fact, these transfers were fostered by some specific factors: ownership, transaction costs and exploitation of specific advantages linked to market imperfections. In this case, Headquarters formulates the global strategy and specifies the results expected from each subsidiary. The local units receive and implement the global knowledge and sometimes adapt it to their context. The predominance of this model can be justified by three theoretical approaches: reducing the transaction costs, dependency on Headquarters resources (Pfeffer and Salancik, 1978) and the agency theory (Jensen and Meckling, 1976). The Headquarters play the role of "leader" while subsidiaries play the role of "agents". We can assume that this practice is used exclusively by MNCs, which design and implement a global strategy (Bartlett and Ghoshal, 1989). This strategy is based on a second assumption that customers' needs are homogeneous throughout the world, resulting in products standardization (Vrontis and Thrassou, 2007; Vrontis et al., 2009).

With the new design of the MNC as a differential network (Bartlett and Ghoshal, 1989), valuing subsidiaries has grown. As a result, the "bottom up" transfer, also called « *Reverse transfer* » (Håkanson and Nobel, 2001) is more and more developed. Considering that the subsidiaries have a close collaboration with local customers and suppliers, the wealth of local contexts has become a source of technological know-how, production, knowledge management or marketing (Björkman et al., 2004). The subsidiaries can be seen as major players once they contribute to increasing the knowledge capital of the Headquarters and "sister" units. In fact, knowledge transferred from subsidiaries is more than just exploited. It can be newly developed (Almeida and Grant, 1998) through a learning/experimentation process. Unlike the "top down" transfer, "bottom up" flows characterize any MNC following a multidomestic strategy. This means, according to Bartlett and Ghoshal (1989), the implementation of a local innovation process within subsidiaries.

These two complementary facets of knowledge transfer appear to be very dichotomous. Indeed, dyadic knowledge transfer between two actors has been studied either on the Headquarters' or on the subsidiary's side. This remains an extraction of knowledge from its original context and its move to a new context. On the one hand, the top down transfer, knowledge circulates between different institutional contexts. In this case, local adaptations are very difficult. On the other hand, the "bottom-up" transfer depends heavily on the absorption capacity of the Headquarters (Cohen, Levinthal, 1990) and its degree of NIH (Not Invented Here) syndrome sensitivity (Katz and Allen, 1982). In order to overcome these difficulties, MNCs have to devise new practices based on communication and reciprocity to foster more interaction between Headquarters and subsidiaries (Monteiro et al., 2008). Mixing local and global knowledge becomes so very important. According to Bartlett and Ghoshal (1989), this could be established when MNCs have transnational strategy. Network, exchange, hybridization are the key words of this orientation. The following section focuses more on this aspect.

Knowledge hybridization

Hybridization appears as an organizational practice based on activities of successive adjustment between the initial model of Headquarters and the subsidiary, leading to the joint construction of a final hybrid model. But what about its characteristics, content and added value?

Characteristics

Hybridization can be implemented when two actors (or more) are interacting in a given context leading to a new managerial model. That means that this practice is more than the simple adaptation to the local environment. It is emerging as *"the interaction between different national systems, legal or institutional, different political contexts, different labour markets and structures of skills, different infrastructures"* (Tolliday et al., 1998). According to this definition, knowledge transfer will not be possible if hybridization does not occur. In this context, knowledge must be modified in a first step and then it becomes possible for organizations to transfer it in a second step.

Many researchers studied the hybridization in various forms of collective actions such as networks, clusters, alliances or acquisitions. This is more linked to inter-organizational collaboration. In the inter-firm networks, companies develop close and dynamic linkages to achieve a common strategic action (Gulati et al., 2000). In the specific case of clusters, the competitiveness can be enhanced through knowledge hybridization between two main actors: the industrial cluster (firms) and the institutional infrastructure (higher education campuses, technology transfer agencies, R&D units) (Asheim and Isaksen, 1997). An economic coordination can also be established through the local user-producer interaction and the combination between local and global available R&D competencies (Lundvall, 1992). Hybridization can also occur in a learning perspective in the context of strategic alliances (Hamel, 1991; Doz, 1996). In this configuration, inter-organisational relationships are channels that promote and enhance information flows and other resources from one position to another within a social structure. For cross-alliances and joint ventures, resource combinations between partners are seen as a key for success (Antonelli, 2005).

Studying knowledge hybridization within an inter-organizational relationship is indeed important but it is not relevant for MNCs. In fact, the context, the aim and the relative power between the actors are different. We noticed that MNCs often prefer the "top down" knowledge transfer with standardized procedures, although these multi-dimensional organizations become more and more conscious about the lack of efficiency of this practice. In fact, applying top down transfer means that Headquarters cannot use the resources of subsidiaries in an efficient way and this can lead to a reduced innovation performance. To avoid this situation, a company can develop a new hybridized practice to improve its transnational innovation capabilities. Within MNCs, knowledge hybridization could result from multiple interactions between diffusion (global) and adaptation (local). On one hand, Headquarters tries to keep its knowledge in each subsidiary. So it diffuses processes, methods, human resource management and marketing practices and also technical know-how to ensure the same way of working throughout the group. On the other hand, adaptation is the adjustment of global practices to the specific institutional host countries. The effectiveness of knowledge hybridization depends on the subsidiaries' involvement, the reciprocity and communication (Yahiaoui, 2007).

Content and added value

Despite the importance of the balance between global and local in transferring knowledge, few researchers studied the hybridization practice within MNCs. In the field of International Human Resource Management (HRM) for example, Yahiaoui (2007, 2010) studied the adoption of transferred HRM practices by Headquarters to their foreign subsidiaries and highlighted that certain practices are strongly hybridized or unilaterally transferred such as the career management. Others are neutral or insensitive and are either moderately transferred or moderately hybridized such as compensation or recruitment. She highlighted the importance of allotting more space for isomorphic needs through the analysis of the reactions of subsidiaries' stakeholders, and the interactive management practices involving the co-decision making between Headquarter and the subsidiaries. This co-hybridization of HRM practices leads to the development of new practices more suitable to the subsidiaries local context. Therefore, several components of the hybridization process influence these practices and should be taking into account factors such as the nature of the practice, HR organization and its level of centralization, firm structure, categories of employees, stakes for the actors, local training programs, organizational procedures, international HRM policies and strategies, etc.

Considering hybridization in the innovation context, many researchers identified various types of knowledge to be mixed with the global ones, such as: local needs, local constraints, local results and commercial knowledge (Gupta and Govindarajan, 1991; Bartlett and Ghoshal, 1989; Subramaniam and Venkatraman, 2001). By taking into account these types of knowledge, the Headquarter obtains other hybrid knowledge to conceive a new transnational product.

This variety of context leads us to highlight the importance of hybridization in producing new knowledge. It enhances the integration of global considerations and local specificities (institutional pressures, national cultures) on different levels and the improvement of the Headquarter-subsidiaries relationships and communication (Chebbi et al., 2011). In the strategic context, the combination of local and global knowledge creates suitable innovations to be adopted by customers in several countries ("glocal" products). In fact, for MNCs, the convergence between the knowledge of the Headquarters and that of the subsidiaries succeeds in becoming an integrated process (Subramaniam, 2006; Thrassou et al., 2012a, b).

Towards a MNC hybridization framework as an organizational innovation

It has already been stressed that "top down" and "bottom up" flows of knowledge fall respectively under the global strategy and multi-domestic innovation; and that hybridization relates more to transnational strategy. By mobilizing the design of Bartlett and Ghoshal (1989), it was considered that the creation of new knowledge is made through the combination of local requirements with a high degree of standardization, leading to hybridization. Therefore, knowledge hybridization, in MNCs, is defined by this research as "a *process which combines universal/global practices with local ones; a mixture between knowledge of actors implicated in common strategic action*". As described previously, this process seems dynamic, involuntary and non-deterministic. Indeed, the multiple interactions, between the Headquarters and its subsidiaries, can take the place of ad hoc attempts at adjustment. This knowledge creation process joins the model of knowledge conversion developed by Nonaka and Takeuchi (1995).

Within the innovation field, hybridization could be considered as an organizational innovation. While technological innovations have been the subject of numerous researches, organizational realities are less apprehended (Damanpour et al., 1989; Godowski, 2003). According to the literature on organizational innovation in MNCs, more importance must be placed on new organizational practices (Malnight, 1996). Indeed, for the divided, decentralized, and network structures, the transfer has become a dominant practice, an organizational routine widespread in these complex organizations. To be more competitive, new practices should be created. Thus, organizational innovation is defined by this research as "*the implementation of a managerial practice seen as new by the organization, which affects the functioning of its social system both in the relations between individuals and in their own work*".

According to Rogers (2003), this is linked to a "reinvention" process since the transferred knowledge is transformed. This is what Boyer et al. (1998) qualify as "creative hybridization". On the other hand, when the subsidiaries use their strong resources as an argument to apply pressure and to change the content or the sense of each innovation, it becomes a "resistive hybridization" (Ferner et al., 2005).

As summarized in figure 1 below, in order to combine global and local knowledge, the exchanges between actors (Headquarter – subsidiaries) are essentially based on a continuous communication and an important degree of involvement. Thus, a dynamic negotiation process is very important to take into account subsidiaries' knowledge. The subsidiary has to convince the Headquarters to integrate this knowledge in different levels. For example, it could be the case of the new product development process. Towards this aim, the subsidiary must identify its own market needs within its local context (Vrontis et al., 2006).

The success of the implementation of knowledge hybridization requires a high degree of reciprocity between the actors, an integration of the transnational innovation capabilities and the awareness of the embedded knowledge within the local context. Consequently, the NIH (Not Invented Here) syndrome must be ousted. This Hybridization takes place between headquarter and subsidiary but it occurs also between subsidiaries.

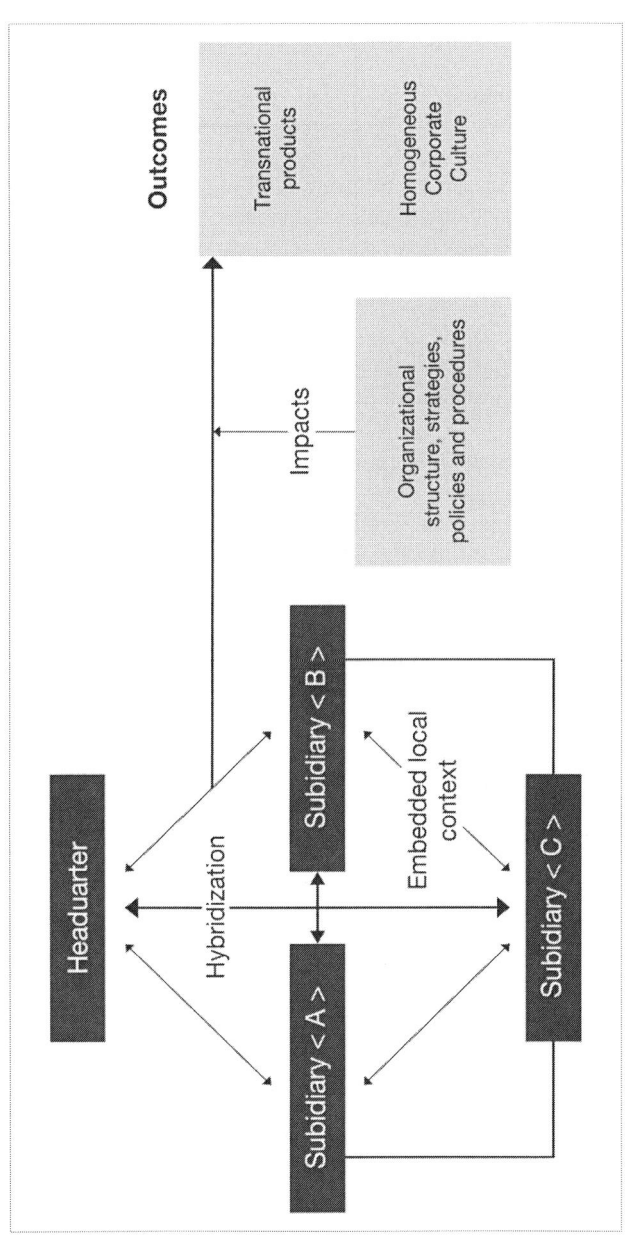

Figure1. The knowledge hybridization process

Conclusions

This chapter presents hybridization as an innovative organizational practice in MNCs. In fact, the knowledge combination from the Headquarter and its subsidiaries constitutes a new practice that leads to various added values on different levels such as a homogeneous corporate culture of MNC and transnational innovation capabilities (Chebbi and Yahiaoui, 2012). This new practice breaks off with all centralization of knowledge transfer and underlines the importance of taking into account the local specificities such as the institutional and cultural pressures (Yahiaoui, 2007; 2010), local needs and constraints, commercial knowledge, etc. (Chebbi et al., 2011). Otherwise, hybridization is often an involuntary process. It is based on the involvement of each actor from the subsidiaries. Besides this, the innovation process is enriched with both global and local practices while improving the competitiveness of the whole enterprise. This chapter puts in evidence the importance of hybridization for developing new products within MNCs. In order to increase the understanding of this new practice, an aggregated analysis of its development mode is deserved which will contribute to future studies of transnational innovation strategy.

References

Almeida, P. and Grant, R. (1998), "International Corporations and Cross-Border Knowledge Transfer in the Semiconductor Industry", Working Paper, Carnegie Bosch Institute, Washington DC.

Antonelli, C. (2005), "Models of Knowledge and Systems of Governance", *Journal of Institutional Economics*, Vol. 1 No. 1, pp. 51–73.

Asheim, B. T. and Isaken, A. (1997), "Localisation, Agglomeration and Innovation: Towards Regional Innovation Systems in Norway?", *European Planning Studies*, Vol. 5 No. 3, pp. 299-330.

Bartlett, C. and Ghoshal, S. (1989), Managing Across Borders: The Transnational Solution, 2nd edition, Harvard Business School Press, Boston.

Björkman, I., Barner-Rasmussen, W. And Li, L. (2004), 'Managing Knowledge Transfer in MNCs: The Impact of Headquarters Control Mechanisms', *Journal of International Studies*, Vol. 35, No. 5, pp. 443-455.

Boyer, R. (1998), "Hybridation et modèle productif : géographie, histoire et théorie", in *Actes de GERPISA : Pourquoi les modèles productifs voyagent*, No. 24, pp. 7-50.

Bresciani, S., Thrassou, A. and Vrontis, D. (2012), "Innovation in Italian Family Business", *World Review of Entrepreneurship, Management and Sustainable Development,* Vol. 9, No. 1, pp. 195-215.

Carrier C. (1997), *De la créativité à l'intrapreneuriat*, Presses Universitaires du Québec, Québec.

Chebbi, H. and Yahiaoui, D. (2012), "Local subsidiaries initiatives: cultural determinants and Outcomes", *World review of Entrepreneurship, Management and Sustainable Development*, Vol. 8, No. 2.

Chebbi, H. and Yahiaoui, D., Thrassou, A. and Vrontis, D. (2012), "The Exploration Activity's Added Value Into the Innovation Process", *Global Business and Economics Review,* pp. (ISSN: 1097-4954, Inderscience).

Chebbi, H., Barin Cruz, L. and Chtourou, W. (2011), "Towards A Sustainable Strategic Formation Process", *Revue M@n@gement,*Vol. 14, No. 3, pp. 183-207.

Cohen, W. M. and Levinthal, D. A. (1990), "Absorptive capacity: a new perspective on learning and innovation", *Administrative Science Quarterly*, Vol. 35, No. 1, pp. 128-152.

Damanpour, F., Evan, W. M. and Szabat, K. A. (1989), "The Relationship between Types of Innovation and Organizational Performance", *Journal of Management Studies*, Vol. 26, No. 6, pp. 587-602.

Doz, Y. (1996), "The Evolution of Cooperation in Strategic Alliances: Initial Conditions or Learning Processes?", *Strategic Management Journal*, Vol. 17, pp. 55-84.

Ferner, A., Almond, P. and Colling, T. (2005), "Institutional Theory and the Cross-national Transfer of Employment Policy: the Case of Workforce Diversity in US multinationals", *Journal of International Business Studies*, Vol. 36, No. 3, pp. 304-321.

Flynn M., Dooley L., O'sullivan D., Cormican K. (2003), 'Idea management for organizational innovation', *International Journal of innovation management*, vol. 7, n° 4, December, pp. 417-442.

Getz I. (ed) (2002), Créativité organisationnelle: regards sur l'individu, l'entreprise et l'économie, Insitut Vital Roux,Vuibert.

Godowski, C. (2003), "Essai sur la dynamique d'assimilation des innovations managériales. Le cas des approches par activités", *Comptabilité - Contrôle - Audit*, special issue, May, pp. 71-86.

Gulati, R., Nohria, N. and Zaheer, A. (2000), "Strategic Networks", *Strategic Management Journal*, Vol. 21, No. 3, pp. 203-215.

Gupta, A. K., and Govindarajan, V. (1991), "Knowledge Flows and the Structure of Control within Multinational Corporation", *Academy of management Review*, Vol. 29, nNo. 4, pp. 695-714.

Hâkanson, L. and Nobel, R. (2001), "Organization Characteristics and Reverse Technology Transfer", *Management International Review, Special Issue*, Vol. 41, No. 4, pp. 392-420.

Hamel, G. (1991), "Competition for Competence and Inter-partner Learning within International Strategic Alliances", *Strategic Management Journal*, Vol. 12, special issue, Summer, pp. 83-103.

Hatchuel A., Weil B. (2003), 'Peut-on structurer l'innovation?', *Industrie et technologies*, pp.114-115.

Inkpen, A. C. and Dinur, A. (1998), "The Ttransfer and Management of Knowledge in the Multinational Corporation: Considering Context", Working Paper, Carnegie Bosch Institute, Washington DC.

Jensen, M. C., Meckling, W. H. (1976), "Theory of the Firm: Managerial Behaviour, Agency Cost and Ownership Structure", *Journal of Financial Economics*, Vol. 3, No. 4, pp. 305-360.

Katz, R., Allen, T. J. (1982), "Investigating the Not Invented Here (NIH) Syndrome: A look at the Performance, Tenure, and Communication Patterns of 50 R&D Project Groups", *R&D Management*, Vol. 12, No. 1, pp. 7-19.

Kotabe M, Dunlap-Hinkler. D., Parente, R. andMishra, H. A (2007), "Determinants of Cross-national Knowledge Transfer and its Effect on Firm Innovation", *Journal of International Business Studies*, Vol. 38, No.2, pp. 259–282.

Lundvall, B. (1992), *National Systems of Innovation: Towards a Theory of Innovation and Interactive Learning*, Pinter publishers, London.

Malnight, T. W. (1996), "The Ttransition from Decentralized to Network-Based MNC Structures: An Evolutionary Perspective", *Journal of International Business Studies*, Vol. 27, No. 1, pp. 43-52.

Monteiro, F. L., Arvidsson, N. and Birkinshaw, J. (2008), "Knowledge Flows Within Multinational Corporations: Explaining Subsidiary Isolation and Its Performance Implications", *Organization Science*, Vol. 19, No. 1, pp. 90-107.

Nonaka, I. and Takeushi, H. (1995), *The Knowledge-Creating Company*, Oxford University Press Inc., New York.

Pfeffer, J. and Salancik, G. (1978), *The External Control of Organizations: A Resource Dependence Perspective*, Prentice-Hall, New York.

Rogers, E.M. (2003), *Diffusion of innovations*, Free Press, New York.
Smith, C. and Elger, T. (2000), "The Societal Effects School and Transnational Transfer: the Case of Japanese Investment in Britain", in Maurice, M., Sorge, A. (Ed.), *Embedding Organizations*, Benjamins J. Publishing company, Amsterdam, pp.225-240.
Stoycheva K., Lubart T. I. (2001), "The Nature of Creative Decision Making", in Allwood C.M. and Seelart M. (Eds.), *Creative Decision Making in the Social World*, Kluwer Academic, Amsterdam, pp. 15-33.
Subramaniam, M. and Venkatraman, N. (2001), "Determinants of Transnational New Product Development Capability: Testing the Influence of Transferring and Deploying Tacit Overseas Knowledge", *Strategic Management Journal*, Vol. 22, No. 4, pp. 359-378.
Subramaniam, M. (2006), "Integrating Cross-Border Knowledge for Transnational New Product Development", *Journal of Product Innovation Management*, Vol. 23, No. 6, pp. 541-555.
Szulanski, G. (1996), "Exploring Internal Stickiness: Impediments to the Transfer of Best Practice within the Firm", *Strategic Management Journal*, Vol. 17, Special issue: Knowledge and the Firm, Winter, pp. 27-43.
Thrassou, A. and Vrontis, D. (2008), "International Strategic Marketing of the Small Construction Consultancy Firm - The Case of Cypriot Firms", *International Journal of Entrepreneurship and Small Business*, Vol. 6, No. 2, pp. 296-314 (ISSN: 1476-1297- Inderscience).
Thrassou, A., Vrontis, D., Chebbi, H. and Yahiaoui, D. (2012a), "A Preliminary Strategic Marketing Framework for New Product Development", *Journal of Transnational Management*, Vol. 17, No. 1, pp. 21-44.
Thrassou, A., Vrontis, D., Chebbi, H. and Yahiaoui, D. (2012b), Transcending Innovativeness Towards Strategic Reflexivity, Qualitative Market Research: An International Journal, Volume 15, Number 4, 2012.
Tolliday, S., Boyer, R., Charron, E. and Jurgens, U. (1998), "Introduction", in Boyer, R., Charron, E., Jurgens, U. and Tolloday, S. (Ed.), *Between Imitation and Innovation: The Transfer and Hybridization of Productive Models in the International Automobile Industry*, Oxford University Press, Oxford, pp. 1-19.
Vrontis, D., Thrassou, A. and Chia-Hung Wei (2006), "A Critical Evaluation of Strategic Market Entry Theories and Practices - the Case of Hewlett-Packard", *Journal of International Business and Entrepreneurship Development*, Vol. 3, No. 1/2, pp.152-170.

Vrontis, D. and Thrassou, A. (2007), "Adaptation vs. Standardisation in International Marketing- The Country-of-origin Effect", *Journal of Innovative Marketing,* Vol. 3, Issue 4, pp. 7-21(ISSN: 1814-2427-Business Perspectives).

Vrontis, D., Thrassou, A. and Lamprianou, I. (2009), "International Marketing Adaptation versus Standardisation of Multinational Companies", *International Marketing Review,* Vol. 26, Nos. 4 and 5, pp. 477-500.

Williams, C. (2007), "Transfer in Context: Replication and Adaptation in Knowledge Transfer Relationships", *Strategic Management Journal,* Vol. 28, No. 9, pp. 867-890.

Yahiaoui, D. (2007), "L'hybridation des pratiques de GRH dans les filiales françaises implantées en Tunisie", PhD. Dissertation, Jean Moulin Lyon 3 University, France.

Yahiaoui, D. and Golli, A. (2010), "The Hybridization of HRM Practices in Tunisian Subsidiaries of French Multinationals", *Annual Meeting of Academy of Management (AOM) 'Dare to Care: Passion and Compassion in Management Practice and Research',* Montreal, Canada, 6-10 August.

Chapter Two

Rethinking Talent Management in Organizations: Towards a Boundary-less Model

Carrie Foster, Neil Moore and Peter Stokes

Introduction

Talent management has been promoted as an important success factor for organizations ever since Steven Hankin from the consultancy firm McKinseys coined the term The 'War for Talent' in 1997 (Agrawal, 2010; Collings and Mellanhi, 2009). This has become even more the case in the turbulent arena of innovative business practice of the twenty-first century. In terms of a *prima facie* definition talent can be a special skill or ability that a person may possess. When linked to strategy the long term control and management of talent has on-going benefits and can enhance the potential of an organization. This gives rise to the hybrid term *strategic talent management.* In recent years, strategic talent management has emerged as a central aspect of many Human Resource (HR) strategies and is based on a belief that managing talent delivers organizational performance and business results (Lockwood, 2006).

The expansion of academic and practitioner literature on the subject has generally focused on how organizational leaders should manage and develop talent in a strategic and systematic way. Much of this writing is concerned with achieving competitive advantage through HR processes which tend to adhere to particular assumptions and ways of viewing, representing and executing talent selection, recruitment and retention in line with the strategic aims of the organization (Iles, 2010; Lewis and Heckman, 2006).

While a considerable amount of energy has been dedicated to exploring talent management, it is noteworthy that academic commentaries that aim to expand more theoretical or conceptual understandings have been surprisingly under-developed (Collings and Mellahi, 2009; Lewis and Heckman, 2006). In the practitioner realm, although much laudable work has been conducted in specific areas such as leadership development little attention has been focused upon releasing the talent potential of the *wider employee population*. Thus, in its normative context 'talent management' is foremost about providing a platform for ensuring that recruitment and retention processes deliver sustained stability and the desired knowledge, skills and attitudes for a limited and privileged number of identified roles and individuals. As outlined above, typically, these roles are considered to be strategically important to future organizational performance whilst nevertheless remaining firmly rooted in the current organizational activities and culture.

Nevertheless, in the same way a production line can be efficient and effective but not leave extensive room for flexibility, extant strategic talent management processes often dedicate limited energies to what may be considered to be 'non-standard' talent. In essence, many presentations of talent management seem to operate akin to a mass production process rather than on an individual basis. In other words, current models of talent management arguably show relatively minor contextual variegation in relation to the many factors that may be at play in relation to talent in a given setting. For example, in relation to leadership and talent management, issues of talent are likely to be driven by the given situational context, the environment and culture and the performance requirements of the organization at a given time (Smith, 2011). The next stage of this conceptual discussion and exploration takes stock of the existing literature on talent management with a view to identifying over looked and unrecognized domains that will provide a challenge to the current boundaries around the area.

The Literature on Talent Management

The discussion thus far has made an initial attempt to broach the concept of talent and, in particular, has raised questions regarding the issues of variety in relation to the strategic processes of talent management. One of the challenges in addressing these issues is the confusion over differing definitions of the field because of the variable use of the term to describe *inter alia* an output, a process and/or a mind-set within the field of HR

(Lewis and Heckman, 2006). For the purpose of the present discussion, we will start by citing a widely espoused conventional meaning of talent management as referring to Human Resource Management (HRM) processes which encompasses a *bundle* of HR practices and strategies - recruitment, selection, induction, engagement, development, performance management, reward, succession planning and career management (Green, 2011). Moreover, talent management has been defined as:

> *"…activities and processes that involved the systematic identification of key positions which differentially contribute to the organisation's sustainable competitive advantage, the development of a talent pool of high potential and high performing incumbents to fill these roles, and the development of differentiated HR architecture to facilitate filling these positions with competent incumbents and to ensure their continued commitment to the organisation."* (Collings and Mellahi, 2009).

Therein are many of the common treatments of the area based on 'systematic', 'competitive advantage' and the notion of a small and elite 'pool'. This is echoed in the language employed by representative bodies. For instance, the Chartered Institute of Personnel and Development (CIPD) defines talent management as:

> *"…the systematic attraction, identification, development, engagement/ retention and deployment of those individuals with high potential who are of particular value to an organization."* (Iles, 2010).

Therefore, perhaps logically, talent management in the organizational setting has tended to develop into a strategic management tool aimed at delivering the skills and knowledge that the organization supposedly requires at a time when they believe they will require it. By focusing on recruitment and retention strategies the organization seeks to construct the future shape of the talent that the organization requires to remain competitive and deliver strategic objectives. Indeed, the emergence of the very notion of talent management developed around the same time as HRM practices started to become influential. Thus, it is little surprise that talent management is aligned with the often metric-oriented and reductionist approaches of 'Hard HRM' which emphasises the deployment of the organization's human capital to achieve strategic goals and tends to dedicate less space to more critical notions of variety, irregularity, shifting boundaries and delineations (Beardwell and Claydon, 2010; Stokes, 2011).

Although talent management can be tactical, the normative purpose of strategic talent management is to deliver a high performing organization and sustainable organizational effectiveness. Some potential confusion over talent management can be attributed to the co-development of 'strategic' HRM over the last twenty years. As the profession has sought to move away from its rather staid payroll, 'tea and tissues' personnel reputation in search of a seat at the boardroom table, HR practices have begun to evolve from a focus of managing employees to that of delivering business outcomes (Tyson, 1995) however, this evolution is far from complete.

In relation to talent management, McKinsey's earlier mentioned proposition regarding the 'War on Talent' was prompted by the lack of excellent leadership talent within the marketplace and the idea that organizations would have to battle to attract and hold onto individuals demonstrating leadership skills and potential. The issue with this proposition - the foundation stone of strategic talent management and indeed many other definitions is that they imply that only a small proportion of employees have 'talent' which might merit managerialistic attention and managing and which contributes to organizational performance (Francis, 2012). In a business and organizational setting, talent and the management thereof most often refers to a HR process with the 'talent' being a *particular* human capital resource which the organization requires, or will require, in the future in order to be successful. In this context, talent management refers not to a process of managing general talent, i.e. all employees, but a specific focus and fit of talent that is considered to be strategically important to the organization. In practice, this tends to be limited to leadership and the key expertise that the organization requires for it to achieve its strategic goals (Garrow, 2008). This is reinforced by Hansen (2007) who writes that a Towers Perrin Survey, indicated that senior HR leaders use the term talent

> "...to identify the core group of leaders and key contributors who drive the business forward. These defined talent pools make up, on average, no more than 15 per cent of the workforce."

It is the contention and argument of the present discussion that this may represent a myopic perception.

Rethinking the Literature on Talent Management: Exploring the Concept

Talent management is widely discussed and HR practitioners and management consultants analysing and debating organizational and individual performance extensively use the term 'talent'. However, what is meant by the concept of talent, is rarely explored in-depth and, even when it is, a wide range of interpretations are generally on offer (Tarique and Schuler 2010; Edenborough and Edenborough, 2012). In this vein, Iles (2010) suggests that talent is about:

> *"...those individuals who can make a difference to organisational performance, either through their immediate contribution or in the longer term by demonstrating the highest levels of potential"*

However, he goes further to note that, in fact, the word 'talent' is more commonly used as a way of describing employees or positions (Iles, 2010). From this we can see issues of identity affirmation and the associated status and power that are ascribed to those allegedly bearing 'talent'.

In the wider public domain, the term 'the talent' is commonly used when referring to, for example, entertainment celebrities. Here 'talent' refers to those individuals who make a living from an ability to perform on stage or screen. In this context the intention is to encourage a search for 'undiscovered talent' and, in attempts to do so, the quest often unearths 'raw talent.' However, what constitutes talent is very much about perspective and is driven as much by personal preferences of 'good' and 'bad' as by something clearly definable. For instance, a popular television show cites successful individuals as having the 'X-Factor' with the 'X' referring to an indescribable quality that constitutes or denotes a special talent. The end result is that the winners of the show, that is the 'talent' who, by winning are believed to have the X-Factor, aren't necessarily guaranteed a successful or sustainable career. This is because they might not after all possess the indefinable, unexplainable and unidentifiable X that will make them successful outside of the talent show. The type of talent that is associated most often with this type of entertainment show, and also with celebrated artistic and sporting ability, is often believed to be a *natural* talent - an innate ability that enables the individual to be excellent in an specific area or perform with excellence with little training, development or intervention from external sources.

This points up a difference with many corporate and managerialistic perceptions of talent where talent is portrayed as a palpable and tangible artefact that can be clearly delineated and managed. Nevertheless, the search for talent in the organizational context is perhaps more successful than 'X-Factor'-type searches because the capabilities that are recognized are arguably more readily definable qualities that are supported by a number of talent management tools and processes, which, in turn, can be validated - for example, the ability to use a particular marketing or accounting or business development tools. According to Lewis and Heckman (2006) a notable aspect of talent in an organizational setting is that it is something that can be replicated, learnt or taught as opposed to something that is innate. However, in contradiction of this it could be suggested that Lewis is merely pointing up what might more readily be termed skills rather than talent.

Thus, talent in this context presents something of a paradox - it must be both something that is capable of being duplicated whilst at the same time delivering a unique competitive advantage that cannot be copied or imitated by competitors (Lewis and Heckman, 2006; and Lawler, 2008). However, many of the descriptions used to define talent in an organization are similar or the same as talent 'competencies' used in other organizations. Talent definitions are by necessity broadly illustrated by action-orientated statements like for example 'Drive for Results.' This breadth is necessary in order to cover the context in which the talent is being assessed, usually across a multitude of organizational functions and roles. This breadth simplifies the processes of assessing talent but also adds complexity because measuring talent becomes difficult and is likely to be based on perspective and judgement. For instance 'Drive for Results' is easy to measure in a sales role, where it is easy to determine whether or not targets have been met. But how can talent in 'Drive for Results' be measured satisfactorily in an engineering, medical, or intellectual role? Does one use quantity or quality of work done? Similarly, in situations where outputs are intangible or outputs are the result of complex interactions, how do we decide what constitutes a demonstration of talent?

However, being naturally pre-disposed to an area of ability can potentially be applied to any human activity whether that is the ability to excel in science, maths, social skills, organization, child rearing, and animal husbandry and so on and so forth (Fleming and Asplund, 2008). It might indeed be argued that everybody has an innate talent at something. It is just that in our society some forms of talent are considered to be *more valuable* and highly prized compared to different or mundane but nevertheless important, skills such as the ability to, for example, dust and vacuum. Those talents that we possess innately (often supported by the things we are interested in) can be improved upon by training and personal development. Talent can be 'wasted' if practice and focus is not given in the area in which an individual possesses a natural gifting. Whether the innate talent is great or not, research has demonstrated that 10,000 hours or ten years of practice, coupled with feedback and opportunity can lead to world class excellence in most areas (Fleming and Asplund, 2008; Syed, 2011).

Furthermore, with regard to the role of context it should be noted that different cultures may well value different forms of talent. For example, a Japanese organization may value the skill or talent to achieve consensus in meetings whereas certain American corporate settings might value somebody with a talent to achieve his or her goal no matter what the cost. For instance, Ready (2009) emphasizes that cultural differences and their impact upon talent management processes and procedures are likely to become more prescient as globalization accelerates. With this in mind, it has to be recognized and acknowledged that the present study is written by United Kingdom-based authors writing broadly within a western tradition and perspective and this may infuse the argument in both explicit and even implicitly imperceptible manners. The role of national or geo-spatial perception may well be an important factor in the construction of the concept of talent.

In sum, despite the development of a range of talent management processes in the areas of recruitment, selection, development and career management extant definitions of talent tend to lack a degree of depth or sophistication. Rather what constitutes talent most often becomes a matter of perspective and is dependent upon managerial perceptions and organizational contexts. In addition, current approaches to managing talent in organizations are lacking on a number of counts. Firstly, they have a propensity to develop norms of talent that the organization is seeking. In other words the perspective is one that is relatively mono-dimensional and managerialistic. Secondly, there is no account of talent that is *unrecognized* or *unprocessed* by the 'talent management system'. Thirdly, existing talent management approaches are poor at dealing with talent that is outside the norm. In the light of the discussion hitherto, there is therefore scope to revisit and to some extent re-contextualize, the manner in which talent management is perceived and approached.

Surfacing the Role of Perception in Talent management

In principle, it might seem plausible that anyone *should be able to recognize talent*, and anyone can be *recognized as having Talent*, although in practice it is not always that evident. This raises the issue of subjectivity and perception in relation to the assessment, judgement and management of talent and reflects the trend for these aspects to be widely discussed in organization and management studies in recent decades (Weick, 1995; Alvesson and Willmott, 1996; Clegg et al., 2008, Buchanan and Huczynski, 2010).

It is important not to see issues relating to subjectivity and perception as necessarily negative or overly problematic when making decisions regarding talent. Boudreau and Ramstead (2005) argues that while rational processes and control systems are at the centre of talent management, instead, talent management processes should provide a framework that provides a starting point for decision makers to evaluate specific circumstances and challenges.

Perhaps of greater importance is the problem that unidentified and/or underutilised talent, on either an organizational or an individual level, is an untapped resource which when ignored may have a negative impact on organizational performance (Mellahi and Collings, 2010). For instance, being chosen or rejected as part of a talent management process may distort employee self-perceptions. Those not chosen may mistakenly believe that they have no talent and consequently may fail to reach their potential. Whereas those people chosen, may believe that they are more talented than they really are leading to 'diva-like' behaviour which is forgiven by the organization because the 'talented' allegedly 'deliver' (Reeves, 2003). This tendency has been seen in the recent financial crisis where bankers have been portrayed as 'masters of the universe'. Indeed the attitudes and behaviour of many those working within the sector have been widely considered in media reporting as factors which contributed to the crisis.

An important aspect of perception is the role played by context. Particular capabilities that are considered to constitute a valuable organizational talent will be decided by the setting in which the individual resides. True, individuals may be identified as part of a normative HR department process such as performance appraisal or talent management assessment systems, however, alternatively it might be that an individual 'moves in the right circles', or has made a timely and positive impact on a decision-maker who is involved in the talent inclusion and review process (Lawler, 2008; Makela, 2010). Indeed, sometimes, due to not being the 'right fit' for an organization, an individual's talents are recognized only when they move organization or are in the 'right place at the right time.' Spatial and temporal contingent factors are clearly also important in understanding and appreciating the notion of talent. The failure of many talent management systems is thus the inability to clarify what talent is in a rich manner; an oversight of not necessarily developing talent-spotting capability within those involved in the decision-making process; and, a weakness in the ability to identify and develop talent both within the strictures of extant talent management processes and within those individuals whose talent is unrecognized by the generic talent definitions (Mellahi and Collings, 2010; Schuler, 2011).

Remodelling Talent management: A Heightened Role for Context and Perception

In examining the ways in which talent is discussed, measured and defined it has already been indicated that there is no single definition of talent, and de facto this points up that talent is rather more based on perception and context. In the traditionally styled castings of talent management outlined above, talent can be defined as knowledge, skills or ability that an individual or organization perceives as a recognizable capability that has an intrinsic value. It is therefore what others perceive as valuable that denotes whether an individual's possession and demonstration of a capability can be labelled as talent. The purported 'War for Talent' is therefore a war for capabilities that are perceived to be in short supply and also perceived to be of value to organizations in driving performance and strategic objectives of an organization. The below model outlines a synthesis of the current approach to talent management in organizations;

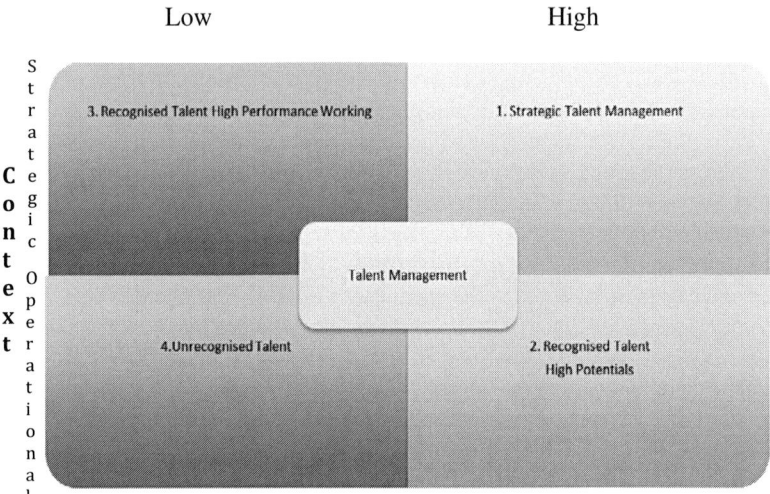

The *Perceived Value* axis shows whether the talent of an individual is considered to be of higher or lower value within the organizational setting. The *Context* axis relates to whether the talent is considered to be of value at an operational level or at a strategic level. This generates four quadrants:

1) **Perceived High Value/ Strategic Context: Strategic talent management** – A capability that has been recognized as important in the delivery of strategic objectives resulting in additional investment and recognition usually within the organizational setting. For example, Leadership Development Programme Participants (Collings and Mellahi, 2009).

2) **Perceived High Value/ Operational Context: Recognized Talent High Potentials** – A capability that has been recognized as important in the delivery of tactical objectives, resulting in additional investment in training and development. For example, High Potential and Apprenticeship programmes.

3) **Perceived Low Value/ Strategic Context: Recognized Talent High Performance Working** – A capability that has been recognized and is rewarded for consistently delivering performance objectives, though this may not warrant additional investment or recognition

beyond that available to any who reach the required performance level. For example, individuals who consistently perform above average but in areas that contribute little perceived added value or competitive advantage.

4) **Perceived Low Value/ Operational Context: Unrecognized Talent** – A capability that has not been discovered or adds no perceived discernable value to an organization's competitive advantage. This may refer to capability that is considered 'normal' or 'un-extraordinary' and, in regards to recruitment and selection, may be viewed as a low value 'easily replaceable' skill and/or area of knowledge.

The Literature on Talent Management: Changing Assumptions and Perceptions and Future Directions

A consequence of recognizing, developing and labelling a small select group as 'talent' is that it may have a negative effect upon employee retention targets. For example, successful Future Leader Programmes often develop knowledge, skills and attitudes in participants which make those individuals highly attractive to alternative employers. Enhanced mobility of this type results in compensation and wage pressure between organizations that focus on 'developing talent' and those that 'buy in talent,' as well as the dilution of perceived competitive advantage (Craig, *et al.* 2008).

By focusing efforts on nurturing the talent of the top 10% of senior employees' talent management has limited its chances of success to the few, and will be unlikely to impact greatly on organizational performance as a whole. Indeed Reeves (2003) advocates that efforts should be refocused so that talent management aims to increase the performance of the majority of employees - "the competent 80%". He suggests that even a small incremental increase in performance of each individual will result in a magnified performance improvement in the organization as a whole.

> *"Many companies are now realising that in their pursuit of creative geniuses they have neglected the massed ranks of the competent. In their search for the soloist they have forgotten the orchestra."* (Reeves, 2003)

Current talent management processes mean that individuals are 'chosen' as being future leaders based on their performance in their current role, whilst others are overlooked or denied the same development opportunities because they do not conform to current perceived leadership talent requirements or strictures. This reduces the opportunity for diversity in leadership and produces homogenised 'talent' which is restricted to a reductionistic strict set of criteria. In essence the labelling of individuals as talent or non-talent regardless of future performance potential and/or the changing knowledge and skill sets required by the organization may jeopardize future success.

This dilemma is best illustrated by the explosion of the internet and the emergence of social media. Twenty years ago the Internet did not exist. Before Facebook in 2004, and Twitter in 2006, the requirement for 'social media' talent did not exist. Today, there are job search sites dedicated to social media jobs, offering jobs as diverse as SEO management, community management, online marketing and digital design. In the current era, the importance of social media talent, not just in adding value to an organization, and the cost of avoiding financial consequences cannot be underestimated. Many organizations suffer crises via social media. Here, a social media crisis is defined as

> *"an issue that arises in or is amplified by social media, and results in negative mainstream media coverage, a change in business process, or financial loss."* (Owyang, 2011).

As organizations embrace virtual life, and with the increasing influence of social media in every area of organizational life, there is now a need for talent that has an understanding of social media; but what about twenty years from now? The impact of social media on organizational life could not have been imagined twenty years ago, so the premise that strategic talent management processes can develop leadership for the future requirements of an organization is difficult to justify.

A key lesson emerging from the above discussion is the identification, recruitment and retention of the right knowledge and skills for the organization's needs as it requires it, which will always outpace traditional talent management methodologies. In her book *Navigating the Badlands*, O'Hara-Devereaux (2004) highlights the changing context of the organizational landscape. Despite being a relatively new management concept, HRM practice within many organizations has not been widely adopted especially in UK contexts and current models of talent management are essentially based in the management and systems of the industrial rather than the post-industrial era. Alternatively expressed, managing talent is often undertaken in the same way organizations would manage the efficiency of manufacturing production lines rather than adapting to the social structural shifts and adaptability required for the Information Age. This has resulted in what O'Hara-Devereaux terms the 'Talent Tantrum' where the traditional organizational hierarchy fails to engage with the very talent they are trying to attract proposing that:

> *"To achieve the desired business results, organisations must get to know key talent at a much deeper level and negotiate the terms of engagement across generations and cultures in a more customized fashion."* O'Hara-Devereaux, 2004).

As well as traditional organization design and structure being replaced with more flexible matrix structures, the modern economy has seen the traditional boundaries between the organization, its' market, customer base and even competitors soften and, in some cases, merge. Globalization, collaboration between competitors, the breakdown of barriers with suppliers and the inclusion of the customer in product and service design is resulting in the emergence of the boundary-less organization and boundary-less talent (Ohmae, 1994, 2005). The result presents new challenges for managing talent and HR practices that require flexible thinking and the need for creative, inclusive and diverse talent management practices.

Talent management has evolved from a simple HR process focused on recruitment and selection to a methodology encompassing HR practices that explore how the human capital in an organization can be utilized for competitive advantage (Lawler, 2008; Collings and Mellahi, 2009). In traditional talent management an organization, and more specifically a select number of organizational leaders, hold the keys to the progression of individuals who have been selected to be part of their talent management programme. It is the organization that decides who should be included on the programme, how and when talent should be developed, and what opportunities the individual will have to pursue to release their talent potential. Trying to *control* the talent, rather than *offer support* and *nurturing* means that the talent may become stifled and fail to deliver its full potential. However, successful talent management is not about controlling access, rather it is about creating a work environment in which employees are engaged and feel valued for the contributions they make (Altman, 2008).

Traditional HRM has emerged as part of the neo-liberal market economy, with the focus on people management as an organizational capital resource to be controlled and manipulated rather than the development of people processes within the organization to release the talent potential of the 'human' in order to deliver sustainable organizational performance. The rhetoric regarding the War for Talent, and pursuit of 'leaderism' (Martin, 2012) avoids the truth which is that strategic talent management has limited its execution to a pursuit of short term thinking, self-interest of the 'heroic' strategic talent and imbalance in the distribution of organizational reward, development and promotion opportunities which erodes trust and fails to recognize the true talent potential of an organizations employee population. The result is organizational performance that is unsustainable in the long term.

The deficiencies of the existing approach to talent management have rendered it unfit for its intended purpose of optimising organizational performance and sustainable business results. To achieve enhanced organizational effectiveness it is recommended that talent management strategies adopt an inclusive approach which is focused upon liberating talent potential within the organizational context and that a new model of talent management is developed to meet the challenges of the twenty-first century (Ready, 2009).

Towards a Boundary-less Approach to Talent management

Drawing on the preceding discussion, there is scope to propose that the future of talent management is associated with an approach that is orientated towards, and more recognizing of, a boundary-less approach.

According to Stokes (2011) a boundary:

> "...usually indicates the limits of a domain or area encompassed by the confines of the boundary.... it is important not to think of boundaries as simply physical entities or artefacts. Boundaries can be created in a wide range of manners – for example, spatially, linguistically and temporally."

The creation, recognition and imposition of boundaries are congruent with notions of modernism and positivistic thinking. This epistemological stance underpins conventional strategic talent management that are predicated on assumptions of the possibility of clearly definable categories and representation, linearity, scientific rationality and an attempt to couch everything in objectivized assessment and measurement. Boundaries also contribute to the representation and reproduction of labels such as 'insider' and 'outsider'. In talent management terms such labelling may result in individuals being categorised as 'talented' or 'untalented'. Such linearity fails to capture the 'messiness' of organizational life and does not reflect the subjectivity associated with identifying and developing talented individuals. Moreover, the exclusivity associated with mainstream talent management initiatives can result in 'othering'. Othering is a process whereby:

> *"...through, discourse or representation, a particular identity or set of characteristics is produced for, and transposed onto, another person, group or object...This can often have the effect of diminishing a person's sense of feeling human and their overall sense of integral identity."* (Stokes, 2011).

Clearly, the alienation and exclusion of 'untalented' employees by the imposition of mainstream talent management programmes has the potential to be divisive and lead to organizational fracture and dislocation. Furthermore, the creation and reproduction of such boundaries results in talent management initiatives which are unfit to meet the challenges of the twenty-first century. In particular, Cappelli (2000) advocates that contemporary talent should be seen as a resource that *flows* through an organization. He suggests that the manager's task is to work with the 'flow of talent' that enters, progresses through, and then exits the organization. Managers should act as facilitators and enablers who shape and facilitate the direction and speed of talent. From this perspective the imposition of rigid definitions of talent and the adoption of boundaries are not conducive to the effective management of the flow.

As has been outlined above the contemporary business environment has become increasingly complex, diverse and dynamic. This has resulted in the emergence of new career structures and employment pathways that in turn have produced a world, which is more rhizomatic, than, fixed in nature. In biology the rhizomatic structure or behaviour is one that spontaneously and unpredictably generates and reproduces. Mangrove swamps provide a rhizome illustration where plants have branches shooting off other branches and stems that intertwine and interconnect in a complex and seemingly confused and messy manner. It might be argued that modern organizational settings have a similar 'messiness' and set against the legacy of out-dated conceptualizations of mainstream talent management programmes there is a possibility that conventional approaches may inhibit the development of collegial rhizomatic organizational structures such as those adopted by exemplar companies such as Semco in Brazil or Oticon in Denmark.

In the case of Semco, a Brazilian manufacturing company, Ricardo Semler took control of the organization in 1982 and dismantled its rigid management structure. He believed autocracy stifled employee potential and consequently he decided to remove boundaries and to introduce a more flexible organizational structure that was based upon worker participation, profit sharing and the free flow of information. By 1998 Semco's transformation was well underway and Semler commented that

> "...the rewards have already been substantial, we've taken a company that was moribund and made it thrive, chiefly by refusing to squander our greatest resource: our people" (Killian et al; 1998).

Similarly, in 1988 when Lars Kolind became CEO of Oticon, a Danish hearing aid technology company, he decided that the company required a radical overhaul. He decided to introduce a

> "...new organisational model with no formal hierarchical reporting relationships, a resource allocation system built around self-organised project teams, and an entirely open-plan physical layout."

Kolind described his structure as 'a spaghetti organisation of rich strands in a chaotic network'. He explained that he had a vision that employees would work according to a common goal, and that employee empowerment would be maximised. Here walls were broken down and boundaries removed so that people from different backgrounds could work together and inspire each other (New Frontiers, 2012).

The cases of Semco and Oticon illustrate the benefits of organizations adopting more organic and rhizomatic approaches to their growth and development. In particular, the cases emphasise the importance of organizations removing boundaries and barriers that inhibit the development of heterogeneous talent. Indeed Capelli (2000) suggests that contemporary approaches to talent management should not be universal, rather individualised strategies that are tailored to particular employees, or groups of employees, should be adopted. He goes on to comment that 'The key is to resist the temptation to use mechanisms across the board.' The need for a boundary-less approach has also been noted by Collings and

Mellahi (2009, 2010). They argue that the emergence of workers who have boundary-less careers (i.e. careers characterized by inter-firm mobility) necessitates a re-thinking of traditional talent management approaches. Increasingly, flexible talent management programmes that recognize talent, which may lie outside of the mainstream, are required, although boundary-less career pathways present new challenges to the organization in regards to the retention and management of knowledge and skills that are competitively advantageous (Yamashita and Uenoyama, 2006).

In order to cope with the challenges of the new millennium, Ready (2009) advocates the establishment of a proactive talent agenda and a new 'talent compact' between organizations and their employees. He suggests that these need to be based on authenticity, connectivity and meritocracy and that the hallmark of relationships of this type should be the dual principles of *promises made* and *promises kept*. In terms of authenticity, Ready (2009) explains that an organization needs to be

> "...true to itself in its policies and practices, including, of course, its talent management practices".

Connectivity requires employees to work together, removal of 'silo thinking' and the spanning of boundaries. Meritocracy advocates fairness and the equal treatment of employees regardless of where they are located within an organization. The notion of *promises made* emphasises

> "...the company's sense of purpose...and the opportunities it provides for talent to grow and develop at a pace in keeping with the growth of the enterprise."

The term *promises kept* reflects

> "...the culture and the climate that the company has created that will enable it to keep its promise." (ibid, p6).

Creating a talent management system that accommodates talent built around the individual requires some consideration. Indeed a primary issue in recognizing and working with individual talent is the need to redefine and re-contextualize talent to encompass elements that lay outside of mainstream categorizations (i.e. boundary-less talent management). In order to achieve this we propose that organizations should expand their notions of what constitutes talent and adopt alternative typologies such as Strategic Talent, Talent Within, Expert Talent and Genius Talent.

34   Chapter Two

This is, of course, in strong contrast to the approach of fitting talent to the roles that the organization needs filling. By focusing on the environment and liberating talent, managers must ignore the clarion call to focus on what the organization wants (Powell and Lubitsh, 2007). Boundary-less talent shifts the focus of talent management from exclusion by selection to inclusion and liberation of the individuals' talent, within the context of the organization as a whole, which may include the management of talent that is both internal and external to traditional organizational boundaries. Boundary-less Talent not only encompasses the traditional proposition of strategic talent management which focuses on those regarded as strategically important but also encompasses employees who offer talent potential which is outside of the 'norm' (i.e. Expert, Genius and/or Talent Within).

A Model of Boundary-less Talent management

Below is the initial stage of a proposed model of Boundary-less Talent management. It is important to say that pictorially we are of course obligated to represent our ideas with words, pictures and linear representations. However, taking full account of the discussion above, we also point up the ephemeral and blurred nature of such lines.

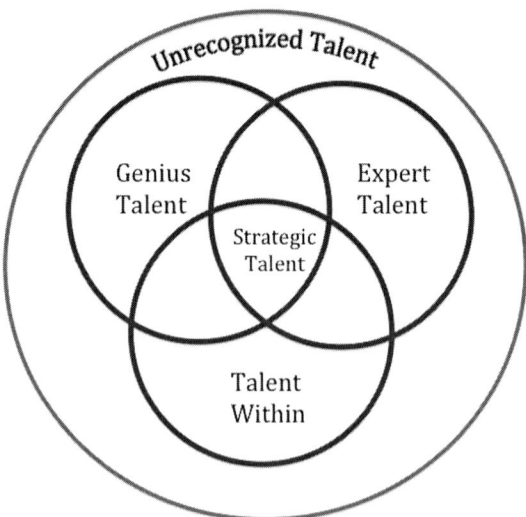

Therefore re-contextualised talent can be re-categorized as follows:

Strategic Talent

A capability that has been recognized as important in the delivery of strategic objectives, resulting in additional investment and recognition usually within the organizational setting. Significantly in the boundary-less talent management model this is recognized as '*current* strategic talent' in recognition that the strategic talent requirement of the organization is essentially temporal in nature and will change over time.

Talent Within

An individual's capability that *has been recognized* and may be regarded as strategic talent as the needs of the organization change. Talent Within may also take the form of Expert Talent which emerges as an individual's knowledge, skills and ability are developed. On the proposed premise that all individuals are talented in some way organizations need to help employees release their potential by creating job roles around the talents they possess. The individual has a responsibility to be aware of their talent and develop their capacity to use it. Boundary-less Talent management requires organizations to build processes to identify, develop and manage the Talent Within as well as working with individuals to enable them to identify their own talent and understand how best to use their strengths in the workplace. Leaders must help integrate the needs of the individual with that of the organization in order to create an environment in which individual goals are achieved in accordance with organizational objectives.

Expert Talent

Individuals that are recognized as being experts in their field are occasionally recognized by organizational talent management processes if their expertise is considered to be strategically important; most often in areas of engineering, science and academic research. However, an individual's expertise is most usually recognized outside of traditional talent management processes, and indeed outside of the organizational context. Just as academic journals are peer reviewed, so too is the expertise of an individual.

Expert Talent may be acquired by an individual through education, training or through experience. Expertise might be recognized in a local setting, such as a club or group to which they belong, or more widely through their delivery of seminars, lectures, articles, books, journals or social media. Their expertise will usually be in a niche area such, but may translate from one area in which they have recognized talent into another area of expertise. For example, sports personalities very often become leadership and management coaches transferring their experience in the sporting arena to expertise in the organizational setting.

Genius Talent

A capability that is considered to be extraordinary, difficult to replicate and beyond the capabilities of those who can gain a perceived value from the talent. It is well known that Albert Einstein, someone who is generally acknowledged as a genius when measured by the norms of academic achievement actually was considered a failure at school. The fact that his discoveries, theories and experiments have added something above and beyond the norm suggests that his 'talent' is extraordinary. Where individuals are recognized, as being Genius it would appear that their capability is a result of a combination of heightened natural ability and their environment. These factors result in the individual contributing something that is valuable beyond that of those who can gain a perceived value from the talent. For example, Einstein's Theory of Relativity does not add much value to HR, but even someone who does not understand the theory or its implications recognizes his talent.

Moreover, Genius Talent has an individualistic element that no amount of training, development or experience can replicate; the elusive X-Factor. A person either has the capability to do something that way, or you do not. Genius talent has a quality that, to our knowledge, only the Genius holds. Genius Talent is readily accepted in fields such as music, arts and in sports. In any field of expertise, corporate, academic or sport there are those who not only work hard but also demonstrate another level of talent, to that which others would struggle to achieve, regardless of development and experience. Genius is perhaps less applied in organizational or corporate realms but it is perhaps not unreasonable to suggest that there is scope to do so.

Unrecognized Talent

Unrecognized Talent presents perhaps the greatest challenge within the *status quo* of extant strategic talent management systems. It is, of course, possible that this form of talent may, when seen and identified, take any of the above-mentioned forms. In other words, akin to the tale of Einstein's life, a genius, for example, may be occluded and not facilitated by organizational processes. It is, it should be stated, also the possibility that those individuals with talent that has not been recognized do not wish that skill or capability to be publically seen. Even less, may they want it to be managed or employed for their organizational lives?

One of the ways in which Unrecognized Talent might be nurtured or coaxed will be to rethink the ways in which the scan for talent traditionally takes place. There is a real need for spaces to be created that engender and facilitate willing talent to be presented and shown in a manner in which it is, itself, comfortable with. This mean inevitably, as indicated above, as in the cases, for example, of Semco and Oticon, the introduction of processes that are shaped round individuals and groups of individuals rather than artefacts, structures and products.

Shaping Performance of Boundary-less Talent

Measuring the effectiveness of boundary-less talent cannot be based on traditional people measures and requires a different set of criteria. Boundary-less talent is needed in the organizational context because the knowledge, skills or expertise of all individuals can contribute positively to organizational competitive advantage. Equally, it has to be acknowledged that certain forms and presentations of talent are likely to cause conflict and clashes and may even inhibit competitive advantage. Therefore, it is necessary to re-think the ways in which various forms of talent are managed. In other words, management processes may need to be rhizomatic and occasionally chaotic and messy in nature.

Fully released talent potential means that one human can be worth more than the sum of a single individual. Where this type of synergy exists measures of effective performance should be based, not only on the ideas or output results that an individual alone can generate but also on the added value that is delivered when talent potential is released

The creative use of Boundary-less talent management needs to encouraged, but will be dictated by the commercial realities of the organizational enterprise. The present argument is not seeking to develop a form of Utopian response. Rather it is designing and advocating an alternative to the limitations and myopias of existing approaches. Perhaps a key reality and challenge of motivating and managing the performance of talent potential comes if the individual's talent has no commercial value. In these instances other areas of performance, such as their competence at the task in hand, the support they give to their peers and colleagues and their awareness of the organizational requirements, will need to be assessed.

Too often individual performance objectives are generic across a team. In recognizing the importance of individual talent in the creation of job roles and the allocation of tasks, the organization must ensure that performance objectives are individualised and are tailored to the task that the individual is required to perform.

Conclusion

Talent management has evolved over the last twenty years as part of the development of HRM. However, its focus has been predominately on developing leadership talent. Strategic talent management has often, paradoxically, been characterised by short term thinking, self-interest in 'heroic' strategic talent, an imbalance in the distribution of organizational rewards and the development and promotion of opportunities which erode trust and fail to recognize the true talent potential of an organization's employee population. The result is that organizational performance is unsustainable in the long term.

Managing talent outside of traditional perceptions of organization boundaries is a substantial challenge for modern entities but not one always recognised. Inherent in this are a number of tensions including the paradoxical need to collaborate yet compare, to protect intellectual property yet share knowledge to grow; and the need for companies to retain talent but move in and out of boundaries in order to fully release their talent potential.

The modern economy has resulted in the emergence of boundary-less organizations, boundary-less careers and boundary-less talent. These create new challenges for managing talent and necessitate HR policies and procedures that are flexible, creative, inclusive and diverse. This conceptual discussion has proposed that a new model of Boundary-less Talent Management be considered which adopts a soft-HRM approach and not only encompasses the traditional proposition of strategic talent management which focuses on those regarded as strategically important but also encompasses the employees which offer talent potential which is outside of the 'norm' that is to say Expert, Genius and/or Talent Within and perhaps most important of all Unrecognized Talent.

References

Agrawal, S. (2010), *Talent management Model for Business Schools: Factor Analysis,* The Indian Journal of Industrial Relations, Vol. 45, No. 3, pp. 481 - 491.

Alvesson, M. and Willmott, H. (1996), *Making Sense of Management: A Critical Introduction*, London: Sage Publications.

Altman, W. (2008, March 8-21), *Tuning into Talent.* Engineering and Technology.

Beardwell, J. and Clydon, T. (2010), *HR Management A Contemporary Approach (6th ed.,.* Pearson Education Ltd.

Boudreau, J. and Ramstead P., M. (2005), *Talentship and the New Paradigm for HR management: From Professional Practices to Strategic talent Decision Science.* HR Planning, Vol. 28, No. 5, pp. 17-26.

Buchanan, D. and Huczynski, A. (2010), *Organizational Behaviour (7th ed.)*, Essex: Pearson Education Limited.

Cappelli, P. (2000), *A Market-Driven Approach to Retaining Talent,* Harvard Business Review, Jan-Feb.

Clegg, S., Kornberger, M and Pitsis, T. (2008), *Managing and Organizations: An Introduction to Theory and Practice,* London: Sage Publications.

Collings, D. and Mellahi, K. (2009), *Strategic Talent Management: A Review and Research Agenda.* HR Management Review, Vol. 19, pp. 304-313.

Craig, E., Pham, C.T. and Bobulsky, S. (2008), *Rethinking Retention: If You Want Your Best Executives to Stay, Equip Them to Leave,* Accenture Institute for High Performance.

Edenborough, R. and Edenborough, M. (2012), *The Psychology of Talent - Exploring and Exploding the Myths,* Cambridge, Massachusetts, USA: Hogrefe.

Fleming, J. and. Asplund, J. (2008), *Understanding the Nature of Talent.* The Gallup Management Journal, Vol. 10, No. 1.

Francis, H. H. (2012), *People and Organisational Development: A new Agenda ofr Organisational Effectiveness*, London: CIPD.

Frank, F.D., Finnegan, R.P., and Taylor, C.R. (2004), *The Race for Talent: Retaining and Engaging Workers in the 21st Century*, HR Planning, Vol. 27, No. 3, pp. 12-25.

Gandossy, R. and Kao, T. (2004) *Talent Wars Out of Mind, Out of Practice*, HR Planning 15-19

Gardener, T.M. (2000), *In the Trenches at Talent Wars: Competitive Interaction for Scarce Human Resources – A Qualitative Study*, CAHRS Working Paper Series, Paper 96.

Garrow, V. (2008), *Talent management Issues of Focus and Fit*, Public Personnel Management, Vol. 37, No. 4, pp. 389-402.

Germain, J. (2010, Spring), *How to Drive your Troublesome Talent Forward to Success*, British Journal of Administrative Management, pp. 18-19.

Green, M. (2011, May), *Learning's Role in Integrated Talent management*, Training and Development.

Hansen, F. (2007), *What is Talent?* Workforce Management, Vol. 86, No. 1, pp. 12 -13.

Iles, P. P. (2010), *Talent Management as a Management Fashion in HRD: Towards a Research Agenda.* HR Development International, Vol. 13, No. 2, pp. 125-145.

Killian, Perez and Siehl (1998), *Richardo Semler and Semco S.A.* Thunderbird The Amercian Graduate School of International Management.

Kolind, L. (2012), *Rethinking management's first principles > Oticon* http://www.managementlab.org/files/u2/pdf/case%20studies/OticonCaseStudy_.pdf accessed 28.6.12.

Lawler, E. (2008), *Talent, Making People your Competitive Advantage.* San Francisco: John Wiley and Sons.

Lewis, R. and. Heckman R., J. (2006), *Talent Management: A Critical Review.* HR Management Review, Vol. 16, pp. 139-154.

Lockwood, N. (2006), *Talent Management: Driver for Organizational Success.* SHRM Research Quarterley.

Makela, K. B. (2010), *How do MNCs Establish Their Talent Pools? Influences on Individuals' Likelihood of being Labeled as Talent.* Journal of World Business, Vol. 45, pp. 134-142.

Martin, G. (2012, January 16), *Is There A Bigger And Better Sustainable Future For Talent Management?* Retrieved January 16, 2012, from CIPD: http://www.cipd.co.uk/comment-insight/comment/talent-sustainability-coming-.aspx

McCauley, C. and Wakefield, M. (2006, Winter), *Talent Management In The 21st Century; Help Your Company Find, Develop And Keep Its Strongest Workers*, The Journal for Quality and Particpation.

McKenna, E. (2012), *Business Psychology and Organizational Behaviour (Fifth Edition),* Psychology Press.

Mellahi, K. and Collings, D., G. (2010), *The Barriers to Effective Global Talent Management: The Example of Corporate Elites in MNEs.* Journal of World Business, Vol. 45, pp. 143-149.

Ohmae, K. (1994), *The Borderless World: Power and Strategy in the Interlinked Economy,* London: Harper Collins.

—. (2005) *The Next Global Stage: The Challenges and Opportunities in Our Borderless World*, London: Perarson/Prentice-Hall.

O'Hara-Devereaux, M. (2004), *Navigating the Badlands; Thriving in the Decade of Radical Transformation.* San Francisco: Jossey-Bass.

Owyang, J. (2011, August 31), *Social Media Crises On Rise: Be Prepared by Climbing the Social Business Hierarchy of Needs.* Retrieved February 9, 2012, from Web Strategy: http://www.web-strategist.com/blog/2011/08/31/report-social-media-crises-on-rise-be-prepared-by-climbing-the-social-business-hierarchy-of-needs/

Powell, M. and Lubitsh, G. (2007*), Courage in the face of Extraordinary Talent Why Talent Management has Become a Leadership Issue.* Strategic HR Review, Vol. 6, No. 5, pp. 24-27.

Ready, D. (2009), *Forging the New Talent Compact*, Business Strategy Review, Summer.

Reeves, R. (2003), *Who Carries the Tune?* Management Today, p. 31.

Schuler, R. J. (2011), *Global Talent Management and Global Talent Challenges: Strategic Opportunities for IHRM.* Journal of World Business, Vol. 46, pp. 506-516.

Smith, N. Q. (2011), *A Strategic Appraoch to Role-Based Talent Management* (Vol. 48). Training.

Stokes, P. (2011), *Critical Concepts in Management and Organization Studies.* Basingstoke: Palgrave Macmillan.

Syed, M. (2011), *Bounce - The Myth of Talent and the Power of Practice.* London: Fourth Estate.

Tarique, I. and Schuler, R., S. (2010), *Global Talent Management: Literature Review, Integrative Rramework and Suggestions for Further Research.* Journal of World Business, Vol. 45, pp. 122-133.

Tulgan, B. (2001), Winning the Talent Wars, *Employment Relations Today,* Summer.

Tyson (1995), *Human Resource Strategy: Towards a Theory of Human Resource Management*, London: Pitman Publishing.

Weick, K., E. (1995), *Sensemaking in Organizations* Foundations for Organizational Science, Sage Publications Inc.

Yamashita, M. and Uenoyama, T. (2006), *Boundaryless career and adaptive HR practices in Japan's Hotel Industry* Career Development International, Vol. 11, No. 3, pp. 96-118.

CHAPTER THREE

SOLIDARITY AS A "COMMONS" TO BE PROMOTED: ORGANISATION OF COLLECTIVE ACTION FOR A MORE RESPONSIBLE MANAGEMENT

BERNARD PARANQUE[1]

The question of collective action and cooperation fills many a page of the academic literature (Cefai, 2007; Thévenot, 2006; also see Ostrom 2010, 2008), if only with the renowned prisoner dilemma[2] which demonstrates that the cooperative solution has little probability of being selected in the absence of trust, therefore of information, between the players involved. The question remains to see if this stylised fact has a true operational scope beyond the case of the experiment in itself. Indeed, in this experiment, which is under the assumption of the liberalism paradigm, the "prisoners" are not given the opportunity to coordinate. Although it can be understood in this case, it is difficult to acknowledge as a reflection of human relations as a whole. For the latter, the need to interact for coordination purposes is the condition for collective action. Cooperation does not necessarily take place under duress, but to the contrary, might be sought after for what it embodies: the expression of solidarity for common purposes.

---

[1] The author thanks John Weeks (SOAS – University of London) and Hugh Willmott (Cardiff University) for their very useful comments. All errors remain mine.
[2] This famous example from game theory, aims to explain why two persons might not cooperate even it is in their interest to do so (Nowak, 2006, 2012).

Liberalism was born out of an affirmation of the freedom of the individual faced with absolute monarchy and the role of the Church. It therefore emerged as a utopia[3] as defined by Ricœur (see also Jaume, 2010: 9, 58)

> What is at stake in any utopia is the possibility of imagining a different way of exercising power. (Ricoeur, 1997: 256)

As a result, as the utopia of absolute monarchy, liberalism has become the ideology of capitalism, again as defined by Ricœur

> At the end of the day, what is at stake in any ideology is the legitimisation of a given authority structure. (Ricoeur, 1997: 256)

A parallel may thus be drawn with the thinking of Marx: it too emerged initially as a utopia over and against the established order. At first, liberalism did not assert itself as a new system but rather as a critique and an affirmation of a specific ontology. There is therefore a high degree of similarity between these two theories, both of which emerged to challenge an established order, even if the latter was more concerned with describing an ideal system, while the former focused rather on how the historical order which had produced this state of affairs could be overcome.

In other words, this historical dynamic can lead us to examine the new emergent phenomenon which needs to be defined in order to overcome the affirmation of private property as a means of liberation (even if the latter is hampered by its now outdated form, in which an individual must "alienate" their freedom in order to live).

This questioning arises from the present challenge people faces: how to be free citizen? To be free, people needs resources or the ability to produce resources, revenues. Liberalism focuses on private property and neoclassical economy on shareholder value maximization. In other words, each of us tries to maximize our own utility function with the hope that from that will emerges social and collective welfare. Some doubts about that are legitimate and another way to promote the last could be proposed.

---

[3] See Audier (2012: 288) quoting Hayek in "Les intellectuels et le socialisme" in Essais de philosophie, de science politique et d'économie (2007: 292), talking about the "courage of utopia" about the role of intellectuals in the promotion of socialism and the lack of it from liberal.

So the collective action in the dominant paradigm will be examined and a contextualisation of this concept in order to connect it with the utopia proposed by liberalism proposed. The Social and Solidarity Economic is presented as a common framework to promote common use and practice with the help of some principles given by Ostrom which help us to propose a new way to coordinate collective action.

The conditions of collective action and the limits of the dominant paradigm in finance

Collective action, or cooperation, is characterised by *"problems of information, anticipation and evaluation"* (Salais et al., 1999: 193). In fact the issue is, both on a collective and an individual level, to agree not only on a reality to be constructed but also to act together with this purpose in mind

> the stake behind these negotiations is the model of interpretation chosen to "construct the reality" that they (the protagonists) come up against as the problem to be solved. (Salais et al., 1999: 197-198)

In other words, this necessary negotiation is the expression of an understanding that officially recognises

> the agreement of the protagonists on their description of the world thus [allowing] them to coordinate their projects. (Salais et al., 1999: 236)

and its construction

> upon social processes for the elaboration of the models according to which reality is represented. (Salais et al., 1999: 239)

This requires the ability to produce relevant information. Whereas to collect information, the latter must first be produced, which in turn requires the ability to define and finalise needs in order to produce the corresponding information

> [...] information can only be passed on if it has first been developed using a common language and if, consequently, it can be adjusted on either side within a congruent system (for example, the presence of identical codes). (Salais and Storper 1993: 76-78)

None of this figures in the neoclassical theory (NCT) for which, in addition, the firm is a mere protagonist and the very concept of organisation is absent. It therefore only takes an interest in trade with the help of calculations to optimize the individual utility functions. The "firm"[4] is thus a dot on a segment, determined by these choices between work and capital factors. In other words, it has no substance and no content and is, at best, a bubble. And yet, all may note the existence of organisations of different and varying forms (association, Limited Company, Public Company, cooperative, economic development association, etc.) whose substance is undisputable although variable. More broadly, from the Theory of Transactions (Coase, 1937; Williamson, 1986) to the Agency Theory (Jensen and Meckling, 1976), the problems of coordinating economic action are sources of debate and proposals, but the questioning more often than not remains within the paradigm of methodological individualism (Birnbaum and Leca, 1991). Nevertheless, understanding and managing the coordination of economic action remains a challenge, particularly due to the intrinsic nature of the latter: complexity and its corollary, diversity, are at the heart of the process. Consequently, the underlying epistemological challenges require the support of work in other disciplines.

The idea is to question one of the strengths of NCT that

> resides in its capacity to separate the analysis of the action at a given time from everything that created the conditions for this action. (Przeworski, 1991: 88).

Although it is people that act (identified as protagonists, employees or other individuals), their actions are set down in a biography that begins with the development of cognitive capacities as tools to build their relationship with the world.

In financial theory, it is through the maximisation of the shareholder's utility function – maximisation of shareholder value – that this well-being is achieved in the long run[5] (Jensen 2001). The debates around the form and role of financial markets and, more broadly, financial systems, insist upon their place in satisfying needs. On one hand, we have the assertion that the maximisation of shareholder value, with all of the control issues that this engenders, is the best means, within a market economy, by which to achieve collective well-being; on the other hand, there is the assertion of

---

[4] In inverted commas to establish a generic term insofar as legally, the company does not exist ; see works of the Collèges des Bernardins at http://www.collegedesbernardins.fr/index.php/component/content/chapter/1364.html
[5] See presentation at http://www.people.hbs.edu/mjensen/.

the necessity (need) to take into account the interests of all the stakeholders of the firm, from the customers to all of the suppliers, through the employees and populations. The debate becomes interesting in the light of Jensen's assertion of the need to understand the maximisation of value from a collective stand point and that collective, social well-being is only achieved if, firstly, "all of the values" borne by each stakeholder are maximized and, secondly, that this maximization takes place over the long term. This is therefore the recognition of the firm, a source of wealth, as a historical and complex organization. However, an operational difficulty appears if we want managers to maximise the thus extended value insofar as the objectives of the different stakeholders have no reason, *a priori*, to converge. This criticism is true as much from the standpoint of value maximisation (how to manage several objectives at once) as from that of the stakeholders theory (how to define a common objective).

The question is therefore to know how this coordination can emerge and be forged.

What of the collective project?

There is a common point to all of these reflections: the quest for collective well-being, for happiness (Mill, 1988). When human beings become a part of society, or a company, they do so to fight against rarity, the risk of famine, death (Manent, 1987; Audard, 2000). They give up, as it were, their right to freedom as a counterpart to a commitment to react effectively against these threats. This requires that the terms of debate have been previously established to define how authority is exercised in order to lead the collective project to a successful conclusion.

It is therefore necessary to reintegrate individuals into their history, into their histories, in order to shed light upon the conditions for collective action. Each individual's career must be explained in order to clarify the conditions in which different interests and motivations converge. This involves the explicit recognition not only of the project, but also of the individual as a product[6] as "*producing in society – hence socially determined individual production*" (Marx, 1980: 17 / 1973: 81).

---

[6] On this subject, see introduction to Volume 1 of «"Grundrisse » (Marx, 1980 / 1973 and on.). For the reference in English the source is www.marxists.org/archive/marx/works/date/index.htm. When reference is given in the footnote the English one is mentioned with "/" after the French one.

Hence, it is not possible to talk of the individual acting in a group without this historical element which is not only the history of mankind or History, but also the history of a single individual who is a product of society, i.e. a single individual, and therefore socialized, in action

> personality is a biography within a history: the deployment of activities in human evolution, is temporal in essence. (Sève, 2008: 486; underlined by ourselves)

Thus, far from any confusion on "the nature of human beings", Marx establishes the essence of the latter in all social relationships (Marx, 1976: 3). There is no "state of nature" or "Reason" to which to refer to define freedom, but there is history, produced by mankind

> The human being is in the most literal sense a ["political animal" the expression is from Aristotle], not merely a gregarious animal, but an animal which can individuate itself only in the midst of society (…). When we speak of production, then, what is meant is always production at a definite stage of social development – production by social individuals (Marx, 1980:18-19 / 1973: 81).

The point is not to set up meetings on life experiences but to take into account the social dynamics that underpin any project and therefore the diversity of personal expectations converging towards a collective project. In the case of a producers' co-operative, one survey revealed that generational effects could emerge and oppose the young salaried members of the cooperative likely to take risks and the elder members, closer to retirement and eager to ensure that the risks would not be a threat to their future (Bouchon et al., 2010). It is possible to call this the mapping of motivations and expectations, a territory for collective action, which is not purely geographical.

It is therefore necessary to have rules, not general ones but generic ones which allow, not to impose principles, but to help develop an agreement on the terms for exercising power and for the evaluation of collective action.

How can we therefore provide ourselves with the means to coordinate our actions to achieve their concrete elements and which do not defer their achievement to some distant point in time?

Liberalism and individualism

If one is willing to follow on with him from Hobbes and Locke (Manent, 1987), labour is thus the source of wealth (even if for Hobbes the motivation is the fear of the death), in other words, of wealth creation. It is thus a source of value with an important characteristic: its implementation creates more wealth than it requires to be implemented. This is what enables a surplus to be produced. The value of labour strength[7] is thus nothing less than the benchmark by which the wealth produced can be measured (Marx, 1974: 177 / 1863 § 4, for example). Wealth is measured by the labour time socially required to produce it (Marx, 2010: 154-155[8]). This is the law of value, otherwise known as the law of necessity. That said, the development of productive forces – man's mastery of his environments – makes it possible to multiply man's ability to meet social needs by means of science, technology and training: in short, through knowledge. This enables enormous productivity gains to be achieved through the division of labour, as Smith and Ricardo have shown. The decrease in working hours – paid working hours – is nothing less than an expression of these productivity gains and their distribution throughout all human societies (unequally and differently in time and space). The counterpart of reducing required working hours is the increase in free time, if only to consume the new goods produced.

> The only extra-economic fact in all this is that man does not need all his time to produce his means of subsistence, and that he has free time over and above the time required to work for subsistence: free time which he can also use for surplus labour. (Marx, 1980b: 133 / 1973: 637)

This does however assume that man can control his work and has the required resources, whether financial or social, to carry out this surplus labour. Marx makes this point very clear

> In this area, the only possible freedom is that all social men, producers together, adjust their exchanges with nature in a rational manner, controlling it together instead of being dominated by its blind power, and accomplish these exchanges expending a minimum of energy, in conditions which correspond as closely as possible to what is most befitting to their nature as human beings. Nevertheless, this activity still constitutes the kingdom of necessity. The development of human strength

---

[7] And not the value of labour – and this is a major break with his predecessors, even if they sensed this difference (Locke, 1992).
[8] Marx, 1864: [469e-469g].

as an end in itself begins beyond that: the true kingdom of freedom, which can only blossom in the soil of this kingdom of necessity. The fundamental condition of this is a shorter working day [in (Sève, 2004: 62)].

What is established here constitutes the conditions for the practical expression of human freedom, without which the questions of sovereignty and representation are meaningful only to a lesser degree.

Marx's analysis clearly highlights the issue of private property (Marx, 2010:130-131[9]), also emphasised by Hobbes, Locke and indeed Montesquieu (Manent, 1987), whose influence he acknowledges when he deals with the development of trade which, through the capture of the surplus produced by labour, leads to the appearance of companies, particularly share companies. The development of financial instruments, as well as of the first financial markets, led Marx to deal particularly with forms of society which "promoted" the notion of private property. In this regard, he emphasises the contradiction which is there in his work right from the outset

> The constitution of share companies. The consequences: 1/ The huge extension of the scale of production and companies which would have been impossible with isolated capital. At the same time, enterprises which were the preserve of the state become private companies. 2/ Capital (...) refers here directly to the form of social capital (the capital of individuals in direct association with each other) as opposed to private capital. (...) 3/ The transformation of a genuinely active capitalist into a mere director and administrator of others' capital, and of capital owners into mere owners (...). In share companies, the function [of manager] is separated from the ownership of the capital. This result of the supreme development of capitalistic production is the nexus through which the conversion of capital into producers' property must pass, no longer converting it into the private property of individual producers, but into the property of associated producers: directly into company property (Marx, 1978: 102 / 1894: 305).

Property which may or may not be collective, such as cooperatives or "traditional" share companies

> The cooperative factories of the labourers themselves represent within the old form the first sprouts of the new (…). The capitalist stock companies, as much as the cooperative factories, should be considered as transitional forms from the capitalist mode of production to the associated one, with

---

[9] Marx, 1864: 383-385.

the only distinction that the antagonism is resolved negatively in the one and positively in the other.... (Marx, 1978: 105 / 1894: 306).

Marx was keen to grasp how individuals could be enabled or prevented from revealing their personality and freedom (Marx, 2010: 159). He showed that since it ignored the practical realities of the system within which we find ourselves, liberalism could not keep its promise. In particular, his analysis of the State shows that despite everything, right from the outset, he had identified the weakness of liberal thought which consists in the concealment[10] of the power plays relating to the ownership of the means of production and to the private control of previously accumulated labour, in terms which recall Locke's analysis of property (Locke, 1992) or Montesquieu's analysis of the separation of powers (Manent, 1987: 119).

> Since private property has separated itself from the community, the State has acquired its own existence alongside, and outside, civil society; but this State is nothing other than the form of organisation the bourgeoisie has had to provide itself with in order to offer a reciprocal guarantee of its property and interests, both externally and internally (Marx, 1976: 73-74 / 1968).

Marx goes on to clarify

> the State is therefore the form in which individuals in a dominant class establish their common interests and in which the whole of a given era's civil society is enshrined. It allows for all common institutions to pass through the intermediary of the State and take on a political nature. This gives rise to the illusion that law represents an action of the will – what is more, free will, detached from its actual basis. The same goes for the right to law in its turn (idem: 74).

Manent says as much regarding Montesquieu's influence, when he notes that the latter

> instead of starting with law as a foundation of freedom, starts with power, which is a threat to it; instead of looking at the origin of power, he studies its effects (Manent, 1987: 123).

He also remarks that it is with Rousseau that

---

[10] Although in some respects he does not completely escape this, by allowing or at least opening the door to the interpretation which holds that collective appropriation of the means of production consists in their nationalisation by the State; the latter "representing" individuals (but how?).

modern man became bourgeois; he ceased to be a citizen (Manent, 1987: 147).

This is at the heart of Marxian thought[11] the issue of power and

> the contradiction within the world of humanity; it is born out of labour and inequalities in property, precisely because its original foundation is the difference in labour capacities and unequal strengths (Manent, 1987:167).

These inequalities cannot be seen simply as "natural" – they are fundamentally social in nature (Sève, 2008).

The Social and Solidarity Economy: field and resource

The object of this chapter is to demonstrate that the SSE pursues collective well-being but in a different way, placing solidarity at the heart of its action system. However, this then raises the question of how this collective action is managed and the way in which it copes with the issues of opportunism and "stowaways".

It is easier to define the Social and Solidarity Economy with respect to its intended outcomes rather than through a legal framework. However, it should be specified that the SSE

> places the human being at the centre of economic and social development. Solidarity within the realms of the economy relies upon a project that is at once economic, political and social, and which leads to a new approach to politics and the forging of human relationships, based on consensus and citizenship action (Mayer and Caldier, 2007: 102).

The works of Elinor Ostrom (2010) is used. She has worked on common physical property "Commons" and studied the systems of ownership under which they may be managed. The question she raises is whether, between the State and the market, there could be forms of management for intermediate collective action, based on coordinated private ownership (Bollier in Ostrom et Hess 2011: 27-40)? The archetypal example is that of private owners' management of a common resource such as fish for fishermen or water for farmers. It is the distinction between public goods and private goods. A public good

---

[11] For the use of this term rather than that of Marxism or Marxist, see Sève (2004 p. 190).

is naturally non rivalrous, meaning that consumption of the resource does not deplete the amount available to other users, and not excludable, meaning that knowledge resources are not naturally defined by boundaries that permits exclusion of users. (Madison et al., 2010: 666)

Could we manage resources in a specific manner which allow a collective use of the resource out of the public sphere and (partially) the private market[12] ?

How can we make the jump from these cases to the SSE? It would seem that in the case of the SSE, it is less a question of knowing how to manage a common resource, even if the operational question remains, than providing the means to better coordinate and manage collective action around a common objective, even if the latter is variable. This joins the "Commons" insofar as it is a question of agreeing on and acting according to common principles. It is different in that the object is no longer the physical resource as such, but the conditions for collective action towards a common goal, a "mediating" resource to some extent.

> The commons paradigm does not look primarily to a system of property, contracts, and markets, but to social norms and rules, and to legal mechanism that enable people to share ownership and control of resources (Bollier, 2011: 29; see also Gosh, Levine or Schweik in Hess and Ostrom, 2011).

A crucial element is therefore governance, to establish the SSE projects sustainably on the market. This aspect is even more important as it has been suggested that the creation of a cooperative might be not so much a defensive response to globalisation rather than an offensive solution to reduce the financial constraints linked, in certain countries, to the failing of the capital market. (Casadesus-Masanell at Khanna, 2003).

The issue of commons has been studied in-depth and developed by Elinor Ostrom (2010) regarding natural resources. In a conference she gave in Paris on the 23rd June 2011, at the initiative of the CIRIEC, the CNAM, the Social Economy Chair of the ESCEM and the RIODD, she underlined the importance of understanding commons as a specific ownership system with a distribution of user rights; for each system of resources there is an *ownership system* with its own system of governance.

---

[12] For cultural commons see Macey, 2010.

Ostrom's position concerns

> questions relative to the best way to manage natural resources used as a common-pool by several individuals (…) (Ostrom, 2010: 13).

The usual answer is binary; either they must be handed over to the State so that nobody is excluded, or left up to the market. However, observation shows that the answer can be different, combining the private ownership and collective management of a common outside of the State or market. In these cases, the important aspect is "the perceptibility of the actions of each member" (ibid: 19). The stake is therefore, and above all, that of trust amongst participants.

The goal is not to apply the criteria developed by Ostrom as such, but to draw inspiration from them to help formalise the conditions for collective action and to define common guiding principles (Schweik, 2011). Although it is obvious that managing a physical resource is very different from managing actions within the scope of the SSE, there is an underlying point that is common to both issues. Before managing a resource, the protagonists involved must first come to an agreement and this is no doubt where Ostrom's major contribution resides, by establishing a junction: how to define a collective objective and the means by which to achieve it. Independently of the material nature of resources, the crucial aspect is the way in which the protagonists, within a precise ownership system, will reach an agreement, or not, to manage either a physical resource or to mobilise the means by which to fulfil a need. The first, in order to be operational and formalised, requires explicit rules to manage collective action and the coordination of private interests. The second mobilises the protagonists, not around a resource but around a project whose purpose is to fulfil a social need for which means must be mobilized (human, financial, technical…). In addition, in the case of SSE, we are looking at collective action which is sometimes/often established in opposition to the market whereas this question does not arise for "Commons", as it has already been decided: the collective management of a common resource by stakeholders who might already be present on the market (fishermen selling their catch, farmers selling their fruit harvests…).

The question therefore arises as to the interest of formalising the management of these solidarity actions, especially as this could be perceived as a desire to "lay hands" on the project and to deflect it away from its values. Indeed, SSE actions are often engaged to target "excluded" populations for whom specific solutions must be found (disabled workers, collective day-nurseries, home-help, etc.). In fact, this means finding a solution to something that the market cannot/does not wish to cater for. The stakes behind solidarity, mutualisation, non-commercial relationships are profound. And yet the question of the inclusion of these people, of the opportunity with which they are, or are not, provided with, the possibility of gaining access to everything that Society has to offer, including via commercial relationships, is clearly there. Hence, the questions of collective action coordination are raised within a space of solidarity, more often than not outside of the market, as the latter is considered to be a constraint and not an opportunity to build the value of emerging activities in this field. To become a market player whilst remaining true to values requires the latter to be clearly established operationally through principles that govern the action and management of the organisations with their own performance indicators. This requires common rules.

Which action principles?

Ostrom defines 8 principles of common agreement for sustainable common pool resource institutions (Ostrom, 2010: 114). The question here is not to set up this type of institution but to draw inspiration to build an analytical grid to help establish appropriate development strategies.

1. Clearly defined boundaries. What are the boundaries of the community? How can its foundations be identified in terms of links?
2. Congruence among appropriation, provision rules, and local conditions. Identify the way the community functions based on its values, the procedures and forms of contributions of its members, and the principles that authorise the use of the output of activities by each person.
3. Collective choice arrangements. How should operational rules be instituted, at what level of formalisation, and what are the procedures to modify them?
4. Monitoring. How is it possible to ensure respect for the spirit of the community, and what should the sanctions be for offenders?
5. Graduated sanctions. What are they, and how are they defined and applied?
6. Conflict resolutions mechanisms. Assess the capacity of the group to manage itself and manage change or divergence in available choices when faced with corporate behaviour.

7. Minimal recognition of rights to organise. Identify the structure of the community and the way diversity in commitment to the project, together with its constraints, can be managed.
8. Nested enterprises. Account for the company's activities in the market and its interconnections with other businesses (in particular outside SSE).

An understanding of this system that resides outside of the market and yet cohabits or even plays with the market (see the experience of the SCOP, Mondragon for example, Casdesus-Masanell and Khanna, 2003, Arando et al., 2010) is vital for the sustainability of the SSE[13].

Common resources, common property are provided by nature or produced by human beings with the knowledge that anything taken by an individual is/can be done so to the detrim45ent of others, as each person is tempted to take as much as they can to avoid being rationed (Ostrom, 2007).

For our purpose, we might imagine two risks for the SSE "community" and the protagonists involved: 1/ certain members can use collective work to "privatise" it, as can happen when a solidarity action for access to quality vegetables creates a new market, which becomes solvable and therefore gives rise to commercial opportunities; 2/ the company might be tempted to "merchandise" the produce of this work to develop its offer as, for example, in the case of the professional insertion of disabled workers who might be considered simply as cheap labour.

The challenge that the community must therefore meet for its own sustainability is to reduce the risk of opportunism: that a protagonist (individual or company) takes over, to the detriment of others, all or part of the resources generated by a project by deflecting it from its original purpose.

---

[13] Regarding this, " The Institutional Analysis and Development Framework and the Commons" (http://www.lawschool.cornell.edu/research/cornell-law-review/up load/Ostrom-response-final.pdf,) provides some interesting elements for our analysis based on the "Response" that Ostrom (2010b) brings to an chapter on open source software (http://www.lawschool.cornell.edu/research/cornell-law-review/upload/Madison-Frischmann-Strandburg-final.pdf) in the same issue (Madison M.J, Frischmann B.M. and Strandburg K.J., 2010).

It is thus important to define the boundaries of the community/group and therefore to clarify the congruent forms of ownership with their objectives. Five ownership laws have been defined by Ostrom to qualify "ownership":

1. Access: The right to enter a defined physical area and enjoy nonsubtractive benefits (for example, hike, canoe, sit in the sun).
2. Withdrawal: The right to obtain resource units or products of a resource system (for example, catch fish, divert water).
3. Management: The right to regulate internal use patterns and transform the resource by making improvements.
4. Exclusion: The right to determine who will have access rights and withdrawal rights, and how those rights may be transferred.
5. Alienation: The right to sell or lease management and exclusion rights. (Schlager and Ostrom, 1992, in Ostrom and Hess 2007: 11).

Creating the conditions for collective action does not simply boil down to managing the entrepreneurial project but requires the definition of the boundaries that characterise the action space and the intensity of involvement for the different stakeholders. Consequently, beyond the technical aspects, it is also important to define the corresponding social space. If we come back to the dimensions proposed by Ostrom, we have eight points:

- "Boundary": Identify the characteristics of the participants in order to determine the boundary (ies) of the collective project, i.e. identify who is targeted and who is involved;
- "Position": The positions of each party must be clarified in order to define responsibilities and the action/intervention capacities of the protagonists;
- "Choice": We must then understand the range of action, i.e. what the protagonists and stakeholders of the project can, must or must not do;
- "Scopes": What are the results of the actions? What does the community produce and how does it define that which is allowed, expected and prohibited (if it does this)?
- "Aggregation": This is a question of understanding how the actions organised produce a result with regard to the aims set by the community;
- "Information": How does the community ensure the production, diffusion and appropriation of the information necessary for its action;

- "Payoff": This is the identification of the form and manner in which the benefits of community action are expressed and how its operating costs are distributed.
- "Nested firms". Control, appropriation, rules, conflict resolution, governance rely on different level of nested firms and imply to be coherent inside the community.

Organisation and collective action

The organisation that carries the project must express the original motivations and values behind the project and operate according to the necessary daily action and management conditions by which to achieve the collective goal as developed between the different people and by which ensure their commitment.

Although it is relatively easy to imagine what might be (that the project seeks to achieve), it is far more difficult to define and daily implement the means and the appropriate behaviours by which to ensure its day-to-day realisation. Indeed, the initial project arises from a demand and/or a necessity, be this disability, access to resources, the need for autonomy…It rarely arises from a reflection on the means as (the need for democracy within a firm, building on opportunities…). Whereas, in all cases, these projects will be faced with the question of means: who will the customers be? Which suppliers will guarantee supply? How to deal with training requirements for the team? How to obtain the necessary loan…?

When these questions arise, more often than not they are urgent or are dealt with in obvious manners: this supplier is available, this customer has approached us. But their expectations and their values might not be coherent or might not meet those of the project carriers. How to be certain that their own constraints won't "contaminate" the project dynamics? For example, how to develop a fair trade network with local and located producers, when the demand from end consumers, from the market, is to eat fruit and vegetables all year round, and not, therefore, seasonally?[14]

---

[14] This was the object of debate during a lecture with students regarding the banana trade. How to support local producers within the framework of the development of fair trade whilst reducing the impact of product supply on the environment during transport to Europe? Can these aspects be dissociated, by saying « I only purchase seasonal produce » if the farmers, due to the weight of history and former choices, have no other choice; if embedded in power struggles, they need time to diversify

The answer to this type of question, and hence the organisation and governance, must reflect the way in which power is exercised and the methods by which it is enforced.

In other words, how are, or how should, decisions be made. Therefore, have the principles for decision making been defined: are they based on each party's contribution meaning that financial capacity would be privileged, or are they based on each party's degree of commitment, in which case motivation and skills would have the upper hand?

The forms of governance will interpret these choices. The rules adopted, depending on whether they place the accent on the principle "one person, one vote" or "one action, one vote", favouring specific expressions of action coordination and the involvement of protagonists (Dunlavy, 2006). They will have a major effect on the way the project is undertaken and the concretisation of the values carried by the group. The right to speak is also the recognition of the legitimacy to speak out regarding decisions. In this respect, if the project carriers agree to share the right to speak out, what about the employees that they have recruited?

From this point of view, the study of cooperatives can be of great interest (even if the question of equality faced with capital has not been entirely solved (Baretto, 2011)), insofar as, beyond the fact that the question is well-documented, they are based on three main principles: interdependence, solidarity and democracy (Gios and Santuari, 2002). The advantage is that they can also be the object of a dual problem. What are the governance stakes regarding the sustainability of the collective project and the need for its re-evaluation over time? What advantages and disadvantages do they present as compared to traditional firms in terms of performance, which implies questioning the nature of the latter, financial or societal? What are the obstacles to this type of collective management of production means and what are the social and cultural conditions required for its appropriation? All of these questions could form a basis for international research cooperation, all the more relevant as the question of the efficiency of this type of organisation is raised. The question remains relevant on condition that the reference model and its underpinning paradigm are described. This requires the clarification of the latter which is that of the maximisation of shareholder value as a means for collective well-being

---

their produce ? How far must we have the capacity to develop compromises, including with regard to our own demands?

and to compare this with a societal performance that cannot be reduced solely to the efficiency of the firm but rather to that of the entire group that it involves: customers, suppliers, population…. Consequently even if some issue the hypothesis that

> the implication [cooperative employees might accept lower salaries in order to keep their jobs] is that cooperatives will underperform limited liability firms, though it is important that the poor performance causes the cooperative to exist, rather than the act of cooperation inducing inefficiency (Casadesus-Masanell and Khanna, 2003: 4).

when a company is taken over by the employees to prevent it from closing down. Thus, once again, it is important to agree upon the objects of comparison and more precisely on the relevance of the connection, i.e. the choice of indicators. Indeed, be it in terms of work productivity, sustainability or investment, the finding of an underperformance is far from being validated (Schwartz, 2011; Arando et al., 2010).

Conclusion

As a conclusion, this chapter does not present any results but proposes to engage in comparative studies on the forms and principles of governance within the field of the Social and Solidarity Economy to clarify the conditions of democratic expression in the management of entrepreneurial projects. It is an invitation to develop a comparative research programme to study the forms of the collective organisation of production or commercialisation whilst analysing the conditions in which informal work can pass into the formal sector without necessarily forgoing the values held by the communities of people within which it is established. With regard to this, the challenge of agricultural development throughout the world might be an opportunity to observe how potentially structuring projects around the development of tourism could be used as leverage to mobilise local smallholding farmers who would thus have a potential source of customers whilst ensuring a democratic model for the governance of the project.

It is obvious that such a project is of even greater interest when it takes into account the different systems of values that underpin collective action (http://www.worldvaluessurvey.org/wvs/chapters/folder_published/chapter_base_54).

As Franck Fischbach says

the question would then be to find out whether we can escape from the coercive and continual power of value by drawing directly from another notion of time which would no longer be the set and spatial time of the presence of value itself, but a moving, fluid and dynamic temporality (2009: 136).

This value could be that of usage and not purely trade, coordinated by the mediation of the collective project developed according to rules that are suitable to all. Case study approach could be a good way to understand better how people act collectively and how they build the required coordination.

There is a need to go beyond the private property under the capitalist rules to contribute to the emergence of 'having' logic base to a logic focusing on commons as a result of production activity and/or as a effect of collective action as a appropriation mean

> of the cultural world and of the civilisation as a whole. (Fischbach, 2009b: 234)?

So how to contribute to define

> an alternative conception of property as a way to benefit of self pleasure (idem: 238)?

Is it possible to agree with Fichte who define this conception

> in a exclusive right to a free determined activity (idem: 244)?

In other words, could we find an agreement on the fact that

> the true opposition (...) is not between private property and collective property but between private use and common use (idem: 249)

and on the proposal to built

> a common use of goods and wealth, against their private and privative consumption which dominate today. (idem : 262)?

References

Arando, S. Freudlich, F. Gago, M. Jones, D.C. Kato, T. (2010), Assessing Mondragon : Stability and managed change in the face of globalization. William Davidson Institute, Working Paper n° 1003, November. Available at SSRN: http://ssrn.com/abstract=1726449.

Audard, C. (2000), Qu'est ce que le libéralisme? Ethique, politique, société. Folio, Essais, Paris.

Audier, S. (2012), Néo-libéralisme(s) : une archéologie intellectuelle. Grasset, Paris.

Baretto, T. (2011), Société coopérative de production et démocratie dans l'entreprise. Collèges des Bernardins, L'entreprise, formes de la propriété et responsabilités sociales –
http://www.collegedesbernardins.fr/templates/standard/images/pdf/ehs/baretto-2011-scop-et-democratie.pdf.

Bollier D. (2011), The growth of the commons paradigm, in Hess C. and Ostrom E. (2011), Understanding Knowledge as a Commons, MIT Press, Cambridge, USA.

Bouchon, C. Michard, B. and Plasse, A. (2010), Influence du statut juridique et de la gouvernance sur les conditions de mise en œuvre d'une politique efficace de Responsabilité Sociétale des Entreprises. Etude comparative des Sociétés Anonymes (SA) classiques et des Sociétés Coopératives de Production (SCOP), mémoire de recherche Master, Euromed Management, Marseille.

Cefai, D. (2007), Pourquoi nous mobilisons nous ? La Découverte MAUSS, Paris.

Coase, R. (1937), The nature of the firm : Origin, meaning, influence. in Williamson O.E. et Winter S.G. 1991. The Nature of the firm, Oxford University Press.

Casadesus-Masanell, R. and Khanna, T. (2003), Globalization and trust: Theory and evidence from cooperatives. William Davidson Institute, Working Paper Number 592, June. Available at
http://papers.ssrn.com/sol3/papers.cfm?abstract_id=577703.

Dunlavy, C. A. (2006), Social conceptions of the corporation: Insights from the history of shareholder voting rights. Washington and Lee Law Review, Vol. 63, p. 1347. Available at SSRN: http://ssrn.com/abstract=964377 .

Fischbach, F. (2009), Comment le capital capture le temps. Marx Relire le Capital, coordonné par Fischbach, F. pp. 101-138. PUF Débats philosophiques, Paris.

—. (2009b), Sans objet : capitalisme, subjectivité, aliénation. Librairie Philosophique J . Vrin, Paris.

Gios, G. and Santuari, A. (2002), Agricultural cooperatives in the county of Trento (Italy): Economic, organizational and legal perspectives. Journal of Rural Cooperation, vol. 30, n°1, pp. 3-12. Available at http://purl.umn.edu/60951.

Gosh S. (2011), How to build a commons: is intellectual property constrictive, facilating or irrelevant?, in Hess C. and Ostrom E. (2011), Understanding Knowledge as a Commons, MIT Press, Cambridge, USA.

Hess C. and Ostrom E. (2011), Understanding Knowledge as a Commons, MIT Press, Cambridge, USA.

Jaume, L. (2010), Les origines philosophiques du libéralisme. Flammarion - Champs Essais, Paris.

Jensen, M. C. (2001), Value maximization, stakeholder theory, and the corporate objective function, October. Available at SSRN http://ssrn.com/abstract=220671.

Jensen, M., and Meckling, W. H. (1976), 'Theory of the Firm: Managerial Behavior, Agency Costs and Ownership Structure', The Journal of Financial Economics, Vol. 3, No. 4, pp. 305-360.

Locke, J. (1992), Traité du gouvernement civil. Flammarion, Paris.

Macey, G.P. (2010), Cooperative institutions in cultural commons. Cornell Law Review, Vol. 95, May 5, pp. 757-792, 2010. Available at SSRN: http://ssrn.com/abstract=1601102

Madison, M.J, Frischmann, B.M. and Strandburg, K.J. (2010), Constructing commons in the cultural environment. Cornell Law Review, volume 95-4, May, pp. 657-710. Available at http://papers.ssrn.com/sol3/papers.cfm?abstract_id=1265793.

Manent, P. (1987), Histoire intellectuelle du libéralisme. Hachette, Paris.

Marx, K. (1976/1968), L'Idéologie Allemande. Editions Sociales, Paris / The German Ideology. Progress Publishers.

—. (1974/1863), Théorie sur la plus-value. Tome 1. Editions Sociales, Paris / Theories of Surplus Value. Progress Publishers

—. (1978/1894), Le Capital, Livre 3, Tome 2. Editions Sociales, Paris / Capital Volume III. International Publisher, NY.

—. (1980/1973), Manuscrits de 1857-1858, Grundrisse, Tome 1. Editions Sociales, Paris / Grundrisse. Penguin.

—. (1980b/1973), Manuscrits de 1857-1858, Grundrisse, Tome 2. Editions Sociales, Paris / Grundrisse. Penguin.

—. (2010/1864), Le Chapitre VI, Le Capital, Livre 1, Editions Sociales – GEME, Paris Capital. Book I. The process of production of capital. MECW, Vol. 34, pp. 339-467.

Mayer, S. and Caldier, J-P. (2007), Le guide de l'économie équitable. Fondation Gabriel Péri, Paris.

Mill, J.S., (1871,1988), L'Utilitarisme. Champs, Flammarion, Paris.

Nowak, M. (2012), Les cinq piliers de l'entraide, Pour la Science, n° 419, septembre, pp. 68-72.

—. (2006), Five rules for the evolution of cooperation, Science, Vol. 314, pp. 1560-1563.

Ostrom, E. and Hess, C. (2007), Private and common property rights. Workshop in Political Theory and Policy Analysis, WP 07-25, Indiana University, available at http://papers.ssrn.com/sol3/papers.cfm?abstract_id=1304699 .

Ostrom, E. (2007), The challenge of crafting rules to change open access resources into managed resources. Workshop in political theroy and policy analysis, Indian University, electronic copy available at http://ssrn.com/abstract=1304827.

—. (2008), Building trust to solve commons dilemmas: Taking small steps to test an evolving theory of collective action. Games, groups and the global good. Simon Levin, ed., New York. Available at SSRN: http://ssrn.com/abstract=1304695.

—. (2010), Gouvernance des biens communs. De Boeck, Bruxelles.

—. (2010b), Response, the institutional analysis and development framework and the commons. Cornell Law Review, Vol. 95-4, May, pp. 807-816.

Przeworski, A. (1991), Le défi de l'individualisme méthodologique à l'analyse marxiste. In Birnbaum, P. and Leca, J., 1991. Sur l'individualisme, (sous la direction de). Presse de la Fondation Nationale des Sciences Politiques, Références, pp: 77-108.

Ricœur, P. (1997), Idéologie et Utopie. Seuil, Paris.

Salais, R. and Storper, M. (1993), Les mondes de production – enquête sur l'identité économique de la France. École des Hautes Études en Sciences Sociales, Paris.

Salais, R. Baverez, N. and Reynaud, B. (1999), L'invention du chômage. Presse Universitaire de France, Quadrige, Paris.

Schwartz J. (2011), Where did Mill go wrong? Why the capital managed firm rather than the labor managed enterprise is the predominant organizational form in market economies. The John Marshall Law School. Chicago. July 14. Available at SSRN: http://ssrn.com/abstract=1886024 or

http://dx.doi.org/10.2139/ssrn.1886024.
Schweik C. M. (2011), Free/open software as a framework for establishing commons in science, in Hess C. and Ostrom E. (2011), Understanding Knowledge as a Commons, MIT Press, Cambridge, USA.
Sève, L. (2004), Penser avec Marx aujourd'hui, Tome 1: Marx et nous. La Dispute, Paris.
—. (2008), Penser avec Marx aujourd'hui, Tome 2: L'Homme. La Dispute, Paris.
Thévenot L. (2006), L'action au pluriel, sociologie des régimes d'engagement, La Découverte, Paris.
Williamson, O.E. (1986), Economic, organisation, firms, market and policy control, Wheatsheaf Books.

Chapter Four

Mindset and Behaviour Effect on Firm Performance

Stefano Bresciani, Demetris Vrontis and Alkis Thrassou

Introduction

Creating and sustaining a competitive advantage is the core of strategic management (Porter, 1985; Barney, 1991; Prahalad and Hamel, 1994). Organisations wishing to build a sustainable, competitive advantage must focus on building organisational capabilities that are valuable, rare, and not easily imitable by competitors (Barney, 1991). The current economic environment is characterised by radical changes effected, among other factors, by the globalisation of markets, the introduction and development of new technologies, as well as variability and demand segmentation (Thrassou and Vrontis, 2009). These trends have a significant impact on the internal as much as on the external environment of the company; and they affect not only production through new systems called "lean" such as Just in Time or Flexible Production, but also organisational structure itself. The new organisational models include structures that tend to be more flat and flexible. The increase of mobility, not just in terms of capital, but also of human resources, has widened the geographical spaces, setting the companies on a comprehensive plan, also facilitated by the information revolution that overturned all the physical constraints of the various processes in different divisions/countries. The context is more and more dominated by a strong and growing competition between companies and within a global arena, forcing organisations to shift the focus of competitive advantage from the classical sources to new notions altogether. For this reason, the greatest risk to which companies are exposed is inactivity, or simply the lack of response to a fast changing external environment. In fact, in order to survive in the developing economic environment, organisations must be able to use tools of various types and at all levels to become more profitable and competitive.

In the last decades, this intensifying organisational phenomenon has captured the attention of researchers on different subjects (Foss-Laursen, 2000; Laursen-Mahnke, 2000; Leoni-Cristini-Mazzoni-Labory, 2000; Wilkinson, 2000; Valdani, 2000; Ham-Kleimer, 2002; Tardivo, 2008; Jackson, 2010; Zheng et al., 2010), who increasingly agree that to be competitive in turbulent markets, organisations must understand how to react quickly to sudden changes happening in the industry in which they compete. In order to achieve this, corporations have modified their internal organisations, evolving to more lean and flexible structures, which enable them to react quickly and adapt their businesses. This is reflected in the way corporations search for sources of competitive advantage; moving their attention from "hard" elements, such as privileged access to resources (e.g. capital), to "softer" elements, such as the management of human resources, innovation (Bresciani et al., 2012; Thrassou et al., 2012a). The soft elements are the focus of much research and represent the overall theme of this chapter.

This change can happen in different ways: change can be planned or unplanned (or emerging), wanted or unexpected, continuous or discontinuous (or episodic), incremental or through quantum leaps, and finally transformational or transitional. According to theorists Linstone and Mitroff (1994) an organisation, during a change, must take into account three different perspectives in the planning and implementation of its processes: the technology available, the organisation of reference and personnel perspectives. It thus appears very interesting to try to understand whether a firm's performance is affected by mindset and behaviour, where "mindset" are the principles, values and beliefs of an organization (both implicit and explicit) and "behaviour" is the way the members of the same organization act within it.

Theoretical background

Contextual framework

The relationship between "human resources" and "performance" is a theme that has been widely discussed over the last twenty years, especially during '90s in the US (Arthur, 1994; Osterman, 1994; Huselid, 1995; Macduffie, 1995; Koch and Mcgrath, 1996; Ichniowski and Shaw, 1999;

Lazear, 2000) and in Great Britain (Guest and Peccei, 1994; McNabb and Whitfield, 1997; Guest, 1999; Hiltrop, 1999), where a number of research studies have been published in prominent international journals. The main outcome of such studies has been that human resource management has an important impact on an organisation's capacity to be competitive and can be considered to be a major source of competitive advantage (Delery and Doty, 1996; Guest, 1997; Boselie et al., 2001, Sundar, 2012). Research in the area of organisational culture is relatively new: in particular the investigation of the relationship between "culture" and performance. Before reviewing related literature though, this chapter investigates the meaning of organisational culture and performance.

"Culture" is a loose term used to describe, amongst other things, the group of values, principles and guidelines particular to an organisation which are shared by all its members. The first, and probably the most widely used, definition of culture is "the way we do things around here" (Bower, 1966), which has been the basis of all the subsequent elaborations. The first to introduce the concept of organisational culture were Deal and Kennedy in 1982, whose description included all the expectations, rituals, taboos, rewards and sanctions at the base of an organisation.

In 1986, Schein described culture as "the values and fundamental principles shared by the members of the organization, which act at unconscious level of people and set a sort of filter through which the organization perceives itself and the environment around". The values and principles tend to be implicit and drive people's behaviour. Very few researchers though try to distinguish culture in terms of its elements of mindset and behaviour. The elements of the mindset being the implicit and explicit principles, values and beliefs, and the elements of behaviour being the visible and invisible acts deriving from the mindset in which they are adopted.

Whilst the term "performance" can have different definitions, it is normally linked to a monetary value of a firm. Performance can be expressed through different indicators: Peters and Waterman (1982) considered variables such as asset growth, equity, market value/book value ratio; ROI, ROE and ROS; Kotter and Heskett (1992) added the dimension of growth of stock prices on markets; Zook and Allen (2001) integrated additional variables into a holistic approach whereby performance is defined as the capability of creating value. Other authors argue that it is incorrect to take into consideration exclusively financial variables

(Thrassou et al., 2012b). In particular Collins and Porras (1994), who introduced a new way of evaluating performance which focuses on the capability of an organisation to maintain a leadership position for a long period (5, 10 or 15 years) in their business sector. It is important to note that the performance concept is not absolute; since a good level of performance or a better financial statement compared to competitors will not necessarily lead an organisation to survive after a period of tough competition.

A review of the research studies, which explore the relationship between mindset and behaviour, is presented below. These studies started early in the 1980s and are clustered by decade.

1980s

The first to bring this topic to a wider audience were Peters and Waterman in 1982 with their seminal work, *"In Search of Excellence: Lessons from America's Best-Run Companies"*. In their research they identified 43 companies that for a period of more than 20 years had constantly out-performed their competitors and had returns above average in their business sector. The criteria they utilised to identify the "top performers" were asset growth, ratios such as Market Value/Book Value, ROE, ROI and ROS. The analysis highlighted the main factors that contribute to such success to be a set of attitudes and actions undertaken by the management, in particular: relationship with customer, entrepreneurship, focus on human resources, lean organisation and alignment of management with corporate values.

The main merit attributable to the two authors is the fact that they created interest in an unexplored field that clearly deserved much attention. However, their model failed to discover why a company's performance can still drop, even after a period of excellence.

1990s

Following the studies conducted by Peters and Waterman (1992), Kotter and Hesket analysed a wider sample of 207 large companies belonging to different business sectors over a period of 11 years. Using financial criteria (net income growth, ROI and stock price growth), they identified companies that could have been considered performance champions. They highlighted the fact that in their relative contexts, the champion companies were those that demonstrated a perfect alignment between culture and stakeholders' interests with strong leadership skills at all levels of the organisation.

A different approach was taken by Collins and Porras (1994), where the emphasis was on a more qualitative analysis. They identified the top performers by surveying the opinions of CEOs from different business sectors; asking them, which were the best organisations in the market. Their main findings were that top performers had: a strong emphasis on the "construction" of the organisation; a shared attitude when considering different alternatives in the decision making process; and a strong alignment on the common objectives between employees.

In 1998, Jain considered new criteria to determinate the excellence of companies. In addition to financial criteria, he considered "strategic thinking, core values and purpose, vision and empowerment". As a result of his analysis on a sample of Indian companies, he observed that the main common factors were: involvement at all levels in the decision making process; communication of values and objectives; clear guidelines to reach objectives; and a strong loyalty to the company.

Recent studies

There have been a large number of new studies on this topic since the start of the new millennium. Foster and Kaplan (2001), in cooperation with McKinsey & Company, provided a strong contribution to the field with their research on more than 1000 enterprises belonging to 15 different sectors, over a period of 38 years. Foster and Kaplan claim in their research that organisations capable of outperforming their industry for a long period (more than 15 years) have never existed. There have been organisations capable of outstanding performances for a limited number of years, or more often for shorter periods. This is due to the fact that "the management" of an organisation acts with the goal of continuity and consistency over time and since the market is dynamic and its performance continuously changes, the management cannot be expected to be able to create value at the same rate as the market. The authors conclude that enterprises should be re-designed continuously in order to change with the market, and be able to adapt to it, rather than limit themselves to more efficient. Clearly such a goal is not easily attainable.

In 2001, Weick and Sutcliffe published a very original work. The aim of their research was to demonstrate that an organisation was likely to perform better than another organisation if it was capable of competing under conditions of strong-pressure and could rapidly adapt, even to sudden, unexpected changes in the scenario or environment. Their research objective was achieved by investigating top-performing organisations, which were in environments where a small mistake could lead to severe consequences, (e.g. high risk fields such as air traffic control, first aid in hospitals, fire brigades and nuclear plants). The rationale being that an organisation operating in such a sector was "designed" to reach an optimal level of efficiency under circumstances of extreme stress, particularly during unexpected events. According to the authors, there appear to be five common characteristics in these top-performing organisations: preoccupation/obsession with failure; reluctance to simplify interpretations; sensitivity to operations; commitment to resilience; deference to expertise.

Whilst Foster and Kaplan's research is renowned for its analytical perspective, and Weick and Sutcliffe are known for their originality, Zook and Allen's research (2001) is of interest due to the conclusions of their empirical observations. Having studied more than 2000 enterprises belonging to different fields for many years, the two authors selected a sample of enterprises, which created value for an extended period of time, producing a return for shareholders, which was higher than the cost of capital. On the assumption that the majority of growth strategies based on diversification fail and destroy (or do not create) value because of distance from the core business, their research highlighted that the strategy of acquiring market share in a well defined core business represents the key for the creation and maintenance of competitive advantage. In particular they have identified three key drivers for winning growth strategies: achievement of the full development potential of the core business; expansion in businesses very close to the core business; ability to rapidly re-define the core business when facing a very turbulent market.

More recently, Nohria et al., (2003) analysed 160 enterprises from 40 different sectors over a 10 year period. By analysing the 40 clusters (each including 4 companies), the researchers identified 4 categories of performance within each cluster:

- *The winning enterprise* - the company which has already achieved a better performance than the other 3 in the group

- *The loser enterprise* - the worst performer in the group
- *The climber enterprise* - the one that has kept a growing trend during the observation period
- *The tumbler enterprise* - the one that has been getting worse over the years

The research noted that the organisations that produce the highest (and lasting) value for their partners and/or shareholders are those that have adopted what they call the "4+2 rule". Where the 4 are optimum practices in the areas of strategy, operations, culture and structure, and the 2 is the adoption of at least 2 practices among four options (talent, leadership, innovation, mergers and partnership)[1].

Finally and though in a more conceptual context, it must be noted that the past decade has seen an increasing trend of interpretations of performance based on the notion of value; as opposed to more mechanistic measurements such as financial or even structural ones. Though in this context, financial success is accepted as the ultimate goal of profit oriented organisations, performance as the ultimate means of achieving profit is viewed differently (Vrontis and Thrassou, 2007; Thrassou and Vrontis, 2009). Performance is thus linked to value and as subjectively perceived primarily by consumers, but also by all stakeholders of an organisation including employees, shareholders and society. The concept was in fact developed and applied across various industries (Thrassou et al., 2008; Thrassou and Lijo, 2008; Vrontis et al., 2008, 2010, 2011), but also across different contexts altogether (Thrassou et al., 2009, 2011). The highest performing organisations, in this frame of thinking are those that ultimate manage to achieve a comprehensive win-win situation for all stakeholders, whereby winning is the perception that value gained is higher than value deprived.

Connecting mindset, behaviour and performance

The literature indicates a correlation between certain mindsets and behaviour and performance, even if researchers speak mostly of culture rather than mindset and behaviour (Goffee and Jones, 1996). There is also evidence of a correlation between mindset and behaviour, characterised by focus on execution, strong alignment and capability of renewal, and a

---

[1] Among the examples mentioned: Dollar General, Flowers Industries, Home Depot, Nucor, Schering-Plough, Target e Wal-Mart.

firm's performance. However, the arguments are hardly unquestionable and the evidence of such correlation is weak. In fact, if one examines the methodology adopted by the researchers and scholars (for example Peters and Waterman, 1982; Delery and Doty, 1996; Guest, 1997; Boselie et al., 2001) a number of critical issues emerge, in particular concerning the method used to form the sample of organisations to be analysed. There are in fact a number of critical issues and question marks.

First of all, all researchers have compared organizations that are very different in industry, product, technological know-how and so forth; a scientific setback, since these variables can, and indeed do, have a great impact on the performance of an organization. Then, the sample of organisations analysed could have belonged to different time periods and this can be very misleading since the economic context may vary dramatically with potentially major influences on the performance of an organization. Moreover, all the organizations used in the analysis were "top-performers", and this could represent a distortion factor since, to identify the sources of over-performance, one should on the one hand identify and isolate the variables influencing the "top-performers" and on the other hand verify that these do not exist (or are lower) in the "non-performing" organizations. Finally, the definitions of performance often are not the same (although there *is* agreement on the use of financial performance) (Peters and Waterman, 1982; Kotter and Heskett, 1992; Zook and Allen, 2001).

Methodology

In order to overcome the aforementioned issues, a sample with very similar organisations has been chosen. 21 corporate bank branches, all from the same bank (a major Italian financial institution), were analysed over the same period, covering a wide range of performance levels, from very low to exceptional. Of course, they belonged to the same industry (banking), they were offering almost the same product (portfolio products), they leveraged exactly the same infrastructure (IT and Knowledge Management system) and they had resources with very similar profiles (in terms of education and experience).

The financial performance measurement used to assess the performance of each bank branch was Average (Gross) Revenue contributed by each corporate banker employed by that branch. An average is used because the intention is to measure the performance of an organization as a whole and not merely of individuals. The authors are aware of more finely-tuned measures of corporate values, such as Free Cash Flow for the Firm (FCFF) discounted by the weighted cost of capital. But this level of sophistication is not needed here. Measurements such as FCFF take into account financial structure, level of investment and accounting policy and are appropriate when comparing company value between companies. In our case, all these factors are the same since we compare branches of the same company. Therefore, a simply understood metric like average revenue is accepted as valid and appropriate.

For the analysis of the mindset and behaviour dimension, the extent to which an organization is effective alongside nine elements (i.e. "outcomes") is investigated. Outcomes are visible, in fact they are the result of the behaviour of the individuals of an organization that are themselves generated by their collective mindsets (Figure 1). The investigated nine elements are described below (Figure 2).

Figure 1: from mindsets to outcomes

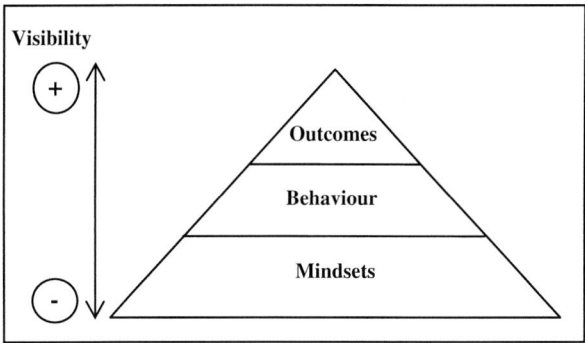

Source: Research findings

Figure 2: investigated elements

Elements	Outcomes (how effective is/in what ways does the organisation…)
Leadership	Ensure that leaders shape and inspire the actions of other organisational members to drive better performance
Direction	Articulate where the company is heading, how to get there, and align people around the vision
Environment and Values	Shape the quality of employee interactions (eg, work space design) and foster a shared understanding of core values
Accountability	Design structure/reporting relationships and evaluate individual performance to ensure that people are accountable and take responsibility for business results
Coordination and Control	Measure and evaluate business performance and risk
Skills and competences	Ensure that the requisite institutional skills and talent exist to support the company's strategy and create competitive advantage
Motivation	Inspire and encourage employees to perform and stay with the company
External orientation	Engage in constant two-way interactions with customers, suppliers, partners or other external groups to drive value
Innovation	Generate flow of ideas and change such that the company can sustain itself, survive and/or grow over time

Source: Bresciani and Sola (2006)

Empirical analysis and results

The survey involved 21 branches (75% of all branches), with 252 responses representing 60% the total people of all branches. All professional hierarchical levels and all geographical regions are included in the results, covering the whole of Italy.

Mindset and behaviour

Overall the results have a very wide range (min. 42%, max. 69%). There is not any element that can be considered distinctive (> 80%). In other words that can be considered to be a unique or primary source of strength. Five elements are above 50%: leadership, direction, accountability, skills/competence, and external orientation; with the highest scoring obtained by accountability and leadership. All these indicate that overall, this network organization is not particularly outstanding, at least not as a whole.

Mindset and Behaviour Effect on Firm Performance 75

Figure 3: mindset and behaviour analysis

Location	Outcomes								
	Leadership	Direction	Environment and values	Accountability	Coordination and control	Capability	Motivation	External orientation	Innovation
Location 1	96%	87%	80%	83%	74%	100%	70%	94%	60%
Location 2	86%	88%	80%	80%	74%	92%	75%	78%	64%
Location 3	93%	66%	85%	79%	65%	76%	73%	80%	63%
Location 4	100%	85%	58%	69%	55%	95%	62%	70%	40%
Location 5	76%	65%	68%	84%	51%	74%	62%	56%	54%
Location 6	69%	54%	46%	57%	60%	71%	63%	80%	60%
Location 7	68%	58%	44%	73%	43%	65%	55%	61%	60%
Location 8	69%	56%	40%	79%	63%	75%	40%	58%	47%
Location 9	77%	68%	66%	84%	22%	77%	51%	52%	20%
Location 10	67%	58%	49%	76%	43%	62%	37%	70%	58%
Location 11	72%	61%	57%	79%	40%	52%	40%	56%	36%
Location 12	67%	43%	47%	67%	47%	60%	27%	75%	76%
Location 13	77%	64%	43%	68%	44%	73%	35%	51%	34%
Location 14	57%	51%	29%	75%	33%	49%	49%	72%	50%
Location 15	57%	60%	38%	60%	42%	54%	32%	55%	31%
Location 16	63%	52%	28%	55%	52%	72%	24%	47%	44%
Location 17	62%	47%	35%	75%	30%	53%	40%	44%	28%
Location 18	54%	31%	32%	70%	35%	50%	43%	60%	40%
Location 19	61%	36%	21%	48%	39%	51%	16%	56%	32%
Location 20	47%	64%	32%	25%	36%	48%	16%	23%	16%
Location 21	24%	27%	21%	29%	17%	26%	7%	15%	11%
Average	68%	60%	49%	69%	42%	66%	44%	61%	44%

Note: the values are normalized (basis 100) from a result from 1.0 out 5.
Source: research findings

Financial results

The following is data regarding the performance of the organizations of the sample (Figure 4).

Figure 4: Financial results ('000 Euro)

Corporate centres	Total employees	Total Revenue	Individual Average (Gross) Revenue
Location 1	2	1227	613,7
Location 2	6	3465	577,5
Location 3	8	4320	540
Location 4	2	1278	638,8
Location 5	10	4098	409,8
Location 6	12	7678	639,8
Location 7	16	8868	554,3
Location 8	10	6181	618,1
Location 9	16	7324	457,7
Location 10	24	12672	528,0
Location 11	6	3060	510,1
Location 12	8	3058	382,3
Location 13	10	3956	395,6
Location 14	18	9091	505,1
Location 15	24	12294	512,3
Location 16	8	3734	466,8
Location 17	20	7879	393,9
Location 18	18	9094	505,2
Location 19	16	7210	450,6
Location 20	8	3397	424,6
Location 21	10	3771	377,1

Source: research findings

It is important to understand that the features of each centre do not allow a direct comparison and therefore there is a need for normalization. In particular, if we consider two corporate centres which have the same number of employees (eg: 10), but with a different balance of functions: in the first one 5 resources are responsible for the sales and the other 5 are assisting them (back office) and in the second one 6 are responsible for sales and 4 are assisting them.

The results, in the second case, should clearly be better than in the first one. In order to avoid such distortion, the authors have normalized the number of employees (where necessary) by realigning the number of employees of each centre by using the sales people as metric. In other words using the previous example the first centre will have as number of employees 10 and the second 12.

Figure 4 puts in evidence that the range of the average revenues per resource varies from a minimum of 377.000 Euros to a maximum of 640.000 Euros and that there are 3 clusters: top performance (4/5 centres), medium performance (12 centres) and low performance (5 centres).

Relating mindset and behaviour with financial results

General findings

Coupling the two sets of data (mindset and behaviour and organization's performance results) it was possible to find a good correlation of $R(X,Y)=0,67$ (Figure 5). This correlation means that a certain mindset and behaviour, characterized by strong alignment, focus on execution and capacity of renewal is well related to performances. In other words, as the scoring of mindset and behaviour grows, the performance follows, clearly showing an impact on net revenues (a growth of 10 basis points of the survey corresponds to a growth of 35 thousands Euro for the centre considered).

The significance of the correlation must be tested. Given the statistically small number of observations (<30), we are in a clear case of a t-student distribution for the coefficient of correlation with 20 (n-1) degrees of freedom, where n=21.

The null hypothesis H_0 is therefore that R=0, the alternative hypothesis that we are trying to test being that R>0. At a 95% significance level ($\alpha=5\%$), tables of probability give a critical value Tav (critical value a 95%) of 2.086. Calculating the test statistic, we have:

$$Tav = \frac{R\sqrt{(n-2)}}{\sqrt{(1-R^2)}} = 3.67$$

Since 3.67 > 2.086, we can reject the null hypothesis and then conclude that a correlation does exist between the two sets of data, with a 95% confidence interval.

Figure 5: the correlation between mindset and behaviour and performance

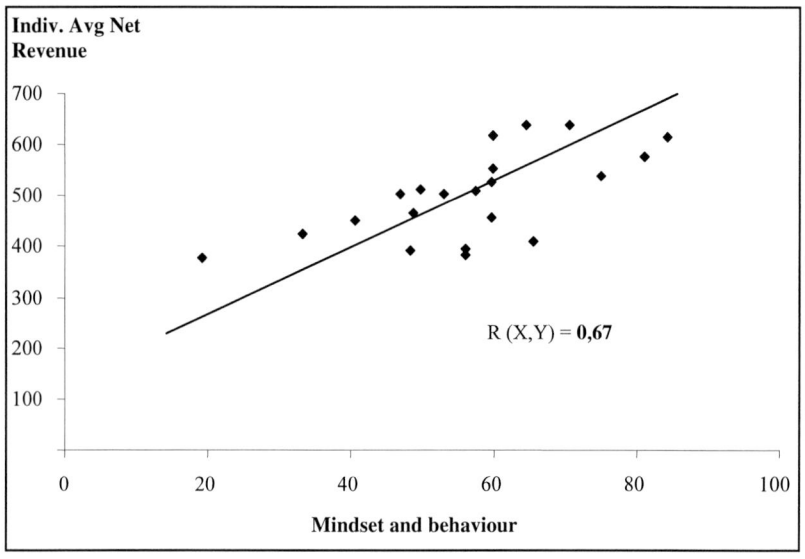

Source: research findings

Regional patterns

The sample was also investigated by segmenting it at a macro-regional level with the aim of verifying if regional patterns existed. In particular, the goal was to understand if external variables such as level of competition have an impact at regional level (they did not at national level since the banking industry in Italy has a similar pattern of market share at national level).

Figure 6: the correlation between mindset and behaviour and performance (North-West Area)

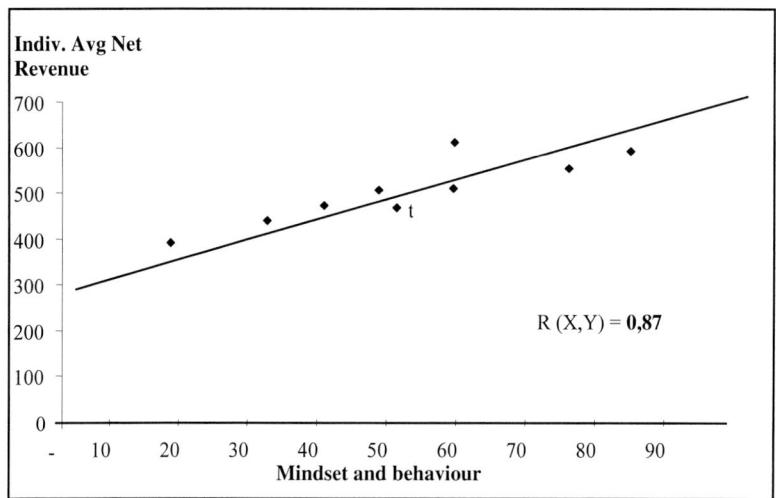

Source: research findings

The results of this analysis have been very interesting. Two regions (North-West and Centre-South) have a good correlation (above national level), meaning that in those areas the external variables, such as competition, do not have an important influence (Figure 6 and 7).

In these regions business augmentation and shareholder significance are set based on investments intended to attain and preserve clients. Therefore, for financial institutions and investment banks to be successful, they must have the tendency to maintain strong relations with their stakeholders.

The correlation function in the Centre-South area presents a strong slope, in other words when the survey results increase the economics results increase in a superior manner with respect to the general ones.

Figure 7: the correlation between mindset and behaviour and performance (Centre-South Area)

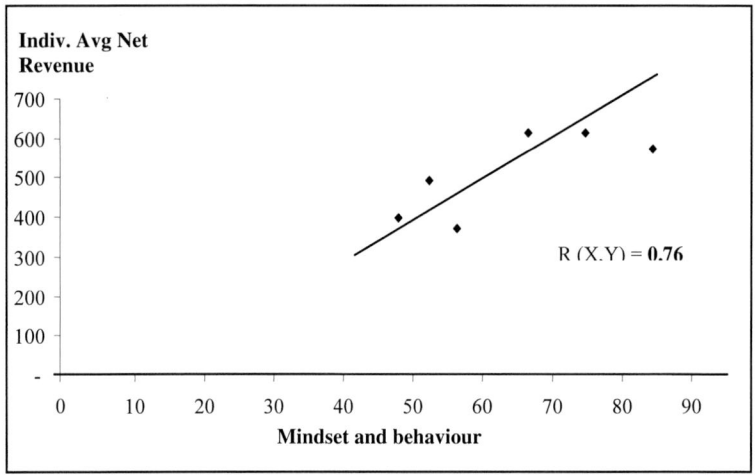

Source: research findings

This aspect confirms that in this region the competition level has a very positive impact. One region (North-East) has a negative correlation, meaning that in this region the competition level is anomalous compared to the level in the rest of the country (Figure 8).

These results are confirmed by managers of the branches localized in different areas. They explained the phenomenon with regards to the different level of competition: in the North-East area, in fact, a competitor exists who has a disproportionately large part of the market. For this reason the average performance of this area is lower than that of the general branch population.

The case is particularly relevant to the corporate branches in Venezia, Trento and Bolzano, where despite excellent overall results, the economic aspects score lower than the average. However, in order to retain customers, those branches have excellent services that satisfy them.

Figure 8: the correlation between mindset and behaviour and performance (North-East Area)

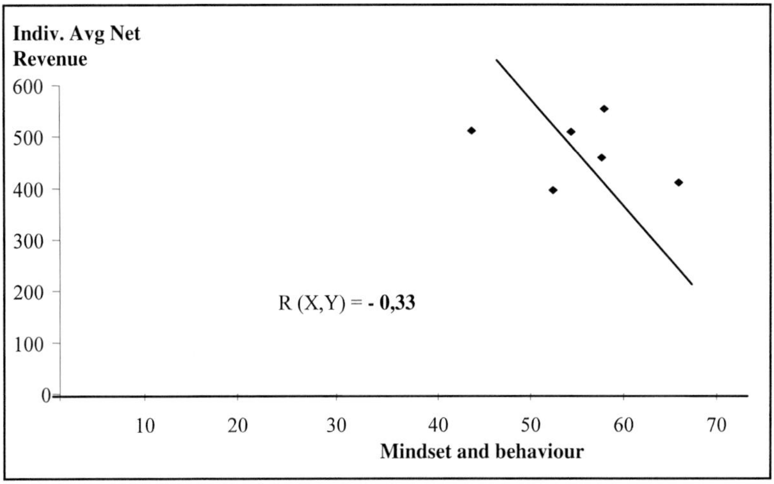

(Scatter plot: Indiv. Avg Net Revenue vs Mindset and behaviour; R (X,Y) = - 0,33)

Source: research findings

Conclusions

The results of the research confirm what executives and practitioners have believed for long time: that organizations with a particular mindset and behaviour are more likely to achieve a sustainable competitive advantage. Effectively, performance can depend on client's satisfaction as the ultimate goal, based on a number of studies in the financial industry that substantiates service quality.

The research has additionally contributed to knowledge by providing new elements for academic analyses and by using a new and simple approach. The originality of the sample has allowed the exclusion of a number of key influencing factors, such as: industry, economy, historical context, regional diversity. In conclusion the research has shown a correlation between mindset and behaviour, which is characterised by strong alignment execution, renewal and performance. In other words, it has been shown that organisations facing an increasingly competitive environment, characterized by discontinuous change, need to develop a mindset and behaviour, which has a strong alignment, and focus on execution with a capacity to renew.

References

Arthur, J.B. (1994), "Effects of human resource systems on manufacturing performance and turnover", *Academy of Management Journal,* Vol. 3, No. 37, pp. 670-687.

Barney, J.B. (1991), "Firm resources and sustained competitive advantage", *Journal of management*, Vol. 17, No. 1, pp. 99-120.

Boselie, P., Paauwe, J. and Jansen, P.G.W. (2001), "Human resource management and performance: lessons from the Netherlands", *The International Journal of Human Resource Management,* Vol. 7, No. 12, pp. 1107-1125.

Bower, M. (1966), *The Will to Manage: Corporate Success Through Programmed Management*, McGraw Hill, New York.

Bresciani, S., Sola, D. (2006), "The Influence of Mindset and Behaviour on a Firm's Performance: An empirical demonstration", paper presented at 21st Workshop on strategic human resource management, March 30-31, Aston Business School, Birmingham, U.K.

Bresciani, S., Thrassou, A. and Vrontis, D. (2012), "Human Resource Management – Practices, Performance and Strategy in the Italian Hotel Industry", *World Review of Entrepreneurship, Management and Sustainable Development*, Vol. 8, No.4, pp. 405-423.

Collins, J. and Hussey, R. (2003), *Business Research: a practical guide for undergraduate and postgraduate students*, Palgrave Macmillan, London.

Collins, J.C. and Porras, J.I. (1994), *Built to Last: Successful Habits of Visionary*, Harper Business, New York.

Deal, T.E., and Kennedy, A.A. (1982), *Corporate cultures*, Addison-Wesley, Reading, MA.

Delery, J.E. and Doty, D.H. (1996), "Modes of theorizing in strategic human resource management: tests of universalistic, contingency, and configurational performance predictions", *Academy of Management Journal*, Vol. 4, No. 39, pp. 802-835.

Foss, N.J. and Laursen, K. (2000), "New HRM Practices, Complementarities, and the Impact on Innovation Performance", Working Paper 5, Department of Industrial Economics and Strategy, Copenhagen Business School, Denmark.

Foster, R. and Kaplan, S. (2001), *Creative Destruction*, Doubleday, New York.

Goffee, R. and Jones, G. (1996), "What's Holds the Modern Company Together?", *Harvard Business Review*, Vol. 74 No. 6, pp. 133-148.

Guest, D.E. (1997), "Human resource management and performance: a review and research agenda", *The International Journal of Human Resource Management*, Vol. 3, No. 8, pp. 263-276.

—. (1999), "Human Resource Management – The Workers' Verdict", *Human Resource Management Journal,* Vol. 3, No. 9, pp. 5-25.

Guest, D.E. and Peccei, R. (1994), "The nature and causes of effective human resource management", *British Journal of Industrial Relations,* Vol. 2, No. 32, pp. 219-241.

Ham, H. and Kleimer, M.M. (2002), *Do Industrial Relations Institutions Impact Economic Outcomes?: International and U.S. State-Level Evidence*, NBER Working Paper 8729.

Hiltrop, J.M. (1999), "The quest for the best: human resource practices to attract and retain talent", *European Management Journal,* Vol. 4, No. 17, pp. 422-430.

Huselid, M.A. (1995), "The impact of human resource management practices on turnover, productivity, and corporate financial performance", *Academy of Management Journal*, Vol. 3, No. 38, pp. 635-672.

Ichniowski, C. and Shaw, K. (1999), "The effects of human resource management systems on economic performance: an international comparison of U.S. and Japanese Plants", *Management Science*, Vol. 5 No. 45, pp. 704-721.

Jackson, M.C. (2010), "Reflections on the development and contribution of critical systems thinking and practice", *Systems Research and Behavioral Science*, Vol. 27, No. 2, pp. 133-139.

Jain, A.K. (1998), *Corporate Excellence*, AIMA - Excel Books, New Delhi.

Joice, W., Nohria, N. and Roberson, B. (2003), *What Really Works: The 4+2 Formula for Sustained Business Success*, Harper-Business, New York.

Koch, M.J. and McGrath, R.G. (1996), "Improving labour productivity: human resource management policies do matter", *Strategic Management Journal*, Vol. 17, No. 5, pp. 335-354.

Kotter, J.P. and Heskett, J.L. (1992), *Corporate Culture and Performance*, Free Press, New York.

Laursen, K. and Mahnke, V. (2000), "Knowledge Strategies, Firm Types, and Complementarity in Human Resources Practices", May, INSEAD Conference, Mimeo, University of Fontainebleau, France.

Lazear, E.P. (2000), "Performance pay and productivity", *American Economic Review*, Vol. 90, No. 5, pp. 1346-1361.

Leoni, R., Cristini, A, Mazzoni, N., and Labory, S. (2000), *Disegni organizzativi, stili di management e performance d'impresa. Risultati di un'indagine in un campione di imprese industriali*, AIEL National Conference, October, Mimeo, Ancona.

Linstone, H.A. and Mitroff, I.I. (1994), *The Challenges of the 21st Century*, State University of New York Press, New York.

Macduffie, J.P. (1995), "Human resource bundles and manufacturing performance: organisational logic and flexible production systems in the world auto industry", *Industrial and Labor Relations Review,* Vol. 2, No. 48, pp. 197-221.

McNabb, R. and Whitfield, K. (1997), "Unions, flexibility, team working and financial performance", *Organisation Studies*, Vol. 5, No. 18, pp. 821-838.

Osterman, P. (1994), "How common is workplace transformation and who adopts it?", *Industrial and Labor Relations Review*, Vol. 47, No. 2, pp. 173-188.

Peters, J.T. and Waterman, R.H. (1982*), In Search of Excellence: Lessons from America's Best-Run Companies*, Warner Books, New York.

Porter, M.E. (1985), *Competitive Advantage: Creating and Sustaining Superior Performance*, The Free Press, New York.

Prahalad, C.K. and Hamel, G. (1994), "Strategy as a field of study: why research for a new paradigm?", *Strategic Management Journal*, Vol. 15 Special Issue, pp. 5-16.

Schein, E.H. (1984), "Coming to a New Awareness of Organizational Culture", *Sloan Management Review*, Vol. 25, No. 2, pp. 3-16.

—. (1986), *Organisational Culture and Leadership*, Jossey Bass, San Francisco.

Sundar, S.B. (2012), "Efficient teamwork performance on organisation culture in construction", *International Journal of Physical and Social Sciences*, Vol. 2, No. 4, pp. 177-199.

Svielby, K.E. (2001), "A knowledge-based theory of the firm to guide strategy formulation", *Journal of Intellectual Capital*, Vol. 2, No. 4, pp. 344-358.

Tardivo G. (2008), "L'evoluzione degli studi sul Knowledge Management", *Sinergie*, No. 76, May-August, pp. 21-42.

Thrassou A., Kone C. and Panayidou A. (2008), "Women Shoppers in Cyprus- Behaviour, Beliefs and Perceptions of Self", *International Journal of Management Cases*, Vol.10, No. 3, pp. 606-620.

Thrassou A. and Lijo P.R. (2008), "Motivators and Critical factors in Mobile Banking Communications - The Case of Kuwait", *Journal for Global Business Advancement*, Vol. 1, No. 4, pp. 327-349.

Thrassou, A. and Vrontis, D. (2009), "A New Consumer Relationship Model: The Marketing Communications Application", *Journal of Promotion Management*, Vol. 15, No. 4, pp. 499-521.

Thrassou, A., Vrontis, D., Chebbi, H. and Yahiaoui, D. (2012a), "A Preliminary Strategic Marketing Framework for New Product Development", *Journal of Transnational Management*, Vol. 17, No. 1, pp. 21-44.

Thrassou, A., Vrontis, D., Chebbi, H. and Yahiaoui, D. (2012b), "Transcending Innovativeness Towards Strategic Reflexivity", *Qualitative Market Research*: An International *Journal*, Vol. 15, No. 4, pp. 420-437.

Thrassou, A., Vrontis, D. and Kotabe, M. (2011), "Towards a Marketing Communications Model for Small Political Parties - A Primary Principles Strategic Perspective for Developed Countries", *Cross Cultural Management: An International Journal*, Vol. 17, No. 3, pp. 263-292.

Thrassou, A., Vrontis, D. and McDonald, M. (2009), "A Marketing Communications Framework for Small Political Parties in Developed Countries", *Marketing Intelligence and Planning*, Vol. 27, No. 2, pp. 268-292.

Valdani, E. (2000), *L'impresa pro-attiva. Co-evolvere e competere nell'era dell'immaginazione*, McGraw Hill, Milano.

Vrontis, D. and Thrassou, A. (2007), "A new conceptual framework for business-consumer relationships", *Marketing Intelligence & Planning*, Vol. 25, No. 7, pp.789-806.

Vrontis, D. Thrassou, A. and Ching-Wei Ho (2008), "The Marketing Implications of the 'Undesired Self' – the case of Chinese Y-Generation", *Journal for Global Business Advancement*, Vol. 1, No. 4, pp. 390-408.

Vrontis, D., Thrassou, A. and Lamprianou, I. (2009), "International Marketing Adaptation versus Standardisation of Multinational Companies", *International Marketing Review,* Vol. 26, Nos. 4 and 5, pp. 477-500.

Vrontis, D., Thrassou, A. and Razali, M.Z. (2010), "Internal Marketing as an Agent of Change – Implementing a New Human Resource Information System for Malaysian Airlines", *Journal of General Management*, Vol. 36, No. 1, pp. 21-41.

Vrontis, D., Thrassou, A. and Rossi, M. (2011), "Italian Wine Firms: Strategic Branding and Financial Performance", *International Journal of Organisational Analysis*, Vol. 19, No. 4, pp. 288-304.

Weick, K.E. and Sutcliffe, K.M. (2001), *Managing the Unexpected: Assuring High Performance in an Age of Complexity*, Jossey-Bass, San Francisco.

Wilkinson, F. (2000), "Human Resources Management and Business Objective and Strategies in Small and Medium Sized Business", Working Paper n. 184, ESRC Centre for Business Research, University of Cambridge, Mimeo.

Zheng W., Yang B. and McLean G.N. (2010), "Linking Organizational Culture, Structure, Strategy, And Organizational Effectiveness: Mediating Role Of Knowledge Management", *Journal of Business Research*, Vol. 63, No. 7, pp. 763-771.

Zook, C. and Allen, J. (2001), *Profit From the Core: Growth Strategy in an Era of Turbulence*, Harvard Business School Press, Cambridge.

CHAPTER FIVE

STRATEGIC DECISION-MAKING DURING UNCERTAINTY: IMPLICATIONS FOR SMES

CONSTANTINOS THEODORIDIS AND CONSTANTINOS V. PRIPORAS

Introduction

Making decisions is a sequence of actions involving the understanding of a context, the development of alternative solutions, and finally the selection of the optimal solution for the given problem. Rational decision-making obeys to laws (Simon, 1979), including one that suggests that decision-makers have the absolute knowledge of the alternatives they can choose from. Behavioural theorists, influenced by the seminal work of Cyert and March (1965), opposed to that claiming that in the real world it is literally impossible to grasp all the available alternatives, let alone the inability of individuals or groups of decision-makers to predict the consequences of their decisions. This debate resurfaces whenever a major crisis takes place (for example, a massive amount of research was published in the late 1980's-early 1990's after the Black Monday of 1987 and the savings and loan crisis in the USA in the late 1980s). However, the vast majority of the research on decision-making during uncertainty is informed by data coming from bigger organisations that are based in the USA, the UK, Canada, or the Central European countries. Within this chapter the authors attempt to the shed light on the strategic decision-making made in SMEs in Greece, particularly in the retail SMEs, using as an example the retail location strategy.

The book chapter starts with a comprehensive review of the concept of the environmental uncertainty and it is followed by sections on uncertainty in retailing, the nature of strategic decision-making in retail SMEs, and a brief account of the developments in the Greek retail sector. A case study is reported right after that and the findings are discussed under the prism of the explanatory framework that is provided by the advances of the complexity theory. The book chapter closes with implications for academics and practitioners.

The concept of environmental uncertainty

Miliken (1987) suggested that individuals experience uncertainty because they perceive themselves to be lacking sufficient information to predict accurately or because they feel unable to discriminate between relevant and irrelevant data. In the first part of the literature review environmental uncertainty literature will be discussed. In the second part of the literature review the retail location decision-making literature will be discussed with particular interest on establishing a linkage between environmental uncertainty and retail location decision-making.

State uncertainty

Miliken (1987) suggests that *state uncertainty* is experienced when administrators perceive the environment (or a particular component of it) to be unpredictable. In his work Miliken (1987:136) describes the environment as follows:

> "Top-level managers might be uncertain about what actions relevant organisations or key organisational constituencies (i.e., suppliers, competitors, consumers, the government, shareholders etc.) might take, or they might be uncertain about the probability or nature of general changes in state in the relevant environment (i.e., sociocultural trends, demographic shifts, major new developments in technology")."

Gerloff et al., (1991) suggest that state uncertainty has a situational character. They specifically suggest that in a given situation, a given manager may lack confidence or has doubts that the available data reveals the significant events and trends of the environment and as a result the manager would experience state uncertainty. Duncan (1972) had also argued that uncertainty is not a constant feature in any organisation. Rather, "it is dependent on the perceptions of organisation members and thus can vary in their incidence to the extent that individuals differ in their perceptions" (1972: 325).

Effect uncertainty

Miliken (1987: 137) defines *effect uncertainty* as "an inability to predict what the nature of the impact of a future state of the environment or environmental change will be on the organisation". Effect uncertainty does not involve the lack of understanding of the environment, e.g. a retail manager may know that the number of single-parent families is growing but he or she may feel unable to predict how this trend is going to change the sales of his or hers product. As Gerloff et al., (1991) note, effect uncertainty involves a lack of understanding of cause-effect relationships. To a large degree effect uncertainty arises from a firm's inability to anticipate or influence how its customers and competitors will shape its own future (Miller and Shamsie, 1996). Past research has shown that companies that have the means to influence their environment experience less effect uncertainty than others that have not (Itami, 1987; Wernerfelt and Karnani, 1987).

Response uncertainty

Miliken (1987: 137) defines *response uncertainty* as "a lack of knowledge of response options and/or inability to predict the likely consequences of a response choice". This type of uncertainty becomes especially important in situations involving a need to take actions, such as a pending threat or opportunity (Gerloff et al., 1991). As Gerloff et al. (1991) notes at this level of uncertainty managers are wondering "What action are we going to take?" Milliken (1987) suggests that this level of uncertainty is directly related with decision making because it is about the importance of choosing between alternatives. Miller and Shamsie (1999) have researched response uncertainty in terms of new product line development. In conjunction with Miliken's observation, Miller and Shamsie suggested that this type of uncertainty (that they call *decision response uncertainty*) is dependant on social, demographical and economic variables (e.g. decision makers' experience, job tenure, product line diversity, cost etc.). Their research findings are consistent with the ones of Downey *et al.* (1977) who focused their research on managers' cognition and perception of environmental uncertainty. A key issue that emerges from both Miller and Shamsie's and Downey *et al.*'s research is the significance of a changing (as noted by the first) or dynamic (as noted by the latter) environment on the perception of response uncertainty. The findings of both are important because they explore the relationship of change and uncertainty and at the same time introduce the idea that the managerial decision making process is influenced by the state of the environment as it is defined by the two latter variables.

A detailed account of the development of the concept of environmental uncertainty can be found in Kreiser and Marino (2002), and Lopez-Gamaro et al. (2011).

Uncertainty in retailing

The concept of uncertainty has been discussed by a number of academics and has been seen from a number of different perspectives. Jones and Simmons (1993) have extensively discussed the impact of uncertainty on the retail location decisions. They suggested that the changes that are happening in the business environment increase the perceived level of uncertainty for the retailers. They also mentioned that retailers in order to respond to the changes they introduce modifications to their companies, which means that they are changing in order cope and potentially get advantage of the uncertainty. Alexander and Freathy (2003) suggested that in the rapidly changing world, the companies would probably use new technological advancements to initiate revolutions that they (the companies) would be able to take advantage of. This is a finding that had also emerged in an earlier study of Schrader et al. (1989). Their research concluded that technological advances had become the focal point of the development of retailers then (it was a period of great development for the Point Of Sale system) and in comparison to other sectors the long-term strategic planning was less active.

Strategic decision-making in SMEs

Decision-making in SMEs is characterised by some features that complicates decision-makers' task (Gibcus et al. 2009). First, managers or entrepreneurs are asked to make decisions in an environment of limited and imperfect information. These companies lack the financial resources to access information and the human resources that are needed to scan the environment, collect data and information, and transform them to meaningful input for the company. Second, the business environment of SMEs is complex and dynamic (Covin and Slevin, 1991). The complexity and dynamism of the environment varies between sectors: for example, in innovation-intensive ones companies reinforce the dynamism of the environment by launching new products or services and competitors' replies maintain the dynamism. Singh et al. (2008) pointed that high-growth SMEs are adapting faster to their external environment by developing programmes for improving their skill and capabilities with a view to offer innovative products and services in the niche market they serve.

The personal relationships that are developed within and outside the companies increase the complexity of the environment as more actors participating in the environment of the company can become important or even essential and their behaviour within the complex environment is highly sensitive.

Another feature of decision-making within SMEs is that it is determined by a limited number of individuals, therefore the key people – or even a single person that makes decisions - within a company is pivotal to the decision-making process. Papadakis et al. (1998) suggested that internal measurable characteristics of an organisation like size, the type of ownership, the past performance of the organisation, and the formal systems that support decision-making, are related to the decision-making process. In a later paper Papadakis and Barwise (2002) suggested that the length of the involvement in a specific position in the company as well as the education of the manager influence the decision-making process. Considering that a lot of the decision-making in SMEs is based on biases and heuristics (Busenitz and Barney, 1997), the experience of the decision-maker to handle the changing environment and the knowledge to deal with fragmented pieces of information that are coming from sources of questionable validity and reliability is crucial.

The experience and education of the decision-maker is also linked to the development of intra-organisational and inter-organisational networks that are a valuable source of information. Lybaert (1998) stressed the importance of networks in SMEs decision-making and suggested that there is a relationship between the size of the SME and size of the networks they use. Ottesen et al. (2004) argued that SMEs' intra-organisational and inter-organisational management networks provide a source of information that is controlled since the members and actors of the networks are selected and continuously assessed for their reliability, validity and credibility. Therefore decision makers constantly filter the information sources they use but there is always the possibility that the strength of interpersonal relationships and habitual reliance on specific networks or their members might skew the information input to the company.

Greece under focus

The business environment in Greece has changed in a number of ways during the last twenty years. This is the result of social, economic, political and technological factors that have impact upon "a system of small, independently owned and operated shops, which has been protected by tight legislative controls on store operations" (Bennison and Boutsouki, 1995). The change of the laws that were restricting competition in the retail sector was one reason for the rapid change. The new laws extended the limit of the opening hours from 50 to 68, removed control of minimum and maximum prices, and allowed grocery stores to sell products like bread, milk and fish. From the demographic point of view two major changes can be identified. The first one is the growth of the number of emigrants in Greece. According to the Greek National Statistics Services (2005) the number of emigrants has increased from 150,000 in 1990 to 600,000 in 2005, a growth of about 300%. According to the same source (2001) the majority of emigrants have settled in Athens and Thessaloniki (the larger urban centres of Greece). Anthropologists and sociologists that have researched emigrants' attitudes in Greece suggest that their buying behaviour is determined by their income and their ethnic origin, thus they frequently purchase products from discount stores, outlets and small independent stores operated by individuals of the same ethnic origin (Droukas, 1998; Fakiolas, 1999). Another factor that has had an impact on the change of the Greek retail sector was that banks made it easier for individuals to get personal loans. The 2005 annual report of the Bank of Greece indicates that from 1995 to 2004 the amount of personal loans have increased by 72%. Commentators have related this rapid growth of debt with the growth of sales of big department stores (To Vima, 2004).

The massive economic crisis Greece faces has affected the structure of society entirely including citizens/consumers, economic sectors as a whole and individual businesses. The crisis created a completely new economic environment, with conditions in which many businesses (producers, suppliers and retailers) have never performed. However, the degree of impact may differ in various sectors since the decrease of demand is more visible in some sectors or in some sub-sectors.

Retailing in general is one of the major sectors that experience tremendous difficulties and it is in the beginning of its new transformation. In 2011 numerous closures, decreased sales, stronger competition, the existence of a significant movement towards lower-priced products were some of the events that characterised the sector. Even successful companies from e-tailing (internet retailer e-shops), have been struggling as the uncertain economic environment increased pressure on operating profits (Euromonitor, 2012). Since mid-2009, when the economic turmoil began to hit the Greek economy, until mid-September of 2011, about 65,000 stores have terminated their operation (Smith, 2012). Non-grocery retailers face the biggest problems in terms of demand, turnover and store closures. For example, many well-known domestic and international apparel and consumer electronics retailing chains (e.g., Sprider Stores, Vardas, Radio Korasidis, MediaMarkt) shut down a number of stores in order to survive.

The food retailing sector enters in a new phase due to various significant changes. Carrefour's announcement that it is pulling out of Greece, and selling its Greek supermarkets to the Marinopoulos group (Nikolas, 2012) creates a new situation in terms of competition and leadership in the market. Also, it is very difficult for a foreign retailer to enter the Greek market (Manifava, 2012). Consumers continue to buy the necessary goods by taking also advantage of any promotional offerings in hypermarkets, supermarkets, and discounters. In addition, consumers turn increasingly towards private label products due to their lower prices since the economic crisis influences dramatically consumer spending. However, an interesting development is the fact that Greek consumers turn towards products made in Greece (Kosmides, 2011).

All the above compose a very competitive environment in which the retailers are called to operate. It is anticipated that strategic actions will take place such as investments in private label products due to the increased demand. Other predicted developments include a series of acquisitions (smaller retailers will be acquired since they felt the economic pressure more), and some big retailers will open new stores as part of their expansion policy (Manifava, 2012).

Characteristics of strategic decision making in Greek companies

Bourantas and Papadakis (1996) have shown that decision-makers in Greek-owned companies follow less rational decision-making processes compared to those found in firms in the US. Generally speaking, Greek management is associated with fewer rules of formalisation, and less hierarchical decentralisation. This is also consistent with Zey's (1992) research, which has shown that rational models have dominated many business areas particularly in the United States and the Western Europe, while Papadakis et al. (1998,:137) noted that Greek private firms have less formal rules and comprehensive decision-making processes than U.S. or British ones, and so are more likely to make decisions in a more "emotional" manner. The preference of Western scholars for these rational models of explanation has been critiqued by Eisenhardt and Zbaracki (1992) who suggested that theorists should be more concerned with real-life processes, rather than being rooted in the normative tradition. A recent study by Dimitratos et al. (2011) confirmed Eisenhardt and Zbaracki's assertion as their research on SMEs from Greece, Cyprus, UK, and the USA showed that their internationalisation strategic decision-making process massively differ, depending on national culture characteristics.

Case study: Making location strategy in Greek retail SMEs

Methodological note

Given the lack of empirical research in this area, an exploratory investigation was considered the most justifiable approach (Churchill, 1991). A "critical case" (Dawes-Farquhar, 2012) was selected aiming to recruit respondents from the major sub-sectors of the Greek retailing sector. Two sets of four in-depth interviews (two phases), informal discussions varying in number and length with each one of the respondents, and observations were made. Interviews took place at the working place of the respondents. All interviews lasted about an hour and were recorded. All interviews took place in Greek, which is the native language of both researchers and respondents. The audiotapes were transcribed and translated by the authors.

The purpose of this research is to help the authors create a better understanding of the decision making process of retailers under uncertainty. For that purpose the cognitive mapping technique was employed (see figure 1 for example).

Cognitive maps can be referred to as a method used to elicit the structure and the content of people's mental process (Daniels et al. 1995), and which provides a mental model. Spicer (2000) defined cognitive mapping as a suite of techniques and methodologies which are designed for the elicitation and representation of individual knowledge and understanding. Cognitive mapping techniques are one of the tools to draw cognitive maps.

These techniques are used to explore graphical descriptions of the unique ways in which an individual views a particular domain (field of thought or action) (Langfield-Smith, 1992). As a research tool cognitive mapping has its strengths and weaknesses; a detailed account can be found in Ahmad and Ali (2003). Table 1 summarises the details of the sample.

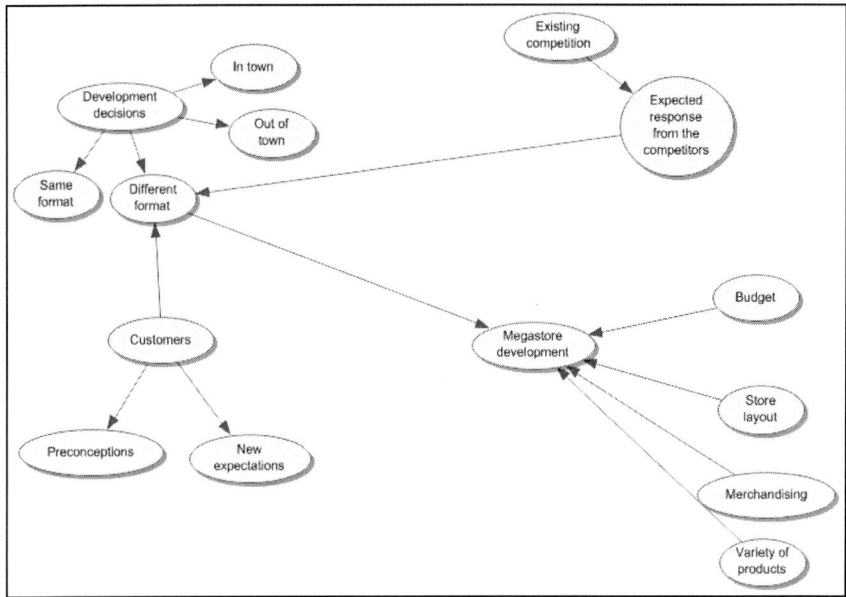

Figure 1: R2's mental map of his decision to open a new store
Source: Adapted by the original mental map

Table 1: Details of the selected cases

	Sector	Main contact
Respondent 1 (R1)	Grocery	The north-Greece locational manager of a leading discount Super Market chain
Respondent 2 (R2)	**Health and cosmetics**	The regional manager of a leading cosmetics retailer
Respondent 3 (R3)	**Electricals**	The owner of a leading electrical retail company
Respondent 4 (R4)	**Fashion**	The owner of a male fashion retail company

The nature of environmental uncertainty

Two major themes emerged in the first part of the interviews. The first one relates to the components of the environment that are creating environmental uncertainty, and the second one is related to the type of uncertainty that retailers are experiencing.

With respect to the first theme, taken together the interviewees suggested that there are eighteen components of the business environment that are causing the state of uncertainty. Most of these components are parts of the external environment of the company, but there are also few that come from the internal environment of the company. Four components were identified as important by all the interviewees.

The first one concerns the laws and specifically planning legislation. As R1 suggested *"planning legislation is very old and cannot cover the needs of the developers that want to bring fresh ideas from abroad"*. R3 added, *"Laws can be very flexible. If you know the right people things are very easy, but what happens if you don't..."* Laws and corruption is a serious problem of the Greek public sector. According to Transparency International the perceived level of corruption in the Greek public sector by Greek citizens is the highest observed between EU-15 and one of the highest between EU-25 (http://ww1.transparency.org/cpi/2005/cpi2005_in focus.html#cpi).

The second one is information circulation. R1 and R2 take information circulation as granted and they experience uncertainty because they are not sure if they are using information in the most effective way. For R3 and R4 information circulation is a matter of capital investment. They believe that they know how to take advantage of the information but they address the issue of the cost of the information and the time needed to get it.

The third one concerns competition. In this case international retailers are afraid of the flexibility of local retailers and local retailers are afraid of the size and power of international retailers. R2 mentioned that *"...there are about ten large independent cosmetics stores in Thessaloniki, and it is very difficult to keep an eye on them. Their size and structure allows them to change fast and approach niche markets. For instance it took us more than a year to introduce a line of ecological perfumes when they did it just a week after a couple of Greek actresses protested against chemical cosmetics"*. On the other hand R4 suggested *"I hear rumours that Zara is looking for a store in Kolonaki*[1] *and the other day I somebody tells me that Zara wants to relocate all their stores from hi-streets in shopping malls because hi-street retailing has saturated in Greece. And the problem is that it's not just rumours. These things are happening in front of my eyes every day."*

The fourth component concerns consumers. Consumers are mentioned in many different ways by the interviewees. Their concern mainly involves consumers' loyalty. It was stated by all four that consumers are not loyal and they cannot understand to what kind of changes consumers are sensitive to. For example R1 mentioned that *"When we decided to advertise our low prices we had a massive fall of our sales, we are a discount chain but consumers don't want to know that!"* Even though all the respondents have some kind of marketing intelligence available to them they all agreed that they just have a partial idea of consumers' needs. This is the barrier for them to serve them effectively.

R1 and R2 largely mentioned the same environmental components. They believe that components of the environment that are mediating their relationship with the top management of the company are very important to the way that they are experiencing the uncertainty. R2 suggested that:

"...sometimes I wonder if senior managers know what they are asking of me."

For these two respondents management expectations and goals are important. They suggested that top management expectations, the strategic goals of the company and profitability expectations are three components of the environment that are a major cause of the uncertainty experience.

R3 and R4 are primarily concerned about the components of the environment that affect the competitiveness of their company. A major issue for them is the expansion of international retailers in Greece and how this influences their companies. They attribute both the emergence of opportunities and threats to the expansion of international retailers. R3 suggested that:

"... the expansion of DSG and Mediamarkt was a shock for both companies and consumers. Our competitors focused on retaining their

---

[1] Kolonaki is the wealthiest district in Athens. R4 has one store there.

market-share but for me it was a great opportunity to grow now that all my competitors try to defend."

For both R3 and R4 the survival and growth of their companies are their focus. They relate the experience of uncertainty to the existence of their company and they consider as most important the components of the environment that can create opportunities and threats for their companies.

R1 and R2, contrary to R3 and R4, are employed by international retailers. The components of the environment that are acknowledged as significant for the international retailers appear to be different than local retailers. R1 and R2 suggested that they have to conform to formal rules and policies, and this can be very difficult especially when they have to deal with the government. R1 suggested that:

"… when I have to get a license from the local authorities or from the town-planning bureau it is very easy if I act as an individual. Everybody there can be bribed. But it is not the same thing when I act as a manager. I have to follow the laws and the rules because it is the reputation of the company on the stake".

There are signs that there are significant differences in the perception of uncertainty between managers and company-owners and local and international retailers. These differences are presented in table 2.

With respect to the second theme, the interviewees suggest that they are not all experiencing the same type of uncertainty. For R1 uncertainty is *"what I cannot predict"*, for R2 it is *"…when I don't understand what senior managers are asking of me"*, for R3 it is *"…when I cannot make decisions"*, and finally for R4 it is *"…how I will manage to survive"*. R1 and R2 are experiencing state uncertainty, while R3 and R4 are experiencing effect uncertainty. R1 and R2 cannot understand their environment, while R3 and R4 cannot decide how they are going to react to the environmental stimuli.

R1 and R2 have only a partial view of the company and the environment, and thus they do not have an overall idea of the environment they are operating within. On the other hand R3 and R4 have a wider view of the company and the environment as they are the owners of their companies. They have a better understanding of their company and the external environment because they are exposed to the internal and external environment of the company. Their uncertainty comes from their inability to choose between alternative replies to the environmental stimuli.

Table 2: Components of the environment causing uncertainty

	Components of the environment	Local	International
Political factors	1. Laws	X	X
	2. Regulation		X
	3. Banks	X	
	4. Interest rates	X	
Technological factors	1. Information systems		X
Capital management	1. Information circulation	X	X
	2. Data		X
	3. Property owners	X	X
	4. Estate agents		X
Competitiveness	1. International retailers	X	
	2. Competition	X	X
	3. Consumers	X	X
	4. Costumers	X	
	5. Suppliers	X	X
	6. Survival	X	
Management	1. Strategic goals		X
	2. Senior managers		X
	3. Profitability		X

Uncertainty and strategic retail location decisions

The findings of the empirical research indicate that retail location decisions are influenced by the environment and particularly by changes that happen in the retail environment. A key finding of the research, which is not consistent with the existing literature but it is supported by the empirical research, is that retail change is not necessarily only a factor that causes environmental uncertainty but it is also retailers' response to uncertainty. It is the means of overcoming uncertainty and coping with it. In fact, it is a response that not only aims at coping with uncertainty but also it is a way for them to compete. A conceptual framework is suggested that links existing theory with the empirical findings reported here (Figure 2).

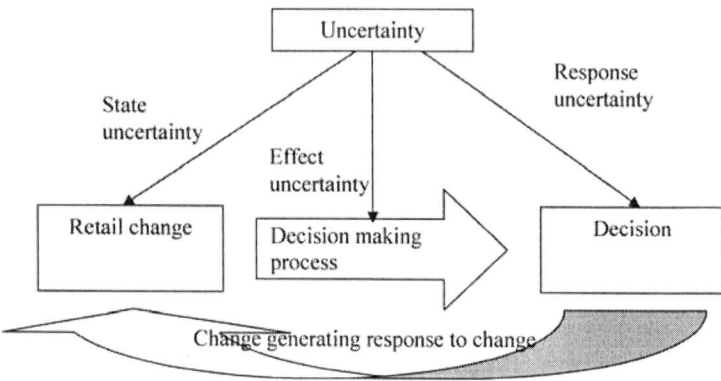

Figure 2: Conceptual framework deriving from research

The framework is informed by the authors' reflection on the relevant literature and the evidence of their exploratory research. As it was argued before, managers experience state uncertainty when they believe that available data and information they have is not enough in order to understand a phenomenon (Duncan, 1972). Retail change is a phenomenon (Brown, 1987) and the understanding of the phenomenon is influenced by the state uncertainty effect.

Evidence from the exploratory research indicate that effect uncertainty influences the decision making process. This happens because the respondents feel unable to predict the changes in their business environment, which is the typical symptom of effect uncertainty (Milliken, 1987). When respondents have to make decisions, and particularly retail location decisions, they are influenced by the effect uncertainty because they are not confident about the outcome of their decisions. So, they are hesitant in making decisions and in order to become confident (reach the threshold of confidence) they are making decisions that are the most effective according to their conceptualisation of the environment.

When managers come to making a decision they experience response uncertainty. Response uncertainty was defined as the inability to predict the likely consequences of a response choice (Miliken, 1987). This is particularly important when decisions involve retail location because a need for a strategic response to a threat or opportunity is implied. The evidence of the exploratory research indicates that respondents attempt to reduce response uncertainty by making decisions that exploit the opportunities or meet the threats by attempting not only to adapt to their environment but furthermore to change the environment up to the extent their company can.

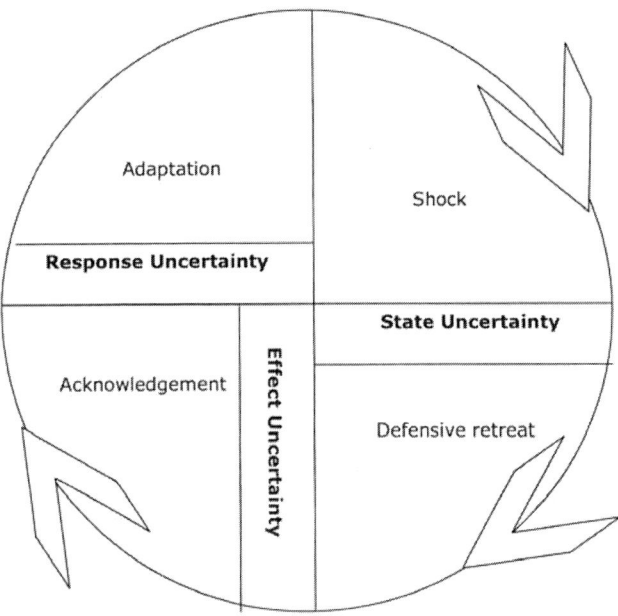

Figure 3: Conflict theory of retail change with the impact of environmental uncertainty

As Brown (1987) noted, the conflict theory of retail change came as an explanation of the emergence of innovative retail formats. Conflict theory basically suggests that retail change is an action – reaction sequence. These are: shock, defensive retreat, acknowledgement, and adaptation (Stern and El Ansary, 1977). Brown (1987), discussing the implications of conflict theory, notes that all four phases are dependent on managers' perception of the event. The shock happens when the manager understands that there is a change in the environment, which is a basic feature of state uncertainty. In the phase of defensive retreat managers are evaluating the changes that have happened in the environment, which is the state of effect uncertainty. In the phase of acknowledgement managers have finally understood the changes in the environment and they are selecting the right action from a set of alternatives. This is when the state of response uncertainty is experienced. Finally the managers are making a decision and based on that they adapt their company to the environment. The evidence from the empirical research indicates that this decision is usually an action that will initiate a new change process. This process is presented graphically in figure 3.

Understanding the strategic decisions through the complexity theory lens

Recent advances in strategic decision-making research are towards the direction of the need of a holistic explanatory model that will be able to capture the changes in the environment that make strategic decision-making a difficult task. During uncertain times this becomes even more complicated because decisions are made in circumstances of high dynamism and volatility that are crying out for urgent responses. A trending approach to this quest is the application of science, and particularly of the physical laws governing complex adaptive systems (Davis et al., 2007, Theodoridis and Bennison, 2009). Brown and Eisenhardt (1997) described complex organisations as systems that exhibit complex, adaptive, and emergent behaviours because they are made up of multiple interacting agents. In organisational sciences complexity is treated as a structural construct that characterises both the organisations and the environments (Anderson, 1999). Complexity is understood and conceptualised in different ways by academics and practitioners (Cilliers, 2000) and it raises rather exotic thoughts about chaotic situations, even though scholars see signs of chaos everywhere (Levy, 1994).

Complexity and organisations

As suggested before the concept of complexity is seen from a number of different ways and has seen different uses during the years. For example there are references of complexity from Simon (1955) who posed that there is a limit to the complexity that individuals can handle over a given period of time; therefore complexity is dependent and time defined. Eisenhardt and Brown (1998) suggested that time refers not only to the management of a complex system but also to the understanding of it, which probably is the most demanding and resource intensive part of it. Authors like Boisot (2000), gave a Darwinian view of the adaptation to the complex environments. He stressed that failing to adapt in a timely manner ultimately leads to the natural termination of the organisational life.

The systemic characteristics of organisations are a factor that explain their ceaseless process of adaptation and change (Morel and Ramanujam 1999). Companies that fail to achieve the dynamic equilibrium with their environments become outdated and ultimately "die". Using anthropomorphisms is a common trait of complexity vocabulary as they are rooted in the Darwinian laws of adaptation. Cilliers (2000: 24) provided a detailed account of the features of the complex systems (see Table 3).

Table 3: Characteristics of the complex adaptive systems,

1	Complex systems consist of a large number of elements that in themselves can be simple. These elements can be of diverse types - e.g. people, coalitions, organisations, processes etc (Morel and Ramanujam 1999).
2	The elements interact dynamically and their interactions are non-linear, therefore they cannot be predicted.
3	There exhibit feedback loops.
4	Complex systems are open, and operate in non-equilibrium conditions.
5	Complex systems have organic properties like memory and history. The behaviour of a complex system is not determined by its elements but by the nature of the interaction among the elements. The interaction of elements produces emergent patterns of behaviour (Morel and Ramanujam 1999). Since the interactions are emerging and dynamic, predictions about the system cannot be made by just inspecting their components.
6	Complex systems are adaptive meaning that they can organise their structure without the intervention of an external actor.

Source: Cilliers (2000:.24), adapted

The fundamental behaviours of organisations that operate in complex settings are either to adapt or absorb to the feedback that is given by the environment (Ashmos et al. 2000). This approach has common grounds to the debate on being a first mover or a fast follower (Song et al., 2012). The transformation is inevitable; however adapting or absorbing is not a magic recipe that can always reply to the environmental challenges. Therefore companies must move from the adaptation to the absorption of the environmental complexity taking into account the circumstances, their resources, and their capabilities. Kauffman (1995) presented companies as organisms that are fed with information, create energy in order to evolve – or co-evolve – and become compatible to their environment. Ashmos *et al.* (2000) have similarly concluded that organisations operate under multiple goals and multiple challenges, therefore they develop – intentionally or not – responses that reply holistically to the emerging challenges. The notion of multiplicity is central to the complexity theory. A response to a certain challenge has multiple consequences, or a piece of incoming information is related to numerous different challenges. That makes decision-making complex and unpredictable and is the fundamental connection between environmental uncertainty and complexity theory. Not knowing the current state, the future state, or the impact of a certain course of actions to the environment are the core of the environmental uncertainty theories and at the same time are the major reasons that organisations show complex behaviours.

Therefore if the company cannot cope with the challenges and adapt, or make the first move in a more prescriptive strategic approach, it will probably develop a bounded rational understanding of the environment and wait to absorb the energy that is created by the transformation from the order to the disorder – what is called as the *entropy* of the system in the thermodynamics – defending its position and waiting for an environmental setting that will meet its capabilities. This is not necessarily a conscious decision! The example of the case study reported above is enlightening. Companies of different sectors, with different access to information and resources showed similar – but not the same – patterns of behaviour to the emerging challenges. The comprehension of the environment was off different level and detail, the resources that could have been allocated are different, and the responses to the challenges are also different. However the pattern of action is similar. Internal and external powers drove the companies to decisions, strategic decisions of high stake and long-term commitment, with present and future implication for the company and the sector. The complexity absorption response was accomplished by emphasising formal role relationships and thereby minimising connections. It is a defensive response, yet this is not a sign of a successful or unsuccessful strategy. Stacey (1992), for example, stressed that managers tend to establish stability and succeed, or experience instability and fail. Adapting or absorbing is not a forecasting technique, it is not meant to be used to assess the performance of the company let alone its future success. It is a way to view the evolution of organisations, understand them, and potentially explain the reasons they succeed or failed in order to learn and create knowledge for future reference.

Complexity theory and strategy development

The basic assumption that needs to be made when strategies are reviewed under the prism of the complexity theory is that companies made strategies decisions in order to achieve advantage over competitors in a given strategic landscape. Companies interact with each other, but also interact with the other elements of their environments, such as consumers, suppliers, labour, the political authorities, banks and other financial institutions. All those have been identified in the case study above as factors that cause uncertainty. So, is strategy itself a complex process that generates uncertainty to the managers of the SMEs? The evidence of the research shows that it is. Strategy refers to the long term engagement to a goal, the allocation of resources, and the investment of capital and time on that goal. Each one of these prepositions entails some kind of art and science, some guessing and some calculation, some gut feeling opposed to evidence based planning. Basically, it involves strategic decisions that are made with limited information, limited resources, and within limited time. This reduction of the environment to a manageable proportion is what is called *scaling* in the complexity theory vocabulary, but it is also the same thing that is described as bounded rationality by behavioural decision-making theorists.

Bechtold (1997) approached strategy development as a dynamic process. It is as a vital activity of organisations, it gives them – as well as the decision-makers – identity, and it is planned and implemented in a different and opportunistic way by complexity adapting and complexity absorbing organisations. This can be viewed in terms of the flexibility and the length of their strategic plans, their understanding of environmental uncertainty and stability, their resistance to change, and their development of mechanisms that support them at times of change. As Stacey (1993) highlighted for some of them, strategy is not developed as a long-term plan but rather emerges spontaneously from chaos through a process of adaptation, real-time learning and political negotiations. In addition to that he added that a distinction between companies that have adopted or try to adopt a chaos-theory approach to strategy development and those that follow the normative view of strategy development is necessary. Not in terms of the likelihood to succeed but as a tool to understand them.

Further implications

This chapter aimed to draw the attention of the readers to an alternative way to understand strategising in retail SMEs. It is not the intention of the authors to provide a recipe book of strategy; on the contrary their intention is to show that there are no recipe books. Strategies shall comply with basic rules however successful strategies are based on the unique internal and external circumstances that govern the operation of the companies. Therefore, the recommendation that is made through this chapter is to spend more resources on developing a process of understanding the context rather than understanding a given and finite environment. The major capability that is unique and non-imitable for the company is the alignment of the resources in a way that managers or decision-makers will be (or feel) confident to make decisions. This is a core competence for the organisation and can lead to long term and non-substitutable competitive advantage. Theodoridis and Bennison (2009) have for example shown that the organisational structure is a potential means for achieving competitive advantage for the retail SMEs in Greece; indeed Wood and Reynolds (2013) had similar findings in their research into big retailers in the UK. For the academic researchers this is a field of further enquiry as the European South still experiences the economic crisis and yet strives to compete against the international competitors – let alone the competition from the online retailers. For the practitioners it is a field of opportunity. Consultancies may find this area of great interest and can provide consultation of business process, re-engineering processes that may lead to an organisational structure that will be open to inputs and outputs, to the environmental entropy, and the challenges of the turbulent environment.

Acknowledgements

The authors would like to thank the anonymous reviewers of the EAERCD 2007 conference, as well as Professor David Bennison for their valuable comments. This research was supported by the Greek State Scholarships Foundation.

References

Ahmad, R. and Ali, N.A. (2003), "The use of cognitive mapping techniques in management research: theory and practice", *Management Research News*, Vol. 26, No. 7, pp. 1-16.
Anderson, P. (1999), "Complexity theory and organization science",

Organization Science, Vol. 10, No. 3, pp. 216-232.

Ashmos, D.P., Duchon, D. and McDaniel R.R.Jr. (2000), "Organizational responses to complexity: the effect on organizational performance", *Journal of Organizational Change Management*, Vol.13, No. 6, pp. 577-594.

Bank of Greece (nd), "Governor's Annual Report" available at http://www.bankofgreece.gr/BogEkdoseis/ekthdkth2005.pdf (accessed 12 August 2012).

Bechtold, B. L. (1997), "Chaos theory as a model for strategy development", *Empowerment in Organizations*, Vol.5, No. 4, pp 193-201.

Bennison, D. and Boutsouki, C. (1995), "Greek retailing in transition", *International Journal of Retail and Distribution Management*, Vol. 23, No.1, pp. 24-32.

Boisot, M. (2000), "Is there a complexity beyond the reach of strategy?" *Emergence*, Vol. 2, No. 1, pp. 114-134.

Bourantas, D. and Papadakis, V. (1996), "Greek management: Diagnosis and prognosis", *International Studies of Management and Organization*, Vol. 26, No. 3, pp. 13-32.

Brown, S. (1987), "Institutional change in retailing: A review and synthesis", *European Journal of Marketing*, Vol. 21, No.6, pp. 5-36.

Brown, S. L. and Eisenhardt, K. M. (1997), "The art of continuous change: Linking complexity theory and time-paced evolution in relentlessly shifting organizations", *Administrative Science Quarterly*, Vol. 42, No. 1, pp. 1-34.

Busenitz, L. W. and Barney, J. B. (1997), "Differences between entrepreneurs and managers in large organizations: Biases and heuristics in strategic decision-making", *Journal of Business Venturing*, Vol. 12, No. 1, pp. 9-30.

Cilliers, P. (2000), "What can we learn from a theory of complexity?" *Emergence*, Vol. 2, No. 1, pp. 23-33.

Churchill, G.A. Jr. (1991), *Marketing Research Methodological Foundations*, 5th ed. Dryden Press, Orlando, FL.

Covin, J.G. and Slevin, D.P. (1991), "A conceptual model of entrepreneurship as firm behavior", *Entrepreneurship Theory and Practice*, Vol.16, No. 1, pp. 7-25.

Cyert, R. M., and March, J. G. (1965), "A summary of basic concepts in the behavioural theory of the firm", in G. Salaman (Ed.), *Desicion Making for Business: A Reader*. Sage, London, Thousand Oaks, New Delhi, pp. 62-73.

Daniels, K., de Chernatory, L. and Johnson, G. (1995), "Validating a method for mapping managers' mental models of competitive industry structures", *Human Relations*, Vol. 48, No. 9, pp. 975-991.

Dawes-Farquhar, J. (2012), *Case Study Research for Business*: Sage Publications, London.

Davis, J. P. K. M. Eisenhardt, et al. (2007), "Complexity theory, market dynamism, and the strategy of simple rules", Working paper, Stanford University, Stanford, January.

Dimitratos, P., Petrou, A., Plakoyiannaki, E. and Johnson, J. E. (2011), "Strategic decision-making processes in internationalization: Does national culture of the focal firm matter?", *Journal of World Business*, Vol. 46, No. 2, pp. 194-204.

Downey, H.K., Hellrieger, D. and Slochum, J.W. Jr (1977), "Individual characteristics as sources of perceived uncertainty variation", *Human Relations*, Vol. 30, No. 2, pp. 161-174.

Droukas, E. (1998), "Albanians in the Greek informal economy", *Journal of Ethnic and Migration Studies,* Vol. 24, No. 2, pp. 347-366.

Duncan, R.B. (1972), "Characteristics of organizational environments and perceived uncertainty", *Administrative Science Quarterly*, Vol. 17, No. 3, pp. 313-327.

Eisenhardt, K., and Zbaracki, M. (1992), "Strategic decision making", *Strategic Management Journal*, Vol.13, No. 2, pp. 17-37.

Eisenhardt, K. M., and Brown, S. L. (1998), "Competing on the edge: Strategy as structured chaos", *Long Range Planning*, Vol. 31, No. 5, pp. 786-789.

Euromonitor (2001), *Retailing in Greece – Country Report*, Euromonitor.

—. (2012), "International country report: Retailing in Greece", available at: http://www.euromonitor.com (accessed 3 July 2012).

Fakiolas, R. (1999), "Socio-economic effects of immigration in Greece", *Journal of European Social Policy*, Vol. 9, No.3, pp. 211-230.

Gerloff, E.A., Muir, N.K. and Bodensteiner, B.D. (1991), "Three components of perceived environmental uncertainty: An exploratory analysis of the effects of aggregation", *Journal of Management*, Vol. 17, pp. 749-768.

Gibcus, P., Vermeulen, P.A.M. and De Jong, J.P.J. (2009), "Strategic decision making in small firms: a taxonomy of small business owners", *International Journal of Entrepreneurship and Small Business*, Vol.7, No. 1, pp 74-91.

Jones, K. and Simmons, J. (1993*), Location, Location, Location. Analyzing the Retail Environment*, Nelson, Toronto.

Itami, H. (1987), *Mobilizing Invisible Assets*, Harvard University Press. Cambridge, MA.

Kauffman, S. A. (1995), *At Home in the Universe: The Search for Laws of Self-Organization and Complexity,* Oxford University Press, New York.

Kosmides, M. (2011), "Focus: food sector suffers as Greek spending slumps", available at: http://www.just-food.com/analysis/food-sector-suffers-as-greek-spending-slumps_id116078.aspx (accessed 3 July 2012).

Kreiser, P., and Marino, L. (2002), "Analyzing the historical development of the environmental uncertainty construct", *Management Decision*, Vol. 40, No. 9, pp. 895.

Levy, D. (1994), "Chaos theory and strategy: Theory, application, and managerial implications", *Strategic Management Journal*, Vol.15, No. 2, pp. 167-178.

López-Gamero, M. D., Molina-Azorín, J. F. and Claver-Cortes, E. (2011), "Environmental uncertainty and environmental management perception: A multiple case study", *Journal of Business Research*, Vol. 64, No. 4, pp. 427-435.

Lybaert, N. (1998), "The Information Use in a SME: Its Importance and Some Elements of Influence", *Small Business Economics*, Vol. 10, No. 2, pp. 171-191.

Manifava, D. (2012), "In the "price battle" will now invest the supermarkets", available at: http://news.kathimerini.gr/4dcgi/_w_articles_economyepix_2_19/02/2012_ 473063 (accessed 3 July 2012).

Miller, D. and Shamsie, J. (1996), "The resource-based view of the firm in two environments: The Hollywood firm studios from 1936 to 1965", *Academy of Management Journal*, Vol. 39, pp. 519-543.

Milliken F.J. (1987), "Three types of perceived uncertainty about the environment: State, effect and response uncertainty", *Academy of Management Review*, Vol. 12, pp. 133-143.

Morel, B., and Ramanujam, R. (1999), "Through the looking glass of complexity: The dynamics of organizations as adaptive and evolving systems", *Organization Science*, Vol. 10, No. 3, pp. 278-293.

National Statistics Secretariat of Greece (nd) available at http://www.statistics.gr/gr_tables/S200_SPO_2_TB_AN_05_1_Y.pdf (accessed 15 April 2008).

Nikolas, K. (2012), "French retailer Carrefur to pull out of Greece", available at: http://digitaljournal.com/article/326858#ixzz1zeyXGbkO (accessed 3 July 2012).

Ottesen, G.G., Foss, L. and Grønhaug, K. (2004), "Exploring the accuracy of SME managers' network perceptions", *European Journal of Marketing*, Vol. 38, No. 5/6, pp. 593-607.

Papadakis, V., Lioukas, S. and Chambers, D. (1998), "Strategic decision-making processes: the role of management and context", *Strategic Management Journal*, Vol.19, No. 2, pp. 115-147.
Papadakis, V. M. and Barwise, P. (2002), "How much do CEOs and top managers matter in strategic decision-making?", *British Journal of Management*, Vol. 13, No. 1, pp. 83-95.
Simon, H. A. (1955), "A behavioral model of rational choice", *The Quarterly Journal of Economics*, Vol. 69, No. 1, pp. 99-118.
Simon, H. A. (1979), "Rational decision making in business organizations", *The American Economic Review*, Vol. 69, No. 4, pp. 493.
Smith, H. (2012), "Greek shoppers look but don't buy as economic crisis bites", available at: http://www.guardian.co.uk/world/2012/jan/30/greek-shoppers-economic-crisis-bites (accessed 3 July 2012).
Song, M., Zhao, Y. L., and Di Benedetto, C. A. (2012), "Do perceived pioneering advantages lead to first-mover decisions?", *Journal of Business Research*, In press.
Spicer, D.P. (2000), *"The role of mental models in individual and organizational learning, including consideration of cognitive style"* Unpublished PhD Thesis, University of Plymouth, United Kingdom.
Stacey, R. (1993), "Strategy as order emerging from chaos", *Long Range Planning*, Vol. 26, No. 1, pp. 10-17.
Stacey, R. D. (1992), *Managing the Unknowable: Strategic Boundaries between Order and Chaos in Organizations,* Jossey-Bass, San Francisco.
Stern, L. W., and El-Ansary, A. I. (1977), *Marketing Channels,* Prentice Hall, Englewood Cliffs, NJ.
Theodoridis, C. and Bennison, D. (2009), "Complexity theory and retail location strategy", *The International Review of Retail, Distribution and Consumer Research*, Vol. 19, No. 4, pp. 389-403.
To Vima (nd), available at: http://tovima.dolnet.gr/print_article.php?e=Bandf=14339andm=D15andaa=1 (accessed 7 July 2007).
Transaparency International (nd) available at: http://ww1.transparency.org/cpi/2005/cpi2005_infocus.html#cpi.
Wernerfelt, B. and Karnani, A. (1987) "Research notes and communications competitive strategy under uncertainty", *Strategic Management Journal*, Vol. 8, pp. 187-195.
Wood, S. and Reynolds J. (2013), "Knowledge management, organisational learning and memory in UK retail network planning", *The Service*

Industries Journal, Vol. 33, No.2, pp. 150-170.

Zey, M. (1992), *Decision making: Alternatives to Rational Choice Models,* Sage Publications, Thousand Oaks, CA.

CHAPTER SIX

A REDEFINITION OF THE PATH OF INDIAN BANKING THROUGH INFORMATION TECHNOLOGY

SAROJ KUMAR DATTA AND SUKANYA KUNDU

Introduction

The financial system of any economy can be considered as its backbone and a determinant of the health of the economy. Banks are one of the major pillars of this financial system and the banking system of a country acts as a prime interface with the financial system of other countries. Hence, any change in the banking system of any country affects the financial system of other countries in a globalised economic environment.

The waves of globalisation affected the economies of developing countries in many ways and with a great impact. During the initial phase of globalization, the more advanced countries underwent, a rapid phase of liberalisation that resulted in sustained macroeconomic stability even during turbulent time, whereas, the least developed countries (LDCs) experienced slow and uneven privatisation that did not prepare them for economic crisis and proved that the macroeconomic stability in these economies were very fragile[1]. One of the major components of structural reforms carried out by the transition economies was financial sector reforms as it was found that a robust and dynamic financial system is essential for sustainable growth of any country. Countries in transition have gone a long way in transforming their financial system, specially the banking system.

---

[1] Globalisation : Trends, Challenges and Opportunities for countries in transition by Mojmir Mrak

The phenomenon of globalisation is outcome of technological development. The impact of globalisation and technological development necessitated a paradigm shift for Indian banking. Nair (2000) found that those banking and financial service providers who can switch over to the electronic environment in the quickest possible period alone would be able to survive. The financial services sector realised that a quick implementation of Internet capabilities and electronic services is a viable option for interaction between financial service providers and their customers (Rotchanakitumnuai and Speece, 2004). Analyzing the impact of IT on the banking sector, Bhasin (2001) commented that IT has transformed the repetitive and overlapping systems and procedures into simple single key pressing technology, resulting in speed, accuracy and efficiency in conducting business.

With rapid technological changes, the consumers' taste and preferences are also changing and their expectation levels are continuously rising. Consumers are the kingpins, driving modern business and their satisfaction is of prime importance to an organisation. Organisational success depends on outperforming competitors by satisfying consumers. Therefore, business needs to adapt to the environment of empowered consumers. Seitz and Stickel (1998) noted that consumer behavior in banking changed partly because of the changes in the available spare time of individuals. Mobility, independence from time and geographical restriction and flexibility have become key words in consumer banking. Timmers (2000) supports this view, highlighting the key features of the Internet – such as 24-hour availability, almost immediate access, and the absence of physical borders. Indeed, the Internet has been one of the key drivers in promoting E-Commerce in the banking sector (Jeevan, 2000).

Information technology and the innovations generated by it are strategic tools for enhancing customers' value and the strength of their relationship. It also enables to reduce the costs of financial transactions, improve the allocation of financial resources, and increase the competitiveness and efficiency of financial institutions. In his recent book, *"Building Social Business"*, Muhammad Yunus (Noble prizewinner from Bangladesh) noted that – in the sixties, no one predicted that Internet would take the world by storm; that laptops, palmtops, blackberries, iPods, iPhones, tablets and kindles would be in the hands of millions. Even twenty years ago, no one could predict that mobile phones would become an integral part of life in every village of the world. Evidently, in 1990, we could not foresee the world of 2010; technology just outpaced our imagination. Similarly, in 2010, perhaps we are just unable to look ahead at 2030.

Chapter Six

The origins of the Indian banking

Banking in India in various forms is as old as Indian civilisation. In ancient times, there were individuals who would lend money against either mortgage of goods (particularly gold) or at an exorbitant interest rate without any such security mortgaged. Those individual moneylenders invested their own funds as capital. They had their own individual norms of doing business. Such type of banking, particularly lending money, was limited to as family business. The traditional instruments used as documents for lending, were called 'hundies'.

The picture that emerged from the available records, clearly established the existence of an indigenous banking system that worked well at least for the money lending purpose, if not for other financial business. The system continued till the arrival of the East India Company in India. With the East India Company establishing its business domination in the country, and the different Agency Houses establishing banking enterprises, the traditional individual bankers had to take a back seat

The commercial banking in India started with the establishment of the Bank of Hindustan in 1770. The history of Indian banking can be deivided two main eras: a) Indian banking system before independence and b) Indian banking system after independence. Again, the Indian banking scenario post-independence has three sub-eras: pre-nationalisation of banks, nationalisation of banks and the present era of liberalised economy with the re-emergence of private banks.

The process of nationalisation of Indian banking started in 1955, with the nationalisation of State Bank of India and that of its subsidiaries in 1959. During this phase, 14 major commercial banks were nationalized. The majority of nationalisation process was over in 1969, and done by the then Prime Minister of India, Mrs. Indira Gandhi. . Finally, in 1980, seven more banks were nationalised and this brought 80% of the banking sector in India under the Government ownership.

As a result of the nationalization process, the Public Sector Banks (PSBs) had huge asset base at their disposal and the widest geographical coverage serving a diverse group of customers. However the Indian Public Sector Banks in their enthusiasm for developmental banking, looked exclusively to branch opening, deposit accretion and social banking, thus neglecting prudential norms, profitability criteria, risk-management and building adequate capital as a buffer to counter balance the ever expanding risk-inherent assets held by them. Reforms in the financial and banking sectors and liberal recapitalisation of the ailing and weakened public sector banks followed.

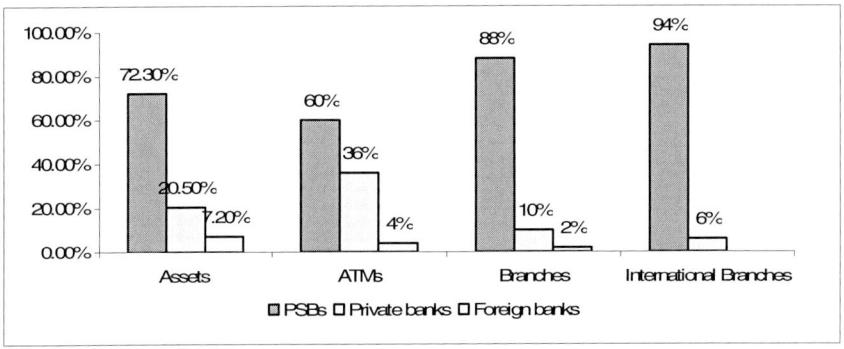

Figure 1: comparison of assets and infrastructure

Indian Public Sector Banks relied upon its branches, which according to its customers led to a situation where banking became an unavoidable, troublesome and time-consuming activity. For customers, particularly for busy executives and business people, banking became very difficult as most of the banking processes such as opening a bank account, withdrawal of money, getting a bank draft etc. consumed a lot of time. Things became worse with the fact that the customers had to go to the bank branches, which remained open for public transactions for limited hours only on working week days. In addition, the transaction hours were in the morning when the executives and business people would be extremely busy. To realise outstation cheque and credit it to customers' accounts, it took up to 45 days as the cheque had to physically travel across the country to the paying branch. There were even cases where the ultimate paying branch returned the cheque to the originating bank because of distortion due to multiple postal stampings on them. A small number of very rich people could escape this situation by subscribing to a small number of foreign banks. These foreign banks had set their standards for opening bank account, minimum balance requirement etc., so high that their service could be availed by only exclusive and small group of HNI customers. These banks were also very choosy about selecting their customers. Hence, the general Indian banking environment at that time can be visualised as having a huge number of un-satisfied customers, which evidently resulted in an ineffective and cumbersome banking operation.

Need for process reengineering

Reengineering of business process aims at transforming the way an organisation conducts its business. It is the search for a new model of organising work which would improve its competitive position in the business environment and thus benefit its customers and all other stakeholders. In this endeavour, a firm must first focus on reengineering its generic business processes, which are of three broad categories: processes pertaining to development and delivery of products and / or services; processes involving interfaces with customers; and processes comprising management activities. The core objectives of BPR are a) Fast cycle capability and competitiveness of the system, and b) Developing boundary-less companies which include customers, suppliers, etc. as part of an integrated, fast cycle system. Improvement on quality and cost follows improvement on thrust area i.e., reduction of total cycle time of business process.

These necessitate the need to foster a fast growing use of IT-initiatives by firms as coping mechanism to an ever changing business environment and to satisfy customers. The Indian banking sector too has recognised that for utmost customers satisfaction, it needs to leverage on the use of information technology (IT). An IT-enabled reengineered business process would help in gaining strategic advantage over the competitors by way of compression of time, overcoming restrictions of geography and / or distance, and restructuring of relationships. Improving competitiveness, without further loosing time, is seen as an essential move for Indian nationalised banks towards this end.

Path of Technology adaptation

IT-initiatives provide business values in three distinct areas: (i) Efficiency – by way of increased productivity, (ii) Effectiveness – by way of better management, and (iii) Innovation – by way of improved products and services.

Service organisations employ technology to enhance customer service quality and delivery, to reduce costs, and to standardise core service offerings (Ibrahim et al., 2006; Bauer et al., 2005). Thus the use of technology was supposed to bring a surge in the satisfaction level of the customers through timely delivery of services and accurate services (Dabholkar et al., 2003) in Indian banking. Constructive uses of new technologies have always contributed positively towards improvement of standards of human life and the economy of the country. In Banking sector too, technology was found to be the most powerful tool to augment the operational performance in terms of timeliness, accuracy, ease of operation etc. at the same time provide convenience in product access and delivery.

Banking industry in the developed countries led the change by initiating excellence in performance for maximum customer satisfaction, which eventually became the norm for the global banking sector. Some of the initiatives regarding infrastructure and data management are:

- Establish infrastructure capable of sustaining 24 x 7 operations, with scalability for future expansion, in line with the international standards of data centre management processes and governance as embodied in norms such as ITIL and CoBIT.
- Established SLAs with vendors for infrastructure management which takes care of :
  Availability – Addressing uptime and downtime, network throughput
  Performance – Transaction per second (TPS) and turnaround times of software, hardware and network infrastructure
  Quality – Number of defects per thousand lines of code.

Many European banks have spent millions to modernise their ATM channel and equip their machines with more functionality to turn routine interactions away from the teller. Other innovations include the use of cash machines to top up mobile phones among others. Following the Basel – II initiatives, IT investments for managing regulatory requirements started capturing a significant slice of IT budgets for the European banks.

In India, the private sector banks brought state-of-the-art technology in its operational systems. With competition increasing, the public sector banks also adopted the new technology. As per the directive issued by the Central Vigilance Commission, it was required to computerise 70 per cent of the banking business by public sector banks before January1, 2001. In 1993, the public sector banks started the basic computerisation process. As on December 31, 2001, 13 banks had achieved the level of computerisation between 75 and 80 per cent while seven banks had computerisation levels ranging between 70 per cent and 75 per cent and seven banks were at a level above 80 per cent. The foreign banks and private sector banks successfully transited from physical cash to any time and anywhere money. 'Click banking' replaced the 'queue banking'. Private sector banks and some public sector banks later started interconnecting their branches and offsite delivery channels. While tracing back the advent of technological development in Indian banking, we can refer to some of the landmark years:

In 1966: Indian Bankers Association (IBA) along with exchange banks association signed first wage settlement with the unions, which accounted for the use of ICT accounting machines for inter-branch reconciliation etc.
In 1970: SBI installed a ledger-posting machine along with a mainframe computer at selected branches, introducing computer based banking.
In 1980: Introduction of computer-linked communication based banking.
In 1983: RBI appointed a committee on computerisation and mechanisation under the chair of Dr. C. Rangrajan. Its objective was to chalk out a plan for mechanisation of Indian banking industry. The committee recommended that computerisation and installation of advanced ledger posting machines (ALPM) at branch, regional and head offices of banks would bring around a new era in banking.
In 1991: Narasimhan committee paved way for the reform phase in .banking.
In 1994: The Saraf Committee constituted by RBI, recommended the use of Electronic Fund Transfer system (EFT), introduction of electronic clearing services and extension of Magnetic Ink Character Recognition (MICR) beyond metropolitan cities and branches.

As per the RBI report, the public sector banks incurred an expenditure of Rs.106.76 billions on computerisation and development of communication networks between September 1999 and March 2006. The report also mentioned that more than 95 per cent branches of public sector banks (at end-March 2006) were fully/ or partially computerised. Out of 27 public sector banks, branches of as many as 10 public sector banks were 100 per cent computerised, while branches of another 12 banks were more than 50 per cent computerised. Branches of only five PSBs were less than 50 per cent computerised.

Recent trends in Indian banking

The environment in the banking industry is going through rapid changes due to the impact of technology. The concept of 'Brick-and-Mortar' banking is gradually changing into the concept of 'Universal banking'. During the last decade, Internet and the concept of E-commerce, M-commerce, etc. entered into the scenario of global banking and financial institutions. With the advent of technology in computing, development of Internet and networking technology and advancement of telecommunication facilities, global players like Citi Bank and GE Capital are now able to reach vast number of clientele spread geographically in different areas through limited branches they have set up.

Chalam (2002) studied the growth and trend of IT application in banking sector. Also Mehta (2003) researched the impact of IT on banks' productivity with reference to Jammu and Kashmir Bank Ltd. Mohamed (2005) carried out a study on six banks (HDFC Bank, ICICI Bank, Indian Overseas Bank, State Bank of India, Standard Chartered / ANZ Grindlays Bank and Citi Bank) located in the city of Chennai to investigate the application of CRM methods in banking and its impact.

Ashish K. Sen[2] (2001) pointed out that new Private Sector Banks have done significant technological up-gradation, thus staying ahead in competition primarily in customer service. Chalam (2002) studied the growth and trend of IT application in banking sector and assessed its impact on banks' performance. He considered the perception of customers on the quality and expectation from such IT-enabled services and the views of employees on such environment. The author inferred that qualitative improvement in the customer service and internal housekeeping due to computerisation of the bank, reflected in quantitative terms of increase in deposits, advances and financial performance of the bank branch. His analysis of these items of pre and post-computerisation periods also revealed that the growth percentage was more attractive during the post-computerisation period. He also concluded that a majority of the customers were satisfied with the improved service offered by the computerised bank branch as well as the staff who were working in the branch. Further, the staff members were also quite happy to attend to their work in the new work environment.

Mehta (2003) carried out an interesting study on the impact of IT on productivity of banks in reference to J&K Bank Ltd... Both qualitative and quantitative evaluation of Computer Based Information System (CBIS) was done to adjudge the efficacy of the new system. The study showed that the overall response towards the change was encouraging.

---

[2] Sen, Ashish K. Former Managing Director, Centurion Bank Limited.

Mobile Banking

Over the last few years, the mobile and wireless markets have been one of the fastest growing markets in the world. Mobile phones have become an essential, as well as, a conveniently available communication tool for almost every individual. Using this technology for funds transfers as well as retail payments holds a huge potential. As such, mobile banking is the most happening area of development in the banking sector and is expected to complement, and to an extent replace, the credit/debit card system in future. While it has the potential to overcome issues relating to cost, infrastructure and resources, it does pose some new issues of its own. The main amongst these pertain to the dependence on service providers, network availability and security. It would also require deep appreciation of management aspects which relate not only to appropriate technology deployment and performance at backend but also to issues such as front end contact with the customer to provide necessary confidence and convenience. All these issues are receiving due attention for prioritised resolution. RBI has also established National Payment Corporation of India to focus attention on development and implementation of requisite technologies for enabling new modes of delivery. Table 1 provides the information regarding adaption of mobile banking in India. For this purpose five top performing public sector banks, three private banks and two foreign banks were selected.

Table 1: Mobile Banking Transactions data over the period March-2010 to March -2012

Bank Name		Volume	Value
STATE BANK OF INDIA	Mar'10	179131	118565.00
	Mar'11	834635	470234.00
	Mar'12	2560751	1074187.00
PUNJAB NATIONAL BANK	Mar'10	18	30.23
	Mar'11	56	231.05
	Mar'12	532	1315.92
UNION BANK OF INDIA	Mar'10	2970	2733.39
	Mar'11	16585	10280.78
	Mar'12	28789	18149.72
BANK OF BARODA	Mar'10	Not available	Not available
	Mar'11	Not available	Not available
	Mar'12	19528	23318.00
BANK OF INDIA	Mar'10	67	119.00
	Mar'11	530	340.00
	Mar'12	1766	912.00
ICICI BANK LTD	Mar'10	37566	80744.00
	Mar'11	98395	261845.00
	Mar'12	278980	811845.00
HDFC BANK LTD.	Mar'10	26599	14950.60
	Mar'11	16486	26372.00
	Mar'12	30021	23406.00
AXIS BANK LTD	Mar'10	3072	918.44
	Mar'11	3618	4162.13
	Mar'12	25673	21731.58
CITI BANK	Mar'10	1207	3095.00
	Mar'11	8728	32738.00
	Mar'12	52446	243703.00
STANDARD CHARTERED BANK	Mar'10	2342	321.20
	Mar'11	4763	890.29
	Mar'12	6466	7382.61

Source: RBI

Electronic Payment Systems

One of the areas where technology has facilitated significant revolution is payment systems. It started with the mechanisation/ automation of certain processes by introduction of cheque sorters and readers, MICR based clearing etc. and has moved on to use information technology for efficient funds transfer mechanisms such as ECS, NEFT, CTS, RTGS. The focus has shifted from the initial needs of capacity management for handling increasing volumes, to efficiency enhancement in transaction processing for the benefit of businesses, markets as well as retail customers. Indian banks have witnessed increased utilisation of these delivery mechanisms and are getting prepared to adapt to the higher level of technology and sophistication to meet the rising expectations of the market participants. RBI has already initiated work towards introduction of new generation RTGS, which would be capable of handling the rising volumes of transactions, provide better functionalities and would have better technological adaptability. Use of electronic payment systems by the customers of these PSBs was assessed by analysing their value and volume of use in day-to-day retail banking. Amount of usage was measured in two different terms: I) number of transactions, referred as volume in the study and II) money worth of transaction, referred in the study as value. The instruments considered primarily were NEFT and RTGS. Bank wise analysis was done for the period between March 2009 and 2012(Table 2 and Table 3).

Table 2: National Electronic Funds Transfer over the period March-2009 to March -2012

		TOTAL OUTWARD DEBITS		RECEIVED INWARD CREDITS	
		NO. OF TRANSACTIONS	AMOUNT (in Rs. crore)	NO. OF TRANSACTIONS	AMOUNT (in Rs. Crore)
SBI	Mar'09	270,085	2,048.32	665,388	4,494.70
	Mar'10	653,670	3,429.34	1,328,914	6,296.39
	Mar'11	1990652	13587.67	2851929	23898.36
	Mar'12	3763484	289026.23	4799881	307898.82
PNB	Mar'09	25,305	80.83	104,263	542.36
	Mar'10	78286	348.74	258021	1800.99
	Mar'11	242532	1550.52	628664	3262.97
	Mar'12	458213	37176.17	1112285	77534.18
UBI	Mar'09	16,444	59.48	74,181	525.89
	Mar'10	57806	199.67	200546	1245.35
	Mar'11	223644	1603.33	433871	3239.12
	Mar'12	464732	24599.35	732814	58233.36
BOB	Mar'09	42,325	132.80	88,256	534.14
	Mar'10	80714	321.82	199523	969.62
	Mar'11	208939	1453.07	442908	2914.26
	Mar'12	356649	28658.57	766161	52291.03

BOI	Mar'09	23,323	111.62	83,115	518.21
	Mar'10	63599	231.81	216929	959.03
	Mar'11	172447	973.63	485998	2902.86
	Mar'12	314674	24843.48	914513	57876.77
ICICI	Mar'09	647,550	1,938.63	697,476	2,529.01
	Mar'10	938035	2606.14	1158719	4015.36
	Mar'11	1589982	6242.59	1856185	13525.39
	Mar'12	2584263	128518.18	2715611	165205.84
HDFC	Mar'09	655,853	4,252.82	544,674	3,668.75
	Mar'10	1331411	5858.16	1086883	6515.38
	Mar'11	2441678	34628.05	1964339	16899.61
	Mar'12	3813080	373817.91	3017909	369892.86
AXIS	Mar'09	175,837	784.89	238,307	1,152.97
	Mar'10	1331411	5858.16	1086883	6515.38
	Mar'11	1077162	5450.45	959942	7604.01
	Mar'12	2033346	136851.95	1555155	133570.70
HSBC	Mar'09	255,721	2,139.96	72,860	954.06
	Mar'10	411654	3203.53	151655	1297.49
	Mar'11	705167	5912.61	215088	4637.34
	Mar'12	956281	108052.65	252238	58396.91

CITI bank	Mar'09	631,555	5,014.11	167,586	1,232.46
	Mar'10	1294726	8106.53	309270	2617.34
	Mar'11	1496285	18578.28	544658	10176.83
	Mar'12	2443690	268473.60	746594	124669.63
STANDARD CHARTERED	Mar'09	243,011	1,607.93	75,958	1,115.62
	Mar'10	498182	3138.78	149959	1852.23
	Mar'11	342095	2950.31	155548	4202.53
	Mar'12	1086989	148732.74	365378	109708.00

Source: RBI

Table 3: Real time gross settlement over the period March-2009 to March -2012

		INWARD		OUTWARD	
		VOLUME	VALUE	VOLUME	VALUE
SBI	Mar'09	323234	3698.46	293564	3825.06
	Mar'10	663414	4458.39	617706	4350.77
	Mar'11	757735	5507.99	663820	5821.76
	Mar'12	989501	7540.27	871585	7334.60
PNB	Mar'09	82098	784.74	112634	759.83
	Mar'10	172584	1176.08	242253	1178.62
	Mar'11	195888	1498.70	245248	1489.00
	Mar'12	273633	1900.26	320586	1875.46

UBI	Mar'09	53184	594.83	74069	576.27
	Mar'10	132020	808.45	171901	782.59
	Mar'11	146925	1057.21	181970	1095.58
	Mar'12	186484	1206.17	231124	1232.80
BOB	Mar'09	54786	481.23	73972	478.43
	Mar'10	124445	811.14	169948	760.16
	Mar'11	150622	948.38	188113	1025.52
	Mar'12	209517	1194.85	254584	1193.03
BOI	Mar'09	47991	869.43	63794	782.66
	Mar'10	107929	1035.89	150988	1009.37
	Mar'11	127565	1368.71	174010	1288.16
	Mar'12	170440	1417.16	230421	1423.81
ICICI	Mar'09	106023	1966.96	77096	1888.40
	Mar'10	229808	2466.03	192408	2405.30
	Mar'11	252229	3615.16	228530	3711.62
	Mar'12	327863	2921.17	303028	2921.38
HDFC	Mar'09	254516	6343.06	209814	6886.21
	Mar'10	660787	9001.43	457422	9803.98
	Mar'11	692992	10931.76	554564	11098.16
	Mar'12	933501	10853.75	759178	11216.13

Indian Banking through Information Technology

AXIS	Mar'09	95643	1633.33	94396	1671.70
	Mar'10	240085	2526.37	219004	2651.72
	Mar'11	272261	3348.73	252408	3292.28
	Mar'12	369664	3453.37	349660	3470.99
HSBC	Mar'09	34528	645.65	25446	658.03
	Mar'10	62720	957.31	42662	1051.27
	Mar'11	57767	1139.22	41324	1240.52
	Mar'12	71994	1494.80	53076	1614.57
CITI bank	Mar'09	55481	1164.33	46098	1269.99
	Mar'10	159579	1922.38	94196	1969.23
	Mar'11	143512	2666.78	92887	2703.22
	Mar'12	180566	3750.41	114439	3571.71
STANDARD CHARTERED	Mar'09	36658	2300.33	49981	2371.21
	Mar'10	91653	2543.62	98576	2639.13
	Mar'11	107184	2537.10	102505	2549.27
	Mar'12	130476	2815.98	125919	2831.31

Source: RBI

ATM/Point of Sales (POS)

Another important benefit derived from information technology deployment is the ability of banks to provide innovative delivery channels. Online banking, debit & credit card payments, ATM access to other bank customers, Point of Sales terminals etc., have all changed the way the customers interact with the banks for their day-to-day needs, thereby creating a huge eco system of convenient banking facilities (Table 4). This substantially reduced the need for physical proximity of bank branches and handling of cash. It also provided access to a large number of global retail banking outlets. There was phenomenal increase in the number of credit cards issued by the banks in India during the last few years. In June 2008, the number of transactions by credit cards at POS terminals was 20.6 million as against 17.2 million transactions in June 2007, reflecting an increase of almost 20 per cent during the year.

Public, private and foreign banks in India

In India, public sector banks are much ahead in asset base compared to private banks and foreign banks. India's public sectors banks are also taking initiatives towards a leading role in terms of information technology usage. Figure 2 shows the comparative figure for the number of mobile banking transaction recorded over the period of March 2010 to 2012. The study takes into account six banks (two banks from each of the three categories, i.e., public, private and foreign banks) which have shown highest amount of mobile transactions.

Table 4: Bank wise ATM and Card Statistics over the period April-2011 to February -2012

Bank Name		Number of ATMs		No. of POS terminals	Credit Cards				Debit Cards			
		On-site	Off-site	On-line	No. of Transactions (Actuals)		Amount of transactions (Rs Million)		No. of Transactions (Actuals)		Amount of transactions (Rs Million)	
					at ATM	at POS	at ATM	at POS	at ATM	at POS	at ATM	at POS
SBI	Apr11	10962	9318	0	21508	2737188	95.6	5482	144809000	4219000	367726	6616
	Feb12	11971	9803	0	43404	3219979	118	6544	158268000	5713000	422697	7971
PNB	Apr11	3033	2195	176	2277	84560	10	184	36192527	647495	49520	740
	Feb12	3056	2845	310	2140	10998	9.00	239.8	37349091	1196369	53776	1197
UBI	Apr11	1832	804	2709	818	35948	3.4	103	12066286	277161	22965	450
	Feb12	2133	1226	2654	795	39765	3.53	107	6340901	389107	19905	617
BOB	Apr11	1018	561	4537	3050	70341	3.2	195	6074724	329175	22062.5	533
	Feb12	1322	611	4310	948	74278	3.3	194	6939684	530848	26909	759

Chapter Six

BOI	Apr11	760	690	1921	8899	78427	59.5	211	1877971	346339	6489	406
	Feb12	853	810	1926	8295	82228	58.4	219	9457658	447182	18814	651
ICICI	Apr11	2724	3467	178960	9256	4088258	47.6	9239	24485090	3908668	105031	6478
	Feb12	3010	5330	153509	8006	4231777	42.2	9691.1	23895310	4350470	104669	7122
HDFC	Apr11	2837	2787	125179	50701	5344558	299	17823	21263901	4606216	85279	6873
	Feb12	3641	3993	177288	64665	6711082	413	23089	23767676	5158212	99859	7608
Axis	Apr11	1745	4595	186708	6432	569770	20.7	1455	39149622	1980268	87919	3433
	Feb12	1517	7227	198297	5759	824036	17.7	2274	47988154	2595259	109571	4226
Citi	Apr11	58	599	10355	29634	4820463	238	14266	3096582	1149124	11225	2606
	Feb12	58	643	9052	27929	5690730	230	15005	3193902	1353475	11055	3017
HSBC	Apr11	72	79	9472	3288	1102183	23.1	2949	464737	258111	2119	602
	Feb12	71	69	9327	2880	1028590	19.9	2791.8	408689	241496	1858.05	578.6
Stan Chart	Apr11	95	224	16	2574	1698682	12	5190	1408552	448972	4771	741
	Feb12	97	209	14	2160	1789148	10	5373	1281790	481094	4484.78	791.4

Source: RBI

Indian Banking through Information Technology 131

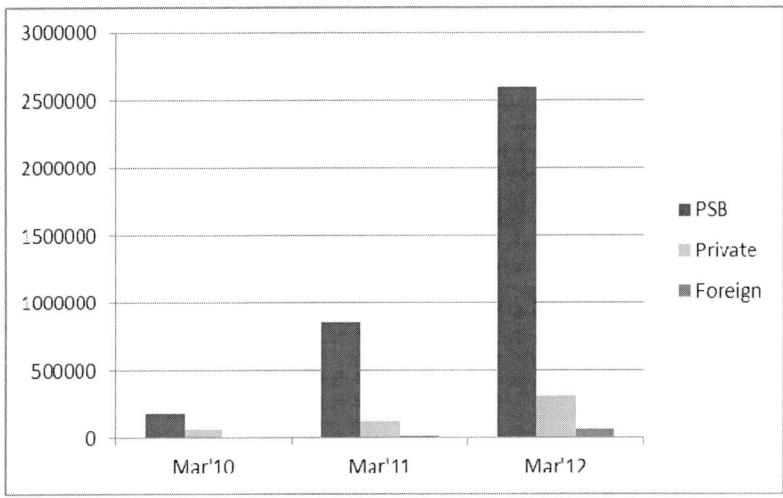

Figure 2: comparative usage of mobile banking (volume wise) over the period Mar'10 to '12 among public, private and foreign banks

Indian PSBs are showing a sharp increase in the usage of mobile banking and they are ahead of private and the foreign players. Private and foreign banks are also showing an upward trend. This confirms customers are accepting mobile banking in India.

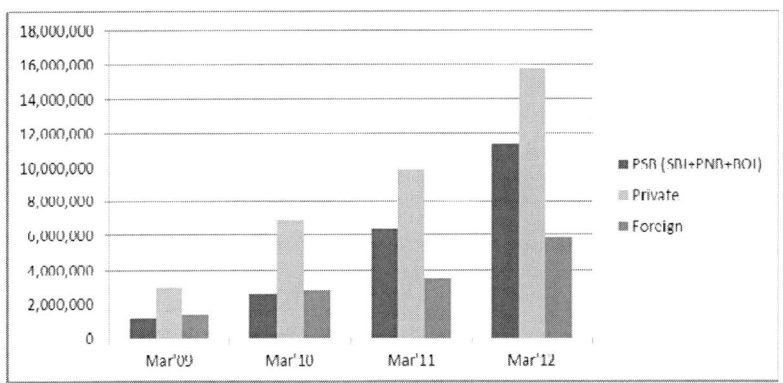

Figure 3: comparative usage of NEFT banking (volume wise) over the period Mar'10 to '12 among public, private and foreign banks

Private Banks hold the leading position in NEFT transactions. Also all the three categories of banks are showing a steady increase in NEFT transactions.

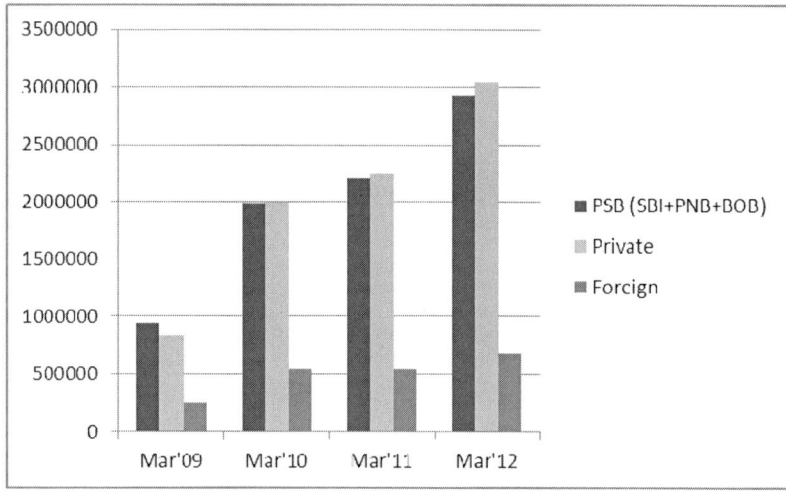

Figure 3: comparative usage of RTGS banking (volume wise) over the period Mar'10 to '12 among public, private and foreign banks

Both public sector banks and private banks are depicting a sharp rise in RTGS that supports the fact that Indian customers are relying on electronic fund transfer.

In terms of volume of usage of credit cards, private and foreign banks are well above the public sector banks. The underlying reason may be due to the fact that credit cards are treated as overdraft in public sector banks and these banks provide credit cards to a selected smaller number of customers in order to ensure that overdrafts do not further add to their non-performing assets (NPA). This is not the case with private and foreign sector banks, who treat credit cards as a business area and promote credit cards aggressively to their customers, as interest rates are much higher for these products and services. However, data on usage of debit card shows that customers mostly use public sector banks' debit cards to transact at ATMs and POS. The reason could be that the public sector banks have more number of ATMs all over the country as compared to the private or foreign banks.

Indian Banking through Information Technology 133

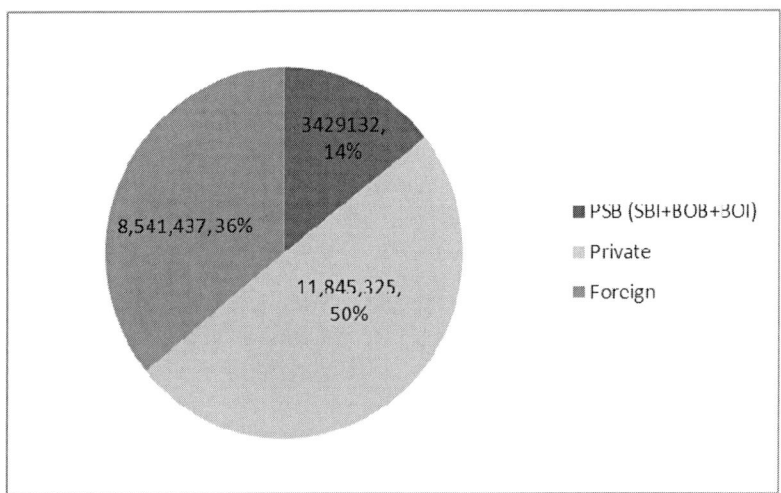

Figure 4: comparative usage of credit card (volume wise) as of March'12 among public, private and foreign banks

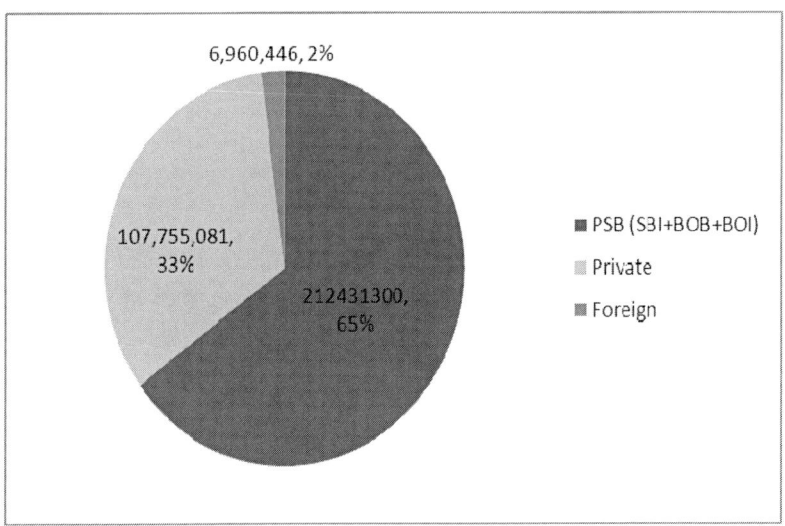

Figure 5: comparative usage of debit card (volume wise) as of March'12 among public, private and foreign banks

Studies on Indian Banking Customers psyche

Saha and Zhao (2005) analysed the relationship between service quality and customer satisfaction in Internet banking; selecting five service quality dimensions and qualitative research approach to get a better understanding of this issue. In addition, quantitative survey was conducted to support the results obtained from the qualitative study. Nine service quality dimensions i.e. efficiency, reliability, responsiveness, fulfillment, privacy, communication, personalisation, technology update and logistic/technical support were identified in this study. The quality performance of all the nine dimensions demonstrated to have a strong impact on customer satisfaction.

Consumer Voice (2006) conducted a survey to study the customer satisfaction level of 3100 customers (credit and debit card holders) during the period from September 2005 to November 2005. The study revealed that most of the customers were shifting from public sector banks to private sector banks, mainly due to convenience provided by private sector banks and restricted working hours of public sector banks. Overall, only 6 per cent of the respondents used Internet banking and most of them were registered with HSBC (16.3 per cent) followed by ICICI Bank (12.6 per cent). Overall, the study concluded that Standard Chartered Bank, Vijaya Bank and Syndicate Bank stole the march, the little known United Western Bank performed impressively and Citibank was the most over-rated bank.

Datta (2008) carried out a pilot study, surveying several branches of Public Sector Banks in the state of West Bengal, India. The findings reflected that the banking service providers perceived information technology as an effective tool to develop fast cycle capabilities and increase their competitive position. The adaptability study reflected that the PSBs intend to bring about changes in banking operation in order to provide better customer service. The study also measured customers' perception on various aspects of banking operation and their expectations. It was found that the level of customer satisfaction improved with the implementation of information technology. The customer gave the highest degree of importance to transaction time (for withdrawal / deposit and opening an account). It was also found that the customer satisfaction level had significantly enhanced following the introduction of ATM facility; introduction of computerised passbook updating facility and computerised teller facility. The study found that for greater satisfaction, customers wanted more ATM facility and expected banks to reengineer operational system so that the transaction time for opening a bank account and for withdrawal / deposit would reduce. Customers were looking for fast cycle capability and competitiveness of the banking system, which are the core objective of BPR. They suggested for a holistic approach to BPR through overall restructuring of the banking organisation and strongly recommended improvement of the HR aspect of business process reengineering in terms of bank employees' skill up-gradation.

Jham and Khan (2008) conducted a study on customer satisfaction in the Indian banking sector and their findings reveal that while private banks have been able to attract young customers with higher educational levels as they are comfortable with multi-channel banking, the customers of the national banks are older and more satisfied with the traditional facilities.

Khatri and Ahuja (2008) analysed customer satisfaction in public and private sector banks and revealed that the Indian banking sector has witnessed heightened competition with so many banks using all their potential and their global strength to their advantage in order to establish themselves in the market. Private Banks seem to have satisfied its customers with good services and they have been successful in retaining its customers by providing better facilities than Public Sector Banks. However, private banks still need to go a long way to become customer's first preference. In an economy of innovative technologies and changing markets, each service quality variable has become important.

Uppal (2009) studied customer service and customer satisfaction for Indian commercial banks and concluded that the speed of rendering service sets apart one bank from another. In the emerging competitive environment and IT era with little or no distinction in the product offering, prompt service is equated with quality service. Time is a major factor that affects the quality and reputation of the banks. E-banks provide quick service and that is why they are becoming popular. Hence, it is very essential that all bank groups should put in place the right kind of systems to further cut down on service time and render instantaneous service to the customers. Only such banks will satisfy the customers' expectations and survive in the scenario of high competition for market shares in the days to come.

Kundu, S. and Datta, S. (2011) studied the use of the delivery channels like Internet, mobile etc. in India. Their paper attempted to find out whether m-banking could be seen as a replacement of i-banking. Nine service attributes were identified and analysis was done on these nine attributes separately for i-banking and m-banking and again for user perception and satisfaction. The results showed that for frequent services like balance enquiry, movie ticket booking, people preferred m-banking; on the other hand for high value transfers and electronic shopping people preferred i-banking.

Kumbhar (2011) attempted to examine the contribution of various dimensions of service quality for customers' satisfaction. The result of the study indicated that all 13 variables were found significant and were good predictors of overall satisfaction in e-banking. However, the result of principle component analysis indicated that, perceived value, brand perception, cost effectiveness, easy to use, convenience, problem handling, security/assurance and responsiveness are important factors in customer satisfaction. Contact facilities, system availability, fulfillment, efficiency and compensation were comparatively less important. Responsiveness, easy to use, cost effectiveness and compensation were predictors of brand perception in e-banking, whereas fulfillment, efficiency, security/assurance, responsiveness, convenience, cost effectiveness, problem handling and compensation were found to be predictors of perceived value in e-banking. Therefore, bankers and e-banking service designers should think over these dimensions and make possible changes in the e-banking services according to the customers' expectations and preferences. It will help in enhancing service quality of e-banking and increase the level of customers' satisfaction.

Siddik and Selvachandra (2011) studied customer satisfaction towards e-banking services of ICICI bank in Chennai city and concluded that the service quality was main reason for the respondents to prefer this bank.. Convenience and popularity of branch were next to service quality in terms of customers' preference. At the same time, customers were dissatisfied with the service rendered by the staffs, and with the delay in sanctioning of loans. The authors suggested that banks should provide sufficient training programmes to mitigate the above problems.

Kumbhar (2011) found that the cost effectiveness of ATM service was the core of service quality dimension and it was significantly affecting the overall customer satisfaction in ATM service provided by commercial banks. However, result of factor analysis indicated that cost-effectiveness, convenience of use, security and responsiveness also influenced customer satisfaction. Therefore, banks should concentrate their efforts on these dimensions to provide better ATM services to satisfy their customers.

Ernst and Young survey (2011) surveyed more than 20,500 global retail banking customers including 1,000 respondents from India. The survey aimed to identify the driving factor of the customers' relationships with their banks. Majority of the retail customers of Indian banking sector were satisfied with the banking system, according to the survey. The positive attitude showed by the Indian banks in handling the global financial meltdown of 2008, increased the trust of people in the banking system of the country. As per the survey, 75% of the retail banking customers in India said that their trust in the banking industry had grown. Benefiting from the conservative banking policies applied by the banking sector regulator Reserve Bank of India, India remained relatively untouched by the global financial crisis.

Agarwal (2012) studied customer satisfaction in banking services in the Aligarh district. Her study reinforced that the banking sector in India is undergoing major changes due to competition and the advent of technology. The customer is looking for better quality of services that would enhance his/her satisfaction. The results of the study showed public sector banks like SBI were much below the expectations of their customers on all dimensions of service quality. Private Banks such as ICICI bank were exceeding the expectations of their customers on all dimensions of service quality. The study suggested the need and relevance of heavy investment on tangibles particularly computer based banking, Internet and intranet services, tele-banking, anywhere and anytime banking, etc., besides physical facilities and communication material.

Discussions and Conclusion

After going through the above studies, we can say that the application of information technology has affected the level of customer satisfaction of Indian Public Sector banks in a strong and positive manner. Today's customers are looking for convenience in banking and they are unwilling to spare much time for their banking operation. This calls for a paradigm shift of banking operation that traditionally is rooted to branch banking system. ATM facilities, e-banking, m-banking etc. (which can be termed as 'any time any where banking') are going to be the key drivers of this new age banking system. Nevertheless, do we assume, in that case branch banking will lose its relevance. The reality is far from it! A study by consulting firm Booz Allen Hamilton in the United States revealed that these bank branches are the key to customer relationships as "90 per cent are gained or lost *in a branch*." In addition, an overwhelming number of customers prefer to go to a branch for majority of their banking activities and use other channels for information processing only. They also recommend that banks should take this opportunity to position themselves as financial advisors, helping their customers in their financial planning process. Thus, banks must reinvent their branch operating philosophy to ensure that their entire experience delivers real financial value to the client; either by providing new knowledge, or by solving problems on financial matters. This will be of great importance to their customers, as proactive branch personnel can resolve an issue on the spot, which might not be possible with a self-service remote operating channel. Banks must also realise that the branch is the only place to allow face-to-face interaction, the importance of which can never be undermined.

Given that urban India is still coming to terms with self-service formats, and that a large population has no exposure to technology, the role of a brick and mortar bank assumes even greater significance. India has only 6 branches per 100,000 people as compared to 31 in the United States. Even if we take only the bankable population of about 300 million, it still works out to 18 branches per 100,000. Obviously, many people are still walking into their local branches in India. Banks must create adequate depth in their relationships through their branches, to ensure that a transition to another channel does not mean a transition to another bank.

While the performance of a few top performing PSBs are comparable to the private and foreign banks in India, many public sector banks are lagging behind in overall performance. It has been observed that most of the public sector banks are not the active users of electronic fund transfer (EFT) product and the majority of NEFT (National Electronic Fund transfer) outward transactions are initiated by new-generation private sector banks, foreign banks and a very few PSBs in India. In June 2008, these banks (as a segment) accounted for a little over 43 per cent each of the aggregate volume of outward and inward NEFT transactions and during the same time, the share of public sector banks in total outward NEFT transactions was only a little over 12 per cent. Again, half of this contribution was from the State Bank of India.

However, the share of retail EFT that remained low in the retail payment system (2.6 per cent during 2006-07) increased to 10.9 per cent during 2007-08. In addition, the coverage of ECS increased and is now available at 70 centers as against 64 centers in the previous year. There has been a growth in the volume and value of transactions put through ECS (both credit and debit) due to increase in both the coverage and awareness about the ease of using this system. However, we must acknowledge that the pace of growth of adaptation of EFT is low in Indian PSBs.

For the Indian PSBs, one of the main hindrances towards adaptation of technology is the lack of tech-savvy skilled personnel. Absence of a competent team of IT personnel is one of the main reasons that the PSBs are lagging behind in overall performance in spite of a much prominent presence in the country. The IT organisation structure needs to have a considerable number of business analyst / domain experts who are well aware of the growing importance of understanding business within the IT department. Indian PSBs lacks in this aspect as compared to the private banks. An alternative would be to outsource the support and maintenance operations.

The Indian banks that have implemented their technology solutions in banking have their focus on the urban population and their financial need. The technology backbones developed by most PSBs are in the metro and urban areas only. This is necessitated from the fact that the volume and productivity of business is much higher in the urban area than in a rural area. This defeats the original purpose for which the infrastructure was envisioned and built. Despite major e-initiative drives by Indian PSBs, the availability of the alternate delivery channels like ATM, phone banking, e-banking and mobile banking is restricted to their urban operations only. Moreover, major banks fail to come out with area specific customisation of products/ services for the Pan-Indian customer base due to its heterogeneous nature, especially in their languages and cultures. But there is a huge rural population that is migratory in nature and present all over India and other countries, who are in need of these banking services. Like, Technology link-up gives instant access to send/receive money from anywhere through Society for Worldwide Interbank Financial Telecommunication (SWIFT) and e-transfer gateways. Moreover, the gap between rural and urban economies narrows down as people gets access to many outside agencies through these payment gateways. Electronic banking channels are add-ons to the urban customers whereas it is an empowerment for the rural ones.

There is a general lack of awareness about the latest technology in banking operations and its use among the Indian public at large. Surprisingly, this limitation is also present among a large number of banking staff who have direct interface with the customers. Many are also not aware of new innovative products/services offered by their own banks using technology. This could be a result of a lack of confidence in their skills; hence, liilte reliance on the new delivery channels used. Thus, the bank staffs continue to recommend the same traditional methods and the customers continue to use them for availing various banking services. As a result, the Indian banking customers as well as the banking system is being deprived of the benefits of the new technology that should percolate to the bottom of the customer-pyramid.

All the technology initiatives that are taken in Indian PSBs helps them to prepare to face global competition by developing their fast cycle capabilities in providing boundary-less services. However, the above discussion reflect how the Indian PSBs are slowly getting equipped with technology tools and progressing considerably in terms of infrastructure, but they are yet to experience high level of competence through the full-fledged usage of the available IT infrastructure.

We can conclude by saying that significant opportunities exist in Indian PSBs to leverage technology as an enabler for gaining competitive advantages for which they need to have clearly defined strategic goals to be leader in the global market.

References

Agarwal, J. (2012), "Customer Satisfaction in Indian Banking Services (a Study in Aligarh District)", *International journal of computing and business research,* Vol. 3 No. 1, pp. 1-14.

Bagchi, A. K. (2006), *The Evolution of the State Bank of India, vol.1, the roots 1806-1876*, penguin books India, New Delhi.

Bauer, Hammerschmidt, and Falk (2005), "Measuring the Quality of e-Banking Portals", *International Journal of Bank Marketing*, Vol. 23, No. 2, pp. 153-75.

Bhasin, T. M. (2001), "Ecommerce in Indian Banking", *Indian Banking Association Bulletin*, Vol. 22, Nos. 4–5.

Chalam (2002), "Impact of Information Technology on the Performance of the Banking Sector", *Research Bulletin of the ICWAI*, Vol. XXI, pp.17–27.

Dabholkar, et al., (2003), "Understanding Consumer Motivation and Behaviour Related to Self-scanning in Retailing: Implications for strategy and research on technology-based self-service", *International Journal of Service Industry Management*, Vol. 14, No. 1, pp. 59-95.

Datta, S. (2008), "Business Process Reengineering and Customer Satisfaction in Indian Banking", *World Journal of Business Management*, Vol. 2, No. 1, pp. 2-10.

Ibrahim, Joseph, and Ibeh (2006), "Customers' Perception of Electronic Service Delivery in the UK retail banking sector", *International Journal of Bank Marketing,* Vol. 24, No. 7, pp. 475-493.

Implementing the Customer-Centric Bank – The Rebirth of the Forgotten Branch, Booz Allen Hamilton, 2003.

Jeevan, M. T. (2000), "Only Banks - No Bricks", Voice and Data, November 11 th, Available [online] http://www.voicendata.com/content/convergence/trends/100111102.asp; Accessed on 7 January 2001.

Jham and Khan (2008), "Customer Satisfaction in the Indian Banking Sector –a Study", *IIMB Management Review*, Vol. 20, No.1, pp. 14-23

Khatri and Ahuja (2008), "Study of Customer Satisfaction in Public Sector and Private Sector Banks of India", *International Journal of Engineering and Management Sciences*, Vol. 1, No. 1, pp. 42-51.

Kumar and Gangal (2011), "Customer Satisfaction in New Generation Banks - a Case Study of HDFC Bank", *International Refereed Research Journal*, Vol. 2, No. 4, pp. 177–186.

Kumbhar, M. (2011), "Factors Affecting the Customer Satisfaction in e-Banking: some Evidences form Indian Banks", *Management Research and Practice*, Vol. 3, No. 4, pp. 1-14.

Kumbhar, V. M. (2011), "Factors Affecting on Customers' Satisfaction: an Empirical Investigation of ATM Service", *International Journal of Business Economics and Management Research*, Vol. 2, No. 3, pp. 144–156.

Kundu and Datta (2011), "M-banking as a Replacement of I-banking – a Study Related to Indian Banks", *Proceedings of* 4th IIMA conference on Marketing in Emerging Economies *in Ahmedabad, India, 2011*, pp. 132-134.

Mehta and Varsha (2000), "Information Technology and Productivity in Banks – A Case of Jammu and Kashmir Bank Ltd.", *Prabandh, Journal of Faculty of Management Studies*, Vol. 2, No. 2, pp. 1-25.

Mohamed, H. Peeru (2005), "Enhancing Marketing Productivity of Banking Services: A CRM Approach", Strategy Summit ICFAI.

Rotchanakitumnuai and Speece, "Corporate Customer Perspectives on Business Value of Thai Internet Banking", *Journal of Electronic Commerce Research*, Vol. 5, No.4, pp. 270-286.

Saha and Zhao (2005), "Relationship Between Online Service Quality and Customer Satisfaction, a Study in Internet Banking, available at http://epubl.ltu.se/1404-5508/2005/083/ltu-shu-ex-05083se.pdf (accessed on April, 2009)

Seitz and Stickel (1998), "Internet Banking-An Overview, Journal of Internet Banking and Commerce", Vol. 3, No. 1, available at: http://www.arraydev.com/commerce/JIBC/9801-8.htm.

Shroff, F. T. (2004), "Impact of Technology on Banking", IBA bulletin special issue, pp. 174-181.

Siddik and Selvachandra (2011), "A Study on Customer Satisfaction Towards e-banking Services of ICICI Bank in Chennai City", *IJEMR*, Vol. 1, No. 4, pp. 112-119.

Timmers, P. (2000), *Electronic Commerce – Strategies and Models for Business-to- Business Trading*, London: John Wiley and Sons.

Uppal, R.K. (2009), "Customer Service in Indian Commercial Banks: an Empirical Study", *Asia pacific journal of social sciences*, Vol. 1, No. 1, pp. 127-141.

CHAPTER SEVEN

VALUE-BASED MANAGEMENT FOR SMALL-
AND MEDIUM-SIZED ENTERPRISES:
FINDINGS OF AN EMPIRICAL STUDY
ON ITS DIFFUSION AND OBSTACLES
TO ITS IMPLEMENTATION

BERND BRITZELMAIER, ANASTASIA PAUL
AND CAROLA NORMANN

Introduction

SMEs are seen as the backbone of the German economy (Schauf, 2009a: 15). According to the SME research institute Institut für Mittelstandsforschung Bonn, 99.7% of German companies subject to value-added tax in 2009 belong to the category of SMEs (IfM Bonn).

The management style of SME entrepreneurs is often characterised by short-term considerations (Wegmann, 2006: 148). In addition, a lot of decisions are taken intuitively (Wegmann, 2006: 185). Because of their increasing need for capital and the growing intensity of competition, SMEs face major challenges (Schlüchtermann and Pointner, 2004: 24-25). Thus, the professionalisation of the management of SMEs is becoming more and more important (Schauf, 2009a: 15).

Increasing emphasis has been placed on value-based management in recent years and it is now considered as one of the key management philosophies (e.g. Britzelmaier, 2009: 11). According to the shareholder value concept, the fundament of value-based management, the main objective of management is to increase the value of the company for its shareholders (Rappaport, 1986: 1). However, value-based management is not only focused on increasing the company value, but also constitutes a managerial approach that enables sustainable economic development (Piontkowski, 2009: 357). Fundamentally, value-based management can be applied by any company independent of its size and its capital market orientation (Krol, 2007: 3). Large listed companies have been using value-based management instruments for years (Arbeitskreis "Wertorientierte Führung in mittelständischen Unternehmen", 2003: 525). The objective of sustainable economic development is also pursued by SMEs (Piontkowski, 2009: 357). Additionally, there are several factors that promote the application of value-based management to SMEs (e.g. Krol, 2009a: 89-128). Nevertheless, value-based management has only spread to a limited extent among such enterprises (Piontkowski, 2009: 357).

On the basis of a description of the theoretical background of value-based management and the characteristics of SMEs, this chapter presents an analysis of the state of knowledge and the diffusion of value-based management among SMEs and identifies possible barriers to the application of this concept.

Fundamentals of value-based management

The first approach of value-based management was the shareholder value concept developed by Rappaport in 1986 (Rappaport, 1986). A company's activities should focus on increasing the company value (Tappe, 2009: 64). On the basis of this concept, other approaches of value-based management, such as Economic Value Added and Cashflow Return on Investment, have been developed (Britzelmaier, 2009: 12).

It should be pointed out that value orientation does not necessarily involve a focus on monetary values. Business activities should always be based on ethically correct behaviour. In western countries, this is characterised by Christian and occidental values; in China, it is characterised by Confucianism and Taoism, for example. Ethically correct behaviour - the orientation of one's own actions along spiritual values - and shareholder value orientation do not exclude each other. A flourishing company preserves and generates jobs; content employees support a good company's performance. Economic, ecological, ethical and social goals do not stringently work in opposite direction, but often have a complementary character.

Investments are only seen as beneficial if a positive net present value is reached under consideration of risk-adjusted capital costs (Arbeitskreis "Wertorientierte Führung in mittelständischen Unternehmen", 2003: 525). The consideration of this principle leads to an ameliorated capital allocation; management and decision-making are focused more in the long run and have a higher strategic focus (Krol, 2007: 3). This approach can be applied independently of the size and the capital-market orientation of a company (Krol, 2007: 3). The focus of value-based management on sustainable and profitable growth is very appropriate to SMEs (Arbeitskreis "Wertorientierte Führung in mittelständischen Unternehmen", 2003: 526). To implement value-based management, value-oriented figures and management instruments have to be integrated in the control system of the company (Krol, 2009a: 85).

Characteristics of small- and medium-sized enterprises

SMEs can be characterised by using qualitative as well as quantitative criteria. There are different quantitative definitions (Tappe, 2009: 12-13). The definition of the SME research institute Institut für Mittelstandsforschung Bonn is commonly used in Germany (Stiegemann, 2007, p.19; Waltermann, 2009: 3). It defines SMEs as companies with less than 500 employees and sales below €50 million (Institut für Mittelstandsforschung Bonn). Quantitative definitions have also been proposed by the German Commercial Code (HGB) and the EU Commission. The plurality of SMEs is not reflected by quantitative criteria (Tappe, 2009: 14-15). They should be completed by qualitative factors to show the characteristics of SMEs (Tappe, 2009: 12).

Besides their legal and economic independence (Krol, 2007: 4), SMEs are characterised by the unity of ownership and management (Tappe, 2009: 15). The owner-manager exercises the functions of both an owner and a manager (Krol, 2007: 4). Thus, the principal-agent problem, which often occurs in large companies, is less important for SMEs (Tappe, 2009: 16). Usually, the owner-manager is the only decision-maker; therefore, he is extremely important for the company (Krol, 2007: 4) and has a major influence on its management (Piontkowski, 2009: 357). Besides the positive features resulting from this person-oriented company structure, there are also negative ones (Piontkowski, 2009: 357). A lot of tasks are exercised in personal union. There is thus a danger of too patriarchal management by an entrepreneur who is not sufficiently qualified (Piontkowski, 2009: 357). Often, the management is also heavily involved in the operating activities (Krol, 2009b: 10). The management style of SME entrepreneurs is often characterised by short-term considerations and a lot of decisions are taken intuitively (Wegmann, 2006: 148). This management style is seen as a reason for the neglect of strategic and formal planning (Piontkowski, 2009: 358). The phenomenon of a lack of specific goals and of an institutionalised planning process is described as a lack of planning (Tappe, 2009: 32).

In most cases, a clear distinction of the personal, meta-economical goals and entrepreneurial (mainly financial) goals is not possible in SMEs (Tappe, 2009: 15). The high importance placed on meta-economical goals, especially in independent companies and/or companies that are family-owned, was also identified by an empirical study (Krol, 2009b: 5-6).

A lot of SMEs are family businesses; this means that the majority of interest is held by up to two people resp. the members of the entrepreneur family, and they are also part of the management board. In general, family entrepreneurs face the same requirements as sole proprietors. However, there is the risk of a conflict of interest between members of the family (Khadjavi, 2005: 60).

Embedding in tight, regional networks of relationships is also typical for SMEs (Arbeitskreis "Wertorientierte Führung in mittelständischen Unternehmen", 2003: 525). Tight relationships to customers, suppliers and employees usually exist for several years (Arbeitskreis "Wertorientierte Führung in mittelständischen Unternehmen", 2003: 525). The importance of these relationships for the company's success is much higher than in major enterprises (Arbeitskreis "Wertorientierte Führung in mittelständischen Unternehmen", 2003: 525). The strong involvement of stakeholders other than the owners in defining the company goals has also been shown by an empirical study (Krol, 2009b).

SMEs often exhibit flat hierarchies because of the small company size, in contrast to major companies (Krämer, 2009: 210). This supports a high level of transparency and leads to short and direct information exchange and a low level of formalization (Krämer, 2006: 214-215). Quick decision-making, realisation and processing reflect a high level of flexibility in SMEs (Hilzenbecher, 2006: 88-89). In addition, SMEs can react quickly and efficiently to changes in the market environment (Hilzenbecher, 2006: 89). Low transaction costs, high efficiency and a high level of innovation are additional strengths of SMEs.

Another characteristic of SMEs is their limited availability of resources. Usually, the management is not supported by staff departments (Krol, 2007: 12). Often, there are no independent control departments (Krol, 2009b: 2). This can increase the risk of strategic planning being neglected. SMEs are also often dependent on only a few know-how bearers (Krol, 2007: 5). Moreover, the information and communication technologies and thus also the documentation in SMEs are more modest than in major enterprises (Arbeitskreis "Wertorientierte Führung in mittelständischen Unternehmen", 2003: 525).

Oftentimes, the financial means of the proprietor are the main source of financing (Behringer, 2009: 46). The financial situation is thus very dependent on the personality and skills of the owner (Helbling, 2002: 189-190). SMEs usually have low equity ratios (Hilzenbecher, 2006: 90). They have to rely more on debt capital because their access to equity capital is limited in comparison to that of larger companies. The capital market offers possibilities for alternative sources of financing. However, most SMEs have difficulty obtaining finance from the capital market because they are not able to fulfil its requirements and are relatively small (Bussiek, 1996: 139). Modern forms of equity financing are mostly rejected (Krol, 2009b: 13). This leads to a high level of dependence on financing from the house bank, which can be seen as a main stakeholder of the company (Krol, 2007: 4). This is supported by an empirical study by Krol, in which nearly 78% of SMEs stated that they use credit from the house bank frequently or very frequently (Krol, 2009b: 13). However, it has been found that more and more SMEs have obtained access to the stock market (Behringer, 2009: 34-35).

Concept and basic findings of the empirical study

Concept of the empirical study

Because there is no generally accepted definition of SMEs, it seems reasonable to introduce an operational definition for this empirical study. Following the commonly used definition of the Institut für Mittelstandsforschung Bonn, an SME is a legally and economically independent company:

- that is not publicly listed,
- that employs up to 500 employees, and
- that generates external sales not exceeding €50 million per year.

If the quantitative criteria are exceeded, more than 50% of the shares should be held by the management.

The aim of this empirical study was to achieve adequate knowledge about the form of management in SMEs in order to characterise the extent to which they act in a value-oriented manner.

To obtain relevant data, a questionnaire was developed on the basis of the empirical studies of Gonschorek, Krol and Tappe (Gonschorek, 2009; Krol, 2009a; Tappe, 2009, Britzelmaer et al., 2009). The enquiry was carried out between April 12th and May 15th, 2010. Participation in the survey was voluntary and anonymous. The collected data were treated strictly confidentially and were not transferred to third parties. To obtain a high response rate, a specific online portal was created. The advantages of this approach over other methods of survey (e.g. via mail or fax) are its convenience and cost-effectiveness.

Two methods were used to collect data. On the one hand, a cover note asking for support and providing the URL address to fill out the questionnaire was posted to the International Controller Association ICV (www.controllerverein.com). On the other hand, the "Hoppenstedt Firmendatenbank", the federal company register and the database of the Chamber of Industry and Commerce in Baden-Württemberg, which provide criteria for the sampling process, were used. In total, 201 German companies that fulfil the criteria presented above were addressed. The collected data were analysed automatically using Q-set-Portal.

Corporate objectives of small- and medium-sized enterprises

The respondents were asked to specify the importance of different corporate objectives for their company. All the listed corporate objectives are very important to the responding SMEs. Each corporate objective was classified as "very important" or "important" by more than 50% of the companies. Thus, it can be reasoned that the systems of objectives of the companies polled are multidimensional (Krol, 2009a: 176). The following figure shows the results.

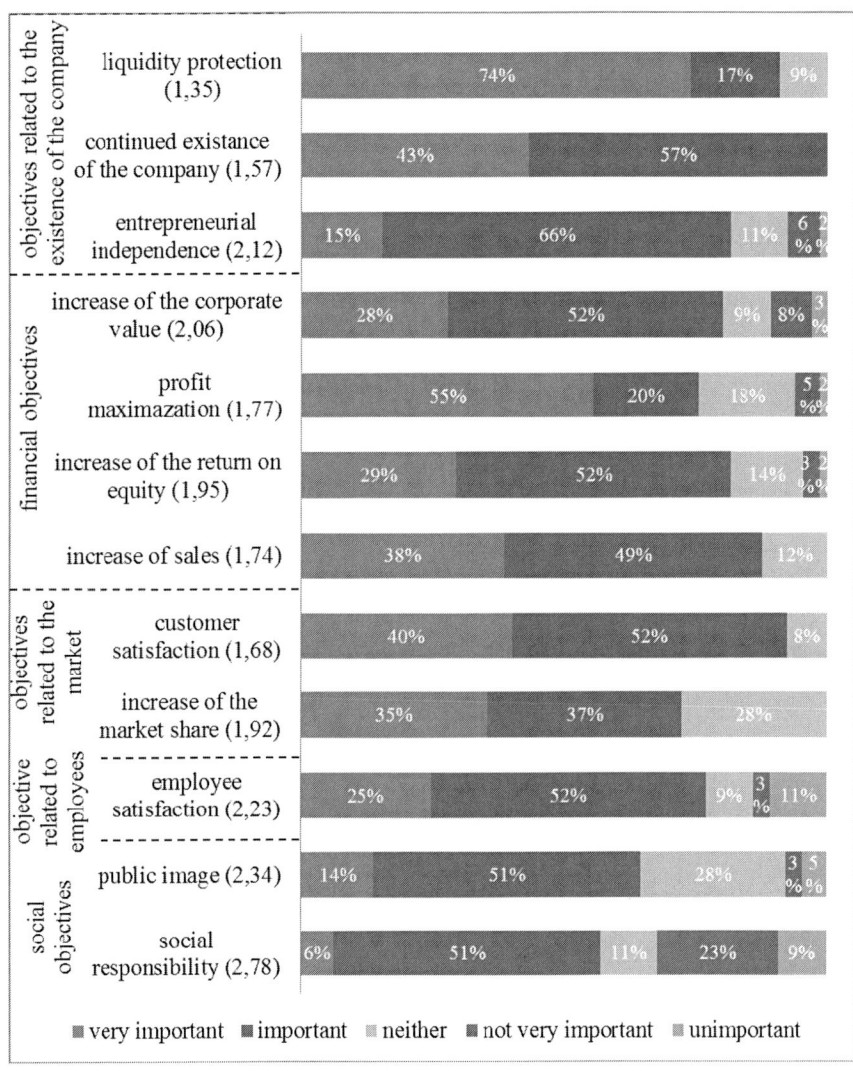

Figure 1: Importance of different goals for the respondents

Comparing the arithmetic means, it is apparent that liquidity protection, continued existence of the company and customer satisfaction are particularly important for SMEs. Since continued existence (100%) and entrepreneurial independence were rated as being very important, it can be assumed that the respondents had a long-term focus on the business operations of SMEs (Tappe, 2009: 205). Analysing the corporate objectives gives some indication of the value orientation of SMEs. It is apparent that the increase of corporate value in consideration of the stakeholder's interests is of high importance. The satisfaction of customers (92%) and employees (77%), as well as the increase of company value (80%), is very important or important for the majority of responding companies. Analysing the means of several corporate objectives, it can be recognised that the financial objectives have a leading role. It is also remarkable that the achievement of financial objectives like profit maximisation and increase of the return on equity have been categorised as not very important and unimportant by 6% and 5%, respectively.

In total, it can be stated that the SMEs polled are characterised by the long-term focus of their corporate objectives and the desire to increase corporate value. However, it remains open whether they actually act in a value-oriented manner.

The following figure shows how much value is attached to the different stakeholders in the process of determining the corporate objectives.

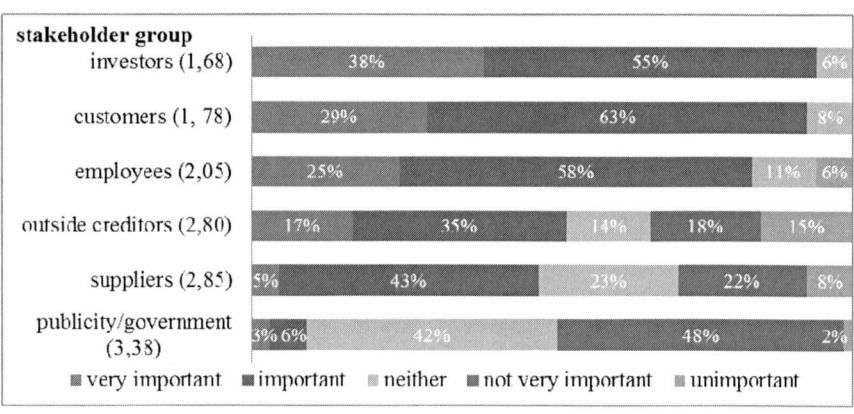

Figure 2: Relevance of different stakeholder groups for the determination of corporate objectives

The majority of the SMEs (94% selected "very important" or "important") stated that the interests of the investors are mainly taken into account when determining the corporate objectives. This is of top priority because, by providing capital, the investors bear the entrepreneurial risk and enable the business to be active (Behringer, 2009: 37). Furthermore, the interests of customers and employees have a great impact on the system of objectives (92% and 83%, respectively, selecting "very important" or "important"). This can be ascribed to their major contribution to the value-added process (Krol, 2009a: 180). Because of the high importance of debt financing, outside creditors were previously described as being highly valued (Krol, 2009a: 180). However, in this empirical study, this stakeholder group, which is important from a theoretical point of view, was "not very important" or "unimportant" for 34% of the respondents. In comparison with the other stakeholders, publicity was considered to be the least important.

The analyses carried out so far indicate that SMEs are focused on shareholders as well as on stakeholders. The fulfilment of the expectations of all stakeholders receives great attention in SMEs, which corresponds to the main principles of value-based management.

Characteristics of the strategy orientation

The enquiry shows that more than half of the respondents (55%) have a strategy that has been written down. Besides this, 48% stated that the set objectives are phrased clearly and definitely ("applies completely" or "applies predominantly"). This is an essential prerequisite for the successful implementation of the company's strategy (see Krol, 2009a: 186 for the rationale). Furthermore, 37% rejected the statement that the management did not have enough time for strategic planning. Nearly every second respondent prepares plans and budgets for all relevant business areas systematically. Despite the percentage of companies where the management is "completely" or "predominantly" occupied with operative tasks being 42%, only 18 respondents (29%) stated that this is a reason for the failure to apply new business administration methods.

Although the majority of respondents take the interests of the employees into account, only 46% declared that they communicate the long-term corporate objectives and strategies "completely" or "predominantly" to their employees. Furthermore, it is negative that external stakeholders like customers or suppliers are "predominantly not" or "not at all" informed about the current business development (42%).

In association with the lack of a long-term strategy, which is often criticised in the literature (e.g. Wegmann, 2006: 148), this empirical study indicated that SMEs are characterised by deficits in strategic planning and a lack of communication of the objectives that have been set out. However, they are aware of the necessity of a strategic orientation. Nonetheless, worse results were expected. As a caveat, it has to be taken into account that the information given in this enquiry is not necessarily consistent with reality. Aspects considered positively can be overemphasised or imagined, intentionally or not (Bortz and Döring, 2002: 231).

Analysis of the financing of SMEs

The questioned SMEs were asked to evaluate different instruments of financing according to their importance for their company. It was shown that bank loans are the most favoured source of financing (68% "(very) important"). This can be confirmed by the fact that the majority (89%) of the companies were interested in long-term cooperation with their bank. In addition, 77% reported their current business development systematically to their house bank. Every second agreed with the statement that the granting of a bank loan had become a highly complex process in the last three years. This may be a reason why leasing as an alternative form of financing is gaining importance in SMEs (Wegmann, 2006: 231). Only 18% are of the opinion that leasing is "not very important" or "unimportant". Nearly all SMEs (91%) reject the possibility of raising capital by taking on new partners. The fear of small- and medium-sized entrepreneurs of losing the sole responsibility for their business activities can be described as one reason for this (Bussiek, 1996: 42-44). Forms of financing like bonds, increase of capital via the capital market, private equity, mezzanine and factoring are seen mainly as "not very important" or "unimportant".

Thus, the results of this empirical study are in agreement with other studies that came to the conclusion that bank loans are the most commonly used form of financing by SMEs (Krol, 2009a: 195-196; Gonschorek, 2009: 200-201).

Diffusion of value-based management in small- and medium-sized enterprises

Findings of previous empirical studies

To date, value-based management for SMEs has not attracted a lot of attention in the economic literature or in terms of practical applications

(Tappe, 2009: 2). Krol investigated the application of value-based instruments in SMEs in an empirical study (Krol, 2009b). For independent SMEs, the increase of corporate value was found to be the most important financial goal (Krol, 2009b: 5). Nevertheless, 81% of the companies polled stated that they make investment decisions "very often" or "often" on the basis of experience rather than calculations (Krol, 2009b: 12). The net present value and the internal rate of return, which are value-oriented assessment criteria, are seldom used (Krol, 2009b: 12). The work of Piontkowski led to the conclusion that SMEs exhibit an underdeveloped application of value-based management, which is also related to instruments and controlling processes that would be suitable for SMEs (Piontkowski, 2009: 363). It was also found that larger SMEs tend to use value-based instruments for management more often than smaller SMEs (Piontkowski, 2009: 362). The analysis of the use of different target figures also shows the rather low use of value-oriented figures (Krol, 2009b: 8). Traditional, non-value-oriented figures like profit and sales are used much more often (Krol, 2009b: 8). Furthermore, regarding the management instruments used, operative management instruments are most common (Krol, 2009b: 16, Beck and Britzelmaier 2010). This and the examination of the methods of investment calculation show the low consideration of value-oriented principles in the management of SMEs (Krol, 2009b: 17).

Findings of the empirical study

Application of different target figures for management

The respondents in this study were asked to state how often they use different target figures. In addition to the five possible answers used previously in the study, two new possibilities were added. The respondents could state that this figure is unknown or that they plan to use it in the future.

By examining the number of companies who apply several figures "very often" or "often", it can be determined that the traditional figures are seen as more relevant for practical application than value-oriented target figures. Figures like return on sales (83%), net income (82%) and earnings before interests and tax (71%) are used "(very) often". Typical value-oriented figures like CFROI (40%), DCF (52%) and EVA (72%) are applied "seldom" or "never". Besides this, 8% of the companies stated that they had not even heard of these metrics. The low intensity of use is seen as being critical in light of the high importance placed on the corporate objective of increasing corporate value. Overall, it can be assumed that SMEs are not familiar with the basics and specifics of value-based management and that value creation is a vague goal for them (see Krol, 2009a: 182-183 and 219 for the rationale).

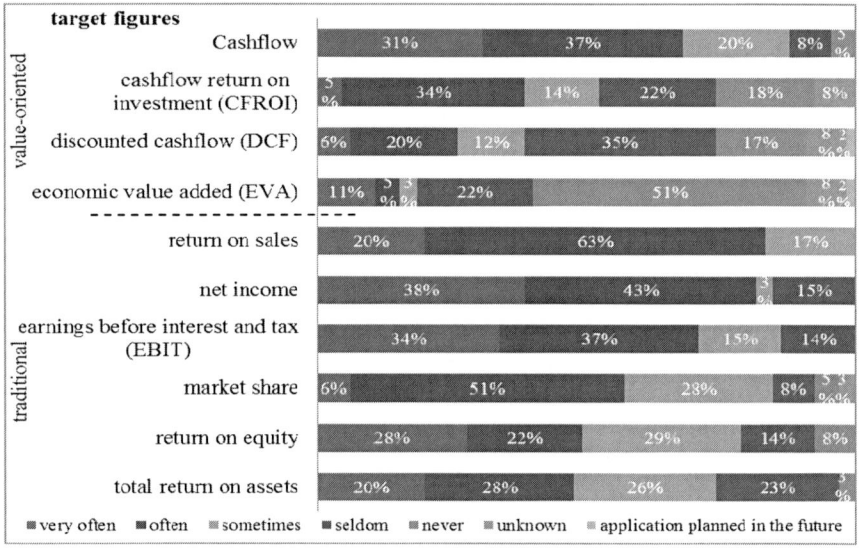

Figure 3: Application of different target figures for management

Application of management instruments

To make a final assessment of the degree of establishment of value orientation in SMEs, it is not sufficient to focus on analysis of the use of value-oriented figures. It is also necessary to analyse the answers related to the application of management instruments (Krol, 2009a: 68 and 78). According to their frequency of use (used "very often" or "often"), the results were grouped into four categories as follows:

- high level of application (51-100%),
- intermediate level of application (26-50%),
- low level of application (11-25%), and
- scarcely used.

The results are shown in the following graph.

Diffusion	Management instrument	Applied "very often" or "often"
High level of application (51-100%)	Liquidity planning	91%
	Cost type and cost centre accounting	82%
	Business analysis	72%
	Budgeting	65%
	Standard costing	63%
	Marginal costing	60%
	Ex post calculation	57%
	Variance analysis	54%
Intermediate level of application (26-50%)	Budgeted balance sheet and budgeted income statement	51%
	Multi-period investment calculation	48%
	Business plan	43%
	Variable compensation systems	42%
	Risk management	38%
	Cash-flow statement	35%
Low level of application (11-25%)	One-period investment calculation	22%
	Balanced scorecard	18%
	Value driver analysis	18%
	Analysis of strengths and weaknesses	15%
Scarcely used (0-10%)	Portfolio analysis	9%
	Process analysis/activity-based costing	9%

Figure 4: Application of management instruments

It can be observed that value-oriented management instruments are not used as frequently as standard management instruments. Multi-period investment calculation, variable compensation systems, risk management and cash-flow statements are only applied at an intermediate level by SMEs. For example, only 42% use a variable compensation system. However, it is necessary that executive managers as well as employees do not only understand the basic principles of value-based management but are also encouraged to act in a value-oriented manner (Weber et. al., 2004: 189).

While the results for balanced scorecard and the value driver analysis show a low level of application (18% each), process analysis/activity-based costing are particularly rarely used. This is seen as critical regarding the contribution of these instruments to successful realisation of a value-increasing strategy (Krol, 2009a: 205-211).

In summary, it was observed that value-based management instruments are not considered particularly important by SMEs. Nevertheless, it is positive that some companies plan to apply a balanced scorecard (17%), variable compensation system (9%), value driver analysis (6%) and process analysis/activity-based costing (6%) in the future.

Obstacles to the application of value-based management in small- and medium-sized enterprises

Findings in the literature and previous empirical studies

The principal-agent problem is considered as one of the main reasons for the application of value-based management in major enterprises (Vogelsang, 2009: 19). Usually, there is information asymmetry between the owners, who are in the role of the principal, and the management, which has the role of the agent (e.g. Britzelmaier, 2009: 19-20). Value-based management helps to enforce management behaviour in the interest of the owner (Piontkowski, 2009: 359). Because of the unity of ownership and management in SMEs, there is no principal-agent problem and such a control function is not necessary (Vogelsang, 2009: 19). Thus, this incentive for value-based management is not important for many SMEs.

A significant obstacle to value-based management is the lack of resources in SMEs (Schomaker and Günther, 2006: 218). It is often the case that a documentation and information management structure, needed for the implementation of complex value-based management systems, is not present (Krol, 2007: 13). This may result in an absence of the information necessary for precise and detailed calculation of the value-based figures (Tappe, 2009: 3). To determine the essential parameters out of the accounting requires economic and financial understanding and considerable effort (Schomaker and Günther, 2006: 218). The companies questioned by Krol stated that lack of resources is the main obstacle to value-based management in SMEs: 38% thought that additional information management systems were necessary, 35% were of the opinion that there was a need for more employees and 30% expected high expenditures

(Krol, 2009b: 18-19). The enquiry of Krol shows that mainly effort and cost aspects are seen as obstacles to the implementation of value-based management instruments (Krol, 2009b: 19).

Owing to the mainly technically oriented careers of SME entrepreneurs, there is a lack of information about value-based management (Krol, 2009a: 3). It was found that 31% of the respondents considered this as an obstacle to implementation (Krol, 2009b: 18-19). This lack of information cannot be overcome because there are no staff departments and an unwillingness to hire outside consultants (Krol, 2007: 12).

The low level of diffusion of value-based management in SMEs can also be explained by the fact that this type of management was developed with particular regard for large, listed companies and does not take the characteristics of SMEs into account (Schomaker and Günther, 2006: 217). At present, there is no generally accepted concept that considers the characteristics of SMEs. This is due, among other things, to the heterogeneity of SMEs. The fact that the specific situation of the company has to be considered to develop and apply a value-based management system makes the development of a universal concept more difficult (Krol, 2009a: 3).

Findings of the empirical study

This study is focused on analysis of the respondents' attitudes towards value-oriented management. First, information about occasions for the determination of corporate value is analysed. It was found that 28% of the companies calculate their corporate value in the case of a sale of the company or parts of it, or in the case of reorganisation. Every second names a credit check and value-based management as important occasions for this. This indicates the value-oriented perception of half of the respondents. The following graph shows the results of the survey on the attitudes towards value orientation.

The statements that value-based management takes only the interests of the shareholders into account and that it is mainly focused on short-term increase of the return on equity are seen as "predominantly incorrect" or "not correct" by more than half of the respondents (58% and 57%). Since 28% agree "completely" or "predominantly" with these statements, it can be concluded that there are some misunderstandings about the focus of value orientation among some SMEs.

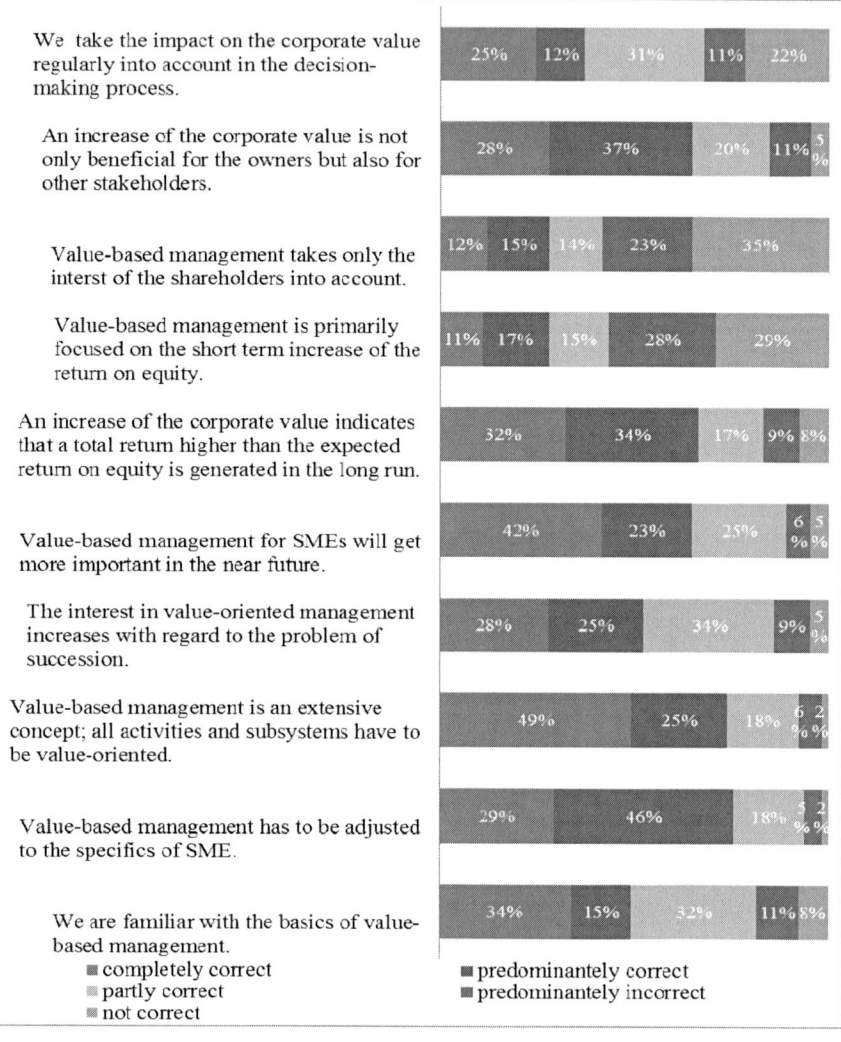

Figure 5: Perceptions of value-based management

The next question was related to evaluation of the contribution of value-based management to the success of the SMEs. The majority of the respondents agree "completely" or "predominantly" with the statement that not only the owners but also other stakeholders benefit from the increase of corporate value. The number of respondents who agree "completely" or "predominantly" to opposite statements[1] was 18.

Furthermore, the majority of the respondents (74%) know that value-based management is an extensive concept, in that all activities and subsystems have to contribute to increase the corporate value (Tappe, 2009: 69-70). In addition, 66% also answered that the statement that an increase of corporate value indicates that the return generated in the long run is higher than the expected return on equity is "completely" or "predominantly" correct.

The statement that value-based management will get more and more important in the near future is also strongly accepted by 65%. More than half of the respondents (52%) stated that the successor problem is a reason for this development. The growing interest in value orientation can be confirmed by the fact that one-third of the questionnaires were filled out by a member of the management.

Another interesting finding is that 46% are of the opinion that the not-value-oriented management instruments currently used are absolutely sufficient for successful management.

Regarding the results, it can be concluded that the majority of SMEs know the basic principles of value-based management. Nevertheless, there are some misunderstandings regarding the focus of value orientation among some SME entrepreneurs.

Previous studies found a low level of diffusion of value-based management in SMEs (Gonschorek, 2009: 98-203; Krol, 2009a: 157-219; Tappe, 2009: 191-294). Therefore, one objective of this empirical study was to examine implementation problems. The following illustration shows the related results.

In this study, 26% believe that their company does not have the necessary knowledge to apply value-based management (statement is "completely correct" or "predominantly correct"). Despite this, 38% of the respondents state that the application of value-based management requires the hiring of additional employees. Nearly every third respondent names the costs

---

[1] "Value-based management takes only the interests of the shareholders into account" and "An increase of corporate value is not only beneficial for the owners but also for other stakeholders".

related to the application of value-based management as a barrier to implementation. According to the economic literature, there is a lack of well-structured IT systems in SMEs. It is not possible to make a definitive statement about this because one-third (32%) agree with this position and one-third (37%) disagree.

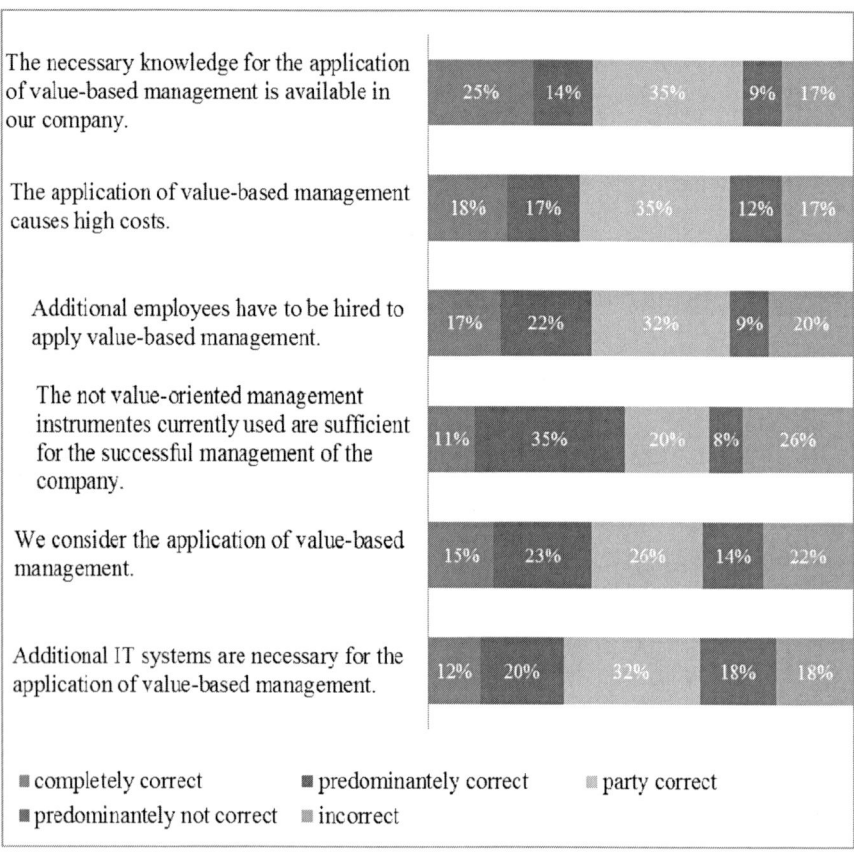

Figure 6: Implementation problems of value orientation

The study showed some evidence that lack of resources is a barrier to implementation of value-based management in SMEs, but this cannot be assessed conclusively.

As there is an assumption that there are other implementation barriers than those dealt with in this empirical study, the respondents were asked to evaluate potential benefits of value-based management. By analysing the answers, it should be possible to determine whether the low level of diffusion of value-based management is related to ignorance of its benefits (Krol, 2009a: 215-219). The results are shown in the following graph.

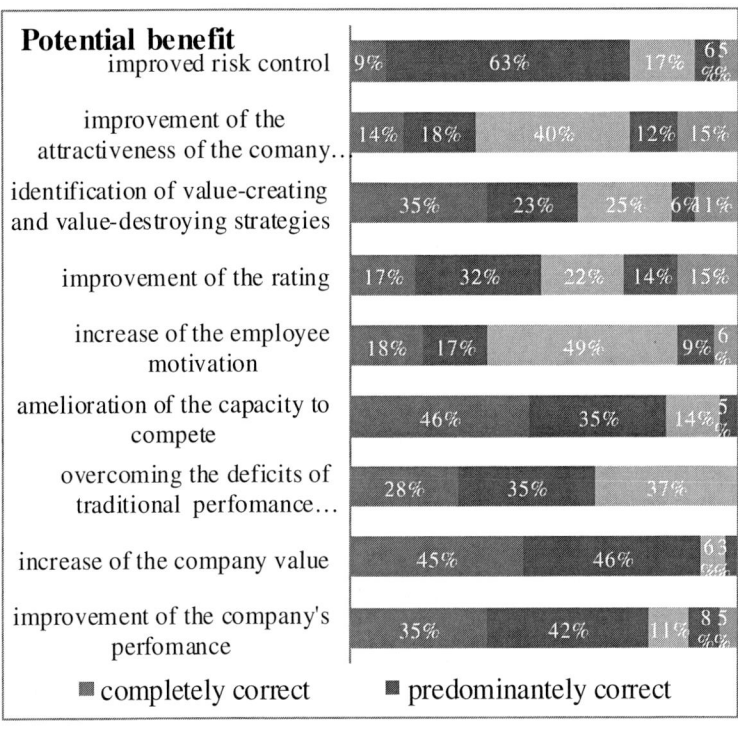

Figure 7: Potential benefits of value-based management

Nearly every respondent (91%) agreed "completely" or "predominantly" with the statement that value-based management results in an increase of company value. The majority of companies (82%) also are of the opinion that value-based management increases the capacity to compete. Regarding the low level of diffusion and the high importance of non-financial objectives, the approval of the statement that value-based management makes a contribution to improve the company's performance was very high (77%). The percentages of SMEs that are of the opinion that value-based management improves risk control and the identification of value-creating and value-destroying strategies were 72% and 58%, respectively. The adherence to such aspects is important for successful implementation of value-creating strategies (Krol, 2009a: 217). The improvement of the rating is only seen as a potential benefit by 49% ("completely correct" and "predominantly correct"). The lowest approval was given to the statements that value orientation increases employee motivation and that a higher value orientation leads to higher attractiveness of the company for potential investors (35% and 32%, respectively). This can be explained by the facts that the idea of selling one's company is not very popular among the majority of SME entrepreneurs and that there are nearly no variable compensation systems for employees (Krol, 2009: 218-219).

On the basis of the high approval of the different potential benefits, it can be concluded that the responding companies are aware of the benefits that can be achieved by value-based management.

Despite the positive results described above, it is a negative finding that only 37% take the impact on the company value "completely" or "predominantly" into account in the decision-making process. The fact that the concept of value-based management was developed for the needs of large listed companies and that the specifics of SMEs are not considered can be seen as a reason for this (Krol, 2009a: 1). The majority of the respondents (75%) agree "completely" or "predominantly" with the statement that value-based management has to be adjusted to the specifics of SMEs. This confirms the assumption stated above.

The respondents were asked to evaluate the requirements for a value-based management concept appropriate for SMEs. Simplicity and practicability can be seen as the most important requirements because all participants agreed "completely" or "predominantly" with this. The comprehensibility of the concept, the ease of use of value-oriented instruments and consideration of the typical lack of resources in terms of personnel and financial means are also important for the SMEs questioned. In addition, 92% also state that the acceptance of value-based management is an important requirement. Thus, value-based management can only be applied successfully if the corporate objectives are communicated transparently to the management as well as to all stakeholders. Furthermore, 52% consider it necessary for the concept to be flexible. This is an indispensable requirement for the implementation and application of value-based management particularly because operational objectives of SMEs can change very quickly, which makes the immediate adjustment of the objective targets necessary.

In total, it can be concluded that value-based management cannot be transferred to SMEs without certain simplifications and adjustments. In addition, its cost-effectiveness has to be ensured. This cost-effectiveness can be evaluated by a cost-benefit analysis. No respondent is of the opinion that the cost-effectiveness of value-based management is not important.

Conclusions

This study focused on the form and diffusion of value-based management in small- and medium-sized enterprises by a synthesis of descriptions of theoretical and empirical findings.

By analysing the answers of respondents to several aspects of this research focus, it was found that the objective of increasing corporate value was considered highly relevant. Although there are several figures and management instruments that can contribute to achieving this corporate objective, a low level of diffusion of value-oriented methods was perceived. Possible reasons for this are the lack of institutionalisation of the controlling department, scarce management support by strategic planning and a lack of resources. Despite these disadvantages, it can be observed that the respondents consider value-based management positively. On the basis of these findings, it can be concluded that the basic principles of value-based management and its potential benefits are known to a large extent by SMEs. However, the hiring of additional personnel and the application of additional IT systems are considered necessary for such a management approach. In addition, the costs related to the implementation of value-based management are stated as a barrier to implementation. The perception of nearly half of the respondents that the existing management instruments are absolutely adequate for the management of the company can be seen as another main obstacle to the diffusion of value-based management among SMEs. The majority of the respondents are of the opinion that the concept of value-based management has to be adjusted to the specifics of SMEs. The findings of this empirical study can be determined by the random sample and cannot be generalised for the main unit of German SMEs (Gonschorek, 2009: 206; Krol, 2009a: 196 and pp. 219-221).

It has to be pointed out that there has been only limited theoretical work on the issue of value-based management for SMEs, and little empirical research has been carried out (Krol, 2009a: 3-4; Tappe, 2009: 289 and 291-292; Britzelmaier et al. 2009). Against this background, it is desirable to do more scientific research on this subject to close this research gap and to promote the establishment of value-based management in SMEs.

References

Arbeitskreis "Wertorientierte Führung in mittelständischen Unternehmen" der Schmalenbach-Gesellschaft für Betriebswirtschaft e.V. (2003), Wert(e)orientierte Führung in mittelständischen Unternehmen. *Finanz Betrieb: Zeitschrift für Unternehmensfinanzierung und Finanzmanagement,* Vol. 5, No. 9, pp. 525-533.

Behringer, Stefan (2009), *Unternehmensbewertung der Mittel- und Kleinbetriebe: betriebswirtschaftliche Verfahrensweisen.* 4th ed. Berlin.

Bortz, Jürgen; Döring, Nicola (2006), *Forschungsmethoden und Evaluation für Human- und Sozialwissenschaftler.* 4th ed. Heidelberg.

Beck Valentin and Britzelmaier, Bernd (2006), Value-based Management in Small and Medium-Sized Companies - Threats and Opportunities, *International Journal of Management Cases,* Vol. 12, No. 2, pp. 14-23.

Berndt, Ralph ed. (2006), Management-Konzepte für kleine und mittlere Unternehmen. Berlin.

Bussiek, Jürgen (1996), *Anwendungsorientierte Betriebswirtschaftslehre für Klein- und Mittelunternehmen.* 2nd ed. Munich and Vienna.

Britzelmaier, Bernd (2009), *Kompakt-Training Wertorientierte Unternehmensführung.* Ludwigshafen am Rhein.

Britzelmaier, Bernd et al. (2009), Controlling in Practice – an empirical study among Small and Medium-sized Enterprises in Germany. In: Vrontis, D., Weber, Y., Kaufmann, R. and Tarba, S. (Eds.), *Managerial and Entrepreneurial Developments in the Mediterranean Area,* EuroMed Press Cyprus, pp. 335-348.

Exler, Markus (2006), Wertmanagement mittelständischer Unternehmen. *Controller Magazin,* Vol. 31, No. 6, pp. 549-553.

Gonschorek, Torsten (2009), *Einflussfaktoren der Anwendung wertorientierter Unternehmensführung im deutschen Mittelstand. Ergebnisse einer empirischen Studie.* Dresden.

Gleißner, Werner (2004), *Future Value. 12 Module für eine strategische wertorientierte Unternehmensführung.* Wiesbaden.

Gleißner, Werner and Meier, Günter ed. (2001), *Wertorientiertes Risiko-Management für Industrie und Handel. Methoden, Fallbeispiele, Checklisten.* Wiesbaden.

Gleißner, Werner and Weissman, Arnold (2001), Das Paradigma der Wertorientierung. In: Gleißner, Werner and Meier, Günter ed. *Wertorientiertes Risiko-Management für Industrie und Handel. Methoden, Fallbeispiele, Checklisten.* Wiesbaden, pp. 45-52.

Haasis, Heinrich; Fischer, Thomas R. and Simmert, Diethard B. ed. (2007), *Mittelstand hat Zukunft. Praxishandbuch für eine erfolgreiche Unternehmenspolitik.* Wiesbaden.

Hahn, Dietger and Hungenberg, Harald (2001), *PuK: Planung und Kontrolle, Planungs- und Kontrollsysteme, Planungs- und Kontrollrechnung. Wertorientierte Controllingkonzepte. Unternehmungsbeispiele von DaimlerChrysler AG, Stuttgart, Siemens AG, München, Franz Haniel & Cie. GmbH, Duisburg.* 6th ed. Wiesbaden.

Helbling, Carl (2002), Besonderheiten der Bewertung von kleinen und mittleren Unternehmen (KMU). In: Peemöller, Volker H. ed. *Praxishandbuch der Unternehmensbewertung.* 2nd ed. Herne and Berlin, pp. 187-197.

Hilzenbecher, Uwe (2006), Wachstumsstrategien für KMUs. In: Berndt, Ralph ed. *Management-Konzepte für kleine und mittlere Unternehmen.* Berlin, pp. 85-110.

Institut für Mittelstandsforschung Bonn (n.d.), *Kennzahlen zum Mittelstand 2009 in Deutschland* [internet]. Available from: <http://www.ifm-bonn.org/index.php? utid=99&id=101> [accessed 22nd December, 2010].

Khadjavi, Kyros A. C. (2005), *Wertmanagement im Mittelstand* [internet]. Eschen. Available from: <http://www.biblio.unisg.ch/www/edis.nsf/wwwDisplayIdentifier/3088/$FILE/dis3088.pdf> [accessed 22nd December, 2010].

Krämer, Werner (2009), Personalführung und Organisation im Wandel. Die Berücksichtigung von Entwicklungen im Umfeld der kleinen und mittleren Unternehmen im Management. In: Schauf, Malcolm ed. *Unternehmensführung im Mittelstand. Rollenwandel kleiner und mittlerer Unternehmen in der Globalisierung.* 2nd ed. Munich and Mering, pp. 195-237.

Krol, Florian (2007), *Value Based Management in Small and Medium Enterprises – Analysis of internal and external impulses and possibilities of implementation* [internet]. Münster. Available from:

<http://www.wiwi.uni-muenster.de/ctrl/md/content/ publikationen/Arbeitspapier_9_1.pdf> [accessed 3rd January, 2011].
Krol, Florian (2009a), *Wertorientierte Unternehmensführung im Mittelstand – Erste Ergebnisse einer empirischen Studie* [internet]. Münster. Available from:<http://www.wiwi.uni-muenster.de/ctrl/md/content/ publikationen/ Arbeitspapapier_10_1.pdf> [accessed 3rd January, 2011]
Krol, Florian (2009b), *Wertorientierte Unternehmensführung im Mittelstand – Eine empirische Analyse von Einfluss- und Wirkungsfaktoren.* Hamburg.
Michel, Uwe (1999), Wertmanagement. Ein umfassender und durchgängiger Ansatz zur kapitalmarktorientierten Unternehmenssteuerung. *Controlling*, Vol. 11, No. 9, pp. 371-379.
Peemöller, Volker H. ed. (2002), *Praxishandbuch der Unternehmensbewertung.* 2nd ed. Herne and Berlin.
Piontkowski, Jan O. (2009), Wertorientierte Unternehmensführung in mittelständischen Unternehmen – Empirische Hinweise auf Anwendung, *Controlling – Zeitschrift für erfolgsorientierte Unternehmenssteuerung*, Vol. 21, No. 7, pp. 357-363.
Rappaport, A. (1986), *Creating Shareholder Value: The New Standard for Business Performance.* New York.
Schauf, Malcolm (2009a), Grundlagen der Unternehmensführung im Mittelstand. In: Schauf, Malcolm ed. *Unternehmensführung im Mittelstand. Rollenwandel kleiner und mittlerer Unternehmen in der Globalisierung.* 2nd ed. Munich and Mering, pp. 1-30.
Schauf, Malcolm ed. (2009b), Unternehmensführung im Mittelstand. Rollenwandel kleiner und mittlerer Unternehmen in der Globalisierung. 2nd ed., Munich and Mering.
Schlüchtermann, Jörg and Pointner, Maria Anna (2004), Unternehmensplanung und Mittelstand – Strategieumsetzung mit Hilfe der Balanced Scorecard. In: Schlüchtermann, Jörg and Tebroke, Hermann-Josef ed. *Mittelstand im Fokus. 25 Jahre BF/M-Bayreuth.* Wiesbaden, pp. 19-44.
Schlüchtermann, Jörg and Tebroke, Hermann-Josef ed. (2004), *Mittelstand im Fokus. 25 Jahre BF/M-Bayreuth.* Wiesbaden.
Schomaker, Martin and Günther, Thomas (2006), Wertorientiertes Management für den Mittelstand. In: Schweickart, Nikolaus und Töpfer, Armin ed. *Wertorientiertes Management. Werterhaltung – Wertsteuerung – Wertsteigerung ganzheitlich gestalten. Mit 202 Abbildungen und 12 Tabellen.* Berlin, Heidelberg, New York. pp. 215-237.

Schweickart, Nikolaus and Töpfer, Armin ed. (2006), *Wertorientiertes Management. Werterhaltung – Wertsteuerung – Wertsteigerung ganzheitlich gestalten. Mit 202 Abbildungen und 12 Tabellen.* Berlin, Heidelberg, New York.

Stiegemann, Karl-Heinz (2007), Sparkassen – Mittelstandspartner vor Ort. In: Haasis, Heinrich; Fischer, Thomas R. und Simmert, Diethard B. ed. Mittelstand hat Zukunft. Praxishandbuch für eine erfolgreiche Unternehmenspolitik. Wiesbaden, pp. 15-25.

Tappe, Rolf (2009), Wertorientierte Unternehmensführung im Mittelstand. Eine Überprüfung der Anwendbarkeit. Frankfurt am Main.

Vogelsang, Till (2009), *Wertorientierte Unternehmensführung im Mittelstand – Eine vergleichende Analyse bestehender Ansätze.* Hamburg.

Waltermann, Hanno (2009), *Unternehmenswertorientierung im Mittelstand. Instrumente zur zielgerichteten Beeinflussung von Werttreibern.* Hamburg.

Weber, Jürgen et. Al. (2004), *Wertorientierte Unternehmenssteuerung. Konzepte – Implementierung – Praxisstatements.* Wiesbaden.

Wegmann, Jürgen (2006), *Betriebswirtschaftslehre mittelständischer Unternehmen: Praktiker-Lehrbuch.* Munich und Vienna.

CHAPTER EIGHT

OPEN INNOVATION SYSTEM AND NEW FORMS OF INVESTMENT: VENTURE CAPITAL'S ROLE IN INNOVATION

MATTEO ROSSI, ALKIS THRASSOU AND DEMETRIS VRONTIS

From a Closed Innovation system to an Open Innovation paradigm

Innovation is hardly a new phenomenon, but over the last few years new concepts and models of innovation have arisen to complement and challenge existing past knowledge and notions. Innovation can be defined:

> "as the commercial or industrial application of something new, such as new product or process or a new type of organization, a new source of supply in the product market" (Schumpeter, 1934: 66).

Schumpeter is considered a pioneer in innovation studies. He started studying how the capitalist system was affected by market innovations and in his book "Capitalism, Socialism and Democracy" he described a process where "the opening up of new markets, foreign or domestic, and the organizational development [...] illustrate the same process of industrial mutation, that incessantly revolutionizes the economic structure from within, incessantly destroying the old one, incessantly creating a new one". This process was called a "creative destruction" process[1]. Schumpeter

---

[1] <<The essential point to grasp is that in dealing with capitalism we are dealing with an evolutionary process. ... [It is a process] that incessantly revolutionizes the economic structure from within, incessantly destroying the old one, incessantly creating a new one. This process of Creative Destruction is the essential fact about

recognized in larger corporations – with some degree of monopolistic power – an advantage to develop innovations, owing to their better resources and greater market power. The Schumpeter model of innovation is a closed innovation system (Figure 1), a vertical integration model where internal R&D activities lead to internal developed products that are distributed by the firm.

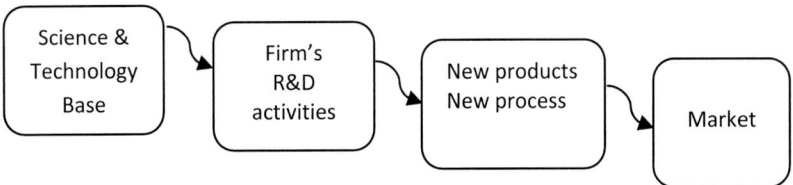

Figure 1. The Closed Innovation Model. Source: authors' depiction

In the closed innovation model

> "research projects are launched from the science and technology base of the firm. They progress through the process, and some of the projects are stopped, while others are selected for further work. A subset of these are chosen to go through to the market" (Chesbrough, 2006: 3).

This model was called also producers' model. In fact, in the past entrepreneurs, economists, policymakers, and managers

> "have assumed that that most important designs for innovations would originate from producers and be supplied to consumers via goods and services that were for sale" (Baldwin and von Hippel, 2011: 1400).

More recently the old closed model has been opposed by a new model: the Open Innovation model (OI). This new paradigm is based on a concept that assumes that both the source of knowledge and the process of technology transfer become external to the enterprise. More specifically:

> "open innovation is a paradigm that assumes that firms can and should use external ideas as well as internal ideas, and internal and external paths to market, as they look to advance their technology" (Chesbrough, 2006: 1)

---

capitalism. It is what capitalism consists in and what every capitalist concern has got to live in>> (Schumpeter, 1942: 82–83).

The Open Innovation System

The Open Innovation System can be considered an opposite to the traditional producers' model. In fact OI is:

> "the use of purposive inflows and outflows of knowledge to accelerate internal innovation, and expand the markets for external use of innovation, respectively" (Chesbrough, 2006: 1).

In other words Open Innovation sustains that internal ideas and knowledge can also be taken to the market to generate new value. In this vision knowledge, research and developments, innovation become an open system (Figure 2). In fact source of knowledge and the process of technology transfer

> "may well be in the same competitive context (competitors, suppliers and clients) or in other actors whose main mission is the creation of knowledge" (Martini and Rossi, 2010: 453).

In this system a lot of actors have an influence on the innovation process: first of all governmental institutions, but also collective associations and formal and informal investors. In this perspective the definition of innovation is broader:

> "Innovation is seen as a continuous cumulative process involving not only radical and incremental innovation but also the diffusion, absorption and use of innovation. Second, a wider set of sources of innovation is taken into account. Innovation is seen as reflecting, besides science and R&D, interactive learning taking place in connection with ongoing activities in procurement, production and sales" (Johnson et al., 2003: 4).

The Open Innovation System is characterized by a plurality of actors and new interactions between these actors. In this perspective innovation isn't considered a single firm process, but rather involving a research system, a productive system and governmental/institutional system. Alongside these actors there are other organizations that do not fit the three above-mentioned players and/or act as an interface between two or more of the same areas, and/or represent a composite of these areas. In the innovation process and in the technology transfer process to business an important role is recognized to investors, exercised both formally and informally (banks, venture capitalists, business angels). This new system is characterized also by new interactions between these actors. Mallone et al., (2005) use the expression of "extended enterprise" where it's particularly difficult to explain the sources flows and transfer of knowledge and technology, internal or external.

Moreover this system is characterized by a decreasing significance of the distinction between methodical private actors and public officials. The reasons for this relate to:

- An increase of public-private structures,
- A growth of public funding in private centers budget, and,
- Above all, by the increasing take-over of final and intermediate research results.

> "In the new OI perspective, the problem of technology transfer acquires new dimensions: from a linear process (between donor and recipient), it becomes a bidirectional process, whose effectiveness depends, not only on the involved subjects, but also on the contexts and their languages" (Martini and Rossi, 2010: 451).

In this new system, the importance of financial structures in the process of production and transfer of innovation is underlined. In fact, finance and innovation are inextricably linked. The innovation process requires multiple of resources – human, technical, organizational and market – but financial innovation is one of the most important. These resources – in fact – permit the acquisition of other resources.

> "Financial resources and the accessibility of these resources are critical to support such business experimentation" (Sharpe, 2009: 3).

Chapter Eight

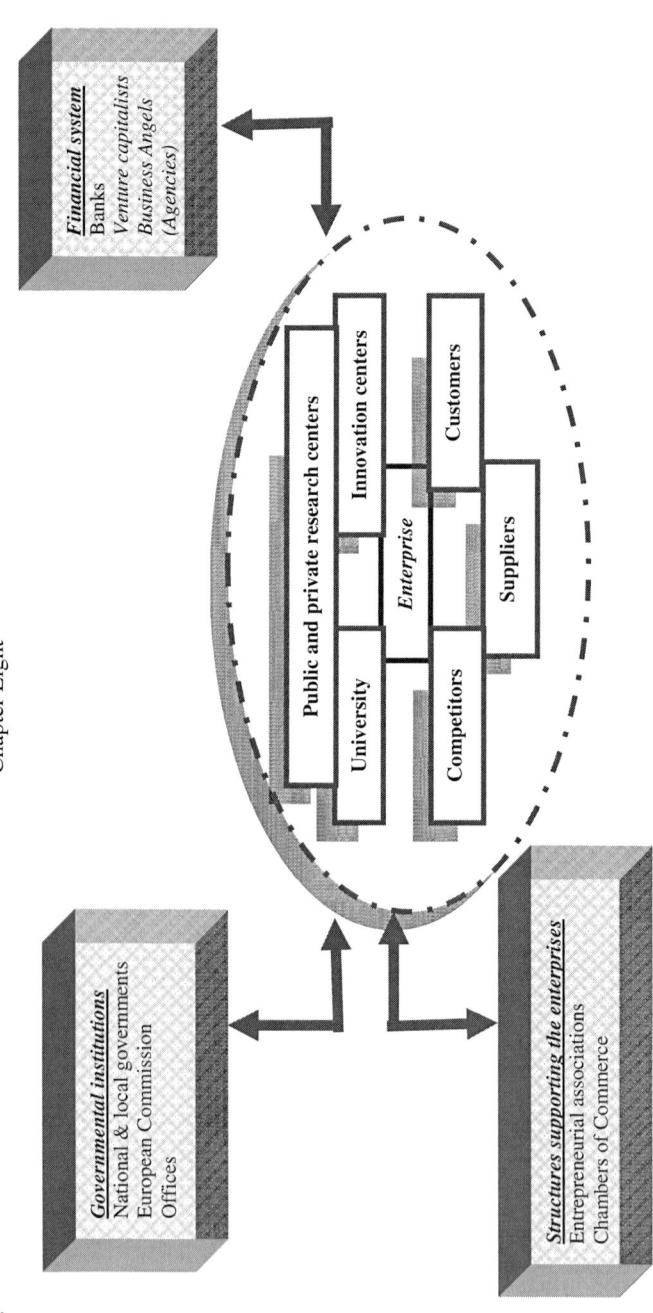

Figure 2. The New Innovation System. Source: Martini and Rossi, 2010

More recent studies have additionally researched innovation as a process. Some with inward focus i.e. studying the individual process components and their interrelationship (Chebbi et al., 2012); some with outward focus i.e. investigating the process within a wider strategic and/or marketing context (Thrassou et al, 2012a,b); some with specific industry focus (Thrassou and Vrontis, 2008; Thrassou and Lijo, 2007; Vrontis and Thrassou, 2011); and some according to firm type (Thrassou and Vrontis, 2006; Breasciani et al., 2012). The common thread is that innovation is increasingly becoming a matter of necessity rather than choice, and therefore in this research's context, one may assume that the relative risk of investment in innovation is decreasing, though not in absolute terms.

Venture Capital and the Innovation System

The sources of finance for innovative enterprises include a multiplicity of equity provision, as well as a wide spectrum of public and private investors. In recent years the lion's share of studies and policy reports on the supply of risk capital has focused on Venture Capital (VC).

> "This has broadly been portrayed as an increasingly necessary, although not sufficient, condition for the formation of new business especially in high tech sectors" (Mina, 2009: 3).

VC can be defined as

> "independent, professionally managed, dedicated pools of capital that focus on equity or equity-linked investments in privately held, high growth companies" (Lerner, 2009: 146)[2].

Furthermore

> "VC is a type of private equity finance involving investments in unquoted companies with growth potential. It is generally medium to long term in nature made in exchange for a stake in a company" (Dagogo and Ollor, 2009: 41).

In short, it is essentially

---

[2] <<Venture capital is a type of private equity finance involving investments in unquoted companies with growth potential. It is generally medium to long term in nature made in exchange for a stake in a company>> (Dagogo and Ollor, 2009: 41).

"a professionally managed pool of equity capital" (Hisrich and Peters, 1998).

VC plays a role in translating Research and Development (R&D) activities into commercial outcomes and is therefore credited with a catalytic role in innovation (Christofidis and Debande, 2001).

> "No matter how we look at the numbers, venture capital clearly serves as an important source for economic development, wealth and job creation, and innovation. This unique form of investing brightens entrepreneurial companies' prospects by relieving all-too-common capital constraints. Venture-backed firms grow more quickly and create far more value than nonventure-backed firms. Similarly, venture capital generates a tremendous number of jobs and boosts corporate profits, earnings, and workforce quality. Finally, venture capital exerts a powerful effect on innovation" (Ghompers and Lerner, 2001b: 83).

In other words, Venture Capitalists invest in technologies firms where growth and returns are expected to be significantly higher than other industries (Rossi et al., 2011).

The analysis of Venture Capital in the literature proceeds in two directions (Sharpe et al., 2009: 4):

> "(1) venture capital as a financial asset class, and (2) venture capital as a means of supporting new technology-based firms. In this paper the second direction is analysed, studying the VC role in the innovation financing process".

The analysis focuses on small and new firms that are recognized as important drivers of innovation (Acs and Audretsch, 1990). Hellmann and Puri (2000) underline that venture capital financing particularly regards small, young and innovative firms. VCs have two different functions: (1) to bring new capitals, and (2) to realize an operative and strategic support to financed firms. For these two reasons Venture Capital is very appropriate for growing or high-tech firms. Bracchi and Gervasoni (2006) support that Venture Capital (and Private Equity) is capable of realizing a virtuous circle that increases innovation intensity (Figure 3).

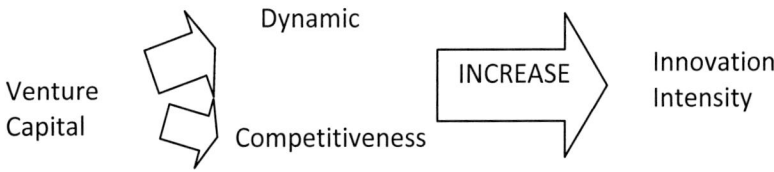

Figure 3. Venture Capital and Innovation System. Source: Adapted from Bracchi and Gervasoni, 2006

Overview of Venture Capital Investments

Venture Capital investments in new ventures can be classified according to the different stages of funding (Ruhnka and Young, 1987). These stages determine the financing lifecycle of the venture and may have different shareholders (Figure 4).

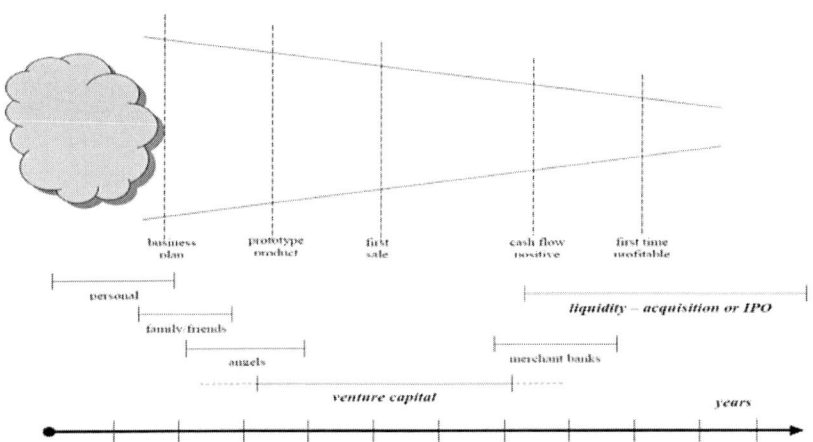

Figure 4. The Venture Capital Investment Process. Source: Callahan and Muegge, 2003

It's possible to realize an analysis of the financing sequence of innovative firms and the role of Venture Capital in growth process. In the first stage the firm has only an idea or product concept, so sources of financing are limited to the entrepreneurship or friends and family. In fact, the entrepreneurs who start a company are the first to invest in it.

> "This may be a significant amount in the case of a firm started by entrepreneurs successful from previous ventures. Normally, the amounts raised this way will be tens of thousands of dollars. This equity will likely include personal debt raised by these individuals that is invested in the start-up as equity. It may include "sweat equity" in the form of under-compensated work. This type of initial investment can extend to employees as well" (Callahan and Muegge, 2003: 648).

This step can be very expensive so subsequently the entrepreneurs acquire funds from friends and family sources. The owners of a new venture can have difficulty to raise equity investments from organized sources, so they go to friends and family to raise funds to sustain and develop their business idea. The capability to go to friends and family and persuade them to invest in a new firm/business/concept/idea is a sign of assurance by the founding entrepreneurs to a real, quality opportunity.

In the second stage the firm has a business plan and a proof-of-concept or a prototype of a product. This is the stage of marketing analysis. Typical sources of financing are business angels. Angels are wealthy individuals who invest their own money (Fenn and Liang, 1998). In other words these are affluent people who provide capital for a business start-up, usually in exchange for convertible debt or ownership equity. They are high net-worth individuals who like to make technology investments. Often they are entrepreneurs who have been successful in the same area of business as that in which they invest.

> "Angels often keep a low profile in their communities, not wanting to be pestered by start-ups looking for money, but preferring to find investment opportunities through their personal business networks" (Callahan and Muegge, 2003: 649).

Many more firms receive funding from angels than from venture capitalists, but the level of funding is much lower (Freear and Wetzel, 1990). The importance of angel investment to a new firm is more than the risk capital that they provide. In fact, they often have deep knowledge of the business, so they frequently carry credibility and contacts with and for their investments. A study in fact underlines the correlation between angel financing and venture capital financing:

> "fifty-seven percent of the firms that had received private investor financing also received financing from institutional venture capitalists; only ten percent of firms that had not received angel financing obtained venture capital" (Madill et al., 2002: 43).

The third stage is characterized by a developed product that has a potential market. In this stage the most important source of finance is Venture Capitalists. VC investments are commonly staged, so that multiple rounds of venture capital investment may be required to take an early-stage firm to liquidity (Gompers, 1995). Each funding round is discussed with a parallel evaluation of the firm. Staging is a control mechanism that permits VCs to monitor the progress of firms. Venture capital firms supply many other things to a new venture in addition to financing: they bring a deep knowledge of the technologies and markets, and as a result can add business value to new firm. Furthermore some VCs have important networks of contacts like other investors, customers and potential partners. This can represent an added value for new company. Finally VC investment bestows prestige upon a firm with positive results in financial and customer markets.

The last stage is the phase of firm growth. The project or product is ordinarily complete in its development and the firm is profitable. In this phase banks and other financial institutions are typical investors, but also VCs may continue to invest. As a firm grows and improves its business model, investment risk can decrease, but the firm still needs funding. In this case a firm can look to institutional investors like merchant banks. These supply late stage venture capital or mezzanine financing. In this step merchant banks have a lot of funds and want to invest in firms with lower risk. Furthermore they prefer investment with short horizon. Usually their investment – in this stage – is in the form of debt with a possible conversion to equity.

VCs have an important role also in this stage, when they disinvest their participation in the new firm. IPO and M&A are typical acts of this stage. In fact a new venture reaches liquidity when it is acquired by another company or when it issues shares during an Initial Public Offering in the public markets. As a result, a venture capital backed new venture must plan and work towards such a liquidity event from the start if they wish to raise venture capital.

These considerations underline that Venture Capital – from the early stage to IPO and M&A stage – plays an important role in financing new technology-based start-ups. Gompers and Lerner (1999) explain the VC cycle that involves investors, venture capital funds and new technology based firms (Figure 5).

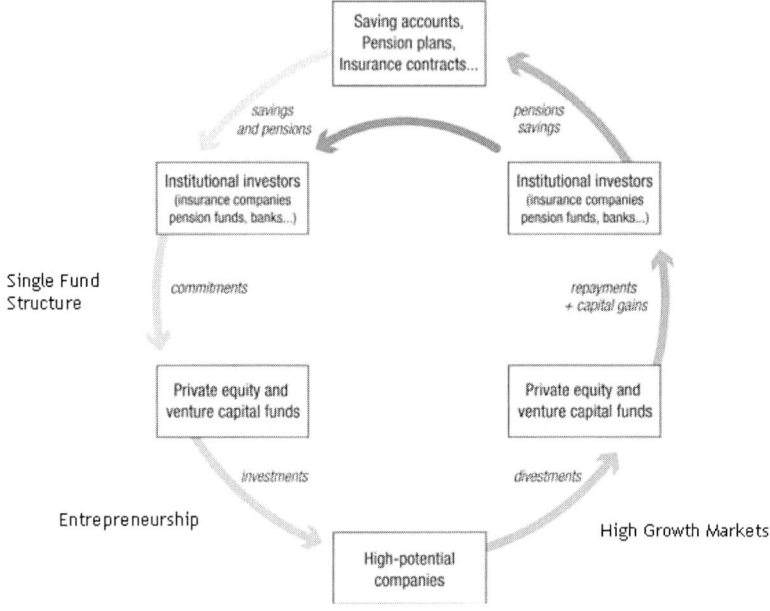

Figure 5. The Venture Capital Cycle. Source: EVCA, 2009

> "The venture capital cycle starts with raising a venture fund; proceeds through the investment in, monitoring of, and adding value to firms; continues as the venture capital firm exits successful deals and returns capital to its investors; and renews itself with the venture capitalist raising additional funds" (Gompers and Lerner 2001: 152).

It's possible to consider three different stages in the venture capital cycle: fundraising, venture investing and exiting venture capital investments. There is a correlation between these stages with each aspect of the venture cycle relating to each other.

Fundraising

This is the first phase of VCS activity. This stage includes deciding on management fees, negotiation of contracts between investors and the fund managers, agreeing the timings of investment disbursements as well as the distribution of profits over the course of the fund management period (Gompers and Lerner, 2004).

Venture Investing

This second phase can be subdivided in three steps: deal flow and screening, negotiation investments and monitoring. This phase of the venture capital cycle is the generation of deal flow and screening investment opportunities. The screening activities are needed to highlight excellent investment opportunities that have the potential for excellent returns. Cultivating good deal flow is an essential activity for the venture capital firm, but is largely completed through informal channels and principally through referral (Langeland, 2007).

The second step of this second phase is the negotiation process. It involves the venture capital manager valuing the firm. This is done with regard to market conditions and future prospects. The fund manager will also complete a number of background checks on the entrepreneur and management and analysis of the firm's proposition and technology base. This is referred to as the due diligence period (De Clercq et al., 2006).

The last step of this phase is monitoring. This is the stage at which non-capital value is added to the portfolio firms through the monitoring, advice and guidance of the fund managers. In the classic venture capital model strategic business support was part of the package. Venture capital investment was considered "more than money" (Bygrave and Timmons 1992; Lange, Mollov et al., 2007).

Exiting Venture Capital Investment

This is the final stage of the VC cycle. It is an obligation taken on when the firm was formed, but may not always be taken at a time that is in the best interests of the firm, the economy, or even the investors. There are different exit ways: IPO, trade sale, secondary sale to another financial institution, buy back by the entrepreneur or write off.

Venture Capital and Innovation: a Literature Review

It's possible to affirm that VC literature is highly fragmented. This is particularly evident when examining different research foci across researches. For the sake of clarity, it is possible to arrange them into two macro-areas: performance and process (Table 1). Although in some articles more than a single focus exists, a classification is possible according to the prevailing focus.

Table 1. Research Focus on VC and Innovations Research

Performance	Processes
Value Growth	*Characteristic of VC Operations*
Gorman and Sahlman (1989), Suzuky (1996), Hellman and Puri (2000), Engel (2002), Engel and Keilbach (2007), Peneder (2007), Caselli et al., (2009)	MacMillan et al., (1985, 1987), Fried and Hisrich, (1994)
Innovation	*Structure of VC Organization*
Kortum and Lerner (2001), Tytkova (2002), Hirukawa and Ueda (2011)	Sahlman (1990), Kaplan and Stromberg (2005)
	Nature of the firm
	Hellman and Puri (2000), Davis et al., (2003)

Source: authors' depiction

The recent rise of VC markets, has been accompanied by renewed concerns regarding their effects. These concerns emphasize the need to evaluate the impact of these transactions on firm performance by examining the effects on short-run stock prices, long-run stock prices, returns to investors, or their impact on innovation process[3].

Gorman and Sahlman (1989); Hellman and Puri (2000); Lerner (1995) have studied what venture capital firms do and theorize how they add value. Hellmann and Puri (2000) and Engel (2002) find that venture capital backed firms grow faster than their industry counterparts. Rapid growth also characterizes venture-backed firms in Japan (Suzuki, 1996).

---

[3] In fact a lot of studies focus their attention on VCs and their effects on innovation: according to National Venture Capital Association (1998) 80% of venture capital investment is towards high-tech industries such as computers, communications, medical and health, and biotechnology.

Peneder (2007), Engel and Keilbach (2007), and Caselliet al. (2009), realize three different studies on Italian, Austrian and German firms. The results of these studies are very similar. Specifically Engel and Keilback (2007) find that firms with a higher number of patent applications are more likely to receive venture funding. Once the firms are venture-funded, they tend to grow more than comparable non-venture firms, while their innovative performance (in terms of patent applications) does not differ significantly.

Regarding innovation, Kortum and Lerner (2001) find that patents granted to venture capital backed companies are cited more often than other patents, suggesting that venture capital backed companies are engaged in important innovative activities. At industry level, Kortum and Lerner (2001) find that in the U.S. venture capital investments account for patent count disproportionately relative to R&D expenditures.

Using German data, Tykova (2000) also finds the positive relation between venture capital investment and patent application. A common interpretation of the results found in the literature cited above is that venture capital (VC) spurs growth and innovation of new firms. Hirukawa and Ueda (2011) confirm a positive correlation between VC and innovation, but they develop two hypothesis: the first one is that venture capital investments stimulate innovation (VC-first hypothesis), the second one is that innovations induce venture capital investments (innovation-first hypothesis)[4].

Another branch of research has used evidence from surveys of VC investment partnerships to describe the characteristics of these investments (MacMillan et al., 1985, 1987; Fried and Hisrich, 1994). Faced with valuation uncertainty, Sahlman (1990) describes and analyzes the structure of venture-capital organizations, focusing on the relationship between investors and venture capitalists and between venture-capital firms and the ventures in which they invest. He suggests that the coping mechanism is to either design investment contracts, which materially skew the distribution of the payoffs from the project to the VC investors or involve the active

---

[4] VC spurs growth and innovation of new firms but "there may be an opposite causality; when there arise abundant opportunities for new firms to innovate and/or to grow fast, these firms demand venture capital investments and as a consequence venture capital markets grow because venture capitalists are complementary assets for such firms" (Hirukawa and Ueda, 2011: 422)

participation of the VC investor to assure that the project has the professional managerial expertise to succeed.

Kaplan and Strömberg (2005) compare the characteristics of real world financial contracts to their counterparts in financial contracting theory.

> "We do so by conducting a detailed study of actual contracts between venture capitalists (VCs) and entrepreneurs. We consider VCs to be the real world entities who most closely approximate the investors of theory" (Kaplan and Strömberg, 2005: 2177)".

The authors show that almost all VC investors receive convertible preferred stock in the firm when they pay in the funds. Optional redemption and put provisions are commonly used to strengthen the liquidation rights of the VC's investments.

> "Regarding the expected profit from VC investment, it is found that the median IPO stock price is 3.0 times greater than the cash infusion (the estimated value of the company) in the initial financing round (payment of the installment options). Over a four-year horizon, this works out to a return of 31% per year (Kaplan and Strömberg, 2005: 2198)".

Hellman and Puri (2000) focus their attention on VC operations and the nature of the firm, stating in fact that

> "VC projects also vary in terms of the nature of the proposed firm" (Davis et al. 2003: 7).

For Hellman and Puri (2000), these firms can be split into innovator or imitator firms. The difference is that

> "innovators are those firms that are the first to introduce new products or services for which no close substitute is yet offered in the market. Imitators are also engaged in relatively new products and technologies, but they are not the first movers in their markets, and therefore tend to compete on aspects other than innovation" (Hellman and Puri, 2000: 962)".

Another important difference is that innovator firms have targets set by internal performance (e.g. development of patents, successful completion of research projects), while imitator firms have targets set by external performance (e.g. sales targets, cash flows or attainment of predetermined market share levels).

On these statements Hellman and Puri (2000) develop their study to find that

> "firms pursuing an innovator rather than an imitator strategy are more likely to obtain venture capital financing. We also find that obtaining venture capital is associated with faster time to market, especially for innovators (page 986)".

They further uncover implications both for firms and VCs:

> "From a finance perspective, our results suggest that the appropriateness of choosing an involved investor depends on the strategic objectives of the company. From an industrial organization perspective, our results suggest that a firm's choice of financing seems to affect its ability to secure first-mover advantages".

In summary, Hellman and Puri (2000) underline the significant role of venture capital for innovative companies and their

> "results refute the sometimes voiced criticisms that venture capital does not support the most innovative start-ups, or that venture capitalists invest in innovative companies only when they are already older and less risky (page 964)".

What do VCs do for innovation?

Sandri (1994) and Caprio and Spisni (1994) define venture capital as a "patient capital", expected to follow the project lifecycle: thus, since high-tech investments are risky and have a long maturity, equity capital should be used more intensively by innovative firms than by traditional ones in order to finance the grow-up phase.

But it's necessary to define better what VCS do for innovation. One of the most influential pieces of empirical work on the content of venture capitalists involvement is the article "What do VCFs do?" of Gorman and Sahlman (1989). They show that the most frequent assistance to portfolio firms is to raise additional funds. Other important roles are given to strategic analysis and management recruiting. Other scholars (Elango et al., 1995; Reid, 1999) found that supply of financial capital and financial expertise are the most important contributions from VCFs.

These considerations are important also for innovative firms, but in these cases, in addition to funding, venture capitalists can provide specialized knowledge and access to a network of contacts. The venture capitalist brings terms, controls, expertise, and financial strength that helps form a well-managed and well-financed company that is more likely to succeed.

The role of VCs in innovative SMEs is important because there are true difficulties in financing innovation. Gompers and Lerner (2001) underline four such problems:

a. high uncertainty,
b. information asymmetry,
c. intangible soft assets,
d. sensitivity to volatile market conditions.

These make it difficult for many firms to raise funds through traditional debt financing. Venture capital fills this void by providing high levels of funding to opportunities with high uncertainty and large information asymmetries – in other words, ventures that may not otherwise have been funded.

Particularly VCs tend to reduce high uncertainty that is a fundamental characteristic of innovation that no amount of study or due diligence can entirely eliminate. Furthermore VCs reduce information asymmetry and this is particularly important because of their particular specialized expertise. Innovators have a superior understanding of their innovation, while investors have a superior understanding of financing. Venture capital is important also for intangible soft assets – patents and trademarks, knowledge, human capital and future opportunities – because the real value of these assets is difficult to measure. Moreover the value and liquidity of innovative firms is highly sensitive to volatile market conditions.

In essence, venture capital provides high levels of funding to business with high uncertainty and huge information asymmetries – in other words, firms that may not otherwise have been funded (Callahan and Muegge, 2003). VCs can have two effects on innovation: (a) a direct effect on the number of innovative projects that are undertaken, and (b) an indirect effect on the average quality of funded projects. The former is analogous to the effect of monitoring by venture capitalists – as in Holmström and Tirole (1997) – in the sense that it relaxes firms' financing constraint, albeit for a quite different reason. The latter effect regards the quality of funded projects that can be measured by the probability of innovation.

The reasons of this positive impact on an innovative firm is that VC - after funding an entrepreneur with an innovative idea - may be able to extract surplus from potential entrants at a subsequent stage, exploiting the informational advantage gained through close interaction with the first entrepreneur (Figure 6).

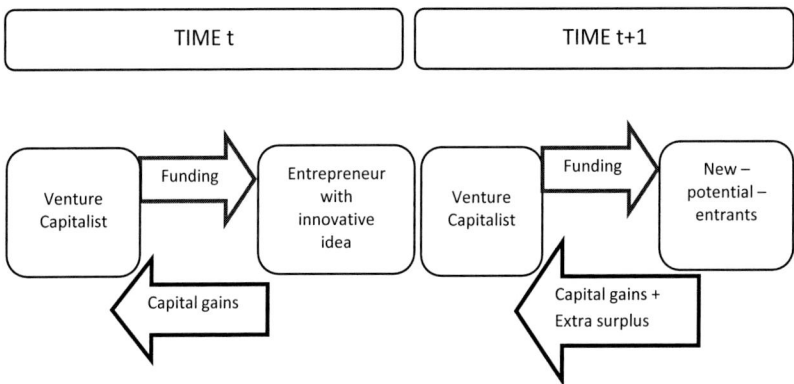

Figure 6. VC positive impact on innovation. Source: authors' calculation

In other words, a number of models in the literature show that venture capitalists (VCs) are:

1. well-informed financial intermediaries,
2. able to face problems related to risky investments in high-technology projects,
3. capable to engage in active monitoring, and
4. skilled to add value to the entrepreneurial team.

VCs place valuable managerial competencies at growing small firms' disposal; their stakes in the equity capital have a relevant image effect, which arouses intangible benefits in objective markets. A network of relationships with other enterprises can be exploited by VCs different problems which might be experienced by innovative firms in the first stages of their life, thus stimulating the firm's growth. In this sense Florida and Kenney (1988) assignee a new role to VCs: they

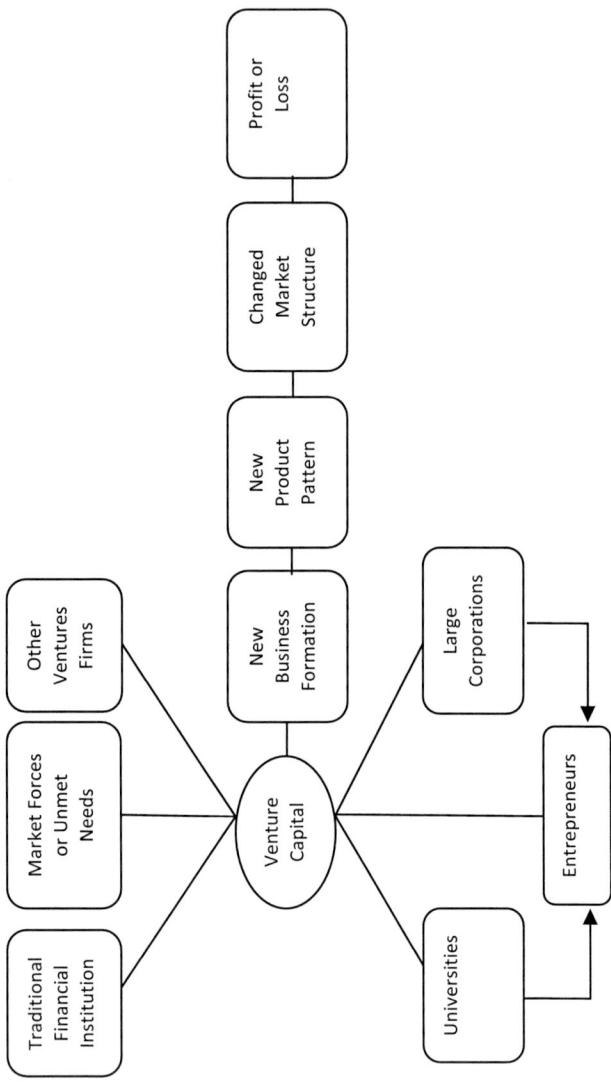

Figure 7. VC in the institutional framework for innovation. Source: Florida and Kennedy, 1988: 127

"forge important linkages among a variety of organizations which are important to the innovation process and act as "technological gatekeepers" accelerating the process of technological change" (119).

"Venture capitalists are situated at the centre of extended networks and actively forge connections which reach into large corporations, universities, financial institutions, and a variety of other organizations which play important roles in the innovation process. From this central vantage point, venture capitalists are uniquely equipped to match personnel and resources drawn from various organizations in the formation of new enterprises" (Florida and Kennedy, 1988: 127).

Florida and Kennedy (1988) consider VCs as the centre of innovation process. It's possible to subdivide this process in four overlapping networks. The first net is used for fundraising and to organize capitals. It consists of investors in the venture capital fund and other venture capital firms that take part in innovation investment. A second network is used to locate and review potential investments and turns to previously successful entrepreneurs, other venture capitalists, lawyers, and accountants as well as contacts in large corporations and universities. The role of other entrepreneurs is important because they can have supplemental contacts that extend to the most promising potential start-ups. A third net cultivated includes professional service firms (i.e. law, accounting firms, market researchers, consulting firms) which serve as sources for industry-relevant information. A final network includes sources of labour, which are used to recruit management and other personnel for start-ups. This net includes also sources for inputs into the production process and possible outlets for finished goods (Florida and Kennedy, 1988).

In this perspective VCs have a fundamental role in innovation process, in fact:

"Venture capitalists are a crucial part of the context within which such breakthroughs occur. Due to the intensive flows of information at their disposal, venture capitalists are well positioned to spot the opportunities that arise as critical barriers are breached. It is at these junctures that they perform "gatekeeping" function, intervening to help create new companies and actualize important breakthroughs, while capturing the "economic rents" that come from being first across such boundaries." (Florida and Kennedy, 1998: 128)

Conclusions and Managerial Implications

VCs have a particularly important role to perform in the growth of innovative firms in their infancy. Their role though, transcends the strict financial contribution to touch upon other aspects of strategic management towards growth. Specifically, VCs contribute significantly also through:

1. management assistance to the portfolio company, analogous to that provided by a management consulting firm;
2. intensive monitoring performance, reflecting the incentives to monitoring arising from equity ownership; and
3. the power to act using the venture capitalist's ability to give the portfolio company credibility with third parties, similar to the role played by other reputational intermediaries such as investment bankers.

Different researches confirm that venture capital backed firms grow faster than their industry counterparts. Though it is a logical assumption that VCs invest in the most promising companies to begin with, the hypothesis does not appear able to alone explain the phenomenon. A possible explanation, further and in conjunction to the above-stated contributions, is that venture capitals have strong incentives to monitor entrepreneurs' performance, deriving from equity ownership. They also receive strong control levers, often disproportionate to the size of their equity investment:

> "the initial investment is typically insufficient to allow the portfolio company to carry out its business plan. The venture capital will decide later whether to provide the additional funding that the portfolio company needs. The company's need for additional funds gives its management a performance incentive in the form of a hard constraint, analogous to the use of debt in leveraged buyouts" (Blossom and Company, 2011: 32).

International experience shows that in most cases, investments have the objective of supporting the early stage of a company development, or even of turning a concept or a project conventionally termed/deemed very innovative into an entrepreneurial activity. The interest of VCs to invest in innovative firms may be explained by the high potential of these firms in combination with their managerial and financial incapabilities. Therefore, the best situation for innovative companies with an excellent technology

> "would be to find a specialized venture capital network, a specialized advisor and specialized investors that believe in and can assist the development of the project by providing the skills, networking and capital

flows necessary for accelerating pipeline and technology development" (Blossom, 2011: 12).

On a catalectic note, for innovative companies, VC appears to be a factor of growth and success. Though cause and effect has no clear boundary in this relationship, all evidence indicates that the amalgam of VC and innovation firms sums up to more than its constituent parts. It is presumably the very differences in their nature that leads to success: on the one hand companies with scientific competences and innovation drive, and on the other VCs, with financial and managerial proficiencies and business drive. In essence, the one compliments and enhances the other; for the good of the individual investments, the individual companies, and collectively, the industry as a whole.

References

Acs, A. and Audretsch, B (Eds.) (1990), *The Economics of Small Firms: A European Challenge*, Kluwer, Netherlands.

Baldwin, C. and von Hippel, E. (2009), 'Modeling a Paradigm Shift: From Producer Innovation to User and Open Collaborative Innovation', *Organization Science*, Vol. 6, No. 2, pp. 1399-1417.

Blossom and Company (2011), *Biotechnology in Italy 2011. The financial perspective*, Milan.

Bracchi, G. and Gervasoni, A. (2006), L'importanza del capitale di rischio per lo sviluppo del sistema economico in Bracchi, G. and Gervasoni, A. (a cura di) *Venti anni di private equità*, EGEA, Milano.

Bresciani, S., Thrassou, A. and Vrontis, D. (2012), "Human Resource Management – Practises, Performance and Strategy in the Italian Hotel Industry", *World Review of Entrepreneurship, Management and Sustainable Development,* Vol. 8, No. 4, pp. 405-423.

Bygrave, W.D. and Timmons J.A. (1992), *Venture capital at the crossroad*, Harvard Business School Press, Boston

Callahan, J. and Muegge, S. (2003), 'Venture Capital's Role in Innovation: Issues, Research and Stakeholder Interests', in Shavinina, L.V. (ed), *The International Handbook on Innovation*, Elsevier Science, Amsterdam

Caprio, L. and Spisni, M. (1994), 'Il capitale di rischio come leva per lo sviluppo delle PMI', *Piccola Impresa/Small Business*, No. 2, pp. 61–85.

Caselli, S., Gatti, S. and Perrini, F. (2009),'Are venture capitalists a catalyst for innovation?', *European Financial Management*, Vol. 15, No. 1, pp. 92-111.

Chebbi, H., Yahiaoui, D., Thrassou, A. and ,Vrontis, D. (2011), *"The Exploration Activity's Added Value into the Innovation Process"*, 4th *Annual Conference of the EuroMed Academy of Business,* Business Research Challenges in a Turbulent Era*,* pp. 361-375, Elounda, Crete, Greece, October 20-21, 2011

Chesbrough, H. (2006), Open Innovation: A New Paradigm for Understanding Industrial Innovation, in Chesbrough, H., Vanhaverbeke, W. and West, J. (eds) *Open Innovation: Researching a New Paradigm*, Oxford University Press, London.

Christofidis, C. and Debande, O. (2001), 'Financing Innovative Firms through Venture Capital', *EIB Sector Papers,* European Investment Bank. Available at http://www.eib.org/attachments/pj/vencap.pdf (Accessed 14 October 2011)

Dagogo, D. and Ollor, W. (2009), 'The effect of venture capital financing on the economic value added profile on Nigerian SMEs', *African Journal of Accounting, Economics, Finance and Banking Research*, vol. 5, no. 5, pp: 37-46.

Davis, M.H.A., Schachermayer, W. and Tompkins, R.G. (2003), 'The evaluation of venture capital as an instalment option: Valuing real options using real options', *Zeitschrift fur Betriebswirtschaft*, Vol. 3 (2004), pp. 77–96.

De Clercq, D., Fried, V.H., Lehtonen, O. and Sapienza, H. J. (2006), 'An Entrepreneur's Guide to the Venture Capital Galaxy', *Academy of Management Perspectives*, Vol. 20, No. 3, pp. 90-112.

Elango, B., Fried, V.H., Hisrich R.D. and Polenchek A., 'How Venture Capital Firms Differ', *Journal of Business Venturing*, Vol. 10, No.2, 1995, pp. 157-179.

Engel D. (2002), "The Impact of Venture Capital on Firm Growth: An Empirical Investigation", *ZEW Discussion Paper*, No. 02-02. Available at http://econstor.eu/bitstream/10419/24804/1/dp0202.pdf (accessed 06 October 2011)

Engel, D. and Keilbach, M. (2007), 'Firm Level Implications of Early Stage Venture Capital Investment - An Empirical Investigation', *Journal of Empirical Finance*, Vol. 14, No. 2, pp. 150-167.

European Private Equity & Venture Capital Association (2009), *EVCA Governing Principles*, Brussels. Available at http://www.evca.eu/uploadedFiles/Home/Toolbox/Industry_Standards/ evca_governing_principles_2009.pdf (Accessed 08 October 2011)

Fenn, G.W. and Liang, N. (1998), 'New Resources and New Ideas: Private Equity for Small Businesses', *Journal of Banking and & Finance*, Vol. 22, No. 6-8, pp. 1077-1084.

Florida, R.L. and Kennedy M. (1988), 'Venture capital-financed innovation and technological change in the USA', *Research Policy*, vol. 17, pp. 119-137.

Freear, J. and Wetzel, W. Jr. (1990), 'Who Bankrolls High-tech Entrepreneurs?', *Journal of Business Venturing*, No. 5, pp. 77–89.

Fried, V. and Hisrich, R. (1994) 'Towards a Model of Venture Capital Investment Decision Making', *Financial Management*, 23, 3, pp: 28-37.

Gompers, P. (1995), 'Optimal Investment, Monitoring, and the Staging of Venture Capital', *Journal of Finance*, Vol. 50, pp. 1461–1489.

Gompers, P. and Lerner, J. (1999), *The Venture Capital Cycle*, MIT Press, Cambridge.

Gompers, P. and Lerner, J. (2001a), 'The Venture Capital Revolution', *Journal of Economic Perspectives*, Vol. 15, No. 2, pp. 145-168.

Gompers, P. and Lerner J. (2001b), *The Money of Invention: How Venture Capital Creates New Wealth*, MA: Harvard Business School Press, Cambridge.

Gompers, P.A. and Lerner, J. (2004), *The Venture Capital Cycle*. MIT Press, Cambridge, MA and London.

Gorman, M.S. and Sahlman, W.A. (1989) 'What Do Venture Capitalists Do?', *Journal of Business Venturing*, 4, 4, pp: 231-248.

Helmmann, T. and Puri, M. (2000), 'The Interaction Between Product Market and Financing Strategy: The Role of Venture Capital', *The Review of Financial Studies*, 13, 4, pp: 959-984.

Hisrich, R.D. and Peters, M.P. (1998), *Entrepreneurship: Starting, Developing, and Managing a New Enterprise* (4thEd.), Irwin, Chicago

Hirukawa, M. and Ueda, M. (2011), 'Venture Capital and Innovation: Which is First?', *Pacific Economic Review*, 16, 4, pp: 421-465.

Holmstrom, B. and Tirole J. (1997), 'Financial Intermediation, Loanable Funds, and the Real Sector', *The Quarterly Journal of Economics*, Vol. 112, No. 3, pp. 663-691.

Johnson, B., Edquist, C. and Lundvall, B. (2003), 'Economic Development and the National System of Innovation Approach', *University First Globelics Conference*, Rio de Janeiro, November 3–6.

Kaplan, S.N. and Strömberg, P. (2005) 'Characteristics, Contracts and Actions: Evidence from Venture Capitalist Analyses', *The Journal of Finance*, 59, 5, pp: 2177-2210.

Kortum, S. Lerner, J. (2001) 'Does venture capital spur innovation?', in Libecap G. (ed.), *Entrepreneurial Inputs and Outcomes*, Volume 13, Amsterdam, Elsevier.

Lange, J.E., Mollov, A., Pearlmutter, M., Singh, S. and Bygrave W.D., (2007), 'Pre-start-up formal business plans and post-start-up performance: a study of 116 new ventures', *Venture Capital*, Vol. 9, No.4, pp. 237–256.

Langeland, O. (2007), 'Financing innovation: The role of Norwegian venture capitalists in financing knowledge-intensive enterprises', *European Planning Studies*, No. 15, pp. 1143-1161.

Lerner J. (2000), 'Money chasing deals? The impact of fund inflows on private equity valuations', *Journal of Financial Economics*, 55, pp: 281-325.

MacMillan, I. Zemann, L. Subbanarasimha, P.N. (1987) 'Criteria Distinguishing Successful from Unsuccessful Ventures in the Venture Screening Process', *Journal of Business Venturing*, 2, pp: 123-137.

Madill, J.J., Haines, G. Jr., Orser, B.J. and Riding, A.L. (2002). 'Managing High Technology SMEs To Obtain Institutional Venture Capital: A Role For Angels', *Eric Sprott School of Business, Carleton University working paper*, presented at the Babson Entrepreneurship Research Conference, June.

Mallone, M., Moraca, A. and Zezza V. (2005), *I centri per l'innovazione e trasferimento tecnologico in Italia: una survey condotta nell'ambito della rete italiana per la diffusione dell'innovazione e il trasferimento tecnologico alle imprese*, available at: www.riditt.it (accessed 20 May 2012).

Mina, A. (2009) 'Risk Capital and Innovation: Literature Review – Part B', *Finance, Innovation & Growth (FINNOV)*, available at: http://www.finnov-fp7.eu/sites/default/files/FINNOV_DP3.1B_0.pdf (accessed 04 October 2011).

Martini, E. and Rossi, M. (2010), 'The Transformation of University-Industry Relations. The Case of Campania', in Roufagalas, J. (ed), *Economic Themes I*, ATINER, Athens.

Peneder, M. (2007), 'Start-ups, Closures and Growth of Enterprises. Evidence for Austria', *WIFO Monatsberichte*, Vol. 80, No. 3, pp. 233-247.

Reid, G.C. (1999), 'Capital Structure at Inception and the Short-Run Performance of Micro-Firms', in Acs, Z., Carlsson, B. and Karlsson, C. (eds.), *Entrepreneurship, SMEs and the Macro Economy*, Cambridge University Press, Cambridge

Rossi, M., Vrontis, D. and Thrassou A (2011), "Financing Innovation: Venture Capital Investments in Biotechnology Firms", International Journal of Technology Marketing, Vol. 6, No. 4, pp.355-377.

Ruhnka, J.C. and Young, J.E., 'A Venture Capital Model of the Development Process for New Ventures', *Journal of Business Venturing*, vol. 2, pp. 167-184.

Sahlman, W. (1990) 'The Structure and Governance of Venture Capital Organisations', *Jounral of Financial Economics*, 27, pp: 473-524.

Sandri, S., (1994), 'Il venture capital come strumento di finanziamento delle piccole imprese', *Piccola Impresa/Small Business*, No. 2, pp. 87–99.

Schumpeter, J.A. (1934), *The Theory of Economic Development*, Harvard University Press, Cambridge, Mass.

—. (1942), *Capitalism, Socialism and Democracy*, Harper & Row, New York.

Sharpe, S. (2009), 'Risk Capital and Innovation: Literature Review – Part A', *Finance, Innovation & Growth (FINNOV)*, available at: http://www.finnov-fp7.eu/sites/default/files/FINNOV_DP3.1A_0.pdf (accessed 12 May 2012).

Sharpe, S., Cosh, A., Connell, D. and Parnell, H (2009), *The role of Micro Funds in the Financing of New Technology Firms*, National Endowment for Science, Technology and Arts, London.

Suzuki, K. (1996) 'Nihon ni okeru venture management no jittai (Facts on venture managements in Japan)', in Yanagi K. and Yamamoto T. (ed.), *Venture management no henkaku*, Nihon Keizai Shimbumsha, Tokyo.

Thrassou A., Lijo P.R. (2007), *Customer Perceptions Regarding Usage of Mobile Banking Services - The Case of Kuwait*, World Journal of Business Management, Vol 1, No. 1, pp. 3-16.

Thrassou, A. and Vrontis, D. (2006), "A Small Services Firm Marketing Communications Model for SME-Dominated Environments", *Journal of Marketing Communications*, Vol. 12, Iss. 3, pp. 183-202 (ISSN: 1352-7266-Routlege, Taylor and Francis Group).

Thrassou, A. and Vrontis, D. (2008), "International Strategic Marketing of the Small Construction Consultancy Firm - The Case of Cypriot Firms", *International Journal of Entrepreneurship and Small Business*, Vol. 6, No. 2, pp. 296-314.

Thrassou, A., Vrontis, D., Chebbi, H. and Yahiaoui, D. (2012a), "A Preliminary Strategic Marketing Framework for New Product Development", Journal of Transnational Management, Vol. 17, No. 1, pp. 21-44.

Thrassou, A., Vrontis, D., Chebbi, H. and Yahiaoui, D. (2012b), Transcending Innovativeness Towards Strategic Reflexivity, Qualitative Market Research: An International Journal, Volume 15, Number 4, 2012

Tytkova, T. (2000) 'Venture Capital in Germany and its impact on Innovation' available at http://caia.org/knowledge-center/bibliography/venture-capital-germany-and-its-impact-innovation (accessed 01 October 2011).

Vrontis, D. and Thrassou, A. (2011) "The Renaissance of Commandaria- A Strategic Branding Prescriptive Analysis", *Journal for Global Business Advancement*, Vol. 4, No. 4, pp. 302-316.

Chapter Nine

Policy Strategies for Innovation in Switzerland

Ruth Rios-Morales, John C. Crotts and Max Schweizer

Introduction

The method by which a small country leveraged itself to a position amongst the world's most innovative and competitive nations in the era of globalization indeed merits assessment. Switzerland has built its once largely agriculture-based economy into a sophisticated model grounded mainly on advanced technology and services. Today, 73 percent of the workforce is employed in the tertiary sector (service sector and service industry), 23 percent in the secondary or manufacturing sector, and four percent in the primary or agricultural sector (Federal Department of Foreign Affairs, 2012a). Much of the success achieved in this economic evolution has been attributed to innovation- focused policy strategies and policy dynamics that have created of Switzerland a competitive market economy. Notwithstanding the global financial crisis, Switzerland's economy remains strong; it has one of the highest Gross National Income (GNI) per capita rates in the world, low unemployment rates with stable economic, political and financial systems (World Bank, 2012a).

The Swiss model of innovation is acknowledged as one of the most successful models in the world (World Bank, 2012b). In 2011, Switzerland ranked first in the Global Innovation Index (INSEAD, 2011) as well as in the Global Competitive Index (World Economic Forum, 2011). As Europe's leader in innovation, scientific research and technology output, Switzerland's knowledge based economy is directly linked with the development of its education, research, and technology infrastructure. This infrastructure has been the result of policy strategies that focused on the country's most competitive resources, producing impressive results. We contend there are lessons to be learned and emulated from such policies. The purpose of this chapter is to examine the policy strategies and policy dynamics of the Swiss model for innovation.

Defining and Measuring Innovation

The definition of innovation has been debated over the years. Different depictions have emerged in academic and non-academic literature, even the quantitative approaches as how best to measure innovation have been widely argued. The gradual transformation of the concept of innovation provides researchers a better understanding of the concept and guides statisticians in their attempt to measure the process by which an invention is transformed into a good or service which yields an economic benefit. Although innovation has been widely associated with technological advancement, innovation may also occur with minor improvements that lead to productivity and economic growth. The Global Innovation Index (GII) embraces a number of definitions which capture global innovation; however, the Organization of Economic Cooperation and Development (OECD) definition of the *Oslo Manual* is a widely accepted definition, describing innovation as follows:

> "An innovation is an implementation of a new or significantly improved product (good or service), a new process, a new marketing method or a new organisational method in business practices, workplace organisation or external relations" (INSEAD, 2011: 4).

We can distinguish three basic types of innovation:

- Innovation as novelty: refers fundamentally to novelty as consequence of innovation that has practical implementations, bringing an added value to the consumer.
- Innovation as change: conveys to inventions that results in transformations, diffusions, and ultimately change.
- Innovation as advantage: in the world of business, innovation refers to improvements that yield competitive advantages. This type of innovation can also include a social dimension in terms of innovative advances.

Measuring innovation on a global scale requires establishing a uniform innovation indicator across very different economies. Calculating innovation is a complex task; one of the most important challenges for computing innovation is access to the statistical data at a global level. Many countries lack the statistical capacity to construct reliable and valid data. There has also been great dispute over how effective some methods of measurement are, as economies differ in economic development, size and population. In recent years, indices have adopted a broader, multidimensional approach that, in addition to the technological and scientific indicators, takes into account a range of social and business indicators. Important indices of innovation have emerged in recent years such as: the Innovation Index developed by the Indiana Business Research Center; the *Oslo Manual* established by the OECD; the State Technology and Science Index developed by Milken Institute; the Global Innovation Index established by the Boston Consulting Group; the Global Innovation Index established by the Boston Consulting Group; and the Global Innovation Index developed by INSEAD.

The most common measures of innovation in use today are at the organisational and political levels. At the organisational level, the measures focus on individuals, team-level assessments, and private companies from the smallest to the largest. At the political level, measures of innovation are more focused on organizational capabilities on a national or regional basis that can be evaluated on a competitive advantage basis attributable to innovation. The Global Innovation Index (GII), developed by INSEAD, is arguably the most innovative measure in that it assesses innovation at the organizational level as well as the ability of governmental bodies to support it. Established in 2007, the GII is not restricted to research and development (R&D) and scientific research, but also captures the social and business models of innovation. In order to increase the validity and reliability of its method of measurement, the GII incorporates a number of datasets into its model from key knowledge partners such as the World Intellectual Property Organisation (WIPO) and the Confederation of the Indian Industry (CII). The GII also submits its rankings to a statistical audit carried-out by the Joint Research Centre of the European Commission.

The Global Innovation Index's conceptual framework incorporates the latest research on the measurement of innovation and introduces two sub-indices; the innovation inputs sub-index and the innovation outputs sub-index. The framework is built around seven different pillars. The first five pillars attempt to capture the elements of the national economy that enable innovative activities, while the remaining two pillars capture actual evidence of innovation outputs. Each sub-pillars are calculated as the weighted average of individual indicators, pillar scores are calculated as the simple average of the sub-pillars scores (see Box 1).

Table 1: The Conceptual Framework of the Global Innovation Index

---

The conceptual framework of the GII is based on the following seven (7) pillars:

1. **Institutions** (innovation input): includes the following indicators; quality of public and civil service, policy formulation, and press freedom.
2. **Human capital and research** (innovation input): includes the following indicators; education, education expenditure, life expectancy.
3. **Infrastructure** (innovation input): includes the following indicators; information and communication technology, energy, general infrastructure.
4. **Market sophistication** (innovation input): includes the following indicators; credit, investment, trade and competition.
5. **Business sophistication** (innovation input): includes the following indicators; knowledge intensive employment, innovation linkages, knowledge absorption.
6. **Scientific outputs** (innovation output): includes the following indicators; knowledge creation, knowledge impact, knowledge diffusion.
7. **Creative outputs** (innovation output): includes the following indicators; creative intangibles, creative goods and services.

Each pillar is divided into sub-pillars and each sub-pillar is composed of individual indicators. Sub-pillar scores are calculated as the weighted average of individual indicators; pillar scores are calculated as the simple average of the sub-pillar scores. Four measures are then calculated:

- The Innovation Input Sub-Index is the simple average of the first five pillar scores.
- The Innovation Output Sub- Index is the simple average of the last two pillar scores.
- The Global Innovation Index is the simple average of the Input and Output Sub-Indices.
- The Innovation Efficiency Index is the ratio of the Output Sub-Index over the Input Sub-Index.

Policy Strategies for Innovation

Innovation has traditionally been considered one of several important drivers of economic development and growth. In today's global economy, the role of innovation has attained a prominent position in strategy development of many countries due to its influence on its competitive position among nations. Given the role innovation plays in economic growth and development, numerous countries have focused important efforts at implementing policies for innovation as evidenced by the prominence innovation is reflected in policy strategies of those countries that have gained competitive advantage over the last two decades (Carlsson, 2006). A number of studies corroborate the correlation between innovation and economic development, and confirm that in recent times, countries have aligned national policies to support innovation in their countries tend to prosper more than those that show no alignment (Greenhalgh and Rogers, 2006; INSEAD, 2012).

Due to the significant role governmental policies can play in support of innovation, the concept of a national innovative capacity has also emerged in the literature (Fransman, 1999). National innovative capacity is defined by Furman, Porter and Stern (2002) as the ability of a country, as both a political and economic entity, to produce and commercialize a new flow of emerging technology over a long term period. Measures of such capacity gauge the degree a nation's institutional capabilities have on innovation (Hu and Mathews, 2005). Central to this source of competitive advantage is to the capacity of formulating policy strategies for innovation, and the achievement of these policies in enhancing competitiveness depend on the effectiveness of such policies and allocation of financial resources in the development of human capital (Garelli, 2002). Furthermore, a successful policy framework for innovation depends to a certain degree on the ability to sustain innovation, as opposed to creating artificial competitiveness. Sustained competitiveness is dependent on many factors such as macroeconomic stability, technological development, human capital conditions, and local capabilities.

> "Competitive success in an innovation-driven global economy needs strong local capabilities and the development of capabilities faces numerous market and institutional failures" (Lall, 2005: 43).

There are several factors influencing the creation of innovation at a national level. However, evidence suggests that the capacity of national innovation depends on the development of an aligned sophisticated educational system (Pavit, 1991). Education, research and technology are the main driving factors of innovation and competitiveness. Education provides technical competence and stimulates creativity (Baumol, 2004), while research and technology are key elements to support the development of a knowledge based economy, which in turn help to maintain macroeconomic stability, support economic growth and attract foreign direct investment (Zhang, 2001). Today, many nations embraced innovation as an instrument of economic growth and competitive advantage with Switzerland a leading example. The Swiss model has adopted governmental policies and policy dynamics that are based on continual support for innovation. We contend the Swiss model is strategic and dynamic, fostering effective policies for innovation, supporting competitiveness, and promoting internationalisation.

Policy Strategies for Innovation in Switzerland

In the case of Switzerland, governmental policies have strongly influenced the development of innovation through education, research and technology. The Swiss model of innovation has been acknowledged as a successful model, in the sense that a small country attains a scientific output that has surpassed most OECD countries (Federal Department of Foreign Affairs, 2012b). According to the Global Competitiveness Report (2011), Switzerland possesses some of the top scientific research institutions in the world that is based upon strong collaboration with the business sector, ensuring that much of the research conducted is converted into marketable products and services. Innovation is secured by Switzerland's patenting system, which is regarded among the most effective systems in the world. In 2010, the patent rate reached 158.95 patents per million inhabitants, one of the highest rates in the world (World Economic Forum 2010). According to the World Intellectual Property Organisation (WIPO), in 2011, Switzerland ranked first at the filings at the Patent Cooperation Treaty. This strong innovative capacity dates back to the 1970s, where Switzerland shared with the United States, the leading position in "international" patenting per capita rate (Furman, Porter and Stern, 2002). It is this capacity for innovation in scientific research along with its ties with the business community that has placed Switzerland as one the most competitive countries in the world. Much of this achievement can be attributed to the government support of innovation through its procurement processes (World Economic Forum, 2011).

> "A country's innovation performance is directly linked to the willingness of companies and academic centers to develop, implement, and share new ideas. Cutting-edge solutions are possible when governments set the right mix of legal environment and business incentives. Switzerland shows how to combine the best results in innovation with economic growth" (World Bank, 2012: 67).

The implementation of appropriate policies has indeed created a positive climate for innovation in Switzerland. The strategic role played by governmental policies for innovation is, according to the OECD (2008), the main reason why Switzerland is outperforming most OECD countries. The main elements that have contributed to the creation of innovation are the implementation of structural educational policies, investment in R&D, strong intellectual property protection and government support of innovation.

Swiss Policy on Education. Although Switzerland has no Ministry of Education, the management of the Swiss education system was ranked first in the fifth pillar (Education and Training) of the 2011 Global Competitiveness Index (World Economic Forum, 2011). The Swiss education system has been an instrumental part of the nation's policy strategies for innovation, whereas providing a qualified labour force is the single most essential element for successful innovation (Swiss-American Chamber of Commerce & Boston Consulting Group, 2008). Thissystem is diverse and decentralised where most authority delegated to the local cantons. The Swiss educational system is divided into four stages: primary, secondary, tertiary and adult education. Students at the age of 16 have the choice to follow a vocational training track for direct entry into the labour market or to follow an academic career (maturité) at university level. The Swiss vocational and professional education and training system is distinguished by its closed links to the local labour market. Students are trained as apprentices in the labour market while having also attending school classes focused on foundation skills. Both activities are organised and coordinated by cantonal education authorities. At the university level, students have even broader choices where there are liberal arts universities, universities of applied sciences, as well as federal institutes of technology. The universities of applied sciences offer professional training at university level where research conducted at these institutions is closely link to the business world. The vocational training and university research connected to the business sector have been acknowledged as the key to systematic innovation in Switzerland (Organization of Economic Cooperation and Development, 2008).

Important reforms have taken place since the 1960s, including governmental policies that provide financial resources allowing the expansion of third level education in the creation of vocational and technological colleges. Switzerland has been investing heavily in human capital. In May 2006, the Swiss population approved a new constitutional provision on education designed to achieve continual improvements in university education, research, and innovation which includes increases in the government's investment in education (State Secretariat for Education and Research 2007). Today, policy strategies that promote education, research, and innovation that are focused on competitiveness, economic growth, and improving quality are designated high priority by the Federal Council.

Support Instruments for Innovation. Supporting innovation, ensuring knowledge transfer, and the building of a strong link between public and private institutions are acknowledged as significant elements in creating an innovative climate in Switzerland. The federal government deploys a variety of means, though the two deemed most instrumental are the Swiss National Science Foundation (SNSF) and the Commission for Innovation and Technology (CIT). The SNSF was created in 1952 to promote scientific research and industry innovation. The SNSF is the most important instrument used by the government in sustaining and funding bottom-up innovation, promoting international research cooperation, and developing target research agenda (Federal Department of Foreign Affairs, 2012b). The SNSF is engaged in supporting and funding the development of young scientists, in ways that insure that scientific research is contributing toward the country's competitiveness and economic development. The SNSF also fosters channels of communication among scientists and the business world. The Commission for Innovation and Technology (CIT) is the innovation promotion agency in Switzerland. The CIT's mission is to guarantee that knowledge and technology are transfer from academic institutions to the business sector.

Investment in R&D. Public and private sector investment in R&D has yielded a strong infrastructure for scientific research and innovation in Switzerland. It is estimated that Switzerland invests around 2.9 percent of its GDP in R&D (Organization of Economic Cooperation and Development, 2008). Today, there are different sources of support for the development of R&D. At the federal level, the Commission for Technology and Innovation began investing in R&D in 2000 (Organization of Economic Cooperation and Development, 2008). In addition, the Federal Council supports financially national education, research and innovative programs, while each canton provides a budget to support R&D activities at cantonal level. The business community also spends generously in research and innovation, accounting for approximately one-third of all R&D (Organization of Economic Cooperation and Development, 2008). The Federal Council's financial support for scientific research and innovation is channeled through the Swiss National Science Foundation and Innovation Promotion Agency. The Federal Council also contributes financially with the European research institutions such as the Space Agency (ESA), European Southern Observatory (ESO), and European Synchrotron Radiation Facility (ESRF), among others (State Secretariat for Education and Research, 2007).

For the period 2008-2011, the Federal Council provided a total of CHF 2,728 million to the Swiss National Science Foundation to support education, research and innovation, which was well over the 2004-2007 budget of CHF 778 million. The 2008-2011 budgets distributed as 83 percent of available funds for basic research and support to measures to promote young researchers, 9.8 percent to support Swiss Priority Programs, 4.1 percent to support the 'Overhead' tool, and 3.1 percent to support the National Research Program. The Innovation Promotion Agency received from the Federal Council CHF 532 million for 2008-2011, which was 32.0 percent higher than 2004-2007 at CHF 403 million. The Innovation Promotion Agency budget for 2008-2011 allocated 62.8 percent of its budget for R&D project funding, 28.9 percent for national and international networks and programs, and 8.2 percent to support start-up projects (State Secretariat for Education and Research, 2007).

Intellectual Property Protection. As previously stated, Switzerland has the highest number of patents per capita in the world (World Bank, 2012b). Switzerland has a long tradition in protecting its intellectual property with the establishment of the Swiss Federal Institute of Intellectual Property in 1888 (Swiss Federal Institute of Intellectual Property, 2012a). This organization was established to be the point of contact for customers regarding industrial protective rights in Switzerland. The German born Nobel Laureate Albert Einstein worked at the Institute from 1902 to 1907; then known as the Patent Office (Swiss Federal Institute of Intellectual Property, 2012b). Although the Swiss Federal Institute of Intellectual Property was established long ago, it is only in recent times that this organization received the status of an independent organization incorporated under public law and supported by the Federal Council budget in 1996. Today the Swiss Federal Institute of Intellectual Property (IIP) is in charge of the process of applying for all patents, trademarks, industrial designs, and copyrights in the country. The Institute also continues to be the main point of contact regarding industrial protective rights, working closely with the Federal Department of Justice and Police, by offering services in the area of trademark research and patent and promotes the intellectual property system, supporting specially small-medium sized enterprises.

Switzerland is also an active and supportive member of the international community, which protects intellectual property. Switzerland has participated in all the major conventions and international treaties related to the protection of intellectual property rights (Swiss Federal Institute of Intellectual Property, 2012a). It is also home to the World Intellectual Property Organization (WIPO) and the World Trade Organization (WTO), both international organization are based in Geneva.

Key Dimensions of the Swiss Model of Innovation

Switzerland has long been an outstanding place for creativity and innovation. Through the years, this country has built up a climate that promotes technological advancement and has produced entrepreneurs with clear vision, courage, with a capacity to take risks. To illustrate, Henri Nestlé, founded the largest nutrition, health and wellness company in the world; Johann Rudolf Geigy, was a pioneer in physiology development and the founder of experimental zoology; Alfred Escher, founded several important organizations such as the Swiss Federal Institute of Technology, Swiss Life and Credit Swiss; and Johann Jakob Sulzer, founded Sulzer, a global provider of oil and gas, hydrocarbon processing, power generation, water and wastewater, automotive, and aviation. Switzerland has been also home to some of the most ingenious people from Alex Mueller- the Nobel Prize winner in Physics for his discovery of high-temperature superconductivity in a new class of materials- to François Louis Callier-- the pioneer of Swiss chocolate making who opened the first Swiss chocolate factory in 1819. In addition, the inventor of cellophane in 1908 was Switzerland's Jacques E. Brandenberger, as well as George de Mestral the inventor of Velcro are further examples of the numerous Swiss inventors searing the nation a reputation as a country with a persuasive pioneering spirit and a history of creativity and innovation (Swiss-American Chamber of Commerce and Boston Consulting Group, 2008).

The strong pioneering spirit of creativeness and innovation continues to be alive and well in Switzerland today. To illustrate, Swiss people are today developing some of the most creative and sustainable projects in the world. The world's largest solar boat - *The Tûranor* - was designed by the Swiss engineer Raphaël Domjan, who is set to further develop renewable technology for tomorrow. *Solar Impulse*, developed by Bertrand Piccard, the first solar powered airplane, is another Swiss invention. This remarkable aviation project may one day revolutionize air transport as we know it by demonstrating that solar powered airplane flight is possible both day and night. Another example of innovative technology developed in Switzerland is the *Gravitation Water Vortex Plant* project developed in the canton of Aargau. The water vortex is micro hydro power plant which is capable of producing energy through a gravitation process that is low cost and produces environmental benefits for aquatic plants, microbes and fish it co-exists with. Such examples provide clear evidence that Swiss scientists, architects and engineers are focused on green technology that may play an important role in bringing solutions to world's climate and energy problems.

The open environment in Switzerland, we contend, fosters a spirit of creativeness and inventiveness which in turn has positioned the country as a world leader in innovation. This climate of innovation is supported by strategic governmental policies that combined with the institutional financial support, intellectual property protection, and the support from a number of significant partners such as the industry, educational sector, and politicians, has made the Swiss economy a success.

Innovation is regarded as an essential factor in the Swiss economy, improving productivity and contributing to sustainable economic growth (Guellec, 2006). These advances are the result of a well-coordinated national policy that has provided the strategic framework on a long-term basis. Policies have been tailored to create an environment that fosters innovation and productivity, supporting the creation of new, innovative and marketable products, encouraging enterprise development, and providing high educational training to support them. Swiss policy makers envision that through these efforts, they will attract international investment that will generate addition return on investment for the country in terms of job creation and wealth.

> "In Switzerland today, the wealth generators are mostly multinational companies in highly innovative industries" (Swiss-American Chamber of Commerce and Boston Consulting Group, 2008: 18).

In conclusion, the Swiss model of innovation depicts three key dimensions that have been the foundation for its strength in creativeness and inventiveness. They are:

a. **Creating a friendly environment for innovation.** Fashioning good conditions for innovation and creativity requires the implementation of policies that support and protect innovation and creativity. In Switzerland, the main elements that have contributed to the creation of environment supportive of innovation are the implementation of policies that protect intellectual property, investment in R&D, financial incentives and support for innovation, and a dynamic promotional framework for innovation.

b. **Fostering innovation.** The Swiss educational system has been instrumental to government policies for fostering innovation. Swiss policy makers recognise that investment in education; research and technology are the main drivers of Switzerland's competitive advantages (Federal Department of Foreign Affairs, 2012b). Innovation is fostered by the financial support from federal, cantonal and private funds made available to selected research programs and projects. Switzerland is home to best universities and research institutes in the world and produces very highly qualified labour force, maintaining the country's cutting edge research and technology.

c. **Staying competitive.** Competitiveness in the present global economy does not only depend on high productivity and fostering innovation through intellectual property protection and financial support towards research and technology, it depends on moving up to the value chain. Staying competitive implies promoting effectively those competitive advantages and building cutting edge research and technology in key industrial sectors. In Switzerland, the promotion of scientific research and innovation has been perceived by Swiss policy-makers as the means to up grade the labour force. Switzerland wants to ensure its leadership in cutting edge scientific research, particularly in the areas of chemistry, pharmaceutics, electronics and metal industries (Federal Department of Foreign Affairs, 2012b).

Creating and promoting innovation has been central to developing competitive advantages in Switzerland. The model of innovation also involves a promotional framework strategy that makes sure innovation and technology are converted into marketable good or service. Switzerland has also developed an attractive and friendly environment for foreign investment; one of the most important competitive advantages is its highly trained labour force that very few nations could offer. Switzerland governmental policies have been tailored to benefit from the country's competitive advantage; creating a culture and environment that fosters, support and protect innovation and entrepreneurship, and promoting Switzerland as a market place for foreign investment.

Concluding Remarks

The role that innovation plays is increasingly being recognized among the world's most developed countries as a means to create competitive sustainable economies. Among those countries that have made significant gains competitive advantage over the last two decades, the focus on innovation is clearly reflected in policy strategies. Switzerland is one of those countries, and has been acknowledged for its policy strategies and policy dynamics that have created of this small country one of the most competitive and innovative countries in the world. Switzerland has also created a stable and prosperous economy, and has weathered the current financial downturn and has remained strong. Moreover, Switzerland perceives the present financial crisis as an opportunity to for further innovation (Bilan Magazine, 2012).

Although Switzerland has a long-standing heritage of innovation and creativity, the establishment of a competitive and innovative market had required efforts in many areas. For innovation to be an element of competitiveness and an instrument of economic growth, the implementation of a well-coordinated long-term plan needs to be put in place. The effectiveness of the Swiss model is based on a well-coordinated framework and policies based on long-term development goals. These policies designed to foster and support innovation and competitiveness must be aligned reconciled with the interests of its key stakeholders in industry, academia and the political sector; their support and participation in the process has been vital to it achieving successful results.

Switzerland is determined to maintain its leadership in innovation and technology on the world's stage. Those that subscribe to this model of innovation must remain focused on moving-up to the value chain. Competition is dynamic and rests on innovation and the pursuit for strategic differences (Porter, 2002). To remain competitive, Swiss policies and strategies must continue to invest in new key scientific and technical areas that it believes it can be competitive. The number of projects carried out currently in the area of renewable energy, chemistry, and bio medical sciences indicates that Switzerland is determined to become a leader in these scientific fields, along with green technology bringing solutions to global climate and energy problems.

References

Baumol, W. J. (2004), "Education for Innovation: Entrepreneurial Breakthroughs vs. Corporate Incremental Improvements", NBER Working Papers 10578, April 30th, 2004.

Bilan Magazine (2012), "La Crise est Synonyme de Boom de la Innovation", Vol. 11, June 6th, 2012, p. 24.

Carlsson, B. (2006), "Internationalisation of Innovation Systems: a survey of the literature", *Research Policy,* Vol. 35, pp.56-67.

Federal Department of Foreign Affairs (FDFA) (2012a), "Economy", available at: http://www.eda.admin.ch/eda (accessed 15 May 2012).

—. (FDFA) (2012b), "Innovation in Switzerland", available at: http://www.eda.admin.ch/eda/en/home/doc/infoch/checin.html#ContentPar_0003 (accessed 23 May 2012).

Fransman, M. (1999), *Is National Technology Policy Obsolete in a Globalized World?,* Oxford University Press: Oxford and New York.

Furman, J., Porter, M., and Stern, S, (2002), "The Determinants of the national Innovative Capacity", *Research Policy*, Vol. 32, Issue 6, pp. 899-933.

Garelli, S. (2002), "The Competitiveness of Nations in a Global Knowledge-Based Economy", International Institute for Management Development (IMD), available at:
http://www02.imd.ch/wcy/fundamentals/, (accessed 03 May 2012).

Greenhalgh, C. and Rogers, M., (2006), "The Value of Innovation: the interaction of competition R&D and IP", *Research Policy* Vol. 35, pp. 562-580.

Guellec, D., (2006), "Productivity and Innovation in Switzerland: an international perspective", Paper prepared for the OECD Workshop on Productivity, Bern, 16-18 October 2012.

Hu, M. and Mathews, J.A. (2005), "National innovative capacity in East Asia", *Research Policy* Vol. 34, pp. 1322–1349.

INSEAD, (2011), "The Global Innovation Index Report 2011: Accelerating Growth and Development", Fontainebleau, France 2011.

Lall, S. (2005), "Linking FDI and Technology Development for Capacity Building and Strategic Competitiveness", *Transnational Corporations,* Vol.11, pp. 39-88.

Organization of Economic Cooperation and Development (OECD), (2008), "Systematic Innovation in the Swiss VET System: Country Case Study Report", available at: http://www.oecd.org/dataoecd/39/14/42397664.pdf (accessed 10 May 2012).

Pavit, K. (1991), "What Makes Research Economically Useful?", *Research Policy* Vol. 20, pp. 109-119.

Porter, M. (2002), "How Government Matters: Influences on Prosperity, Competition, and Company Strategy", Harvard Business School, All-Academy Session, Academy of Management, Washington, DC, August 6, 2001.

State Secretariat for Education and Research (SER) (2007), "Education, research and Innovation 2008-2011: the Federal Council proposed guidelines, goals ad funding", Bern 2007.

Swiss Federal Institute of Intellectual Property (IIP) (2012a), "The Institute", available at: https://www.ige.ch/en/about-us.html, (accessed 25 May 25 2012).

—. (2012b), "Einstein at the Patent Office", available at: https://www.ige.ch/index.php?id=289&L=3, (accessed 26 May 2012).

Swiss-American Chamber of Commerce & Boston Consulting Group (SACC & BCG) (2008), "Creative Switzerland? Fostering an Innovative Powerhouse", Joint Study of the Swiss-American Chamber of Commerce & Boston Consulting Group, Zurich December 2008.

World Bank (2012a), "Data by Countries and Economies: Switzerland", available at: http://data.worldbank.org/country, (accessed 15 May 2012).

—. (2012b), "Golden Growth: Restoring the Lustre of the European Economic Model", International Bank for Reconstruction and Development 2012: Washington D.C.

World Economic Forum (2010), "The Global Competitiveness Index 2010–2011: Looking Beyond the Global Economic Crisis", Geneva, Switzerland 2010, available at: http://www.weforum.org/reports/, (accessed 10April 2012).

—. (2011), "The Global Competitiveness Report 2011-2012", Geneva, Switzerland 2011, available at: http://www.weforum.org/reports/, (accessed 02 March 2012).

World Intellectual Property Organisation (WIPO) (2011), Patent applications by patent office and country of origin (1995-2010), Statistics Database, available at: http://www.wipo.int/ipstats/en/statistics/patents/ (accessed 10 May 2012).

Zhang, K. H., 2001. "Does Foreign Direct Investment Promote Economic Growth? Evidence from East Asia and Latin America" *Contemporary Economic Policy,* April 2001, Vol. 19, Iss. 2, pp. 175-185.

CHAPTER TEN

THE NATURE OF COMPANY IMAGE MANAGEMENT AND THE USE OF BRAND PERSONALITY IN THE SOCIAL NETWORK ENVIRONMENT: SHIFTS TOWARD CONSUMER CONTROL

KIP BECKER AND HELENA NOBRE

Social Networks as Destabilizers of Company Influence

Recognition of the importance of brand and company image, how that image is established as well as social network (SN) factor that might influence the bond is of increasing importance. The pervasive and "always on" nature of Social networks (SNs) has contributed to their phenomenal communications power which has destroyed industries, enabled revolutions and altered the balance of power between consumers and firms. This media takes many forms to include text, images, audio and video and includes forums, message boards, photo sharing, podcasts RSS (really simple syndication), search engine marketing, video sharing, Wikis, social networks, professional networks and micro-blogging sites. These networks are revolutionizing companies and devastating industries replacing, for example, traditional Newspapers as well as TV and radio news programs. Shirky (2009) writes about the earthquake that rocked the Sichuan province in China on May 12, 2008. With 70,000 deaths; 350,000 wounded and 5 Million left homeless. While a major international news story, the first reports came not from traditional news media but from Sichuan residents who sent messages on QQ, China's largest social network, and on Twitter, the world's most popular micro-blogging service (Shirky, 2009). He notes that initial reports were being transmitted while the ground was still shaking and long before the any of the more traditional news media carried the story. It is certainly not by conscience that when the tsunami struck Japan in 2011 that social media not only produced the first videos carrying the story first, throughout the world, but rapidly became the primary means of locating victims, linking separated families and a significant source of fund raising.

While the internet and social networks have become an important means of interpersonal communications they have also, because of the ability to rapidly connect consumers, developed into a major threat. This is highlighted by such recent events the McDonald's Twitter ad campaign (Bradshaw, 2012) which backfired causing consumers to express anger through the social media site and Verizon wireless dropping plans (Bensinger, 2012) to charge a fee for customers paying their bill online. Verizon withdrew the payment policy after social networks called on individuals to drop Verizon service through a petition (change.org) which quickly massed 100,000 social network signatures (change.org). The damage could have been much worse however Verizon recognized, that in their highly competitive industry, it was essential to act swiftly to address the public relations damage to their brand image from the SN threat. No company is immune from brand damage as was clearly demonstrated by hackers breaching Verisign's computer system in 2012, and stealing high level passwords that allowed entrance into the revered Secure Electronic Transaction (SET) security system. The rapid damage to Verisign's reputation from communications that swiftly traveled throughout the social networks of computer professions cannot be over stated.

Each of these different occurrences resulted in a significant impact on the company's brand image and serves as a reminder that the nature of a consumer relationship, and how it is developed or maintained, can directly affect whether it will withstand long or short term disruptions. Prior to social networks word of mouth complaints were quickly isolated leaving the dissatisfied individual a lone voice. With the aid of viral networks these single voices now have the ability to quickly garner the attention of millions making it painfully clear that firms must understand the social network environment and be prepared to take action when brand or company image is threatened.

Each such event serves as a vivid reminder that what may appear to be strong connections between consumers and a company or product brands may in reality be a fragile relationship. In the highly interconnected environment it is highly likely that how the relationship is developed, or maintained, can directly affect whether it will withstand social network disruptions. Decisions whether to maintain a brand relationship repurchase or switch brands can often be more emotional/behavioral than based on facts (Sheth and Parvatiyar, 2002). As such, it is often the potential damage to loyal consumer-brand relationship bonds, not the crises themselves that can have the most severe consequences for a firm. The case of PB oil disaster provides an excellent example of how the mishandling of an environmental crisis escalated into a long term degradation of the company (brand) name. In many cases what differentiates those firms that thrive following a crisis, from those that do not, is the type of relationship bond that had been developed, how it was maintained over time, the type loyal consumer-brand bond that existed at the time of the event and the manner in which the firm responded to the crisis.

One environmental threat to the equilibrium of image not being adequately addressed by firms relates to the new internet social networks which include such platforms as Facebook, twitter, blogs as well as online reviews and rating sites. It is clear that in less than a decade advanced technologies have redefined social interaction. Previously complaints spread by a consumer's word of mouth (WOM) activities were conveniently isolated to a few close contacts making these lone singular voices fairly ineffective. With the aid of viral networks, however, these voices now have the ability to quickly garner the attention of millions. Social media has not only ended the age of one-way messaging but also put extreme pressure on businesses to engage constituents in unprecedented ways. One thing is clear. The internet has changed the balance of power in the consumer's favor and this change has come about quickly. Many firms, or in some cases whole industries, that have not embraced the new shifts in power of communications have felt the consequences. Fogel and Nehmad (2009) found that the continual monitoring of today's highly interactive social network environment now must be added to the list of threats to a firm's image. Managing the social network environment is essential to staying relevant and building a loyal fan base. Those firms that have designed systems to react to social media threats have found that often their brand image and consumer relationships have strengthened.

Taco Bell restaurants, for example, acted quickly through an internet and YouTube campaign to maintain image by addressing concerns that were raised when a group in 2011 requested the American Food and Drug Administration to look into beef percentage in the company's products. In another example the president of Domino's Pizza responded personally when a YouTube video was posted showing an employee putting Pizza in his nose and then serving it. Acting boldly the president, within days, posted his personal YouTube response noting video was a hoax but of grave concern to the firm. He not only cited actions the firm had taken but ended by offering an apology to the loyal employees of Domino's and the firm's faithful consumers who had been deceived. It was clear that these companies recognized the possible damage to their loyal consumer base designing internet media campaigns to preserve the relationship. Broadly the fears of companies, resulting from sufficient actual incidences over the past few years and the often disorganized responses to them, have resulted in the increased awareness of corporate social network business continuity programs designed to mitigate threats to the brand and company image. Previously the major responsibility of business continuity programs was to assure that a firm could operate after facing supply chains disruptions, damaged manufacturing facilities or disturbances in personnel.

The idea that social interaction can be a powerful marketing force is not new. While firms have been striving to understand how to best use influencers of social networks to their marketing advantage it is important to additionally appreciate that these same powerful systems can turn against a firm and possess the ability to damage productivity and reputation. These sources of instant communication have made it possible, due to widespread and low cost information, for rapid disruptions to a firm's image to occur for legitimate or less than legitimate reasons. Such disruptions can put long term pressures on the company-consumer relationship by altering consumer perceptions of the brand and/or the company. Firms that appreciate this new force can often avoid, or lessen, the impact of potential social network damage. It is essential that firms continually monitor, and when appropriate respond to, social media sites to attempt to increase the effect of positive and decrease the effects of negative comments. Appreciating the dynamics of the brand personality, and how those dimensions support a brand relationship, is essential when considering the firm's reaction options to a word of mouth social network threat.

As the popularity of the social online community increases the need for companies to take ever increasing cautionary measures in protecting reputations and brands becomes essential. Jones et al., (2009) have even pointed to an expanding active online consumer defining new roles such as "consumer watchdog, investigative journalist, and opinion influencer".

According to Davis and Moy (2007) the internet has created a new wave of intensely engaged "professional consumers" that they term "prosumers". These active prosumers create news and can rapidly affect a firm's image. Through these new prosumers an incidence of bad service can be echoed around social networks reaching thousands of consumers within minutes. Consider the effect that David Carroll's "United breaks guitars" YouTube video had on United Airlines reputation in 2010. David's band was departing on a United Airlines flight when a person behind him noted that the ground baggage crew was throwing guitars while loading. Upon arrival David found his guitar to be broken and requested assistance. United, following the "old rules" of isolation and non-response was painfully introduced to the need to focus on the "new rules" of communication and respect. Posting a very entertaining and pointed music video YouTube video called "United Breaks Guitars" his band became an overnight success. While costing a mere $150 to produce David Carroll gained national reputation when his musical satire was noted on national news, late night talk shows and ultimately viewed by over 100 million. United Airline's costly and embarrassing lesson could have been avoided if the company had been quick to recognize the intensifying social network word of mouth, swelling number of video viewings, and the escalating damage the video was causing.

Interconnected Consumers are the New Corporate Communications Model

The addition of "new media" into the traditional perspective has significantly altered marketing's focus and strategy. As noted by Deighton and Kornfeld (2009) the flow of information about a brand has become multidirectional, interconnected, and difficult to predict. They state that marketers have lost control over their brands and now participate in a ''conversation'' about the brand. While social networks enable companies to talk to their customers, in a nontraditional sense it, perhaps more importantly they enable customers to talk directly to one another. "The control, timing, and frequency of the social media-based conversations that are occurring between consumers are outside managers' direct influence. Hennig-Thurau et al., (2010) provide a model of consumer interaction that depicted the relationship between company brand, the consumer's attitude toward the brand/company and the influence of consumer through social media. The model depicts the many factors of the new media that serve to place much of the aspects of the consumer – company relationships beyond the company's control

Firms, for a considerable length of time, have recognized the importance of the new social media communication networks. Consider that in 2008, sixty-one percent of business stated that the emergence of blogs and social media had changed the way their organizations (or their client organizations) communicated. Only a year later that number had risen to seventy-six percent (Wright and Hinson, 2009).

Network social groups obtain their power much in the same manner that Inter-connected networks do through the value of each additional member to that network. Robert Metcalf's law, designed to illustrate how computer networks on the internet derived their value on LANS and WANS is equally valuable in helping to illustrate how social network derive theirs. The law states that the "value" or "power" of a network increases in proportion to the square of the number of nodes on the network (Hendler and Golbeck, 2007). This means that as the number of people in a network increases the value of the content they share grows exponentially. For example, if there are 10 people in a social net the power of the structure is 10^2 or 100. If the number is, however, increased by simply one member the power now becomes 11^2 or 121 explaining why viral networks, which can quickly amass thousands of members/viewers, can be so dangerous.

A. Jolly (2001) refers to a company's choice of communication as either "dialogue" or "monologue." Companies traditionally have had a one way communication monologue channel to their consumers, however, these one way communications directed toward consumers are becoming increasingly ineffective. Company Web postings promoting the firm or products as well as paid internet advertisement cannot by itself protect image since it is generally viewed externally as self-serving propaganda. Companies must move to establish interactive dialogue communications with the many social platforms consumers use to exchange ideas, cooperate and even to seek advice from consumers in what is considered as "social casting" (Jones, 2009). Consumers' ability to communicate directly with one another limits the amount of control companies have over the content and dissemination of information. C. Vollmer and G. Precourt (2008) underscore this in their book, *Always On*. They note, in the era of social media "consumers are in control; they have greater access to information and greater command over media consumption than ever before" (p5). Companies must have well thought online social network strategies that call for implicit collaboration between a company and the social network environment in order to shape and protect their image.

Argenti's (2005) recommendation that companies prepare for potential problems; Plan company responses; Analyze constituencies and provide as much certainty as possible are sound advice for social networks as well as it is clear that small firms as well as large ones are increasingly aware of the power of social media and some, to varying degrees of sophistication, are incorporating these tools in their communications portfolios. One aspect of "certainty" would be the understanding of the most important constructs supporting a brand reputation and how those constructs can be used to overcome threats coming from social network communications.

Kozinets et al., (2010) in a historical perspective of word of mouth (WOM) research offers a series of models to explain how WOM, and the company reactions to it, have changed over time. He calls attention to Ryan and Gross's (1946) statement six decades ago that, "conversations among buyers were more important than marketing communications in influencing adoption" (p.71) as one of the first articles addressing consumer interaction. One might argue that in spite of this early observation companies have done little to alter their communications patterns with consumers.

Referring to this stage as The Organic Interconsumer Influence Model Kozinets et al., (2010) recognizes the attempts of one consumer to influence another's attitude toward a product or service without direct prompting, influence, or measurement by marketers (Figure 1).

According to R. V. Kozinets et al., (2010) this stage was followed by the Linear Marketer Influence Model. With this model we see the first organizational attempt to recognize the active role of the consumer and attempts to influence consumer WOM. It was during this stage that companies recognized the concept of the opinion leader and how they could be used to sway consumer preferences (Figure 2).

Figure 1. The organic interconsumer influence model

Source: Kozinets et al., (2010)

Figure 2. The linear marketer relationship influence model

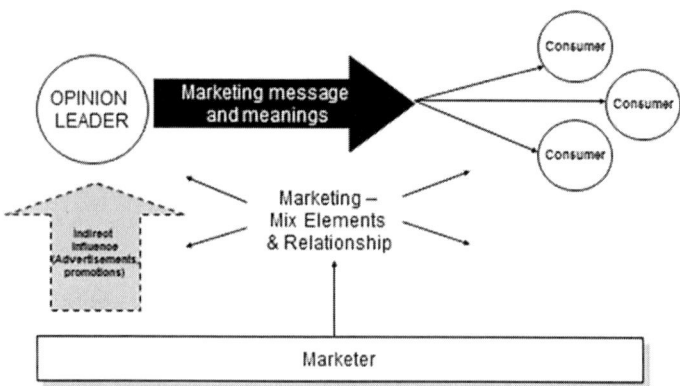

Source: Kozinets et al., (2010)

Building on these prior models the next developmental stage became the Network Coproduction Model (figure 3) where marketers become directly involved in focused "one to one seeding and communication programs" (Kozinets et al., 2010, p. 72). It is in this stage that managers become involved in data analysis from information obtained about interconnected WOM consumer.

Figure 3. Network coproduction model

The Network Coproduction Model

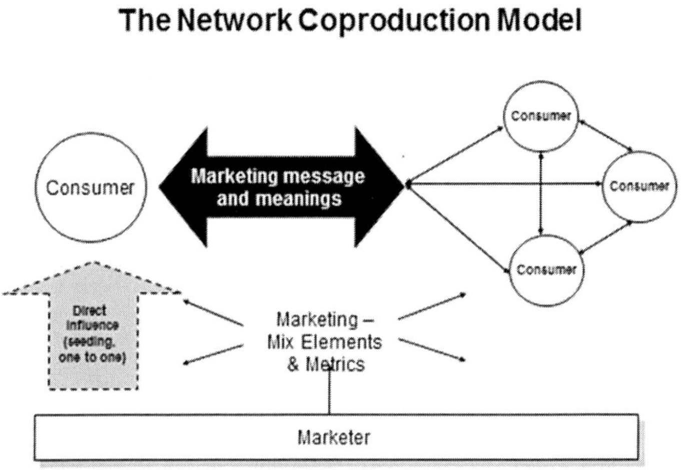

Source: Kozinets et al., (2010)

Becker et al., (2013) proposes a new model (Figure 4), the Consumer Initiated Integrity and Reputation Management Model, that expands the concepts of R. V. Kozinets et al., (2010) to incorporate the new reality that consumers have assumed their own power base which operates external to company influence. While Kozinets et al., recognizes the importance of monitoring the social environment it is felt that a model of company/brand reputation management now needs to reflect the continual interplay and accumulation of many consumer networks as a dynamic ongoing and interconnected process.

Figure 4. Becker Consumer Initiated Integrity and Reputation Management Model

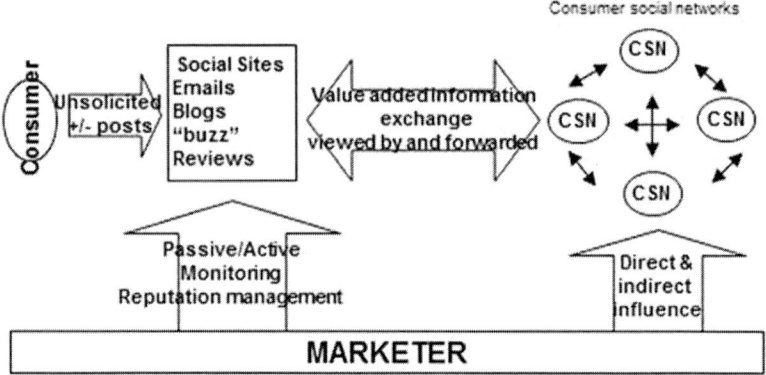

Source: Becker et al., (2013)

In the Consumer Initiated Integrity and Reputation Management Model the marketer recognizes the geometric growth and power of Web Word of Mouth (WWOM) and continually monitors Internet postings while cautiously attempting to influence/respond to them. In response to the recognition that social network members can significantly influence the value (positively or negatively) of a company brand or image there have been a number of new products designed to passively monitor social sites and inform users of potential dangers. These software products are similar to the "old" press clipping firms that monitored news and popular magazine articles. The consumer initiated integrity and reputation management model is more comprehensive in nature, and expands the reputation management list of Argenti (2005) by including social media monitoring and response. The new list includes:

- Plan reputation management strategies to be able to allow the right respond to risks in an immediate manner
- Develop a crisis management process
- Understand all threat environments
- Understand what brand personality attributes support the consumer brand relationship
- Apply new technology to monitor social media
- Set priorities for reputation risks
- Plan scripts and/or policies for response including a broad representation of company departments (management, legal, marketing) as preclearance allows rapid responses

- Assure management understands the disruptive potential of Social Networks
- Analyzing constituencies to include "opinion leaders", " influencers" and "prosumers"
- Provide as much certainty as possible to how the firm will respond and who will be responding

The Interaction between the Social Network Relationship, Brand Personality Dimensions and Reputation Management

Recognition of the importance of brand relationships, how they are established and factors that might influence the bond during situations of brand disruption, to include catastrophic events and product recalls are of increasing importance. Fournier and Lee (1995) point to the need to fashion a flexible brand relationship that allows individuals to adopt new roles as lives, ages and values change. Nobre et al., (2010) suggest that while needing to be adaptable to life and company changes, for the consumer brand relationship to be maintained, the company must be vigilant to assure that both the consumer's personality and the brand's personality remain in equilibrium over during specific instances of brand disruption and longer time frames.

The ever-changing competition in the information age pushes companies to find more creative and flexible means to reach out to and retain their customers as well as protect their brand image. "With focus on brand personalities, one can articulate an understanding of how the brand relationship role is constructed and begin to envision ways in which the brand, acting as an enlivened partner in social network relationships, contributes to the initiation, maintenance or destruction of loyal consumer-brand relationship bonds" (Fournier, 1998: 345). How the bonds are established and maintained can ultimately determine the degree of success that a firm will have when attempting to mitigate the potentially damaging effects of negative social network campaigns.

Outcomes of the work of Aaker et al., (2004) suggest that brand personality significantly influences relationship strength and can help in predicting the strength of consumer-brand relationships. They tested the effects of two contrasting brand personalities, sincerity and excitement as possibility being the two most important in a Personality Model involving five behavioral factors (sincerity, excitement, competence, sophistication, and ruggedness. Of importance in the social network context is that Aaker et al., (2004), has concluded that: (1) sincere brands tend to facilitate strong and stable relationships based on trust but are more susceptible to the transgression effects which may be irreversible. They also noted that (2) the brands of excitement tended to nurture less stable relationships but that customers are more benevolent with their transgression acts and the reparation of problems may actually serve to reinforce the relationship. From these observations we conclude that two types of relationships that would relate to social network brand/image are identified: (1) Intimacy-Loyalty representing "close, increasingly intimate, long-term oriented friendships" characterized with adjectives such as: caring, respectful, honest, trusting, and support and (2) Passion characterized by "initially enthused, but subsequently declining flings." And defined through adjectives such as: exciting, fun, and independent.

From the accumulated prior research findings Nobre et al., (2010) identified two personality dimensions (sincerity and excitement) of the consumer brand relationship they considered as being potentially highly significant to the attributes of Intimacy-Loyalty and Passion. The importance of the identification of what brand attributes, and how they help in defining brand relationship bonds useful in developing, strengthening or maintaining consumer – product/firm relationships during periods of brand stress is clear. Further study (Nobre and Becker, 2012) indicated that excitement and passion accounted for the greatest contribution to the relationship with the passion relationship. In addition, the dimension of Intimacy-Loyalty of Consumer-Brand Relationship as the dependent variable the dimensions of the Brand of Excitement, Sincerity, Sophistication, Peacefulness that Sincerity, accounted for the greatest contribution to the relationship with the Intimacy-Loyalty relationship followed by Sophistication (figure 6).

In terms of relating brand characteristics to brand maintenance, the brand personality characteristics that are most relevant to positioning a brand and maintaining its value through periods of disruption appear to be intimacy/loyalty and passion and those managers can use this understanding to design strategies directed at developing and maintaining brand reputation.

Figure 6. The relationship of intimacy/loyalty and passion to the brand relationship

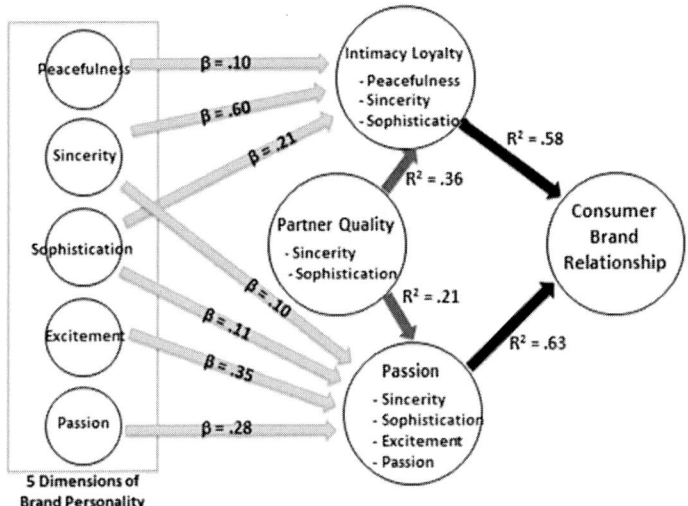

Source: Nobre and Becker (2012)

Broadly the fears of companies, resulting from numerous actual incidences over the past few years and the often disorganized responses to them, have resulted in an increased awareness of the need for social network strategies designed to mitigate threats to brand and company image. Of importance in determining how best to respond to SN threats is an understanding of the company or brand personality characteristics to which the consumer most identifies. Understanding the specific constructs and the unique personality bond in the consumer relationship can assist in determining how best to respond to social network threats. A brand based on intimacy / loyalty would need a different type of company threat response then one in which passion was the underlying consumer bond. This would appear central as a company would most likely not respond to threats toward brands of passion in the same manner that they would toward brand relationships build on intimacy/ Loyalty.

Companies are Failing to Capitalize on the Power of Social Networks

This need to influence social networks, to the degree possible, is highlighted within *The Rising CCO III*, an annual survey conducted by global executive search firm Spencer Stuart and global public relations firm Weber Shandwick (Spencer and Shandwick, 2010). The survey found that thirty-four percent of global chief corporate communications officers report that their companies experienced a social-media based reputation threat during the previous year. That firms have yet to incorporate social networks into their monitoring or business continuity plans is clear as the same report noted that approximately thirty-three percent of the companies stated that they were not prepared for managing social network reputational threats. This low figure raises questions. Without a defined strategy of how to respond and an appreciation of the characteristics of the brand bond between product/company, firms remain vulnerable to attacks operating primarily in a defensive manner.

The ease with which social networks seem to be dismissed as significant business threats in spite of the clear examples is troublesome. The reason for this is ambiguous. One explanation often offered is that members of Facebook's and Twitter are not considered to not be of high importance to company business by managers who, because of their age, are out of touch with the dynamic force and power base of social networks. Another consideration is there may be a general lack of appreciation that the 4P's of marketing (price, place, promotion and product) which were the pillars of the "old" marketing are being replaced by an awareness that companies no longer control the marketplace environment and consumers are communicating among each other about products and services on a 24/7 basis.

While there appears to be only limited SN interactions by firms, it is clear that large, as well as small firms, are increasingly becoming aware of the power of social media and a few, to varying degrees of sophistication, are incorporating SN strategies in their communications portfolios. Having a web site or social media presence is one thing, it is quite another to use resources in an engaged efficient manner. Solely having a profile will not in itself establish a consumer relationship or trust as firms need to be engaged with those sites through continual monitoring and timely responses as well as actively seeking ways to develop consumer trust and loyalty. In short, a social network operations framework must be part of an overall communications strategy, continually monitored and include:

- Who monitors and controls the company social media sites?
- Who is responsible for observing what people are saying on the Internet (chats, ratings and social networks)?
- How posts noted and what are the guidelines for response?
- What is in place to monitor and act to influence reputation externally?
- What kind of information is collected and how/to whom is it forwarded for consideration?
- Who will monitor and control the company social media websites?

One would assume that large companies, by virtue of their resources, would be ahead of curve compared to smaller ones. A recent study (McCann, 2010) conducted by communications firm Burson-Marsteller noted "65% of the largest global companies have Twitter accounts, 54% had Facebook fan pages, and 50% had YouTube video channels" The study also noted that while financially significant for large firms a social media campaign can be "less than 1% of their overall marketing budget.

Recent research reviewing small, medium and large firms on two world stock world stock markets it was determined that while many companies had social media sites (Facebook and Twitter) the number of firms actually monitoring activities on those sites remained small (Becker et al., 2011). In the studies only 25% (36 out of 144) firms from all categories had social media sites while 75% (108 out of 144) firms did not have social media sites. Company size was in direct proportion to site ownership as large companies owned the most, medium companies owned less than those of larger ones, and small companies owned the least.

In their research the size of the firm was related to the frequency of response as large firms had the most responses, followed by medium with small the fewest. While most social network sites surprisingly did not allow for interaction, the majority of Facebook pages were well organized with news of products and services posted regularly. Without interaction, however, one could question if these sites are not really "social media" sites but extensions of the firms static webpages. Twitter's less organized and more informal (and less expensive) display appeared to make a more efficient two-way communications platform for firms of all sizes than Facebook.

How long a firm takes to a social media site posting is quite important as the longer a negative comment(s) is in the SN environment and not responded to the more viral it may become. The studies noted (Becker et al., 2013; Becker et al., 2011) reported that for firms in the United States (NYSE) and Europe (FTSE) the average time to reply for the large firms was 7.14 hours while the small firms replied in 5.35 hours. It is interesting that when small firms responded they did so more quickly than large firms. Companies tended to respond faster on their twitter pages than they did on their Facebook pages. The reason could be that twitter offers a more instant-message like environment that encourages immediate communication. Contrary to expectations the smaller the size, the faster the firm responded as the small companies were the quickest, the medium ones took longer, and the largest companies were the slowest. When small firms did respond they tended to use Twitter, not Facebook, and responded quicker than large firms.

Implications for Management

Generally there appears to be a lack of a strategic framework for thinking about SN communities as most firms were not monitoring, engaged, integrating or leveraging social media adequately. An unexpected finding of several studies was the number of non-monitored social networks and that, regardless of category, few firms were actively involved with their own social media to the extent one would expect (Becker et al., 2013). The overall poor response rate is a worrisome finding. It tends to indicate that while the business world is aware of the power that social networks can yield companies of all sizes, however, remain naïve as to how to establish truly interactive personal relationships. This is interesting given the increasing importance of social networks in developing and maintaining a reputation and image.

The general lack of appreciation of the increasing importance of social networks has been previously noted. Murphy (2006) found an overall lack of either presence or response to sites pointing out that some traditional marketers believe that they have nothing to gain from customer empowerment and that blogging only results in brand bashing. Singh et al., (2008) provided some insight into why many firms have taken a rather passive approach to social networks stating that ,"Marketers have been accustomed to telling the customer the message they want the customer to hear, rather than the message the customer truly cares about" (p. 282).

Reinforcing the importance of the consumer as a partner in the relationship, managers need to develop a comprehensive understanding of how the personalities of their consumer relate to partner quality and the consumer brand relationship. In his study of affective commitment as "rooted in shared values, identification and attachment" and continuance commitment as binding consumers to brands as a result of a difficulty "in getting out of a relationship or perceiving few alternatives outside the relationship" (Fullerton, 2005: 99). In consideration one should note the importance in the difference in Intimacy- Loyalty and Passion driven relationships as they relate to maintaining brand/image loyalty in the social network environment. Consistent with Fullerton' findings, the authors found that Intimacy – Loyalty bonds served to maintain the relationship through developed partner quality while Passion bonds were to a much lesser extent associated with relationship strength.

One might argue that in an intimacy-loyalty brand relationship the brand adds value to the consumer through partner quality in a manner similar to the way that loyalty adds value to the personal relationship (Nobre et al., 2010). It provides a type of psychological glue that secures the bond between partners. When difficulties arise it is this glue that serves to secure relationships, whether personal or brand. When responding to social network threats it is wise to recognize the type of relationship that the consumer has with the brand/company in order to organize responses in a meaningful a manner as possible. It is worth noting that Intimacy-Loyalty bonds have a higher association with relationship strength than Passion bonds and that the consumer-brand relationship was shown to be an important predictor of relationship strength. Brand relationships of intimacy-loyalty seemed to influence the strength of the ties consumers establish with brands in an indirect way through the inferences they make about the quality of the brand as a partner. As such, it would seem that Passion bonds would create a heightened sense of excitement and "in the minute" product support. Passion relationships, however, tend to be favorably evaluated by consumers, and customers tend to be more excited with those brands. If, however, a disruption in that passion were to occur (due for example to product disappointment or a new passion for another brand) repurchase could be questionable. Under Intimacy –Loyalty, however, the nature of the bond could be considered more mature/stable and thus would be more stable under situational adverse brand conditions to a better extent than relationships which have focused on passion.

How consumers differ in perceiving their relationship with brands is often a result of the brand's "personal" characteristics (Reddy et al., 1994). More recently, it has been noted that consumers differ not only in how they perceive but also in how they relate to brands (Fournier, 1998). Sociologists remind us that business dealings are transacted within the broader realm of personal relations and structures or imbedded within the networks of such relationships (Granovetter, 1985), As such, a broader understanding of the bond that develops between customers and brands (Fournier and Yao, 1996) may provide a better appreciation of how of how to address reputation and consumer interaction management in the social network environment.

What is important to recognize is that how a firm organizes the brand relationship prior to disruptive events will directly relate to how that brand image is positioned to withstand situational disruptions. It is interesting to note that in spite of Toyota's severe braking problem in 2009/2010, resulting in deaths, consumers tended to remain loyal repeat the purchase. This was certainly a result of Toyota's prior efforts to establish a dedicated consumer relationship based on a higher sense of a loyal (intimacy/loyalty brand relationship) bonding between consumers and the firm. Of importance to management is the understanding that how a firm organizes the brand relationship prior to disruptive events will directly relate to how that brand image is positioned to withstand situational disruptions. Factors such as passion, which could have immediate sales consequences, may not be able to sustain consumers' loyalty should brand disruptions occur in the manner that products positioned around aspects of brand intimacy and loyalty might. It is additionally interesting to note that while a brand relationship, such as passion, can stimulate sales a relationship such as Intimacy - Loyalty can serve to directly support on ongoing business continuity during times of firm or brand image uncertainty.

References

Aaker, J., Fournier, S. and Brasel, S.A. (2004), "When Good Brands Do Bad", *Journal of Consumer Research*, Vol 31, June, pp. 1-16.

Argenti, P.A. (2005), "The Challenge of Protecting Reputation," available at: http://www.tuck.dartmouth.edu/exec/pdf/FT_protecting_reputation.pdf (accessed 10 March 2012).

Becker, K., Kanabar, V. and Nobre, H. (2011), "Company Integrity Management in the New Social Network Environment: a comparison of large and small firms on Facebook", *Advances in Global Management Development,* Vol. 20, pp. 268-273.

Becker, K., Nobre, H. and Kanabar, V. (2013), "Monitoring and Protecting company and brand reputation on social networks: When sites are not enough", *Global Business and Economics Review,* Vol. 15 Nos. 2/3, pp. 293-308.

Bensinger, G. (2012), "Verizon Wireless Abandons New Fee", *Wall Street Journal,* 1 January, B1.

Bradshaw, T. and Rappeport, A. (2012) McDonnald's Twitter Campaign Hijacked. Financial Times. (January 24, 2012) http://www.ft.com/intl/cms/s/0/6de5a21e-46b3-11e1-bc5f-00144feabdc0.html#axzz26IEx95KD (accessed 13 September, 2012).

Davis, C. and Moy C. (2007), "Coming to Terms with Business Transparency", Admap Magazine, Vol. 487, pp. 19-22.

Deighton, J. and Kornfeld, L. (2009), "Interactivity's Unanticipated Consequences for Marketers and Marketing", *Journal of International Marketing,* Vol. 23 No. 1, pp. 4-10.

Fogel, J. and Nehmad, E. (2009), "Internet Social Network Communities: Risk Taking, Trust, and Privacy Concerns", *Computers in Human Behaviour,* Vol. 25 No. 1, pp. 153-160.

Fournier, S. (1998), "Consumers and Their Brands: Developing Relationship Theory in Consumer Research", *Journal of Consumer Research,* Vol. 24 March, pp. 343-373.

Fournier, S. and Yao, J.L. (1996), "Reviving Brand Loyalty: A Reconceptualization Within the Framework of Consumer-Brand Relationships" (working paper), *Harvard Business School,* Vol. 14 No. 5, pp. 451-472.

Fournier, S. and Lee, L. (1995), "Getting Brand Communities Right", *Harvard Business Review,* Vol. 59 No. 1, pp. 105-111.

Fullerton, G. (2005), "The Impact of Brand Commitment on Loyalty to Retail Service Brands", *Canadian Journal of Administrative Sciences,* Vol. 22 No. 2, pp. 97-110.

Granovetter, M. (1985), "Economic Action and Social Structure: the Problem of Embeddedness", *American Journal of Sociology,* Vol. 91 No. 2, pp. 481-510.

Hendler, J., and Golbeck, J. (2007), "Metcalfe's Law, Web 2.0, and the Semantic Web", *Journal of Web Semantics,* Vol. 6 No. 1, pp. 14-20.

Hennig-Thurau T., Malthouse, E., Friege, C., Gensler, S., Lobschat, L., Rangaswamy, A. and Skiera, B. (2010), "The Impact of New Media on Customer Relationships", *Journal of Service Research,* Vol. 13 No. 3, pp. 311-330.

Jolly, A. (2001), *Managing Corporate Reputations*, Public Relations Consultants Association, London, UK.

Jones, B., Temperley, J. and Lima, A. (2009), "Experts Say Verizon FiOS TV is the Future of TV Service", available at: http://www.ifibercompany.com/Verizon-FiOS-TV-Future.asp, (accessed 10 March 2012).

Kozinets, R.V., de Valck, K., Wojnicki, A.C. and Wilner, S.J.S. (2010), "Networked Narratives: Understanding Word-of-Mouth Marketing in Online Communities", *Journal of Marketing*, Vol. 74 No. 2, pp. 71–89.

McCann, D. (2010), "Social Media Frenzy", *CFO*, January/February 2011 Issue. http://www3.cfo.com/article/2012/2/technology_social-media-roi (accessed 12 September 2012).

Murphy, C. (2006), "Blogging: Waste of Time or Corporate Tool?", available at: http://www.personneltoday.com/Articles/2006/03/21/34506/blogging-waste-of-time-orcorporate-tool.html, (accessed 10 March 2012).

Nobre, H.M, Becker, K. and Brito, C. (2010), "Brand Relationships: A Personality-Based Approach", *Journal of Service Science and Management*, Vol. 3 No.2, pp. 206-217.

Nobre, H. and Becker, K. (2012), "Developing Consumer Brand Relationships built to last brand stress, catastrophic Events and Negative Social Network Campaigns", *Journal for International Business and Entrepreneurship Development,* Vol. 6 No. 2, pp. 107-124.

Reddy S.K., Holak, S.L. and Bhat, S. (1994), "To Extend or Not to Extend? Success Determinants of Line Extensions", *Journal of Marketing Research*, Vol. 31 May, pp. 243–62.

Ryan, B. and Gross, C. (1943), "The Diffusion of Hybrid Seed Corn in Two Iowa Communities", *Rural Sociology*, Vol. 8 No. 1, pp. 15-24.

Sheth, J. and Parvatiyar, A. (2002), "The Relationship Between Customer Loyalty and Purchase Incidence", *Journal of Relationship Marketing,* Vol. 1 No. 1, pp. 3-36.

Shirky, C. (2009), "Clay Shirky Explains How Twitter & Facebook Have Changed Geopolitics", available at: http://www.marketingshift.com/2009/6/clay-shirky-explains-how-twitter.cfm (accessed 8 July 2012).

Singh T., Veron-Jackson, L. and Cullinane, J. (2008), (2008), "Blogging: A New Play in Your Marketing Game Plan", *Business Horizons*, Vol. 51 No. 4, pp. 281-292.

Spencer, S. and Shandwick, W. (2010), *The Rising CCO III*, available at: http://www.webershandwick.com/Default.aspx/Insights/ThoughtLeade

rship/ThoughtLeadership/2010/TheRisingCCOIIIOctober262010 (accessed 10 March 2012).

Vollmer, C. and Precourt, G. (2008), *Always on: Advertising, Marketing, and Media in an Era of Consumer Control*, McGraw-Hill, New York.

Wright, D. and Hinson, M. (2009), "An Analysis of the Increasing Impact of Social and Other New Media on Public Relations Practices", paper presented to 12th Annual International Public Relations Research Conference, 14 March, Miami, Florida, available at: http://www.kyagr.com/pr/report/documents/Wright_Hinson_PR_Miami.pdf (accessed 9 July 2012)

CHAPTER ELEVEN

ETHICAL BUSINESS PRACTICE AND CSR IN TIMES OF ECONOMIC TURBULENCE

ANGELO NICOLAIDES

Introduction

Ethics is a collection of principles or standards of human conduct that govern the behaviour of individuals as well as groups. Business ethics is found at the individual employee level, organisational, association, societal and global levels. It arises from human nature itself and is thus a natural body of laws that must be adhered to by employees and other stakeholders of an organization and in society in general. To many, it is considered to be a normative science as it is concerned with the norms of human conduct. It really is much more than just a collection of values and is an operational dimension all organisations need in a business environment. It is demanded by shareholders, customers, employees and society in general. Managers, as leaders in an organization, are responsible for the promotion of ethical conduct and morality within the organizations that they serve. Sadly, and often to the detriment of stakeholders, this important role of leadership is ignored. However, promoting ethical conduct and providing ethical guidance to employees is just as important as managing the physical output of the organisation. Ethics has a huge impact on business today. At a time when there are global financial crises, and to the day-to-day decision-making that impacts on the work environment and beyond, ethics is an important aspect to consider if an organizational wishes to be sustainable.

Many managers neglect their moral leadership role because they find it difficult to define a universal set of ethical principles and values. Individuals tend to frame their understanding of values from their own personal experiences, philosophy or religions. It is virtually impossible that employees will have a common perception of what is moral and ethical. Consequently, managers need to consider societal rules and laws and what is considered to be appropriate behaviour in any given environment in which their organization operates. Unfortunately, in many organizations what is considered to be ethically acceptable behaviour is in fact nothing more than a mere informal comprehension in the workplace. Ethics and ethical behaviour can take on a life of its own and it will develop rapidly if given an opportunity. It also concerns the obligation of employees to do something beyond themselves, such as consistently treating customers in a spirit of service quality excellence, caring for fellow employees or people in the community. When the needs of the customer come first, ethical behaviour wins the day. It is clear that ethics is thus often an unwritten understanding of an employee's appropriate behaviour to people other than themselves.

Understanding business ethics

Business ethics is a question of values and associated behaviours. The values that are embraced by an organization are discerned through the process of ongoing reflection in what is relatively long and ongoing process. Ethics generally implies having and using one's morals to do the right thing. It is a critical aspect to consider as it gives an organisation much needed credibility, especially in a global environment of great competitiveness between organisations. Once an organisation is perceived to be ethical by its stakeholders, its credibility increases and sales climb. Consumers also prefer to buy from companies that have untarnished reputations.

Ethics is a branch of philosophy which studies questions pertaining to what is right and wrong, or good and bad, acceptable or unacceptable based on societal expectations. For our purpose, ethical and moral behaviour mean the same thing. Ethical behaviour occurs when an individual or organisation does what is good for others in society and the quality of the interaction that takes place. One cannot on the other hand, fail to take his or her self-interest into consideration. We can thus be focused on ourselves but should not only be self-serving in what we do. Ethics and morally 'right' conduct are now more closely integrated with a wide range of "global" issues of basic human rights and conduct. In business, ethics revolves around how risk is managed and the manner in which companies keep records, be they human resource or financial in orientation. Consequently, companies require effective and strong leaders who support ethical conduct in the workplace, and who impact positively on complex social, economic and legal considerations. The world has a plethora of socio-economic problems. Many of these are the direct or indirect result of greed, leading to bribery and corruption, especially in business conduct. The purpose of this chapter is to demonstrate that ethical conduct should be utilized by businesses and they should develop a code of conduct or credo by which all employees in the business will be expected to operate.

Figure 1. Stakeholders of an organization

In the business environment of the new millennium, the behaviour of managers is under greater scrutiny than was previously the case. Something may be legal but not right (ethical) and something may be right (ethical) but not necessarily legal. The access to information of the public at large makes transgressions on the part of employees virtually impossible to keep secret. Unethical business practice, clearly, also leads to the reputations of businesses and even governments, becoming tarnished. The customers of today expect managers to adhere to high standards of ethicality in their behaviour. Added to this is the fact that there are increased governmental regulations in place for all organisational activities to remain ethical (Wright & Noe: 1996). Any behaviours, which are in line with the narcissistic value system that is prevalent in the West and are based on the ethic of self-preservation, are not conducive to effective business practice in the global economy and yet such practice is rife. Conduct which strays from the moral imperatives governing the behaviour of individuals and businesses is deemed to be unethical and tends to destabilize the system in which a business operates. In this regard, the ethic of self-preservation (ESP), is highly destructive in the long-term. Businesses which opt for this particular approach in their dealings with employees and customers do not have a long-term vision in which their sustainability is assured. The needs of all stakeholders (Fig. 1) need to be considered in all dealings that are undertaken by all employees in an organization.

Sadly, more and more businesses are becoming more narcissistic in their cultural orientations (Irvin, 2002). What is needed is a vision which is realistic enough to be achievable and which encompasses 'imaginative insight into what is to be done so that the result will lead the organisation to great heights of excellence in pursuing a purpose or goal' (Van Zyl, 1998).

The Root of Values

Most individuals are interested in ethics and moral behaviour. Since we are all products of particular societal structures and systems, we owe much our identity to the community in which we live. Ethics is thus a complex philosophy since our morality is a mixture of tradition that we receive and our personal opinions. Individual living in the Western Christian world base their ethical beliefs and their behaviour on the Ten Commandments that were handed to Moses on Mount Sinai. Thus understood, ethics is a series of rules that individual should try to live according to. Many Western philosophical works on ethics have been based on a culture whose literary and religious thoughts were founded and moulded according to the Judaeo-Christian Old Testament and the New Testament teachings. There thus exists a deep connection between the ethics of the Holy Scriptures of Judaism and Christianity and the ethics of the great western philosophers. When we think about ethics we very often begin with certain assumptions about human nature and the idea that mankind was born into original sin and in need of redemption. There is an opposite Romantic view which assumes that humanity is programmed to be good.

In Hinduism, Buddhism and Islam we encounter some universal principles of ethics which are compatible with western ethics and in some instances, these may be more austere than in the western modality. To put it plainly,

the values governing conduct are products of the normative responses from within a system and form the basis of all moral reasoning.
Ethics is thus part of a social quintessence that has strong cultural roots and presents itself in actions and behaviours which are ultimately aimed at guaranteeing the survival of the system from which they emanate. The roots of African life, culture and value systems, in Southern Africa, for example, are found in the philosophy of *ubuntu* as well as in the imported Judaeo-Christian tradition. Both *ubuntu* and Christianity call for caring for others and for upholding moral integrity. In *ubuntu,* it is only through others that a person can be considered to be a person- *'Umuntu ngumuntu ngabantu'*. It is only through *imbizo* or participation that all people are treated inclusively and have their suggestions and ideas considered and they are treated with human dignity. *Ubuntu* has its foundation on democratic ideals and welcomes consultation and inclusivity from all role-players in all walks of life and this can be translated into the workplace.

Loyalty and conformity is expected from all employees in terms of *ubuntu*, and these are prized values for each and every member of a group. The development of practices, policies, procedures and processes must be aimed at developing people in the institutions they serve (Mbigi and Maree, 2005). Only by having a common set of mutually inclusive values in place, which are embraced by all employees, can a business have any hope of truly ethical business conduct. *Ubuntu* transcends cultures and is a strong unifier of all peoples irrespective of race or creed. In fact the Platonic-Aristotelian traditions of both individual and social virtue, is highly compatible with *ubuntu* as are many other traditions.

Internalizing value systems

What prevents businesses internalizing ethical value systems? Egoism and self-centredness and especially the ethic of self-preservation are clearly major hurdles to cross. It is nonetheless necessary for the business world to adopt a common set of values from all employees and incorporate these into a code-of-conduct or a credo for use by business. In terms of each value system, no situation can be adequately transformed unless there are totally transformed individuals driving the situation. It is the people who create a new spirit of ethical behaviour in an organisation which makes it possible to nurture new practices and ultimately to sustain them (Mbigi and Maree, 2005).The value systems espoused by businesses should thus include aspects such as codes of conduct and credos as these will guide them to function with integrity and uphold a strong ethical stance even in turbulent economic times. These value systems should be based on a wide range of philosophies, especially including local traditions and value systems as the majority of employees in a given country will embrace a philosophy that they have rapport with.

Ethics can be integrated into organisation values with relative ease as many of the values, for example, integrity, care for others, pride in performance and safety, are all in harmony with what responsible businesses should be instilling in all their employees. Companies must get back to basics and focus on shared ethical principles while forging ethical cultures in the workplace. This requires committed and strong leadership that is seriously concerned about making ethical conduct part and parcel of everyday workplace behaviour.

Five business ethics theories

What are business ethics theories? These include the moral principles, values or codes an organisation implements in its efforts to ensure that employees conduct themselves within acceptable parameters of behaviour that do not transgress legal statutes or moral bounds. Each organisation uses an approach or combination of approaches that it deems to be suitable for its operations. Each theory includes very specific characteristics that spotlight precise ethical principles that may assist in rectifying some or other business issue. Since ethics has a huge impact on whether a business succeeds or fails, employers require guidelines to direct their decision making processes. Such guidelines are found in ethics theories including the Common Good Approach, the Utilitarian Approach, the Rights Approach, the Justice Approach and the *Common-Good Approach.*

Some of the ethics theories are highlighted below:

The **common good approach** strives to promote the common values and moral or ethical principles that exist in a particular society. This then varies from country to country. This approach is in use where organisations implement principles to ensure that their mission is aligned with the society in which they operate.

The **utilitarian approach** focuses on using ethical actions that will promote the most good or value among a society while limiting the amount of harm to as few people as possible. In other words as long as what is done produces maximum benefits for everyone, utilitarianism does not concern itself whether the benefits are produced by lies such as false advertising, manipulation, or even by coercion. This is the oldest business ethics theory, and was propagated by philosophers, such as Jeremy Bentham, James Mill, and John Stuart Mill. Organisations opt for this theory to ensure the outcome of various situations aids the maximum amount of stakeholders. Many managers and employees thus use this type of moral reasoning frequently in their daily decisions making. So long as a course of action produces maximum benefits for everyone, utilitarianism does not care whether the benefits are produced by lies, manipulation, or coercion.

A **rights ethical approach or deontological approach** is premised on the belief that people have basic human rights that should be preserved. All people should be treated with tolerance, respect and dignity. Morality is important in this approach since employees use ethical behaviour in order to achieve the end goal without abusing people. Often business ethics theories apply this approach as they do not impose their missions or products, on their customers.

Justice or fairness as an ethical approach is where all humans are treated equally in society, irrespective of rank, position, class, creed, or race. The philosopher John Rawls promoted this theory. This is also known as the fairness approach in business ethics theories. An ethical action is one that treats all stakeholders fairly and consistently in line with ethical, moral or legal standards in society. The philosopher John Rawls promoted this theory. In terms of this theory there must be a justifiable reason why an employee receives more or less pay than a colleague doing the same work. We need to therefore consider the distributive, procedural, and interactional rules before making ethical decisions. The Justice approach is based on the results received by employees and their understanding of the results. The processes i.e. policies, procedures and rules that are utilized to reach decisions must be procedurally fair. The personal treatment received by an employee during in the administration of a decision-making process must be fair and consistent with how others were treated in a similar situation. There should also be interpersonal fairness in which there is demonstrable respect and consideration in the dispensing of decisions. Explanations for any decisions made must be fair in terms of information.

The **virtue approach** focuses on following ethical principles that should be evident in society and postulates that virtuous actions lead to the achievement of values. By adopting virtuous principles, strategies, and actions can result in organisations comprehending their values including their mission, purpose for existence and profit potential. If employees act virtuously they will be more likely to carry out their roles in a way that is compatible with the organisation's goals. Virtues allow employees to act to gain values.

The role of the virtues is to direct and motivate employee behaviour toward obtaining the objectives of the organisation. For an organisation to succeed, it needs to advocate a set of virtues that are realistic, unambiguous, integrated, and comprehensive and which replace current values if they do not result in what is best for humanity in general.

What happens on the ground?

Work is not purely a contractual relationship with people having obligations to each other. It is essentially a service. When one becomes part of the personnel of a business, he or she is making a commitment to the community and society at large. If value-systems are in place and followed by all employees, every employee will be valued and included in the decision making process and strive to share with others, always acting ethically and morally correctly. In truth many global businesses do not act out ethical behaviour in their conduct with clients, and many employees act unethically in their place of employ.

Many businesses bribe decision-makers in other companies and award them contracts and this in itself affects all employees indiscriminately and influences the behaviour of employees and customers in often unpredictable ways. The truth is that any business which fails to take cognizance of the welfare of its customers, is ultimately dysfunctional, and will eventually lose them to their competitors in the marketplace. Such a business is also likely to ignore the essentiality of a healthy workplace environment and will consequently also experience an abnormally rapid rate of employee turnover. In especially turbulent economic times, a business, which opts to go the ethical route, will have greater prospects for success and will ensure the sustainability of the enterprise. There should be no place for self-preservation at the expense of others, and corruption in business. In most countries, the Constitutions are quite clear on the fundamental principle of honesty. Businesses and individuals are accountable and obliged to explain their actions if these are contrary to the values of society, and they are expected to act ethically, i.e. apply the values of society to their actions at all times. Generally, most societies and businesses are opposed to bribery. This does not, of course, suggest that bribery is not occurring. Clearly, business has a major role to play in promoting acceptable business practice conduct. Once a business opts to use bribery to obtain favoured status, it promotes the corruption of regulatory institutions, whereas it should in essence be trying to strengthen the regulatory framework and all its institutions (Rossouw, 2002).

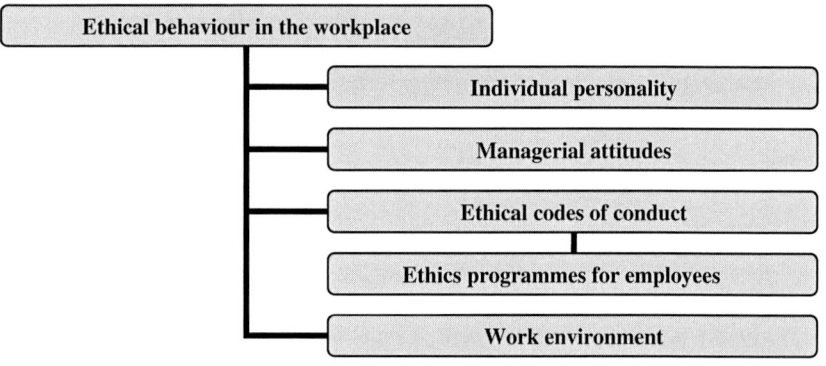

Figure 2. Ethical employee conduct

There are many reasons why employees may act unethically. Greed and the total disregard for business codes of conduct are but two reasons (Bayat and Meyer, 1994). In Africa, as indeed in other parts of the globe, many businesses are dysfunctional because their managers are simply not willing to transform their enterprises in terms of ethical practice, and thus disregard what is in essence managerial wisdom in practice. According to the United Nations, corruption and bribery is rife in most African countries and this fact undermines the prospects for economic investments on the continent by foreign firms. Sadly, the greatest impact of corruption and bribery is on the poor who are unable to absorb its costs (Cookey, 2005). Corruption and bribery, whether at the governmental or business levels, results in reduced investments and even de-investment in some cases. It is common practice for many national and international companies in Africa to conduct business by offering bribes in order to secure business and undercut their legitimate competitors in the marketplace.

In South Africa, there are more and more cases of corruption in business and these are considered to be a manifestation of the moral disintegration of society and the natural result of great poverty and ethnic discrimination (Mafunisa, 2000). In the United States of America and other western nations, corruption, including bribery, lowers the levels of ethical consciousness in the society in which it manifests itself on an ongoing basis (Ferrel *et al*, 2002). The criminal justice process is a major deterrent for corruption in society as many would be perpetrators are fearful of the consequences of their actions (Rich, 1975). As a society accepts relatively minor infractions of the law as being in line with what is considered to be acceptable behaviour, it is likely that people in that society will become ethically desensitized and unethical behaviour becomes reinforced as the norm (Baack *et al*, 2000). According to Kohlberg (1981), people are orientated towards social norms and are judged by others in terms of how they comply when they are what he calls the conventional stage of moral development. By means of contrast, those beyond the conventional stage behave in ways, which can be evaluated according to normative standards that are based on principles. The implication of this is that if ethical behaviour in the workplace is to become part of an employee's mindset, it is essential for the underlying ethical principles to be recognized, understood and internalised by employees.

The consequences of corruption and bribery are destructive in that sound competition is undermined and standards of service tend to fall. Furthermore, products become inferior while prices become unrealistic. Very often, the environment is even threatened. Even more disturbing is the rapid disintegration of morality and conscience amongst the people of the country and the loss of credibility by the country in the eyes of potential or actual foreign investors who logically seek out more politically and economically stable countries (Malan and Smit, 2001).

Does Culture affect Bribery?

Gordon and Miyake (2001) express the opinion that bribery and corruption is a huge obstacle to development in many areas across the globe. In fact, in many developing countries, bribery is expected as a natural business practice and if one is not bribed then something is amiss (Wong and Beckman, 1992). By contrast, in developed countries it is generally accepted that employees should not accept bribes in any shape or form. They should not allow themselves to be influenced to arrive at a business decision by accepting any special favours, gifts or bribes. According to Ferrel et al., (2002), many managers have fallen from favour because of their acceptance of some or other bribe. In certain African and South American cultures, giving a gift to obtain business is more or less a norm, but in the case of the latter, the gift should be given during a social meeting only (Millet, 2004).

In China, gifts should be given to recipients in private, while in the Middle East giving a gift may be construed as a bribe. Culture is then a great influencer.

How is it possible then, for example, that African culture which espouses *ubuntu* tolerates unethical business practice? Clearly, what is a solid philosophy of goodness, has been hijacked by greed and corruption emanating from western business practices. While western business frowns on corruption and bribery, there are nonetheless individuals and businesses which opt to go for the easy way out, bribing their way through business deals and corrupting otherwise ethical people.

What should be happening?

Organisations should be paying closer attention to business ethics. This is imperative during times of fundamental change and economic turmoil. In the complex global business arena, older values that were previously accepted as a given are now strongly questioned. Organisations need to consider the broader community and not just their bottom-line earnings. Consequently, many of the older business ethics related values are no longer desirable. The result is that there is very often no unambiguous moral compass to guide managers and employees through highly challenging and complex dilemmas about what is moral and ethical, good or bad and right or wrong. It is clear that far more attention must be paid to ethics issues in the global workplace as this will sensitize all employees as to how they should behave to the benefit of all stakeholders of the organization.

Businesses should strive for the inclusion of all employees in the decision-making process, irrespective of rank in the operational hierarchy. Corruption in any shape or form must be condemned out-of-hand. The opinions of all employees should be considered seriously and valued. Employees need to feel a sense of worth and ownership in a business and will commit themselves more to their employer as a consequence of such acknowledgement on the part of their employers. This is clearly one aspect, which is lacking in many businesses. Employees generally do simply not trust their employers, who they see as narcissistic promoters of ESP. There is no *esprit d'corps* between the employees and the employer in such businesses and in most cases employees are not treated with the dignity and respect they deserve.

In our example of African society, a manager who disrespects his employees is at once considered to devoid of decency and humanity, and such a manager is not taken seriously at the best of times. African society is for the most part, highly compassionate as evidenced in *ubuntu*. Individuals will share with the have-nots in their society and will strive to uplift them. Such regard for others leads to greater sustainability in African society. Whilst such behaviour is paid lip-service to in most businesses, in practice, it is not supported as most businesses are caught up in ESP. While western business models tend to focus on 'the bottom-line' and narcissism, African businesses are more committed to uplifting society and creating a new workable community in which all can prosper. This is not to say that some black managed companies are also not ESP promoters.

Organisational Culture

Organisational culture refers to the values and ways of behaving in an organization. It includes the values and principles that employees are required to adhere to in their daily work conduct and in their interactions with all stakeholders. Robbins and Judge (2009), provide a very useful list of things that managers could do to promote a more ethical organisational culture. These are highlighted below:

1. Managers must be role models for employees and be visible. Since employees look up to management for guidance, how managers act is crucial to ethical conduct in the workplace. When management demonstrates that it is serious about ethical issues it sets a positive tone in the organisation.
2. It is vital that organisations communicate their ethical expectations to stakeholders in general but especially to employees. An organisational code of ethics must be created and if necessary workshops should be conducted concerning its contents. The code that is adopted should be unambiguous in stating the organisation's primary values and explain the ethical rules that employees are expected to follow and the sanctions that exist in the event of unethical conduct occurring.
3. Ideally, every organisation should have an ethics officer to oversee ethics issues in the workplace. The ethics officer or manager tasked with ethics in the workplace should as a matter of course, conduct seminars, workshops, and ethical training programmes in which the organisation's expected standards of conduct are clarified., to

clarify what practices are and are not permissible, and to address possible ethical dilemmas and how these should be handled.
4. Managers should reward individuals in some or other way for demonstrating ethically sound conduct that is in line with the organisations code of ethics. This means that there should be effective employee appraisals in place which address ethics in the workplace. Conversely, where unethical conduct is apparent, employees should be punished accordingly.
5. Every organisation should provide formal mechanisms for ethical issues so that employees can discuss ethical dilemmas and report any unethical behaviour without fear of reprimand. This might include having a whistleblower, creation of ethical counsellors, ombudsmen, and/or ethical officers.
(http://workplacepsychology.net/2011/02/14/creating-an-ethical-organizational-culture)

Patterns of employee behavior should reinforce ethical conduct. This means that any events, or written or spoken comments, and especially behaviours displayed by employees should exude ethical conduct as a norm rather than as something employees should try to do. It is thus important to continually reinforce important organisational values. It may be useful to hold or support annual community events that symbolize the firm's values and moral grounding. Such activity will serve to at least convert some employees to embrace the expected values. Introspection is vital as organisations that have the best chance of effecting real change in striving for an ethical culture are those with a higher level of self-knowledge of their own cultural strengths and weaknesses. Ethics training is thus very useful in orientating all new employees to what is expected of them in terms of ethicality. This will invariably prepare them to handle tricky situations that invite misconduct.

Senior established employees also require ethics training but such training should include a different curriculum.The culture of every organisation should be a source of pride and inspiration for all the stakeholders including employees, investors and consumers. It should encourage moral and ethical imagination and lead to creative and innovative decision-making processes. It should also foster commitment and loyalty, and serve as an incentive for the development of all employees.

Forging principles and values for behaviour

Basic business ethics concepts should cascade from the top echelons in the hierarchy of an organisation to all employees. Leaders as role models and leadership ethics in general also have a great influence on customer relations and relations with all stakeholders and impacts on how well the values are enforced in the workplace environment. Where there is dishonesty, a business will falter. Many definitions of honesty in the workplace refer to people refraining from lying, and upholding high ethical and moral standards of behaviour. Some allude to integrity. However each and every unethical situation is unique differ. An employee who is honest about everything may essentially not be an effective and efficient employee. He may argue with colleagues all day long. Ethics must be concerned with what is good or right in any given situation. It involves employees making correct moral choices for the good of all stakeholders involved, and it should not be sense self-serving when others may be harmed as a result of what is done.

Principles are general rules and guidelines that intended to be enduring and remain relatively constant. They serve the purpose of informing and supporting the way in which an organisation sets about fulfilling its mission to the benefit of all stakeholders. Principles include for example, employees not accepting bribes for obtaining business, or treating multi-culturally diverse employees equitably. The guiding principles of a organisation are thus the very foundation upon which a business is built and these provide guidance and direction for employee behaviour. The principles we adopt relate to duty, freedom, equity, justice etc. Principles are universal and absolute and demarcate for us the parameters within which we may act. We use these principles to devise rules for conduct. Generally, principles are valued across a range of cultures.

The values of any organisation are the fundamental beliefs that are shared by employees that establish what is deemed right or wrong, or good and just, in any given situation. Consequently, values are distinct from principles. They are based on choices made by leaders and are entrenched in the culture of the organisation. Examples of some values include employees accepting responsibility for their actions and keeping promises to stakeholders. Typical values include aspects such as honesty, integrity, compassion, honour, responsibility, respect and fairness. Our ethical values relate to accountability, social responsibility and loyalty to stakeholders. Business values on the other hand, relate mainly to profit margins and aspects such a gaining a strategic competitive advantage and innovation. When we evaluate the ethicality of something we compare it to a set standard. We thus ascertain if an action we may be considering meets the set standards or if it falls short. So when we evaluate, we determine the worth of a something or an action as compared to a standard. Our Morals are values which we attribute to a system of beliefs, such as in a religion. Such values derive authority from a higher being or higher authority such as society. Many human values are strongly influenced by their sense of morality as defined by higher authority. Ethics refers to our particular actions and decisions that we make in a given situation. When employees act in a manner that is consistent with their beliefs we say they are acting ethically. When their actions do not correspond with their values we see that as unethical behaviour.

Workplace ethics are forged by two important factors. Firstly, any workplace policy must be in accord with the laws and regulations of the place where the organisation operates. This to an extent ensures that basic workplace ethics prohibit any coercion to engage in actions that are considered to be illegal, or that promote discrimination in the workplace. Whatever ethics code is in place in an organisation must also be in line with what is considered to be fair labour practice.

Identifying and defining organisational values

Managers need to set good examples to employees and all stakeholders and keep their promises and commitments. It is also important that the support employees in adhering to ethical standards in terms of the organizations code of conduct or ethics. Organisational values are what guide its mentality and actions. In this regard it is important to be aware of what employees think about and discuss. Having an interactive website will assist in this aspect. Organisations' need to define what really counts as this is their foundation. This is necessary so that effort is not expended on pointless exercises and activities. In clearly defining the organisation's values the foundation is laid for the formation and development of an ethical workplace. The values of the organization must be appropriate for the time, place, and operating environment in which the organisation finds itself.

Organisations with international operations may thus have diverse values depending on the country in which they find themselves. Employees should not purport to follow one set of rules and then act in a manner which is contrary to that set of rules. The values that are adopted should thus be carefully considered. They are after all an abstract set of ideas that guide the organization. The values of the organization are important as differentiators of the organization in highly competitive and turbulent global markets. Managers need to interrogate how the organisation operates and carefully observe employees during the conduct of their work.

All that glistens is not gold

Organisations are not only responsible to their shareholders but to society in general. Money is not as important as reputation. Ethical organisation standards need to resonate with the community and this is critical to the organisations long term success. Organisations obviously need to take care of their commitments to shareholders but this must be done in accordance with the laws of the country in which they operate. Whatever is done must be done ethically within the organisation as well as beyond, in industry and in terms of stakeholder relationships. What remains then is for organisations to be philanthropically orientated as they plough back into the community and exhibit corporate social responsibility. Profits are not the most important aspect and all that glistens is indeed not gold. Whether business ethics or profits are more important should not be a dilemma for organisation directors. If a business has to constantly set profit objectives against business ethics, it ought to re-evaluate its vision, mission and strategic business objectives. It clearly has no place in the modern highly competitive and complex globalized marketplace. Ethics must be viewed as a conduit that makes managers take socially responsible actions to benefit society. An organisation should be successful because its system of competition in the marketplace adopts underlying values of truthfulness and fair dealing with all stakeholders. By being fair to suppliers and customers, the organisation's public image is enhanced and this attracts customers.

Greenwashing

"Greenwashing," is a term derived from the term "whitewashing." It refers to the manner in which many organisations try to portray themselves as being environmentally responsible. Greenwashing makes an organisation appear to be more environmentally friendly than it is in reality. It is essentially a marketing lie used to differentiate the products or services of one organisation over its competitors by promising greater energy and power efficiency or by being more cost-effective than another product in the long run.

It is an unethical practice and it intentionally misleads consumers about the benefits of buying certain products or services. The term was first used to explain misleading cases of environmental advertising. Today it refers to a wide range or corporate activities, including environmental reporting, event sponsorship and even the distribution of educational materials and the creation of "front groups." The main idea behind greenwashing is that it creates the impression to consumers as well as governments that an organisation is taking serious and carefully considered measures to limit its ecological footprint. The creation of an illusion of environmental sustainability could have dire social consequences as consumers will continue to use products and support companies that further promote environmental degradation and reduce the quality of living conditions for future generations (Davis, 1992).

Ethical dilemmas and moral mazes

There are many ethical dilemmas and moral mazes that employees need to manoeuvre through on a day-to-day basis. Madsen and Shafritz (1990) explain that "managerial mischief" includes "illegal, unethical, or questionable practices of individual managers or organizations, as well as the causes of such behaviours and remedies to eradicate them." Generally speaking, business ethics is a question of dealing with ethical dilemmas that have no clear indication of what is right or wrong. There are also "moral mazes" which include a wide range of ethical issues that managers must deal with on a daily basis. These include *inter alia* potential conflicts of interest, wrongful use of organisational resources, bribery, lack of cultural diversity understanding, mismanagement of contracts and agreements.
(http://jpkc.szpt.edu.cn/english/supplement/business%20ethics10.htm)

Employee empowerment against ESP

Another aspect which deserves attention is employee empowerment, which has been receiving greater attention than was the case in the past (Zani and Pietrantoni, 2001). There is no doubt that empowerment of employees goes a long way in fostering an ethical workplace ethos. Much literature supports the view that the major determinant of empowerment, by category, is the psychological variables affecting it (Menon and Hartmann, 2000; Dimitriades,

2002). By empowering or 'granting power' to an employee, a business is seen to be acting ethically as it is considering the employee's human dignity and is according him/her a status of worth. The employee has a sense of having free choice in "initiating and regulating" his or her actions (Spreitzer, 1995) and is able to shape his/her work role and context. In essence, employees have a locus of control in which they believe that they, rather than external forces, determine what happens in their workplace environments and thus feel empowered. There is an erroneous perception in many businesses that because employees are not all in management positions, they are not concerned about ethical questions. In fact, the more they are involved in the decision-making process and participate, the more they will feel the desire to be part of an ethically responsible workplace. Any management style which stifles the individual and does not respect human dignity, is problematic, for in such a workplace ethical behaviour is less likely to be maintained. Such autocratic management styles are thus deleterious to both employees and employers and therefore to the community at large. A business's dynamic core of human interaction cannot be ignored. Any style of management which fosters self-centredness is antithetical to the creation and maintenance of a sustainable business operation. If employees are not sufficiently empowered, they will perceive themselves to be separate entities and will make all decisions based on ESP (Irvin, 2002). They will thus not take into account the effect of their actions on those around them, either in the workplace or in society, and will have their moral reasoning inhibited to the detriment of all who may come into contact with them. A business that empowers its employees will have enlightened leaders who are also the initiators of new values. These leaders will of necessity, strive for creating a sense of commitment and ownership in all employees and make certain that all the values proposed by them are in harmony with the basic goals of the business and be part of its processes.

According to Bass (1990), 'The organisational philosophy includes its assumptions, values, foci of attention, priorities, and goals and the techniques it promulgates to implement its efforts. Clearly its philosophy and culture overlap and reinforce each other in determining "what is the right thing to do" and "what is important and good'. As such, leaders of businesses are thus important developers of business philosophy and drive the value system of their businesses. It is incumbent upon them to co-opt all employees in the decision-making processes concerning the preparation and formulation of the business's philosophy including the code of ethics to be adhered to by all employees. The virtues that employees are expected to develop in the workplace must also be expressed in the culture of the business. Rules on how employees should act when practical dilemmas arise are equally important. In fact the modes of expected behaviour in given scenarios should be spelled out clearly for all employees who should be empowered to act as they see fit within given parameters of behaviour. It is only in this way that ESP can be effectively countered and the welfare of all be upheld in business practice.

Codes of conduct (ethics) and ethics programmes

Organizations are required to establish policies and procedures to ensure that correct employee behaviour results and that it is based on identified and prioritized values which should guide employee behaviour. "Values management" guidelines are usually contained in a code of conduct or ethics and employees are also put on ethics programmes where such exist, usually conducted in-house by an ethics officer or manager tasked with ethics management. The most important outcome of having an effective code of conduct and ethics programme in place in an organization is evidence of the behaviours that are preferred by the organsation. Codes of conduct are meaningless unless they promote what they affirm and produce fair and just behaviours in the workplace. Consequently, appropriate policies, procedures and training must exist that translate those values into appropriate and desired behaviours. Every organisation should commit itself to achieving market leadership through living its values and embracing the principles that are vital to its success. The ethics officer or manager promoting ethics should at all times make a point of stressing to employees that earning the loyalty of customers through ethical products and ethical services, is of prime concern. Especially shareholders should be provided with exceptional value through ethical performance and honestly obtained growth in revenues and profits. Ethically oriented employees must also be recognised and rewarded for their important contributions in an organization. Such issues are highlighted in a code of conduct.

Codes of conduct are formal statements that serve as a guide for how people in an organisation should behave and how they should be making ethical decisions that impact positively on the organisation and society. If the code is effective it will establish the values of the organisation that will drive its actions and the principles that underlie its decision making activities. The code provides an organisation with an opportunity to differentiate itself. It also promotes teamwork and synergy and the job gets done properly. Codes set out strategy for handling ethical dilemmas and moral mazes when these occur. They also deal with other issues, amongst others, such as conflicts of interest, bribery and corruption, how employees behave towards competitors and security of information. Codes of conduct help to establish ground-rules for employee behaviour and thus set a tone of trust in the workplace. The code establishes a foundation for a strong organisational culture and helps an organisation to enforce ethical policies and operate within the bounds of the law.

A code has rules that restrict outcomes and that all employees need to respect. It assists all decision making as it contains principles and values that are espoused by the organisation. It sets the tone for effective operational procedures that help employees maintain an ethical stance in their day-to-day activities. A well formulated code can build trust between the organisation and its stakeholders who are in some way or other affected by its actions. Codes of conduct align with the vision and a mission to the organisation and very often create a good impression of an organisation in the marketplace. More importantly, it helps to prevent employees from violating laws and regulations and also engenders an environment of trust in the workplace and beyond. All employees should have at least a broad knowledge of the code's contents and intentions and be aware of what they can do in a dilemma. The code of conduct enables employees to ascertain how the provisions therein relate to their practices in the workplace, and ethical training sessions hosted by an organisational ethics officer are the best way to accomplish this goal. An effective code will also address the plan of action to be adhered to in the event of an unethical act having being perpetrated by an employee.

Once managers know which ethical risks are facing the organisation, they need to work out how to avoid them. After this, a relevant code of ethics can be developed containing 'must dos' and case studies of ethical dilemmas and moral mazes that employees could likely face during the course of their work. It is imperative that top level management fully supports the initiatives that are taken so that they can provide efficient leadership for the implementation of the code. They are after all potential role-models for all employees. They should thus set the tone. The values and principles upon which the code will be based must be unambiguous and intelligible to all levels of employees. The code must be relevant and workable or it will lack credibility and fail from the outset. All departments in the organisation should give their buy-in on what could and should be included and why this is indeed the case. Once the code is drafted, which will be after a number of workshops, it should be sent for review to a wide range of stakeholders for their inputs and further suggestions. When the code is finally agreed to, an ethics officer should begin to implement it by hosting a number of workshops for all levels of employees. Once these are concluded, each employee should be given a copy to keep and refer to as needed.

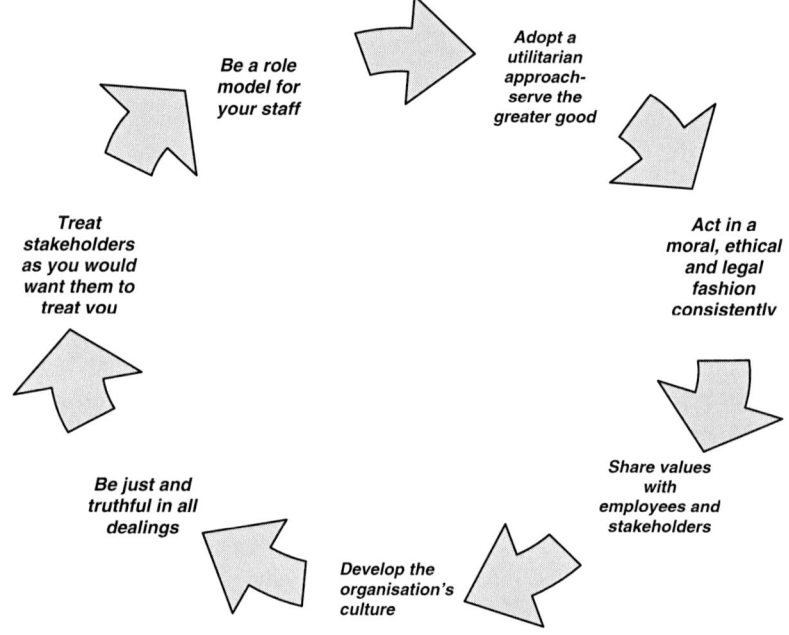

Figure 3. Critical considerations for an ethical senior or middle manager

Developing and finally distributing the organisations a code of ethics is an effective and efficient means of promoting ethical practices within an organisation. It is important to note that the code of ethics cannot cover all eventualities and that the adopted code requires regular monitoring so that new guidelines may be incorporated into it. Managers at all levels in the organisational organogram must strive to encourage ethical practices not only so as to ensure moral conduct, but also to obtain a strategic competitive advantage. An ethics programme in the workplace assists employees to face reality, both the good and the bad. It allows them to be introspective so that they can feel confident that how they behave in the workplace is acceptable. It also allows them to effectively handle whatever ethical dilemma comes their way.

Essentially then, a code of conduct or ethics, and ethics programme, serve the purpose of sensitizing employees to ethical considerations and minimize the possibility of unethical behaviour taking place in the first instance. They assist us to identify and prioritize values which guide behaviour in the organization. In a sense they manage values in the workplace.

Managerial actions to follow in forging desirable workplace ethics

- *Maintain a moral course in turbulent as well as good times*
- *Be the perfect role-model*
- *Think ethically in all situations*
- *Set up an ethics office*
- *Establish a code of conduct*
- *Assume responsibility for creating and sustaining conditions in which employees can behave ethically*
- *Minimize conditions in which people are susceptible to unethical actions.*
- *Promote ethics in the workplace*
- *Promote a strong public image*
- *Communicate expectations to employees*
- *Cultivate strong teamwork and productivity*
- *Manage values associated with quality management, strategic planning and diversity management*
- *Keep your promises*
- *Provide the work force with appropriate training*
- *Promote the social responsibility aspect of business*
- *Live the values of the organisation*

Table 1. Managerial actions

Ethical reasoning is required in any company so that a good corporate image is maintained and for fair and equitable dealings with all stakeholders to be part and parcel of daily practice. There is clear evidence that companies that are viewed as being "excellent" have created great concern for employees that often goes beyond the bottom-line. In such companies, customer service is exceptional and both public and employee relationships are carefully monitored. From a moral point of view, it is important to promote business ethics and always be prepared to pay a price for ethical behavior to exist so that the integrity of a company can be valued and preserved. It is critical that ethical reasoning exist in companies, since complex moral issues arise that often require a learned understanding of due process to stakeholders, justice and fair action.

One needs to start the process of designing an ethics strategy to combat corruption and bribery in the workplace by clearly defining the businesses' strengths, weaknesses, opportunities and threats in terms of both the micro and macro environments (SWOT analysis or PESTLE analysis). Once this objective has been achieved, it is necessary to clearly spell out what the business wishes to achieve in terms of its mission and its long-term strategic plan. It must also address the question of how it will face up to the multiplicity of environmental challenges and opportunities (McDonald, 2000).

It is not simply a question of drawing up a list of values considered to be important, but to rather discuss with employees which values are considered important to ethical business conduct. What is essential is that the values that a business intends to operate by need to be credible and consistent and place values in a hierarchical order of importance from most essential value first. A business cannot simply ignore the fact that it employs people from different religious, socio-cultural and political backgrounds. Each person may thus differ from the next in that he or she emanates from a society, which has a somewhat unique, if not similar, value system. In the South African example provided, given that *ubuntu* and Christian morality are highly compatible, there is great likelihood that a code of conduct or credo based on these will be highly successful once implemented. The values that are selected must be selected and accepted by all employees in the business, irrespective of level of seniority in the business. This requires the value systems of a worker to be respected by his fellow workers and places management in a position where it is obliged to acknowledge cultural diversity in the workplace and sensitize employees to this. After this process, the values accepted by all should be communicated to all through a code-of-conduct or a credo. Without the total formal commitment of the senior management, it is unlikely that the rest of the employees will buy into the code-of-conduct or credo.

Handling ethical predicaments

Organisations are pressurized to achieve results so that especially shareholders can benefit. Often this creates space for unethical conduct as unscrupulous employees do whatever it takes to achieve the set goals. Consequently in an end justifies the means approach, employees often resort to unethical conduct. Such behaviour inevitably affects the organisation in an irreversibly catastrophic manner. The image of the organisation is tarnished beyond repair and there is a huge flight on the part of stakeholders, especially customers and investors.

Ethical crises arise and usually the organisation involved, assuming that it still operates, tries to crisis-manage what could have been avoided. Very often managers will need to manage unethical and illegal behaviour which is related to employment practices such as insider trading in which markets are manipulated, staff recruitment and selection and relationship issues in the workplace such as personal relationships between employees, sexual harassment and even racism. If there is evidence of an ethical crisis developing management should apply the guidelines in table 2.

A number of reputable companies have adopted various techniques that allow for the effective management of unethical activities. The first important step is to create a written company policy that is read and signed by all employees. This clears the air when it comes to deciding what to do after witnessing an unethical behaviour or when one is caught in a moral maze.

The second important step is to provide a clear outline of what is expected of the person who has uncovered the unethical behaviour. It should include the person who should be contacted in such an event. If there are clear instructions, there will be less hesitation in reporting unethical activities, and then they can be dealt with quickly and relatively easily, before they develop into issues that can seriously compromise a company.

The repercussions of unethical behaviours should be clearly stated in a written code of conduct. This will enhance the possibility of unethical behaviour being reported.

> **Guidelines for mangers in an ethical crisis**
>
> - *Ascertain if there is indeed a problem- has the code of ethics been breached?*
> - *Obtain all the possible facts relating to the issue at hand.*
> - *Find out who is involved.*
> - *Obtain clear information on what has transpired.*
> - *Take immediate action against the employee/s involved.*
> - *Ascertain if law enforcement is required.*
> - *Ascertain who should act against the perpetrators internally.*
> - *Give them support and try to understand what has motivated unethical conduct.*
> - *Maintain a focus on how to right the wrong that has been done.*
> - *Identify any alternative actions that could be put into operation to rectify wrongs.*
> - *Clarify any grey areas.*
> - *Call on an ethics committee that has been established to deal with such issues.*
> - *Make certain that other employees are free to air their views without fear of fear of recrimination or suspension.*
> - *Seek to minimize harm to stakeholders while at the same time uphold the organisation's values.*
> - *Try to arriving at a workable and acceptable solution.*
> - *Make sure that such violations do not occur again.*
> - *Draw up, implement, and monitor an effective action plan to inform stakeholders of what has transpired.*

Table 2. Guidelines for Managers

Beyond the 'bottom-line' and CSR

No organisation exists in isolation and is not merely a way of making money. The employees depend on the business and all stakeholders including customers, suppliers and the local community are affected by how the organisation functions and what it does. What is produced by the organisation and how this is made may also impact on the environment. Generally, Corporate Social Responsibility is the obligation of any business to take necessary action to protect and improve the welfare of society as a whole as well. This does not mean that organisational interests become subservient but that things are done morally and ethically acceptably. Managers thus need to achieve both organisational and societal goals. Corporate Social Responsibility (CSR) is about acknowledging an organisation's impact on the community in which the organisation operates and on society in general. Corporate Social Responsibly and ethics go hand in hand. CSR can be beneficial for the bottom line but it requires taking a responsible attitude, going beyond the minimum legal requirements and doing what is ethically and morally right.

Managers need to consider their suppliers and the way they are dealt with. This is especially important if suppliers are, for example, polluting a river in a city. How employees are dealt with is also critical. Organisations must treat their employees with the respect and dignity that they deserve. It is important to not only treat them according to the legal requirements of a country, but to in fact go beyond that. Organisations should be involved in the local community and resources should be used to uplift the environment and reduce pollution. The social responsiveness of the organisation can be improved by conducting regular corporate social audits in which there is an evaluation an organisations performance in meeting its social obligations. A social audit has basic steps in its process which includes monitoring, measuring, and appraising all aspects of the organisation's socially responsible performance or lack thereof. It thus evaluates the extent to which an organisation has conducted itself in the sphere of CSR.

As organisations possess social power, they have a social responsibility to the community. They should always however operate transparently and disclose their activities to their stakeholders. Before any activity is undertaken by the organisation, it must weigh up the cost in terms of the impact on the community. It is incumbent on organisations to bare responsibility in a variety of social problem areas that are normally beyond the scope of their operation, for example, buying books for the library of a school or supplying medicines to those in need. In such instances, managers establish socially responsible programmes.

Managers should as a rule encourage social responsibility and should endeavour to create proactive, positive impact programmes which express the organisations values and guiding principles. For example, the organisation can support community youth groups or old age homes, raising funds for a charity or school etc. Regardless of the specific activity that is supported, CSR and thus ethics, can reach out to groups that are beyond oneself.

There are a multiplicity of areas in which organisations can become involved to protect society and improve the welfare of a community. Many organisations partner governmental agencies in projects such as environmental matters and health issues such as HIV/Aids awareness campaigns.

There are certain economists such as Milton Friedman, who argue that making business managers responsible to the business owners for attaining profit objectives as well as to society for supporting societal welfare initiatives, is in itself a conflict of interest that can cause the demise of an organisation. There are however arguments supporting CSR by organisations since they are an integral part of society and should give something back to the societal stakeholders rather than simply make profits for shareholders. In any event, they have a moral duty to support the community in some way. In many countries, laws have been enacted which require that organisations perform certain socially responsible activities and organisations are monitored to see the effect of their outputs on the environment for example. By adhering to the laws of a country concerning CSR, an organisation is merely offering the minimum standard of social responsibility performance.

A truly socially responsive organisation that is effective and efficient will meet its social responsibilities without squandering organisational resources. It should ascertain which CSR initiative/s to support and then how it will do so. This does not imply that an organisation should be a less profitable business. In fact, CSR will assist business performance to improve since customers are responsive to morally correct behaviour by organisations. The bottom-line should in fact improve when CSR is in operation. Many organizations opt for having a whistle-blower policy in place in which any person may report any wrongdoing on the part of employees or stakeholders so as to preserve the integrity of an organisation. Unfortunately many whistle-blowers are discouraged from "spilling the beans" because of the cheating culture that surrounds the practice.

For an organisation to be successful in CSR initiatives and in meeting social obligations it should ideally:

- Incorporate social goals into the annual strategic planning meetings.
- Prioritize issues and threats and opportunities.

- Identify possible CSR partners.
- Develop collaborative strategies.
- Benchmark against strong CSR supportive organisations.
- Issue regular reports to stakeholders on CSR initiatives.
- Try to measure the actual cost of CSR projects against the annual income statements so as to determine if profits increase-surprisingly, they should!

Socially responsible goals should be set by organisations in what is a win-win scenario. Measurements to gauge organisational approaches to CSR should view business as having both economic and societal progress targets. Measuring of CSR targets should be carried out on a regular basis and CSR should not just be 'lip-service' but actual societal support. The social investment of the organisation must be real and it must truly invest both financial and human resources to try to solve social problems in the community in which it operates. Efforts should be made to improve the quality of life in the area in which the organisation is operating. If the organisation is found to be degrading the local environment, it will be accountable to watchdog organisations, and its profits will surely decrease as a result of any improper conduct which adversely affects society. Ethics and CSR are affected by managerial action or inaction. Managers should thus take steps to build an effective caring organizational culture that supports meaningful CSR initiatives.

Workplace ethics set the standard for right and wrong conduct, making policies far more efficient and the workplace more employee-friendly and structured. Effectively managing ethics in the workplace holds tremendous benefit for organisational leaders and all managers' and in fact all employees at whatever level in the hierarchy. They benefit in a moral and practical sense. In the diverse workforce of the modern organisation, ethics is non-negotiable.

This is particularly true today when it is critical to understand and manage highly diverse values in the workplace. Organisations' that have and effectively use a code of ethics and that have implemented ethics programmes, find that employees feel more confident in knowing which values to hold and when to hold them. They are able to modify their values and thinking and thus their behaviour becomes more ethical and morally correct. Ethics, of course, demands a willingness to change on the part of employees. What is certain is that productivity improves and profits follow suit.

At the organisational level, ethics goes beyond mere personal ethics and values. With good leadership and motivation and training, it becomes a collective undertaking to know what is right or wrong and to do the right thing and morally appropriate standards are maintained.

References

Aupperle, K.E. Caroll, A.B., and Hatfield, J.D. (1985), "An Empirical Examination of the Relationship between Corporate Responsibility and Profitabilty", *Academy of Management Journal* June, pp. 446-63.

Baack, D., Fogliasso, C. and Harris, J. (2000), "The personal impact of ethical decisions: a social penetration theory', *Journal of Business Ethics,* Vol. 24, No. 1.

Bass, B.M. (1990), *Bass and Stogdill's Handbook of Leadership, Research and Managerial Applications,* The Free Press, New York, NY.

Bayat, M.S. and Meyer, I.H. (1994), *Public Administration, Concepts, Theory and Practice.* Southern Book Publishers, Halfway House, *Constitution of the Republic of South Africa.*

Cookey, P. (2005), "UN decries effect of corruption on investment poverty", in *African Standard,* August, pp.16-31.

Davis, L. (1975), "Five Propositions for Social Responsibility", *Business Horizons June*, pp. 19-24.

Davis, J. (1992), Ethics and Environmental Marketing, *Journal of Business Ethics*, Vol. 11, No. 2, pp. 81-87.

Dimitriades, Z.S. (2002), *Employee empowerment in the Greek context. A constructive replication,* International Society for the Study of Work and Organisational values (ISSWOV), Conference Proceedings, Warsaw, Poland.

Ferrel, O.C., Fraedrich, J. and Ferrel, L. (2002), *Business Ethics: Ethical Decision Making and Cases,* Houghton Mifflin Organisation, New York, NY.

Friedman, M. (1989), "Freedom and Philanthropy: An Interview with Milton Friedman", *Business and Society Review,* Fall, pp.11-18.

Gordon, K. and Miyake, M. (2001), "Business approaches to combating bribery: a study of codes of conduct", *Journal of Business Ethics*, Vol. 34, pp.3-4.

http://workplacepsychology.net/2011/02/14/creating-an-ethical-organizational-culture: retrieved 28/5/2012

http://jpkc.szpt.edu.cn/english/supplement/business%20ethics10.htm : retrieved 02/03/2012

Irvin, L. (2002), "Ethics in Organisations : a chaos perspcetive", in *Journal of Organisational Change Management,* Vol. 15, No. 4, MCB University Press.
Kohlberg, L. (1981), *Essays on World Development,* Volume II, San Francisco, California.
McDonald, G. (2000), "Business Ethics: Practical Proposals for Organisations", *Journal of Business Ethics,* Vol. 25, No. 2.
Mafunisa, M.J. (2000), *Public Service Ethics,* Juta, Kenwyn.
Malan, F. and Smit, B. (2001), *Ethics and Leadership in Business and Politics,* Juta and Co., Lansdowne.
Mbigi, L. and Maree, J. (2005), *Ubuntu,* Knowres Publishing, Randburg.
McGuire, J.B., Sundgren, A., and Schneeweis, T. (1988), "Corporate Social Responsibility and Firm Financial Performance", *Academy of Management Journal,* December, pp. 854-72.
Menon, S.T. and Hartmann, L.C. (2000), *Generalizability of Menon's empowerment scale: replication and extension with Australian data,* ISSWOV, Conference proceedings, Warsaw, Poland.
Millet, J. (2004), "Gift giving savvy: how to avoid blunders and faux pas", www.culturalsavvy.com
Rich, V. (1975), *Law and the Administration of Justice,* John Wiley and Sons, New York, NY.
Robbins, S.P., and Judge, T.A. (2009), *Organizational behavior* (13th ed.). Upper Saddle River, Pearson Education, Inc., NJ.
Ross, T. (1988), *Ethics in American Business,* Touche Ross & Co. New York, NY.
Rossouw, D. (2002), *Business Ethics in Africa*, Oxford Southern Africa, Cape Town.
Sethi, S. P. (1975), "Dimensions of Corporate Social Performance: An Analytical Framework." *California Management Review* Spring, pp. 58-64.
Sims, R.R., and Brinkmann, J. (2003), Enron ethics (or: Culture matters more than codes). *Journal of Business Ethics,* Vol. 45, No. 3, pp. 243-256.
Spreitzer, G.M. (1995), "Psychological empowerment in the workplace: Construct definition, measurement and validation", *Academy of Management Journal,* Vol. 38, No. 5.
Van Zyl, J.J.L. (1998), *The Art of Purpose-directed Leadership and Management: Handbook for Orientation Workshops,* Institute of Purpose-directed Management, Pretoria.
Wong, A. and Beckman, E. (1992), "An applied ethical analysis system in business", *Journal of Business Ethics,* Vol. 11, No. 3.

Wright, P.W. and Noe, R.A. (1996), *Management of Organisations,* Irwin, Chicago.
Zani, B. and Pietrantoni, L. (2001), "Gender differences in burnout", *Equal Opportunities International*, Vol. 20, No. 1/2.

Chapter Twelve

A Conceptual Framework towards Succession Effectiveness in Family Wineries: An Innovative Means for Wine Sector Development in Cyprus

Thoukis Georgiou and Demetris Vrontis

Introduction

Honestly, how simple or complex is for a family-owned winery to introduce a succession? What if there are no competent successors apparent? What if, although there are talented successors, they are not interested in exercising entrepreneurship in this challenging and particular business sector? What if competent successors have other work obligations "behind the scenes" and are not "allowed" to be innovative agents of change? Instead, such successors simply pursue the steps of a dominant incumbent! And what if incumbents tend to face succession as a simple and static event (Georgiou et al., 2011) "whose timing is never right". And then, how vulnerable is a sudden death of the existing leader, leaving the business to face difficulties and rivalry from competitors?

These and many other complex dilemmas remain unanswered and risk the development prospects of the Cyprus wine sector as well as the versatile role of rural areas planted with vineyards for the national competitiveness in general. For that reason, for more than thirty years, abundant academic research work from several scholars has been recorded on the topic of executive succession in family firms (Boeker and Goodstein, 1993; Canella and Lubatkin, 1993; Dalton and Kesner, 1985; Hambrick and Fukutomi, 1991; Klein and Bell, 2007; Le Breton-Miller et al., 2004;

Pfeffer, 1981 and Zald, 1965, as cited in Boeker and Goodstein, 1993: 184; Poutziouris, 2001; Schwartz and Menon, 1985).

In a conceptual point of view, when we refer to succession this is defined as a long, ongoing and multidimensional socio-political process that encompasses the transfer of leadership, and eventually the transfer of ownership to the new successor by the means of actions, events and organizational mechanisms (Le Breton-Miller et al., 2004). More specifically, the literature on the topic of succession in family firms mainly positioned succession effectiveness as the result of an outstanding organizational performance that boosts business viability and assures its continuity over the time (Le Breton-Miller et al., 2004; Poutziouris, 2001).

In parallel, succession effectiveness is additionally articulated such as the incumbent's-successor's functional or emotional satisfaction on the basis of various pre-contractual expectations (Klein and Bell, 2007). Poutziouris (2001) stressed even more this social aspect of succession effectiveness and defined it as a pathway of avoiding conflicts among incumbent and family members involved in the business.

Thus, much academic research and various influential studies have looked into the key factors that are believed to foster succession effectiveness. Several scholars considered that specific factors-commonly named as process factors, that are subject to more or less controllable manipulation, appear core to succession such as an ongoing (Le Breton-Miller et al., 2004), multidimensional (Poutziouris, 2001), socio-political process (Canella and Lubatkin, 1993) in which the power and influence exercised by the incumbent and other executives determines its outcome-that of success or failure (Klein and Bell, 2007; Le Breton-Miller et al., 2004; Pfeffer, 1981 and Zald, 1965, as cited in Boeker and Goodstein, 1993: 184).

Similarly, other factors which are identified in the periphery of succession environment, and conventionally are defined as context factors, might be more or less manageable during the process and have a higher or lower degree of peripheral influence on the final outcome of succession. These context factors have been connected to the business-managerial or social-political aspects of the business, focused on a variety of related issues, and are assumed again to determine succession effectiveness (Klein and Bell, 2007; Le Breton-Miller et al., 2004; Poutziouris, 2001).

Hence, "process" and "context" factors are of paramount importance for the concept of succession and are in brief outline as follows: a. incumbent characteristics and qualities, b. incumbent tenure, c. successor skills and attributes, d. successor training and development, e. successor origin, f. incumbent-successor expectations, g. succession ground rules, h. family dynamics, i. board of directors, j. organizational performance, k. organizational size, l. organizational age, m. transfer of capital, and n. succession monitoring and reflective feedback.

Conceptual Understanding of Succession and its Effectiveness in Family Firms

Idiosyncratic characteristics of family firms and succession challenges

Over the past years, family business has been a vital force in the UK and other market economies (Kirby and Lee, 1996; Poutziouris, 2001). According to Poutziouris (2001) estimations, about two thirds of all enterprises are family operated, managed, owned or controlled,. Moreover, family firms range in size from traditional small firms to large conglomerates. In relation to the development of the literature, the pattern of a family owned business was basically seen as a dual system encompassing the business and the family (Klein and Bell, 2007; Le Breton-Miller, et al., 2004; Poutziouris, 2001).

The existing system has in fact a parallel function in which all involved family members are engaged in both a task and emotional state of affairs: (a) the business-managerial task and its development (Le Breton-Miller et al., 2004; Poutziouris, 2001), and (b) the socio-political state of relationships and interactions between all involved parts (Klein and Bell, 2007; Le Breton-Miller et al., 2004; Poutziouris, 2001).

However, the existing literature on this particular form of business organization supports that one of the most essential dilemmas facing family firms is the capability to guarantee proficient family management across generations (Le Breton-Miller et al., 2004). Evidently, a series of characteristics evident in the family business idiosyncrasy and organizational environment (Lee et al., 2003) can affect managerial succession, and eventually the succession of ownership (Le Breton-Miller et al., 2004).

To this regard, among the most beneficial features that are mentioned in the literature which are, entrepreneurial talent, long-term commitment, loyalty to business success, pride in the family, tradition, solidarity (Klein and Bell, 2007; Le Breton-Miller et al., 2004; Poutziouris, 2001), and the degree of idiosyncratic knowledge (Lee et al., 2003; Poutziouris, 2001) might be easily accessible in family firms and supportive to succession effectiveness.

On the other hand, lack of distinctiveness of family firms might place them in a vulnerable situation over time (Le Breton-Miller et al., 2004; Poutziouris, 2001). Among others, anachronistic nepotism, de-formalized procedures, inexistent organizational structures, rigidity to adapt in new challenges, weakness to make strategic decisions, and family feuding might be catastrophic for the future of the business (Poutziouris, 2001).

Hence, a number of researchers (Birley, 1986; Kets de Vries, 1993) emphasized that only a third of family firms survived into the second generation, and from that fraction, a further ninety per cent failed the transition process to the third generation (Birley, 1986; Le Breton-Miller et al., 2004; Morris et al., 1997; Ward, 1987). It is moreover supported from the literature that the typical life duration of a family owned business is estimated to be twenty-four years, which is also comparable to the typical tenure of their founders-incumbents (Beckhard and Dyer, 1983).

According to Barach *et al.* (1988) and Beckhard and Dyer (1983, as cited in Lee et al., 2003, p.657) "nepotism [as a form of implicit prejudice] is generally perceived to be the reason why families hand over their businesses to their offspring or close family members". Therefore, poor successions (Kirby and Lee, 1996) and performance inadequacies (Kets de Vries, 1993) were often the source of business failure due to the inability to ensure competent family leadership across generations (Dalton and Kesner 1985; Le Breton-Miller et al., 2004; Poutziouris, 2001; Schwartz and Menon, 1985). Further reflective challenges have been identified in the current literature assuring succession effectiveness (Finkelstein and Hambrick, 1996; Le Breton-Miller et al., 2004) although the situation is far more difficult in the case of family firms where there are frequently complicating emotional factors and interactions among all involved parties, and multifaceted social bonds and political games within the family (Dyer, 1986; Lansberg, 1999; Le Breton-Miller et al., 2004; Poutziouris, 2001).

What is further supported from the relevant literature is that the level of a business idiosyncrasy (Klein, 1988; Williamson, 1979, 1981) which "is often individual-specific rather than firm-specific" (Castanias and Helfart, 1991, 1992, as cited in Lee et al., 2003, p.658), nepotism (Barach et al., 1988; Beckhard and Dyer, 1983) and the usual absence of a prescribed succession planning (Klein and Bell, 2007; Le Breton-Miller et al., 2004; Poutziouris, 2001) explain more expressly the reasons behind the aforesaid family business failures. Accordingly, a preannounced planning for succession is seen to be foremost vital to the success and continuity of the family business across generations, and thus a crucial mean for the effectiveness of succession (Klein and Bell; 2007; Le Breton-Miller et al., 2004; Miller, 1993; Ocasio, 1999; Pitcher et al., 2000; Poutziouris, 2001).

Effective succession in family firms-An ongoing and interactive process of different factors

Systematic literature review of recorded knowledge on the topic of succession in family firms effected by Georgiou (2010) revealed that succession is certainly a multidimensional process that encompasses the transfer of leadership, and eventually the transfer of ownership by the means of actions, events and organizational mechanisms (Le Breton-Miller et al., 2004; Poutziouris, 2001).

Le Breton-Miller et al., (2004) in their argumentation considered the aforesaid fundamental to plan for both structures in order to empower the new leader and strengthen his or her professional status inside the business. In addition, executive succession was defined as a long, ongoing and dynamic process that may be depended on a series of interacted process and context factors (Klein and Bell, 2007; Le Breton-Miller et al., 2004; Poutziouris, 2001).

It was moreover believed that such factors can synergistically predict succession effectiveness while succession itself is about an open and systemic process needing a continual monitoring and reflective adjusting (Le Breton-Miller et al., 2004). Thus, in a simplistic way, figure 1 illustrates that in the broader business environment, succession effectiveness is dynamically influenced by process and context facilitators which evolve and interact with each other adjusting the process in the light of feedback.

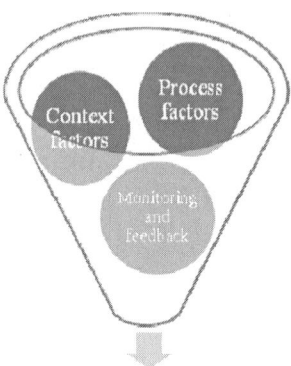

Effective Succession in Family Firms

Figure 1: Succession as an interactive process of different factors
Source: Georgiou and Vrontis (2012)

Succession effectiveness in family firms-A matter of philosophical positioning of different researchers

The systematic literature review (Georgiou, 2010) indicates that various tangible or abstract metrics can distinguish succession effectiveness within family firms according to the philosophical positioning of every researcher. For strictly positivist researchers like Boeker and Goodstein (1993), Dalton and Kesner (1985), Le Breton-Miller et al. (2004) and Schwartz and Menon (1985) the most common explanation of effective succession was recorded to be the result of an outstanding organizational performance.

For more socially sensible scholars, as Klein and Bell (2007), however, who have taken a broader scope on the subject, they have seen succession effectiveness as the incumbent-successor satisfaction based on a set of pre-contractual expectations. Le Breton-Miller et al., (2004) and Poutziouris (2001) in relation to their narrative theoretical development, expressed the issue of succession effectiveness as the family business viability and continuity over time. It was further extremely interesting to note that succession effectiveness was even articulated as the pathway of avoiding conflicts among family members while keeping the family in unity (Poutziouris, 2001).

In this regard, Poutziouris (2001) further assumed that in case of an inappropriate design, implementation and administration of a succession process, all the involved parties may exercise internal politics and games of influence that will jeopardize succession effectiveness. In a more general way, we would deduce that the recorded meaning of succession effectiveness has been seen through the lenses of ontological, epistemological and axiological assumptions of every researcher. In other words, it is based on how researchers face and interpret the world through their life philosophy.

Factors Believed to Foster Succession Effectiveness in Family Firms

Frequent succession process factors found in the literature

What it was notably promising to identify from the literature review was getting in touch with some common enablers of effective succession (Georgiou, 2010). All things considered, it was possible to classify them in two thematic groups: a. the process factors and b. the context factors. Primarily, the process group of factors comprises frequent cited processing oriented categories and competency related variables such as a sociopolitical process that seemed to be core to succession (Canella and Lubatkin; 1993, Le Breton-Miller et al., 2004; Pfeffer, 1981 and Zald, 1965, as cited in Boeker and Goodstein, 1993:184).

These process factors which are more or less subject of manipulation, are hierarchically summed up according to their citation frequency in the literature and are outlined as follows: 1. incumbent characteristics and qualities, 2. successor skills and attributes, 3. succession ground rules, 4. successor training and development, 5. successor origin, and 6. incumbent tenure. The aforementioned six process factors are explained and discussed below in more detail.

Incumbent characteristics and qualities

Le Breton-Miller et al., (2004) and Ward (1987) classified the business incumbent as the most important factor of a successful succession at the same time where Le Breton-Miller et al., (2004) placed incumbent [and successor] in the central of an integrative model of effective succession. Castanias and Helfart (1991, 1992, as cited in Lee et al., 2003: 658), Klein (1988), and Williamson (1979, 1981) all suggested the importance of a business "idiosyncratic knowledge" (Lee et al., 2003) which is regularly part of the incumbent's personality rather than firm specific.

Bruderl and Preisendorfer (1998), and Nooteboom (1993b) asserted that idiosyncratic knowledge habitually embraces considerable personal relations and networks. Nooteboom (1993a) claimed further that this kind of knowledge is all about the skill of the incumbent to gain the cooperation of the firm employees. He furthermore associates this suggestion with knowledge and understanding in relation to the internal operations of the family business and responsiveness to the organizational context milieu.

Cabrera-Suárez et al., (2001), Dyer (1986), Goldberg (1996), Handler (1990, 1992), Klein and Bell, (2007), Lansberg (1988), Le Breton-Miller et al., (2004), and Ward (1987) all emphasized the significance of a "quality professional and social relationship" between the incumbent-successor to the process of effective transfer of leadership and knowledge. A relationship based on mutual respect and considerations, agreed goals and cooperation, is discussed to make all involved feel supported and to create a setting of trust and understanding (Klein and Bell, 2007; Ward, 1987) where learning can later surface through an evolutionary process (Cabrera-Suárez et al., 2001; Klein and Bell, 2007; Ward, 1987).

Dyer (1986), Goldberg (1996), Handler (1990), Klein and Bell, (2007), Lansberg (1988), and Le Breton-Miller et al., (2004) pointed out the paramount importance of the incumbent overcoming concern on the subject of succession and failure to "let control go". Therefore moving away from this refutation step will enable the successor to be finally "willing to move ahead and progress". Klein and Bell (2007) conversely, emphasized that mistrust, controlling and aggressive behaviors were shown to be inhibitors of the succession process and resulted in high costs. It is not surprising that Cabrera-Suárez et al., (2001), Dyer (1986), Handler (1990), and Le Breton-Miller et al., (2004) affirmed that incumbent aptitude to "delegate", to "let successor expand his or her own critical thinking" and learn from mistakes, are fundamental for the required transfer of knowledge to the successor and further development as a leader.

Successor skills and attributes

Evidently, the successor is the other key performer in any succession process. The quintessential importance of a "quality relationship" between incumbent and successor has been previously discussed. However, the literature review acknowledged other key variables such as successor "motivation". From Barach and Gantisky (1995), Chrisman et al., (1998),

Le Breton-Miller et al., (2004), Potts et al., (2001b), and Sharma et al. (2001) theorizations, successor "willingness to join and serve with commitment the family firm" appeared to be of major essence.

Moreover, from Handler's (1992) and Le Breton-Miller's et al., (2004) assumptions, it was clear that the more opportunities for "career advancement and personal professional development" the more likely the succession process will be effective. Without a doubt, satisfied successors tend to be more interested and personally involved, more excited and fulfilled and more apt to be effective successors (Barach and Gantisky, 1995; Handler, 1990). Similarly, if successors demonstrate "academic, professional and social skills", they earn credibility and respect within the family organization and therefore it is associated with effective succession (Barach et al., 1998, 1995; Chrisman et al., 1998; Le Breton-Miller et al., 2004; Potts, 2001b). Among others skills and attributes, "decision-making ability", "experience", and "advanced interpersonal skills" were found to be the most important (Chrisman et al., 1998).

Succession ground rules

Le Breton-Miller et al., (2004) claimed that a judiciously established set of ground rules that cover different courses of action, have to be "set early in order to direct the process". This could be a key determinant of succession effectiveness. However, the same author highlighted that deteriorating successions have shown that conflicts take place in family businesses because of misunderstanding those ground rules. They furthermore asserted (Le Breton-Miller et al., 2004) that at least it might need to include a "planning for succession", a "transition period of working together" and development of "shared vision for the future" which is evidently some of the most significant researched variables in the literature. Landsberg (1988) asserted that succession planning specifically means making the required arrangements according to the future needs of the family business in order to guarantee the harmony of the family and the continuity of the business through the next generation.

Le Breton-Miller et al., (2004) and Ward (1987) claimed that the "gradual transfer of power and control" takes five to seven years on average whilst Dyck et al., (2002) and Handler (1990) believed that a "mentoring connection" between incumbent and successor who are collaborating for a transition period, is found to be critical for the succession effectiveness. Moreover, a "smooth phase-out/transition/phase-in" period is facilitated when the incumbent established plans to do so (Klein and Bell, 2007) and thus to develop new challenging activities, even a "new career" outside the family business (Dyer, 1986; Klein and Bell, 2007; Le Breton-Miller et al., 2004) in order to satisfy his or her individual desires and needs (McGivern, 1978).

Similarly, if the incumbent is able to accept related opinions and recommendations of an "internal selection committee" (Le Breton-Miller et al., 2004) or from a committee within the board of directors which is acting according to criteria, then succession launching and reflective monitoring is substantially facilitated (Boeker and Goodstein, 1993; Le Breton-Miller et al., 2004).

Barach and Gantisky (1995), Chrisman et al., (1998), Dyer (1986), Lansberg (1999), Le Breton-Miller et al., (2004), Potts (2001b), Poutziouris (2001), Sharma et al., (1998) all believed that a communicated shared vision for the future is an outstanding family business tool necessary for achieving the goals and objectives, and the passage of the business to the next generation. In this regard, Dyer (1986: 133, as cited in Le Breton-Miller et al., 2004: 310) stressed that "the individual dreams of different generations [must] be woven together into a shared collective dream". This will then compose an essential and trustworthy variable for succession effectiveness and business future decisions (Le Breton-Miller et al., 2004; Poutziouris, 2001).

Dyck et al., (2002) stressed the importance of "sequence timing" and "communication" in executive succession. In the same direction, Klein and Bell (2007), Le Breton-Miller et al., (2004), Poutziouris (2001) and Ward (1987) emphasized that succession must be seen as an early established, clearly communicated and appropriately adjusted with [reflective] feedback planned process. A time frame and timing variables "in a slow and subtle process of role adjustment between the incumbent and successor is a key" (Handler, 1990, as cited in Le Breton-Miller et al., 2004: 314). However, Dyck et al., (2002) emphasized the role of the competitive environment to the timing variable.

As such, a steady organizational context may allow freedom for a continuing and secure transition, while an unstable one may demand a far speeder process "as an incumbent may become obsolete very quickly" (Dyck et al., 2002, as cited in Le Breton-Miller et al., 2004: 314). Of course, timing variables such as the incumbent's health and the successor's educational, personal training and professional development have a quintessential importance for the succession effectiveness (Le Breton-Miller et al., 2004: 314).

Successor training and development

As previously discussed, the training and development of successors to acquire "new knowledge" and "idiosyncratic capabilities" (Lee et al., 2003) as well as to gather credibility and admiration within the family business is of principal importance. (Barach et al., 1998, 1995; Chrisman et al., 1998; Le Breton-Miller et al., 2004; Potts, 2001b). In fact, successor training and development for a family firm leadership role was found to be one of the most important factors among successful successions (Klein and Bell, 2007; Le Breton-Miller et al., 2004; Ward, 1987). Dalton and Kesner (1985), Kets de Vries (1993), Kirby and Lee (1996), Le Breton-Miller et al., (2004), Poutziouris (2001), Schwartz and Menon (1985) all reported that poor successions and performance inadequacies often resulted from incompetent family leadership across generations. Indeed, McGiven (1978) similarly supported that half of all businesses failures in the United States were due to successor incompetency.

In reality, it seemed clear that successor "prior to introduction" to the family organization allows to get in contact with the culture, value system, operations and workforce and provides the opportunity to develop distinctive capabilities out of the firm's idiosyncratic knowledge (Cabrera-Suárez et al., 2001; Barach and Gantisky, 1995; Barach et al., 1988; Dyer, 1986, Klein and Bell, 2007, Le Breton-Miller et al., 2004). In the view of Goldberg (1996), successful successors were linked to significantly more years of "appropriate work experience" than less effective ones. Barach and Gantisky (1995), Le Breton-Miller et al., (2004) and Ward (1987) claimed that former "work experience in an external enriched environment" can provide positive outcomes such as knowledge, reliability, self esteem and reliance.

Dyer (1987) and Le Breton-Miller et al., (2004) proposed the "apprenticeship" of successor as a key family business tool. Thus, family mentors use their idiosyncratic knowledge to educate the apprentice in all the distinctive aspects related with being a manager [of change] in a family business. In that case, Cabrera-Suárez et al., (2001) and Le Breton-Miller et al., (2004) emphasized that greatest apprenticeships often begin at home environment, increase during summer job activities inside the family business and maintain through an officially established career. However, Klein and Bell (2007) highlighted that apprenticeship is facilitated when a close and quality relationship exists between the incumbent and the successor.

Morris et al., (1997) and Le-Breton-Miller et al., (2004) further pointed out that the most effective successions were positively correlated with successor "education" whereas Klein and Bell (2007) and Le-Breton-Miller et al., (2004) moreover stressed that a "formal leadership training plan" benefits family owned businesses. Dyer (1986) and Le-Breton-Miller et al., (2004) expressed that an assortment of experiences and everyday jobs are vital to any well structured training plan that may include administrative duties, wide-ranging management tasks, operational issues and organizational performance responsibilities (Churchill and Hatten, 1987; Le-Breton-Miller et al., 2004; Ward, 1987).

Successor origin

Klein and Bell (2007) and Le Breton-Miller et al., (2004) all claimed that successor origin is a core dimension of succession process and emphasized its long term dynamic nature. In addition, our literature review (Georgiou, 2010) faces succession as "inside" (internal), when the successor is coming from firm's managerial ranks, or "outside" (external) when the top leader is approaching from firm's external span (Boeker and Goodstein, 1993; Dalton and Kesner, 1985; Klein and Bell, 2007; Schwartz and Menon, 1985). Presumably, and according to Brady and Helmich (1984, as cited in Boeker and Goodstein, 1993: 174), outside succession can impose greater change in every organizational level and a sense of uncertainty to actual incumbents in the top management.

In their turn, inside managers could resist an outsiders' selection to create job security and decrease uncertainty. Moreover, Helmich and Brown (1972, as cited in Boeker and Goodstein, 1993: 175) argued that uncertainties for the present executives may be reduced by the selection of an insider successor since a new outside leader is more likely to dismiss subordinates in the executive ranks. Therefore, the insiders' resistance to change might affect the successor's choice and moderate the overall succession process.

Incumbent tenure

A rather less researched but still central factor of the process of succession is that of the seasons of the incumbents' tenure. Hambrick and Fukutomi's (1991) empirical findings confirmed that there are noticeable phases, or seasons, within an incumbent's lengthy executive leadership, and that these seasons influence particular structures and patterns of executive interest, organizational performance and behaviour, and, ultimately the selection of a successor. Evidently, Canella and Lubatkin (1993) emphasized that those business socio-political forces, such as the incumbent's aptitude to influence the selection decision, can impact the successor choice and consequently determine the effectiveness or collapse of the succession process in the future. Lastly, Beckhard and Dyer (1983) empirically supported that the typical tenure of a founder-incumbent is twenty-four years which coincide with the average life cycle of a family firm of first generation.

Frequent succession context factors found in the literature

The recorded literature on the topic of succession effectiveness in family firms involves not_only processing and competency oriented factors_but fundamentals related to the business-managerial and industry specifics (Churchill and Hatten, 1987; Mc. Givern, 1978, in Le-Breton-Miller et al., 2004: 317). The way a particular business operates in a particular evolving industry could be a critical issue to be handled prior to a selection in order to appropriately match successor and competitive challenges (Churchill and Hatten, 1987). In relation to the socio-political profile of succession, social elements such as nepotism, influence, and various politics are also involved (Le-Breton-Miller et al., 2004; Poutziouris, 2001). However, and in contrast to process factors, factors related to the context of the business are only partly subject to manipulation.

Accordingly, Lansberg (1988) and Le-Breton-Miller et al., (2004) asserted that succession as a social and political process, is more or less influenced by cultural norms that must be taken into consideration and managed according to the cultural circumstances and social context of the business. In this regard, context factors are orderly summed up according to their citation frequency in the literature, and include that of: 1. family dynamics, 2. board of directors, 3. incumbent-successor expectations, 4. organizational performance, 5. transfer of capital, 6. organizational size and age, and 7. succession monitoring and reflective feedback. They are examined below.

Family dynamics

Unavoidably, the succession choice involves not only competency, know-how and processing skills but internal socio-political fundamentals of preference and power (Boeker and Goodstein, 1993; Schwartz and Menon, 1985; Canella and Lubatkin, 1993; Le-Breton-Miller et al., 2004) expressed by the owning family and other influential stakeholders. In this regard, the literature admitted the significance of dominant family members in various elements of the business such as "ownership patterns", "governance structures", "succession process", "selection criteria", "managing feuding", "developing consensus" around emerging issues, "counseling" and "guidance" in family councils (Churchill and Hatten, 1987; Lansberg 1998; Le-Breton-Miller et al., 2004; Poutziouris, 2011; Ward, 1987).

Moreover, Boeker and Goodstein (1993) characteristically concentrated on the role of the owning family as the vehicle to "manage capital", a "moderating factor to control decision making" and therefore, a means to "influence successor choice" during succession process. In the same path, Schwartz and Menon (1985) and Boeker and Goodstein (1993) particularly emphasized that family ownership structure and ownership concentration can affect and moderate successor choice much more than any other [context] factor.

Likewise the family can help the successor to meet both competency and social criteria and abilities to develop consensus on key issues (Le Breton-Miller et al., 2004). Consequently, Lansberg (1988) asserted that frameworks, plans and processes towards succession effectiveness must take into consideration the social organizational context in which a family and its business found themselves. Therefore, succession such as a socio-political and familial process is heavily dependent on various cultural norms such as patriarchy, matriarchy, primogeniture, and eventually other individual or group complexities of social nature (Le-Breton-Miller et al., 2004).

Board of directors

The board of directors is seen as a key factor for a successful succession as it could "facilitate commencement and monitoring" of the succession process, and "assure the establishment of the succession plan" for the benefit of the owning family (Barach and Gantisky, 1995; Churchill and Hutten, 1987; Dyer, 1986; Lansberg, 1988; Le Breton-Miller et al., 2004; Malone, 1989; Potts et al., 2001b; Sharma et al., 2001). A dynamic and well-structured board of directors with clear comprehensible duties and responsibilities could act as the "watchdog of the selection process", and thus as a vehicle to succession success (Le Breton-Miller et al., 2004).

Klein and Bell (2007) took a broader view on the issue and evidenced higher succession failures in case of external recruitment, instead of an internal recruitment. Hence, they (Klein and Bell, 2007) underpinned that a "selection-recruitment process" has to be a task role for an entrusted and experienced "internal committee" that would preferably functions under the board of directors. However, long before the start of a selection process, Dyck et al., (2002) and Le Breton-Miller et al., (2004) highlighted the necessity for all involved board members to agree on who is to participate in such a committee, under which criteria, with what procedures of repetitive appraisal and selection, and from what pool of candidates.

Incumbent-successor expectations

Klein and Bell (2007) argued that several expectations exist for both the incumbents and successors before the latter join a family firm. In case where an incumbent is outward looking that switches from the internal limited pool of successors to the opened market of capable talents, this may generate enhanced expectations to "de-emotionalize the business", formalize decision making and other business operations (Klein and Bell, 2007).

In a situation like this, an external successor may feel a sense of being member of an informal and cozy work environment, or even feel attracted by a certain influence a family firm may have on people, behaviors, structures and processes. An outside successor may also have expectations for "higher income", "career advancement", "new status" and "self esteem" (Klein and Bell, 2007; Le Breton-Miller et al., 2004). In this direction, Klein and Bell (2007) supported that a family firm could indeed offer to a new successor the chance to achieve "individual visions and goals", and demonstrate "entrepreneurial passion" in a less bureaucratic and hierarchical environment.

In reality, fully satisfied pre-contractual expectations of both the incumbent and his/her successor are found to be helpful to the succession process as they ensure an enthusiastic and responsible activity within the family business, greater trust, mutual understanding, and knowledge among all involved (Klein and Bell, 2007). Hence, fulfilled expectations are said to contribute to the "family business harmony" (Churchill and Hatten, 1987; Dyer, 1986; Handler, 1990; Le Breton-Miller et al., 2004; Malone, 1989; Potts et al., 2001b). In this regard, Sharma et al., (2001) and Le Breton-Miller et al., (2004) hypothesis is that such harmony supports again the development of a "shared vision for the future" which in its own turn provides a classic element to be encompassed in the succession "ground rules".

Inversely, Klein and Bell (2007) emphasized that a probable "moral hazard problem" might be in a latent situation and occur in case where an external successor becomes extremely autonomous. In such scenario, personal hidden agendas and actions may not be aligned with the best general financial and social interest of the family owning the firm. Such inadequacies on behalf of the successor may result in mutual unsatisfactory expectations, uncertainty, vulnerability to attack from competitive firms, loss of reputation for the involved parties, high switching costs due to dismissal that may put the succession process and the business itself at serious risk.

Organizational performance

This literature viewed organizational performance as a key factor of succession effectiveness. Schwartz and Menon (1985) argued that corporate environmental contexts such as uncertainties and financial distress can influence top management succession, and thus affect the distribution of power. In other words, chief executive selection and recruitment can result in major organization change that drastically affects organization profile. From our literature review (Georgiou, 2010), it was also revealed that a non-linear, statistically significant relationship exists between "organizational performance and succession type" (Schwartz and Menon, 1985).

Consequently, failing firms may replace top executives with an outsider due to dissatisfaction with organizational performance or perceived incompetency. In fact, the appealing "formula" resulted from the theory which tied inside replacement with maintenance and outside replacement with change (Dalton and Kesner, 1985; Schwartz and Menon, 1985). Basically, in the hopeless reality of poor performing firms, an outside succession was seen as an opportunity for turning around stressful business situations; therefore, it is presumably relevant to say that failing firms should go for an outside successor to make critical strategic decisions and to seek to turn around the problematic incidences.

On the other hand, one could presume that firms with a reasonable performance should opt for an inside executive to maintain current successful strategies. However, strong socio-political forces as exercised by all involved parties, the incumbent, an heir apparent, the owning family and the board of directors, can be drastic moderating factors of the above theoretical "formula" (Boeker and Goodstein, 1993; Canella and Lubatkin, 1993).

Transfer of capital

Concerning the transfer of capital, Le Breton-Miller et al., (2004) asserted that two aspects of family owned business succession exist; a. the leadership transition and b. the ownership transfer. Barach and Gantisky (1995), Forbes (1990) and Le Breton-Miller et al., (2004) emphasized that both aspects should be planned and proceeded together. Churchill and Hatten (1987), Lansberg (1988), Le Breton-Miller et al. (2004) and Potts et al., (2001b) suggested that capital transfer should happen immediately after the phase-in period in order to strengthen the new successor with confidence and self-worth.

Organizational size and age

From our systematic literature review (Georgiou, 2010), it was revealed that organizational size, and possibly, age, may attenuate the logic "formula" behind linking outside succession with change and inside succession with maintenance (Dalton and Kesner, 1985). In fact, Schwartz and Menon (1985) statistically justified that corporate size of solvent firms did not drastically affect succession type. However, size did matter for larger poor performing firms in which outside executives are the most prevalent type of successors.

This preference may be partly explained by the deterioration of internal socio-political forces, power structures and the increase of dynamics of external stakeholders (Boeker and Goodstein, 1993). In addition and according to the same authors, no empirical data supported the general argument that top executives in larger firms are more resistant to their replacement and that large failing firms, consequently, make fewer top executive changes than small firms (Dalton and Kesner, 1985; Schwartz and Menon, 1985).

Succession monitoring and reflective feedback

This literature on the topic deduced that succession was not found to be a linear and static process (Cabrera-Suárez et al., 2001; Barach and Gantisky, 1995; Barach et al., 1988; Churchill and Hatten, 1987; Dyer, 1986; Handler, 1990; Klein and Bell, 2007; Le Breton-Miller et al., 2004; Malone, 1989; Potts et al., 2001b; Poutziouris, 2001). On the contrary, any uncertainties and change that may occur should be an effect of frequent actions, observation, feedback and re-adjustment at different stages on the basis of reflection (Le Breton-Miller et al., 2004). They further emphasized (Le Breton-Miller et al., 2004) that such re-adjustments may encompass changes mainly in the ground rules stage, selection criteria, competitive environment and performance trends of succession candidates and incumbents.

Development of a Conceptual Framework for Succession Effectiveness in Family Firms

This chapter seeks to provide the reader with a fundamental direction of what literature has to say in the areas of succession and its factors of effectiveness in family firms. While going through the supportive but fragmented literature on the topic, various studies were identified, selected, searched and directed towards different but important key factors and variables of succession effectiveness. Thus, some studies were found to be more focused on factors such as the "incumbent-successor skills and attributes" as well to their "joint expectations and relationships" during the transition period. Others were mostly centralized on the socio-political aspects of succession, which highlight the moderating "dynamics of the owning family" on ownership structures and governance patterns. Still, others stressed the succession outcomes, linking "organizational performance" with successor choice.

This work is therefore pointing out our merging and synthesizing effort, which proposes a conceptual framework that draws a lot from Le Breton-Miller's et al., (2004) succession model. It aims to specifically be expanded on their findings in the direction of developing a Conceptual Framework towards Succession Effectiveness in Family Wineries, and thus "to professionalize succession [process] as much as possible and safeguard family tradition as much as necessary" (Poutziouris, 2001: 15) in a particular business sector such as the wine sector of Cyprus. Hence, at this stage of our research work, a Conceptual Framework towards Succession Effectiveness in Family Firms (figure 2) is presented as a precursor of our wine specific abstract conceptualization. It is therefore preliminary, generic and descriptive for all businesses, and not explanatory or specific to the family wineries of Cyprus, which is our finale ambition.

Our framework presently theorizes on certain elements which are commonly named as process and context factors. On the other hand, constructed theory on the topic underpinned the assumption that such process and context factors might be performed on individual basis; though, they can certainly interact synergistically in determining again the succession outcome (Boeker and Goodstein, 1993; Le Breton-Miller et al., 2004).

However, several trends, relationships, and interactions that might exist among succession factors [and their variables], or even between other empirical factors which are specific to the wine sector, are not presently placed on the conceptual framework because they are currently missing from theoretical research and normative models are already studied. These trends and connections, as well as the participants understanding and thinking will be empirically examined in the arena of Cyprus family owned wineries in a way to provide substantial and original contribution to conceptual knowledge.

Hence the concepts we discuss now encompass a number of secondary factors resulting from theory that may be restricted to a general business leadership succession, not to a particular succession process in family wineries. As we can see from figure 2, at the heart of the framework, a fundamental factor-"the succession ground rules"-is related to the first stage of critical actions to take in order to gradually launch the succession process itself. At this stage, the creation of a "shared vision" for the future of the family business and early foundation of the "succession planning" has a vital importance in leading the process.

The second stage of the succession process includes five more central factors which are tied to the key performers of succession-that of incumbent and potential successor(s). Thus, the "incumbent's characteristics", "qualities" and accumulated "idiosyncratic knowledge" from the incumbent's "tenure experience", and the "successor's skills", "attributes", "training and development", as well as his or her "inside or outside origin", are all subjective to both socio-political forces and business-managerial circumstances. At the summit of the conceptual framework distinct tangible factors are noticeably embedded in the business-managerial context.

Evidently, the "organizational performance" and "firm size", "firm age" and "ownership transfer" have all a profound and potential importance on the succession effective outcome of the succession. In turn, at the socio-political base of the framework, the "dynamics of the family" and the "board of directors" have again a quintessential value to the same direction.

Succession "is a long-term dynamic issue that requires an ability to constantly adapt in the light of evolving circumstances" (Le Breton-Miller et al., 2004: 324). Similarly, a good quantity of those process factors and variables are thoroughly monitored and adjusted with reflective feedback. These are factors at the heart of the framework that are all connected by a continual monitoring from which a reflection upon and feedback lead to related adjustments and new actions as the business, the owning family and their environment often co-evolve.

However, in contrast to what has been previously mentioned on the issue of monitoring and responsiveness to changes that occur during the succession process, the factors at the summit and base (context factors) exceptionally differ in the extent to which they can be controllable and manipulated by the current management to facilitate effectiveness. Therefore, succession monitoring and feedback factor are placed at the heart of abstract conceptualization in a way to show that core or process factors are more likely technocratic than political, and certainly, are more easily handled and adjusted accordingly.

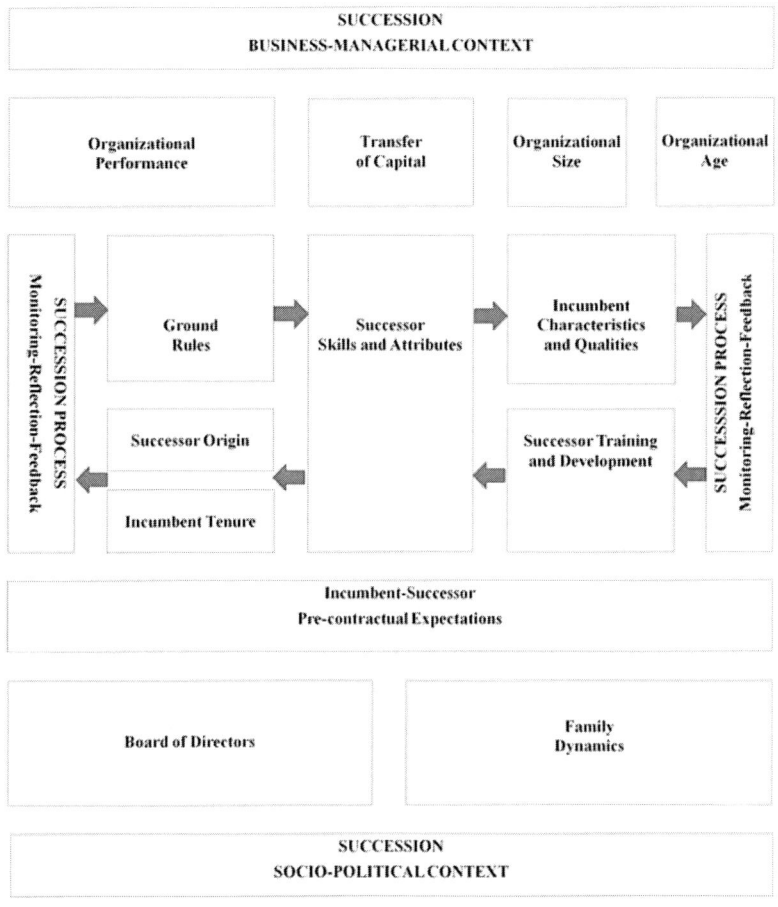

Figure 2: A Preliminary Conceptual Framework for Succession Effectiveness in Family Firms
Source: Adapted from Georgiou and Vrontis (2012)

Why Further Empirical Research is needed in the Cyprus Wine Sector?

From secondary sources of information it is evident that today, in Cyprus, fifty-three out of sixty registered wineries in the governmental archives (Wines Products Council, 2011), are owned, managed and operated on a familial basis. However, in contrast to the conceptual understanding

(Georgiou, 2010; Georgiou et al., 2011; Georgiou et al., 2012), these wineries are facing succession as a situational and static event than a never-ending and dynamic process, which indisputably risks their future development and even their existence!

Moreover, none of the reviewed studies located in the literature deal with the topic of succession effectiveness in the arena of family wineries of Cyprus, which is our empirical research base, implying that "unlike other countries, this is an industry that is difficult to research from inside" (Vrontis et al., 2001: 260). Thus, a gap in the professional practice is evident in this vital and particular area of agricultural economy of Cyprus.

Additionally, even in the more encompassing studies, we cannot assume that the process and context factors emerging from theory were, too, sound predictors of effective winery succession as they overlook essential dimensions related to the specificity of the wine business context. Furthermore, it was confirmed that the majority of studies on the subject-matter were mostly provided from research on large family controlled organizations of diverse industries quoted in the stock markets rather than from smaller privately owned firms (Boeker and Goodstein, 1993; Dalton and Kesner, 1985; Schwartz and Menon, 1985). This assertion coincides with Boeker and Goodstein's (1993), Dalton and Kesner's (1985) and Schwartz and Menon's (1985) claims, that, in several cases, data from privately owned firms were much more difficult to be gathered and treated.

Virtually, the theory constructed has not been accustomed to the specific needs of the wine business industry and that a vital "wine factor" is currently missing from abstract conceptualization. It was also obvious to assume that theoretical orientation of past research, which is the central focus of this chapter, has been placed on the basis of strict quantitative research approaches (Boeker and Goodstein, 1993; Dalton and Kesner, 1985; Schwartz and Menon, 1985) and oddly, that is in contradiction with the socio-political roots of succession (Canella and Lubatkin, 1993).

Thus, again, the generic framework developed is limited in its potential to provide authentic insights into socio-political aspects of succession such as the beliefs, thoughts, feelings, behaviors and practices of research participants within their organizational contexts and unable to explain true mechanisms behind succession effectiveness in individual settings. Consequently, a gap in the conceptual understanding also appears true.

The identification of the aforementioned practical and conceptual gaps reveals that incomplete knowledge still exists in this wine specific business area and created the need for a further thoughtful empirical research, new reflection and meaningful abstract re-conceptualization. This enquiry is considered essential in order to create a deeper organizational, socio-political and emotional meaning from the participants' perspective, and propose a generalized conceptual framework under the prism of wine specificity. Consequently, the main scope of our empirical research is the foundation of a specific Conceptual Framework towards Effective Succession in Family Wineries whereas its philosophy is based on our vision for the brightest future of the wine sector and the rural development of Cyprus.

Conclusion

Recorded studies over a thirty year period of research identified a crucial succession process and context factors and the main performers such as incumbent(s) and successor(s). These were acknowledged as they can potentially show the way to succession effectiveness. In this regard, Le Breton-Miller *et al.* (2004: 324) theorizes that "these processes and actors can play key roles in assuring the health of successions, especially in the face of uncertainties that so often derail the process". It is also concluded that the literature, which systematically enclosed some of the key components of the framework, did not enlighten much on how these factors interact and contribute to the succession success.

We furthermore believe critical that previous research ignores peoples' symbolic world (Saunders et al., 2009) and emotional expressions that otherwise would have been surfaced during the research phase. For this reason, the research participants' thoughts, views, psycho-synthesis and actions are completely omitted. This was even true in the prism of the family owned wineries which is a very specific form of business organization where in addition, and as a third conclusion, no systematic review has been conducted to tackle the complexities, the enablers and barriers of succession in the Cyprus or other countries' wine arena.

It should be moreover noted that our preliminary and generic abstract conceptualization outlined in figure 2 which is proposed on the basis of post-positivism, does not fully encompass the "wine factor" which is essential to add specificity to the framework. Hence, it is suggested that a future research based on mix methodological strategies is necessary to validate this framework in the organizational context of Cyprus family owned wineries. This is of paramount importance in order to provide change and improve future succession processing in Cyprus and other wine producing regions and countries.

A future [action] research direction in the wine sector will therefore be focused on investigation of peoples' thinking and preparation for succession against abstract considerations in a way to provide answers to the gaps mentioned previously. It will also test and validate the Preliminary Conceptual Framework for Succession Effectiveness in Family Firms, and the philosophy on the way to its design. Finally, primary research will contribute to the identification of the usefulness of the framework towards succession effectiveness and its adaptation to the real needs of the family owned wineries.

Nevertheless, the findings from our literature review satisfy our aim and objectives as they provide sufficient insight on the succession topic, research trends and emerged aforementioned theoretical gaps. By adopting a deductive approach (Saunders et al., 2009) our theory proposes a conceptual framework that draws heavily from Le Breton-Miller's et al., (2004) succession model. At this period of time, however, the framework is generic and descriptive, not thoroughly specific and explanatory.

As previously discussed, this is in relation to the fact that there have been no attempts to frame the enablers and complexities of succession in family wineries which is indeed a particular form of business organization. Thus, the concepts we discuss now encompasses a number of factors resulting from a theory that may be restricted to general business leadership succession, and not to a specific succession in family wineries.

Regardless of significant theoretical contribution to knowledge of succession in family firms, the value of this work stems from the fact that no prior research attention has been located and focused on the true dynamics, enablers and barriers behind succession effectiveness in the family wineries of Cyprus and elsewhere. Hence, we believe that further thoughtful research in the Cyprus wine sector, which is our empirical basis, is fundamental as it will be helpful in analyzing and interpreting trends, relationships and functional mechanisms towards succession effectiveness in family wineries. Therefore, our work is expected to offer a firm and inclusive theoretical basis for further empirical research in the wine sector and practical application.

References

Barach, J. A. and Gantisky. J. B. (1995), *Successful succession in family business. Family Business Review.* Vol. 8, No. 2, pp. 131-155.

Barach, J. A., Gantisky, J. B., Carlson, J. A. and Doochin, B. A. (1988), Entry of the next generation: Strategic challenge for family business. *Journal of Small Business Management,* Vol. 26, pp. 49-56.

Beckhard, R. and Dyer, W. G. Jr. (1983), Managing continuity in the family owned business. *Organizational Dynamics.* Vol. 12, No. 2, pp. 5-12.

Bird, B., Welsh, H., Astrachan, J. H. and Pistrui, D. (2002), Family business research: The evolution of an academic field. *Family Business Review,* Vol. 15, pp. 337-350.

Birley, S. (1986). Succession in the family firm: The inheritor's view, *Journal of Small Business Management,* Vol. 24, No. 3, pp. 36-43.

Boeker, W. and Goodstein J. (1991), Organizational performance and adaptation: Effects of environment and performance on changes in board composition, *Academy of Management Journal,* Vol. 34, pp. 805-826.

Boeker, W. and Goodstein J. (1993), Performance and successor choice: the moderating effects of governance and ownership, *Academy of Management Journal,* Vol. 36, No. 1, pp. 172-186.

Bruderl, J. and Preisendorfer, P. (1998), Network support and the success of newly founded businesses, *Small Business Economics,* Vol. 10, No. 30, pp. 213-225.

Cabrera-Suárez, K., De Saá-Pérez, P. and García-Almeida, D. (2001), The succession process from a resource and knowledge-based view of the family, *Family Business Review,* Vol. 14, No. 1, pp. 37-47.

Cannella, A. A. Jr. and Lubatkin, M. (1993), Succession as a sociopolitical process: internal impediments to outsider selection, *Academy of Management Journal,* Vol. 36, No. 4, pp. 763-793.

Castanias, R. P. and Helfart, C. E. (1991), Managerial resources and rents, *Journal of Management,* Vol. 17, pp. 155-171.

Castanias, R. P. and Helfart, C. E. (1992), Managerial and windfall rents in the market of corporate control, *Journal of Economic Behavior and Organization,* Vol. 18, No. 2, pp. 153-184.

Chrisman, J. J., Chua, J. H., and Sharma, P. (1998), Important attributes of successors in family businesses: An exploratory study, *Family Business Review,* Vol. 11, No. 1, pp. 19-34.

Churchill, N. C. and Hatten, K. J. (1987), Non-met-based transfers of wealth and power: A research framework for family businesses, *American Journal of Small Businesses,* Vol. 11, No. 3, pp. 51-64.

Dalton, D. R. and Kesner I. F. (1985), Organizational performance as an antecedent of inside / outside chief executive succession: an empirical assessment, *Academy of Management Journal,* Vol. 28, No. 4, pp. 749-762.

Dyck, B., Mauws, M., Starke, F. A. and Mischke, G. A. (2002), Passing the baton: The importance of sequence, timing, technique and communication in executive succession, *Journal of Business Venturing,* Vol. 17, No. 2, pp. 143-162.

Dyer, W. G. (1986), *Cultural change in family firms: Anticipating and managing business and family transitions,* San Francisco: Jossey-Bass.

Finkelstein, S. and Hambrick, D. C. (1996), *Strategic leadership: Top executives and their effects on organizations,* Minneapolis/St. Paul, MN: South-Western College Publishing.

Forbes, M. S. Jr. (1990), A message from Forbes' president: The spirit remains. *Forbes Magazine,* March 19, Vol. 145, No. 6, pp. 19.

Fredrickson, J.W., Hambrick, D., C. and Baumrin, S. (1988), A model of CEO dismissal, *Academy of Management Review,* Vol. 13, pp. 255-270.

Friedman, S. D. and Singh, H. (1989), CEO succession events and stockholder reaction: The influence of context and event context, *Academy of Management Journal,* Vol. 32, pp. 718-744.

Furtado, E. P. H. and Karan, V. (1990), Causes, consequences, and shareholder wealth effects of management turnover: A review of the empirical evidence, *Financial Management,* Vol. 19, No. 2, pp. 60-75.

Georgiou, Th. (2010), Systematic literature review on family owned business succession, *Proceedings of the 3rd EuroMed Conference-*Nicosia, Cyprus, 4th-5th of November, 2010. *Business Development across Countries and Cultures,* pp. 1338-1339.

Georgiou, Th. and Vrontis, D. (2012), Wine sector development: a conceptual framework towards succession effectiveness in family wineries, 5th *Conference of the EuroMed Academy of Business, Building New Business Models for Success through Innovation, Entrepreneurship, Competitiveness and Responsibility,* Glion-Montreux, Switzerland, 4th-5th of October 2012, pp. 689-709.

Georgiou, Th., Vrontis, D. and Alexandrou, K. (2011), Towards the optimization of family owned winery succession: an action based research in the Cyprus wine sector, *Proceedings of the XXXIV World*

Congress of Vine and Wine, The Wine Construction-Porto, Portugal, 20th-27th of June, 2011.

Goldberg, S. D. (1996), Effective successors in family-owned business, *Family Business Review*, Vol. 9, No.2, pp. 185-197.

Hambrick D. C. and Fukutomi G. D. S. (1991), The seasons of a CEO's tenure, *Academy of Management Review*, Vol. 16, No. 4, pp. 719-742.

Handler, W. C. (1990), Succession in family firms: A mutual role adjustment between entrepreneur and next-generation family members, *Entrepreneurship Theory and Practice*, Vol. 15, No. 1, pp. 37-51.

Handler, W. C. (1992), Succession experience of the next generation, *Family Business Review*, Vol. 5, No. 3, pp. 283-307.

Kets de Vries, M. (1993), The dynamics of family controlled firms: The good news and the bad news, *Organizational Dynamics*, Vol. 21, No. 3, pp. 59-68.

Kirby, D. A and Lee, T. M. (1996). Succession management in family firms in the North East England. *Family Business Review*, Vol. 9, No. 1, pp.75-85.

Klein, B. (1988). Vertical integration as organized ownership: The Fisher Body-General Motors relationship revisited. *Journal of Law, Economics and Organization*, Vol. 4, pp. 199-213.

Klein, S. B. and Bell, F. A. (2007), Non-family executives in family businesses-a literature review, *Electronic Journal of Family Business Studies*, Vol. 1, No. 1, pp. 19-37.

Lansberg, I. (1988), The succession conspiracy, *Family Business Review*, Vol. 1, No. 12, pp. 119-143.

Lansberg, I. (1999), *Succeeding generations: Realizing the dream of families in business*, Boston: Harvard Business School Press.

Le Breton-Miller, I., Miller, D. and Steier, L. P. (2004), Toward an integrative model of effective FOB succession, *Entrepreneurship: Theory and Practice*, Vol. 28, pp. 305-328.

Lee, K. S., Lim G. H. and Lim W. S. (2003), Family business succession: Appropriation risk and choice of successor, *Academy of Management Review*, Vol. 28, No. 4, pp. 657-666.

Malone, S. C. (1989), Selected correlates of business continuity planning in the family business, *Family Business Review*, Vol. 2, No. 4, pp. 341-353.

McGivern, C. (1978), The dynamics of management succession, *Management Decision*, Vol. 16, No. 1, pp.32.

Miller, D. (1991), Stale in the saddle: CEO tenure and the match between organization and environment, *Management Science*, Vol. 37, pp. 34-52.

Miller, D. (1993), Some organizational consequences of CEO succession, *Academy of Management Journal*, Vol. 36, pp. 644-659.

Morris, M. H., Williams, R. O., Jeffrey, A. and Avila, R. A. (1997), Correlates of success in family business transitions, *Journal of Business Venturing*, Vol. 12, pp. 385-401.

Nooteboom, B. (1993a), Firm size effects on transaction costs, *Small Business Economics*, Vol. 5, No. 4, pp. 283-295.

Nooteboom, B. (1993b), Research note: An analysis of specificity in transaction cost, *Organizational Studies*, Vol. 14, pp. 443-451.

Ocasio, W. (1999), Institutionalized action and corporate governance: The reliance on rules of CEO succession, *Administrative Science Quarterly*, Vol. 44, pp. 384-416.

Pitcher, P., Cherim, S. and Kisfalvi, V. (2000), CEO succession research: Methodological bridges over troubled waters, *Strategic Management Journal*, Vol. 21, pp. 625-648.

Potts, T.L., Schoen, J. E, Engel, L. M. and Hulme, F. S. (2001b), Effective retirement for family business owner-managers: Perspectives of financial planners-Part 1, *Journal of Financial Planning*, Vol. 14, No. 7, pp. 86-96.

Poutziouris, P. (2001), Understanding family firms, In Adam Jolly (Ed.), Institute of Directors-*The growing business handbook*, London: Kogan page, Chapter 6.3, pp. 9-15, 4th edition.

Puffer, S. M. and Weindrop, J. B. (1991), Corporate performance and CEO turnover: The role of performance expectations, *Administrative Science Quarterly*, Vol. 36, pp. 1-19.

Rosenzweig, M. R. and Wolpin, K. L. (1985), Specific experience, household structure, and intergenerational transfers: Farm family land and labour arrangements in developing countries, *Quarterly Journal of Economics*, Vol. 100, pp. 961-987.

Saunders, M., Lewis, P. and Thornhill, A. (2009), *Research methods for business students*, 5th edition, Pearson.

Schwartz, K. B. and Menon, K. (1985), Executive succession in failing firms, *Academy of Management Journal*, Vol. 28, No. 3, pp. 680-686.

Sharma. P., Chrisma, J. J., Pablo, A. L. and Chua, J. H. (2001), Determinants of initial satisfaction with the succession process in family firms: A conceptual model, *Entrepreneurship Theory and Practice*, Vol. 25, No. 3, pp.17-35.

Vrontis, D. and Paliwoda, J. S. (2008), Branding and the Cyprus wine industry, *Brand Management*, Vol. 16, No. 3, pp. 145-159.

Vrontis, D. and Papasolomou, I. (2007), Brand and product building: the case of the Cyprus wine industry, *Journal of Product and Brand Management,* Vol. 16, No.3, pp. 159-167.

Vrontis, D., Thrassou, A. and Czincota, M. R. (2011), Wine marketing: a framework for consumer-central planning, *Journal of Brand Management,* Vol. 18, pp. 245-263.

Walsh, J. P. and Seward, J. K. (1990), On the efficiency of internal and external corporate control mechanisms, *Academy of Management Review,* Vol. 15, pp. 421-458.

Ward, J. L. (1987), *Keeping the family business healthy: How to plan for continuing growth, profitability, and family leadership*, San Francisco: Jossey-Bass.

Williamson, O. E. (1979), Transaction-cost economics: The governance of contractual relations, *Journal of Economic Literature,* Vol. 19, pp. 1537-1568.

Williamson, O. E. (1981), The modern cooperation: Origins, evolution, attributes, *Journal of Law and Economics,* Vol. 22, pp. 223-261.

Wines Products Council (2011), *Registry of Cyprus Wine Producers,* Retrieved March 27, 2011, from http://www.wpc.org.cy/index_gr.html.

CHAPTER THIRTEEN

THE INTERNATIONALIZATION OF FASHION RETAIL IN TODAY'S MODULATING ENVIRONMENT

GABRIELLA MANDARA AND CHRISTOPHER M. MOORE

Introduction: Internationalization of Fashion Retail

International activity has become a crucial dimension of the growth of fashion retailers, as measured by proportion of sales and contribution of assets (Alexander and Quinn, 2002; Moore, 1997; Moore et al., 2000).

Even though more and more retailers are seeking to extend their operations beyond national boundaries, the majority of scholars contributions are linked to the internationalization of firms operating in the grocery industry, maybe as a consequence of the global growth of food retailers that caught theirs attention. Moreover, literature about retail internationalization is more focused on production and on reaching economies of scale and there is less attention on the skills that retailers must have, on customers (whose dimension have a different complexity in fashion retailing), as well as on the challenges that fashion retailers have to face in a continuing changing environment.

In fact, despite the success of international fashion retailers (Moore et al., 2010), this particular sector has attracted little research attention (Doherty, 2000; Fernie et al., 1997) and fashion retailers are often cited as part of general conceptual works (Akehurst and Alexander, 1996; Salmon and Tordjman, 1989; Simpson and Thorpe, 1996) or case studies (Christopher and Peck, 1994; Treadgold, 1991). However the characteristics of fashion retailing makes it distinctive from other sectors (Dawson, 1994; Doherty,

2000; Fernie et al., 1997; Moore et al., 2000; Treadgold, 1991). Starting from the work of Dawson (1994) indicating the reasons for success of non-food retailers, Moore (1997) and Fernie et al. (1998), summarized why fashion retailers are more likely to succeed internationally, compared to other retailing sectors (Table 1):

• Small format size: requires limited capital investment, minimum management costs.
• Relative ease of market entry and exit.
• Precise consumer targeting.
• Transferability of a single brand product and store identity.
• Suitability for franchising the concept/brand.
• Associated cachet of connection with foreign retailer.
• Economies of replication.

Table 1: Factors which enables fashion retail internationalization.
Source: Doherty (2000)

Other advantages enjoyed by fashion retailers relate to the single brand nature of their operations which provide for economies in replication and ease of international expansion, often through franchising (Fernie *et al.* 1998).

This chapter proposes a brief literature review on the internationalisation of fashion retailing, showing the most important contributions that, during the time, marked the studies evolution on this research area. It will be followed the logical framework built by Akehurst and Alexander (1996) who identified a range of questions to address the studies on retailing internationalisation, contextualizing it for fashion retailers. The questions are:

- Who are international fashion retailers?
- How are fashion retailers internationalising?
- Where are fashion retailers internationalising?
- When does internationalisation occurs?
- Why are fashion retailers internationalising?

After that, it will be outlined the need for fashion retailers to rethink their internationalisation processes according to the new challenges imposed by the global economic downturn and it will be shown a model able to address the management decision-making process for their international expansion.

Who are international fashion retailers

In 2004 Moore and Fernie provided a taxonomy of international fashion retailers encompassing four categories (Moore and Fernie, 2004: 28):

1. The product specialist fashion retailers.
These are companies that focus upon a narrow and specific product range. These have a clearly defined target customer group either based on demography (such as childrenswear), gender (such as La Senza and Hom Underwear) or a specific interest (such as sport and Nike and Reebok). These retailers usually operate relatively small-scale stores either within busy customer traffic sites, such as adjacent to airports/railway stations or major mass-market shopping areas, such as Oxford Street in London, and Fifth Avenue, in New York. The competitive differential of this specialist group is inextricably linked to the depth of their merchandise range within specific product categories.

2. The fashion designer retailers.
These firms retail merchandise through outlets bearing the designer's name (or an associated name), within two or more countries and market their own label merchandise. In many cases, the merchandise ranges offered by these companies extends beyond clothing to include other lifestyle product areas, such as furniture and household accessories. These retailers have bi-annual fashion show in one of the international fashion capitals (i.e. Paris, Milan, London and New York) and have been established in the fashion design business for at least two years (Fernie et al., 1997). Examples of this group include Gucci, Giorgio Armani, Prada, Valentino and Chanel. These firms typically locate within premium locations within capital and other important cities. Their competitive differential relates to the allure of their brand, their perceived exclusivity and, at times, the innovative nature of their product design.

3. The general merchandise retailers.
These are retailers that offer a merchandise mix that includes clothing alongside non-fashion goods. Examples include department stores such as Dunnes Stores from Ireland, who incorporate fashion ranges with household goods; Marks and Spencer in Hong Kong, who sell an edited range of foods alongside their fashion ranges. Their stores are often located within key expatriate locations. The competitive differential of this general

group is linked to the breadth, and in some occasions, the depth of their merchandise ranges.

4. The general fashion retailers.
Unlike the product specialist fashion retailers which tend to concentrate on only a limited range of fashion product categories, the general fashion retailers offer a more extensive range of fashion merchandise and accessories, either to a broad (e.g. The Gap, Next) or highly defined target segment (e.g. Kookai, Miss Sixty, French Connection, Mango). These groups are usually located in "city-centre" locations, so as to allow for maximum customer access. The competitive differential of this group is linked, in part, to the strength of their brand identity, as well as the breadth and depth of their fashion offer.

Finally, Moore and Doherty (2007) defined fashion luxury retailer as:

"Those firms that distribute clothing, accessories and other lifestyle products which are: exclusively designed and/or manufactured by/or for the retailer; exclusively branded with a recognized insignia, design handwriting or some other identifying device; perceived to be of superior design, quality and craftsmanship; priced significantly higher than the market norm; sold within prestigious retail settings." (Moore and Doherty, 2007: 278)

How fashion retailers develop international operations

The answer to the "How" question is very articulate, because it encompasses the explanation of how international fashion retailers act strategically in new markets and how they enter on them, that is the entry methods they used and, finally which are the patterns of their international development.

Looking at the entry strategies, when a company decides to internationalise, a fundamental decision is whether to use a standardized marketing mix with a single marketing strategy in all countries or to adjust the marketing mix to fit the unique dimensions of each local market. In literature on international marketing, supporters of standardization viewed markets as increasingly homogeneous and global in scope and believed that the key for survival and growth is a multinational ability to standardize goods and services (Fatt, 1967; Buzzell, 1968; Levitt, 1983; Yip, 1996). One of the main supporter of this views was Levitt (1983) who argued that the marketing mix standardization and the creation of a single strategy for the entire global market offers economies of scale in production and marketing (Vrontis, 2005). In contrast with this view, scholars such as

Kashani (1989) specified difficulties in using a standardized approach and argued that, in their internationalisation processes, companies have to adapt their marketing strategy in order to satisfy different needs and uniqueness in each market (Thrassou and Vrontis, 2006). However, scholars like Vrontis (2003) quoted practical evidence, suggesting that companies make contingency choices, which relate to key determinants in each circumstance (Vrontis et al., 2006). Vrontis (2005) outlined that the decision to pursue a standardized or an adaptive strategy depends of a number of factors one of them being entry method.

Also internationalising fashion retailers, typically, must respond to two conflicting pressures: the adaptation to local market conditions in order to fully respond to consumers' needs, and to benefit from operational scale economies (Moore and Burt, 2007). While the globalization of markets continue to weave complex interdependencies between geographically distant locations and tend towards global interconnection and spatial homogeneity, patterns of regional specialization are emphasizing the importance of place and are reinforcing regional uniqueness, because fashion sector is a truly global industry as well as a potent symbol of personal and spatial identity (Crewe and Lowe, 1996).

In fashion retail literature was underlined that, during the time, fashion designs houses, luxury goods retailers as well as general fashion retailers adopted a globalised approach to international expansion (Hollander, 1970; Laulajainen, 1992; Fernie et al., 1997). However today successful global fashion retailers search for retain and centralize tactical and strategic decision-making, and the standardization of their activities provides the economies of scale through the consistent replication of store format elements, marketing communication, product development and management control systems (Moore and Burt, 2007). In fact, thanks to the information technologies developments, fashion companies are able to adapt their offer to the markets needs (Moore and Burt, 2007), an example is the Italian retailer Benetton who adopted the global replication of its formats abroad through its franchising network, but the company, thanks to their process-related technologies, also mimic some of the adaptive characteristics of the multinational derived from the flexibility of just-in-time manufacturing (Moore, 2000).

Considering entry modes for international fashion retailers, despite the fundamental importance of this choice to the success of an international venture, relatively few studies have examined it (Doherty, 1999, 2000).

From the literature analysis it emerges that fashion retailers use the following entry methods:

- Flagship stores;

Flagship stores are company owned, large in scale to showcase the brand. Flagship stores are shops that (Kozinets et al., 2002):

- carry only a single brand of product;
- are company owned;
- operate with the intention of building brand image rather than solely to generate profit for the company.

Essentially, flagship stores are closely related to organic growth because this is a form of in-house store development; however, for its characteristic role, and impact on the market, flagship store is considered as a separate entry method. Flagship stores are located in prestige locations in capital cities to enhance the image of the brand and create awareness in specific geographical markets prior to the opening of stores in provincial cities. In the fashion industry, flagship stores are part of firms marketing communications activities. In fact flagship store ensures a standardized brand images across national markets and, considering that every successful fashion brand is based upon an image (Moore, Fernie and Burt, 2000), flagship stores are fundamental for every retailer. Flagship stores are considered as being at the centre of the internationalisation process for international designer brands and, for many luxury retailers, the opening of a flagship store is the first direct method of entry into new markets. On the basis of their flagship operation, these retailers subsequently build their product's distribution via wholesaling and department store concessions (Moore and Doherty, 2007). Hollander's (1970) observed that flagship location choice contributes to enhances the luxury brand's reputation and status (which he defined as the "New York, London, Paris syndrome"). Moreover, Moore et al., (2010) noted that for luxury brands, opening larger scale flagship stores gives the impression of a large brand that is significant and imposing.

- Organic growth

Organic growth consists on the replication of the company stores abroad within the existing or an integrated organizational framework. Organic growth is today used by some fast fashion retailers to have the close control on market testes. Zara is the fashion retailer brand known worldwide thanks to the organic growth of Inditex company. However this growth option is not the only one used by the Spanish company, as in small or culturally different markets, the group has extended its stores through franchise agreements with local retail companies (Inditex press dossier, 2008). Organic growth was found to be also the primary means of foreign market entry for firms such as Laura Ashley (although the company used in-store concessions and franchising within Europe as well) (Treadgold, 1991) and Hennes and Mauritz (Lualajainen, 1991). However, for fashion firms organic growth is a very expensive entry method, motivated by the need to maintain the strict control over the international expansion (Doherty, 1999).

- Merger and acquisition

For fashion retailers merger and acquisition are a way to enter new international markets gaining new resources and competences, serving different customer groups and strengthening their competitiveness covering all the fashion product categories and segments.

Fashion luxury retailers are implementing very successful acquisition strategy: the group Louis Vuitton Moet Hennessy has grown buying several brands, such as Donna Karan, Christian Lacroix, Emilio Pucci, Celine, Kenzo, Loewe, Fendi, Givenchy, Thomas Pink and Marc Jacobs, as well as a range of drinks brands and jewelry brands. In 2011 the last operation of LVMH concerns the exchange of 16.5 million of its own shares for the 152.2 million shares in Bulgari owned by the company's founding family. With this operation LVMH gains the strong leadership position of Bulgari in the jewelry and watch segment and strengthens its role in the fragrance, cosmetic and accessories segments as well.

- Concession

Concessions to department stores is an entry method widely used by fashion retailers. This is a way that allows fashion companies to avoid the high start up costs for their own retail outlet; it assures a good exposure to an high volume of customers that go to the department store; moreover and probably most important thing, concession allows to test markets and new ideas at a relatively low costs (Moore and Burt, 2007).

Concessions and wholesaling are often used in luxury fashion retailing in conjunction with a flagship operation. Some of the world's most exclusive brands, such as Bottega Veneta, Bulgari, Christian Dior, and Giorgio Armani, operate concessions within Harvey Nichols stores, because concessions offer these luxury retailers international exposure, avoiding the huge cost of owned stores, such as flagship operations.

- Exporting and wholesaling

Wholesaling is commonly used by fashion companies, not only at the early stages of their international involvement, but also in conjunction with their development of a network of retail outlets (Moore and Fernie, 2004). International retailers use agents to act as their representative in a foreign market. The agent is responsible for attracting potential customers, selling ranges to stockiest, taking orders and making sure that these are received and processed by the wholesaler (Moore and Fernie, 2004). As Moore explains, for fashion companies wholesaling is a means of (Moore, 1996: 352):

- entering a foreign market by selling to a local retailer without financial risk or significant resource investment;
- testing market reaction to the brand/product/concept;
- generating a customer following;
- developing relationships with possible franchise partners;
- generating market information, re-sizing etc.

Wholesaling provides an important income stream for international fashion retailers. While luxury retailers indulge in flagship stores and incur their exorbitant costs, much of a luxury brand's distribution of product is achieved through wholesale agreements or concessions in department stores (Fernie et al., 1998; Moore et al., 2000). Wholesaling is also a low-risk way of testing market reaction to a brand and product range, and assists in the establishment of a customer following prior to the establishment of a store network within a foreign market.

For many fashion retailers, wholesaling remains an important distribution method long after they have established stores on a foreign country. As well as being a low-cost option, wholesaling can provide for significant market coverage at relatively low risk. There are, however, certain problems associated with wholesaling. While some suppliers may set down strict criteria for the evaluation of potential stockists, there is always the risk that they may undermine the reputation of the brand through poor visual presentation, unauthorized pricing discounting or poor customer-service provision (Moore and Fernie, 2004).

- Franchising

Franchising has established itself as an entry mode for fashion firms (Doherty, 1999). This entry mode is low cost and low risk for the franchisor, because entering the international domain through franchising a strong brand and concept, puts the financial burden on the franchise partner, limits the financial risk exposure of the firm and leaves capital available to be dispersed among other parts of the company. Having developed a strong brand in the domestic market coupled with a manageable contract, the firm is very well placed to control the brand in the international market because they know exactly what they are internationalising (Doherty, 1999). However there is a debate in literature because franchising has been placed at the lower end of the traditional high cost/high control entry mode continuum (Dowson, 1994; Lu et al., 2011). Specifically Lu et al., (2011) suggested that franchising should be used when firms have low financial capabilities, low international experience, low brand equity, the foreign market is perceived to be cultural distant and high competitive. On the other hand, the presence of a strong brand equity was indicated by Moore and Burt (2007) as a precondition increasing the opportunity to use franchising as an entry mode for fashion firms. In fact, as Moore (2000) outlined, fashion retailers with well defined brand propositions, are more easily able to replicate their core competence across foreign markets. This is because their brand positioning can be re-created through the generation and careful application of a "franchise package". The fact that these branding elements can be contained within a "franchise package" and replicated relatively easily means that these companies can benefit from low cost, low-risk market entry strategies (Moore, 2000).

The franchising as a entry mode let the rapid expansion of many fashion retailers, the most famous example is the Italian fashion retailer Benetton.

In summary, organic growth and franchising are the most commonly used entry methods for fashion companies (Fernie et al., 1997; Doherty, 2000), however the Internet is progressively becoming more mainstream as a retail distribution channel, even though it has not be considered yet as an entry mode for fashion firms. Today Internet is a forceful channel for fashion goods (Beck, 2004) as it not only provides an excellent means for fashion retailers to display their most up-to-date lines via photograph, video and sound technology; the use of web sites has also enabled them to sell direct to their customers. In fact, the Internet allows companies to saving costs segmenting markets more effectively and cheaply. Recently has been outlined the importance of some features that retailers must request as part of their ecommerce website, including an interactive look book and a "buy the look" catalogue, which allows the customer to see a look and add the entire outfit to their cart in a single click (Gilbert, 2012).

However, the shop still represents a fierce competition to the online shop for specific products: high involvement products, such as fashion garments, usually suffer from the lack of shopping experience and the tradability online. Furthermore Internet shopping still presents some resistances from consumers linked to money transactions security (Schoenbachler and Gordon, 2002).

To sum up, what distinguishes the market-entry strategies of international fashion retailers from other categories of retailers is that these often use a range of entry methods concurrently (Moore and Fernie, 2004). The more successful example of this strategy is Benetton company; according to Moore and Fernie (2004: 19):

> Benetton operates 50 stores under the Benetton and Sisley fascias within the UK. Of the 50, nine are company owned and the remainder operate under franchise agreements. In addition, Benetton's has a wholesale distribution network which supplies leading department stores, such as House of Fraser and Debenhams. Benetton's mix of operating approaches is motivated by their desire to balance control over brand presentation (achieved through their company-owned stores), with maximum market coverage achieved at minimum risk (via their franchised stores and wholesale accounts) (Moore and Fernie, 2004: 19).

Finally, looking at the last element of the "How" answer, the pattern of international development of fashion retailers was summarized in a for step process by Moore and Fernie (2004: 19):

> The first stage involves the international designers supplying to prestigious department stores, such as Harrods in London and Saks Fifth Avenue in New York, via wholesale arrangements. Wholesaling are used in order to establish a brand following at a low cost. Once established, their wholesaling arrangements are extended to key retailers in other major cities. The second stage involves the opening of flagship stores within the key fashion capitals and premium shopping streets (like Bond Street in

London, Fifth Avenue in New York and Rue Saint Honairé in Paris). Due to the high rental and operating costs associated with these stores, these tend to be viewed as "loss leaders", which exist in order to promote and support wholesale sales and the movement towards the development of stage three. This third stage involves the development of diffusion brands that are sold in dedicated flagship stores and distributed via the wholesale arrangements. Generally, it is the diffusion brand, which is the most profitable for the internationalising retailer; this is because their middle market, lower-price positioning facilitates significant sales volumes. Given the crucial role that these diffusion flagship stores play within the market development of these firms, many design houses have sought a stock-market listing in order to finance the international expansion of these diffusion stores. The fourth and final stage involves the expansion of diffusion stores to the key provincial cities of the main operating markets (Moore and Fernie, 2004: 19).

Where are fashion retailers internationalising

In literature there are few studies about direction of fashion retailers' foreign market expansion. However, those studies which examined this issue on specific fashion retailers, found that the choice of market to be entered is largely determined by the market positioning of the retailer concerned (Moore and Brut, 2007). For example, Lualajainen (1992) found that the luxury goods retailer Louis Vuitton focused its international expansion upon the world's leading centres, specifically the capital cities of the most prosperous nations. Likewise Hollander (1970) found that a focus upon capital cities expansion was a common trait of the internationalising luxury fashion retailers and he termed this expansion strategy the "New York, London, Paris syndrome". In fact, luxury fashion retailers adopted this strategy of opening flagship stores within the world's leading fashion capital streets (Via Condotti in Rome, Bond St. in London, Via Napoleone in Milan, etc.) in order to communicate with their store that their products are available only in elegant and prestigious locations (Hollander, 1970). While the luxury fashion retailers typically focus their expansion upon geographically disparate foreign markets, other studies found that general fashion retailers tended to concentrate their expansions upon markets that are geographically and culturally proximate to their local market (Moore and Brut, 2007). Lualajainen (1991), describing the international expansion of Hennes and Mauritz of Sweden, argued that those retailers which seek to serve the broad mass market typically opt to enter those markets which are culturally and geographically closer, so as to minimize the associated risk and maximize their control over their operations there. It is only when this adequate coverage is achieved within adjacent foreign markets that consideration is given to entering into markets that are culturally and geographically distant from the home market (Moore and Brut, 2007).

Moore and Burt (2007: 94) identified some patterns relevant to the geographic expansion of fashion retailers:

- European fashion retailers typically confine their foreign market entry to other European markets, as well as the North American market.
- American retailers typically enter into Canada, followed by the markets of Western Europe, specifically the UK.
- European designer retailers have extended their international participation into the Japanese and Pacific Rim markets.

They also noted that, as a consequence of the highly competitive conditions within the European Union, fashion retailers have reoriented their international expansion to include Russia and other markets of Eastern Europe, also as a result of the opportunities afforded by the good economic condition of these countries that are not affected from the global downturn like European and American countries.

When does fashion retailers internationalization occur

The "When" question encompasses the analysis of conditions in which internationalisation occurs, i.e. the success factors and barriers to their international development. This last aspect of fashion retailers expansion received scant attention, it was only outlined that (More and Burt, 2007: 95):

> the main reason for failure within foreign markets was because fashion retailers often underestimate the cultural differences that exist between foreign and domestic markets; as such, these retailers invariably fail to make necessary adjustments to their offer in order to suit local market conditions (Moore and Burt, 2007: 95).

In the same way, recently Ryu and Simpson (2011) confirmed the lack of adaptation to the host market culture as a reason of failure in retailing international expansion.

On the other hand, in literature some key factors contributing to fashion retailer success have been identified: the ability to develop internationally appealing brands (Simpson and Thorpe, 1996; Fernie et al., 1997; Moore

2000; Wrigley and Moore, 2007); the ability to transfer a single brand, product and store identity; the suitability for franchising the concept/brand; the possibility to have economies of replication (Doherty, 2000). In fact, a great role is played by the retailer environment that has to be memorable and capable of easy replication across a variety of markets (Moore, 2000). Moreover it allows to customize the fashion experience (Moore and Fernie, 2004). Furthermore, the power of country of origin was considered as a factor influencing consumers' perception of the style, reliability and quality standards of a garment (Hines and Bruce, 2007).

Why fashion retailers internationalise

From the first work of Hollander in 1970, in literature several motivations for fashion retailers internationalisation have been acknowledged. Hollander (1970) found that the main reason to internationalise is to make money, he also differentiated the motivation to internationalisation according to the "commercial objectives", suggesting that luxury fashion houses developed international chains for reasons of prestige, while department store retailers went abroad because of saturation in the domestic market. Laulajainen (1991) argued that the motivations to internationalise for fashion retailers were linked to three main reasons: the saturation of the home market, the necessity to preempt competitors, and the entrepreneurial/managerial ambition. Following the explanation provided by Alexander et al. (2009) about the reasons why of the retailers internationalisation, the contribution of fashion retailers' scholars has been ascribed to three main approaches: the transition, the reaction, the proaction approach. This last one, is linked to the retailer's willingness and ability to exploit international opportunities before domestic saturation forces the retailer to consider operating in international markets (Alexander, 1995). Also Moore in 1996, emphasized the importance of factors such the entrepreneurial personal ambition or the strength of the brand, attributing them at a proactive approach. However in 2007, Moore and Burt argued that it could not be assumed that the international expansion of all clothing retailers, serving clearly defined customer segments, could be attributed only to proactive motivations. In fact, Hutchinson et al., (2007), considering how time and differing circumstances may serve to influence a fashion retailer's motivation and attitude towards foreign market participation, recognized that company brand identity represents a crucial antecedent for international expansion, but they also emphasized the importance of facilitating factors that provide a context for the motivation to internationalise for small specialist fashion retailers. These facilitating factors have three sources: internal (these include a global vision/mind-set, entrepreneurial personality and the founder's informal/personal relationships in foreign markets), external (like business contacts in foreign markets and government/ consultancy assistance and support), and parent advantage (i.e. change in ownership by a parent company, which provided access to additional financial capital, management know-how, and expertise) (Hutchinson et al., 2007).

Literature on fashion retailers has not been focused on the strategic behavior of international fashion firms in periods of economic downturn. Today the fashion sector has been hit seriously by the global economic crisis. This last one, together with other structural changes involving the sector in the last years (both in the supply and demand side), leads to a modulating environment that improves the importance of some competitive factors such as innovation, time to market and customer service (Savelli, 2011). In the demand side, together with the new austerity, consumers are not only rethinking their spending priorities attitude, but they are also changing dramatically their behavior, so retailers are facing more and more demanding, increasingly discerning, and less loyal customers (Moore and McCool, 2010). In the supply side, there is a growing competitiveness and a decreasing availability of financial resources that limits the R&D investments so strengthening the strategic relevance of brand that becomes one of the main intangible assets on which the competitive advantage and the value creation of a fashion firm can be based (Savelli, 2011). Moreover, over the past decade, the clothing market has suffered from strong deflationary pressures with the influx and intense competition from value retailers, such who are driving down prices within the market while showing consistently strong growth (Moore and McCool, 2010). In fact the past twenty years have seen emerging companies such as H&M from Sweden, Zara and Mango from Spain, and from America, Gap (Moore and McCool, 2010; Keynote, 2006). These large retail groups have enormous purchasing power and are able to extract economies of scale from their operations and economies of scope from their existing and developing supply chains (Hines and Bruce, 2007). Zara in particular had a significant impact on clothing retailers who have been forced to respond to their superior store environments and fast fashion format (Verdict, 2007).

In addition, while historically, multi-brand clothing and footwear retailers in Western Europe and North America have had a significant role to play in the channel; today, in developing regions, such as Asia Pacific and

Eastern Europe, this is much more geared towards single-brand retailing. Today's turbulent economic condition in almost all markets around the world caused the reduction of volumes and margins, the time to market cutback, the rise of customers store loyalty instead of brand loyalty. This led that, actually, internationalisation is led by single-brand clothing retailers, while multi-brand retailers achieve much slower rate of internationalisation and are focused on single markets: they need to be focused on volumes, due to the margins reductions, in order to build up the economies of scale required to earn profits. For these retailers, internationalization is a step by step process, and consequently due to the instable markets conditions, the prospect of international development for multi-brand retailers is less attractive. On the other hand for the single-brand retailers the economies of scale are guarantee by the opening of new stores internationally. Moreover, through their stores, they are able to build their image and awareness and so to attract more customers, that are more likely to spend for international brands. Additionally, single-brand retailers can discriminate prices in new markets and so, due to instable economic conditions around the world, their model is more suited to balance revenues and losses in markets around the world, in order to face the different trends of the market shares internationally (Mandara, 2012).

Figure 1 below, coming from the Euromonitor International 2011' report on international challenges and opportunities for clothing and footwear retailers, well summaries this situation.

Summarizing, only retailers owing a strong store brand can exploit it internationally. The more these retail brands expand internationally their stores, the more they will gain awareness and prestige, and these will attract even more customers on their web stores, allowing them to gain market shares even in countries where they have no stores. This contribute to increase the competition and saturation internationally and to lower profit margins. The result is that mid-fashion companies need to growth and to internationalise even further to gain economies of scale to be price competitive.

Figure 1: Single vs. Multi-brand retailers.
Source: Euromonitor International (2011)

The new process of fashion firms' internationalisation

In today's economic downturn period, the international expansion of firms has not to be considered as an option to growth, but as needed to survive. Design and luxury brands can benefit from a sort of pull effect that drives products into new markets, especially if the country of origin effect adds further value to the brands; but for product specialist and general fashion retailers the situation is different: the competition is very high and companies fight in order to gain selling spaces. These brands have to be pushed in new markets. In addition, in a period of dramatic economic downturn, companies have no money to penetrate countries with their own stores, while wholesales development could not guarantee the brand visibility necessary to win against competitors. Thus firms, in periods of resources scarcity and intense competition, have to rethink their internationalization processes, in order to make them effective and efficient, focusing on the entry strategies and the entry modes able to ensure the growth in an era of economic crisis.

Akehurst and Alexander's (1996) conceptual framework on retail internationalization provided a skeleton to direct the studies on the internationalization of fashion retailers and it can be used as the starting point to schematize the management decision making process for the international expansion of fashion retailers. Mandara (2012) provided a model able to address fashion retailers internationalisation, that was based on a qualitative research on a sample of six product specialist and general international fashion retailers. Specifically she critically examined the "Why", "How", "When" and "Where" questions on fashion retail internationalisation, in order to discover the decision-making factors and build the anatomy of the management decision-making process for the international development of general and product specialist fashion retailers. This model shows that decisions on internationalisation can differ according to the business model adopted by fashion retailers and it also shows how all the strategic choices that management has to consider are strictly linked together and are influencing each other. In view of the importance of brand for fashion retailers, from the scheme in Figure 2 it emerges that the exploitation of the brand is at the top (the head) of the process. Given a powerful and international appealing brand to exploit internationally, in period of economic downturn, the management of a fashion company (especially if a product specialist or a general retailers) has also to consider reactive factors as main motivations to develop international operations, like geographical diversification and home market saturation. The way in which companies decide to implement internationalization encompasses the decision on which entry strategy and entry mode to use in the new markets, and these will determine the patterns of their international development. Moreover, the "how" body of decisions will settle on the directions of the international expansion as well as the success factors and the barriers.

Specifically less was said in literature about the entry modes able to ensure the growth of fashion companies in period of global economic downturn, but Mandara's research investigated the entry modes able to ensure the international expansion of these firms. She found that fashion retailers used mainly franchising, wholesale agreement and the organic growth business model to enter in new markets, but overall, the franchising business model reveals itself as the entry mode more appropriated in order to ensure the international development of general and product specialist fashion retailers, especially in period of economic crisis, when these companies get few resources to invest. She noted also that the growth of franchising companies is only slowed if they can't find a partner able to invest in new stores opening. In countries where it's difficult for fashion companies to find a franchise partner, and where it's expensive to penetrate with flagship stores, companies use the concession or the consignment entry mode. In fact shops in shops in big department stores allow to gain brand image and awareness in new markets in order to develop the franchising business model.

For companies entering markets by wholesaling and organic growth, the situation is different according to the degree of direct investment that they made. For companies that use mainly the organic growth, the economic crisis plays a more intensive effect, because they face directly the slowdowns in consumptions. For companies internationalising mainly through wholesalers, the global downturn affected the international strategies in a less direct way, because the most affected by the consumption's cutback have been distributors. For these companies the entry mode more appropriated in order to growth internationally is the concession to big department stores. This is a way that allows fashion companies to avoid the high start up costs for their own retail outlet, it ensures a good exposure of the shop to a high volume of customers that visit the department store, moreover concession allows retailers to test at a relatively low cost new ideas that, if successful, could result in expansion and ultimately opening their own stores and, if not, still enable them to relinquish the concession agreement itself (Moore and Burt, 2007). The department stores are also able to provide all the information about the changing fashion consumer needs and local testes, in order to help the implementation of the mix approach as entry strategy.

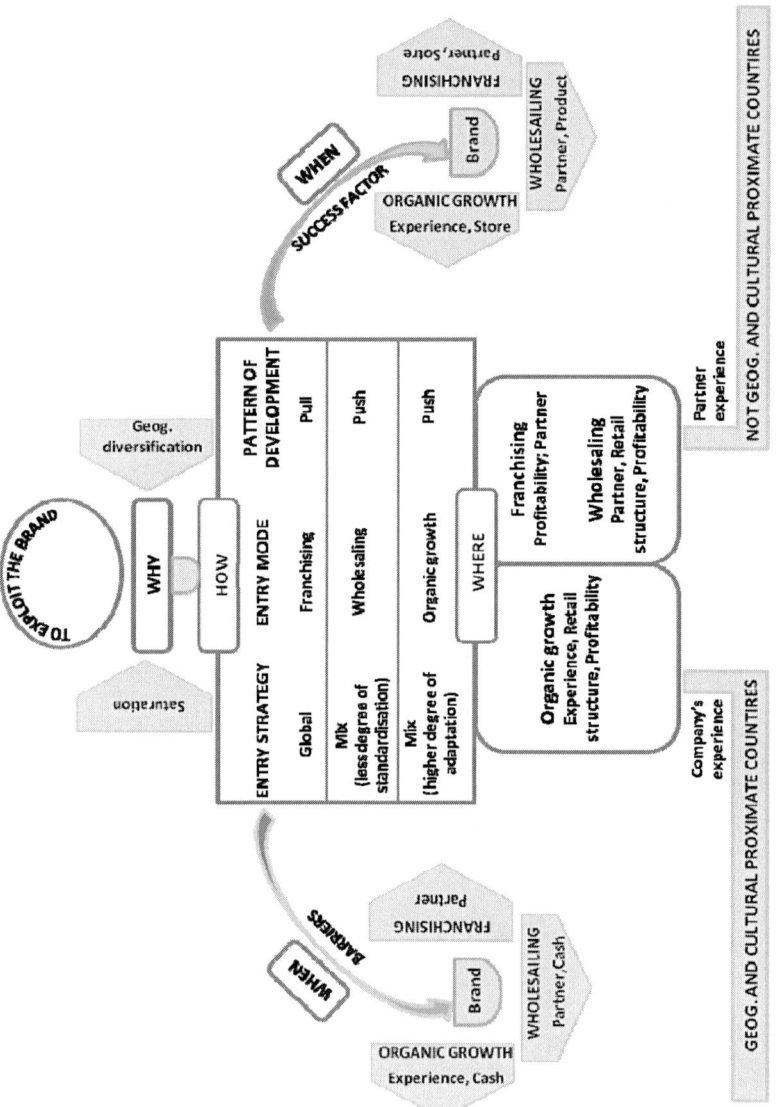

Figure 2: The anatomy of management decision-making process for fashion retailers internationalization.
Source: Madara (2012)

Specifically, if the fashion retailer management chooses:

- Franchising or to pursue a global strategic approach, it will have a pulled pattern of international development as the key success factor is the business model easy replicability internationally. The more the international stores are, the higher the brand equity internationally is, and the more the "franchising package" will be pulled by franchisee partners in their markets. Therefore the management have to consider that, in this case, the critical success factor will be to find a franchisee with a good market experience (because he has to be able to run the business successfully in order to avoid to damage the brand) and with the financial resources necessary to make the communication investments necessary to increase the retail brand awareness and to penetrate the market opening new stores. The availability of such a franchise partner, it will also determine the direction of the international expansion towards different geographical and cultural markets, because the company will rely on partners experiences.

- Wholesaling, it will pursue a mix approach with a lesser degree of standardization because, in this case, companies internationalise their products instead of their business model, hence retailers have to make products appealing for distributors. So management have to consider that the useful success factor will be linked to the availability to find experienced partners able to suggest the product adaptations appropriated for new markets, hence they have to look for them actively. The pattern of expansion will have a push nature and, also in this case, the direction of expansion will be determined by the partners availability in cultural and geographical different markets.

- Organic growth model, or to pursuing mix approach (with a higher degree of adaptation than wholesaling) the retailer will have a pushed pattern of expansion, because it has to find markets for its products actively. Adopting this entry mode, management have to consider that the most important success factor, as well as the most relevant decision-making factor in the choice of where to internationalise, will be the knowledge and the experience on the markets that the company has, in order to make products appealing for the local markets needs or to decide to change its business model, if the adaptations are too demanding and expensive to be realized. In this case, supposedly, the direction of the expansion will be towards closer geographical and cultural markets.

Therefore in this model the phenomenon of fashion retailing internationalisation has not be considered statically, but it has been declined in the negative economic environment that retailers are facing in these years, that are dramatically characterised by resources lack. In addition, since it takes into consideration the strategic choices and the decision-making factors as linked, instead that as standing alone, this model can help managers to take their strategic decisions in a holistic manner in order to rethink their internationalization processes in today's modulating environment.

Conclusions

The retail sector has undergone substantial structural change in the past two decades, with powerful processes that are creating new competitive conditions for retailers (Dowson, 2001). The turbulent nature of changes in the operational environment, in terms of politics, society and to a larger extent economy, has generated in retailers, as a reaction, to need to grow. In fact, the retail industry structural change has as its main characteristic the pursuit of organizational scale economies by retailers in response to the generally low increase in real retail-sales volumes; this lead to the emergence of groups of rapidly-growing large retailers and to a redefinition of the balance of internalized and externalized functions (Dowson, 2001).The rise of large dominant firms is facilitated by a rapid process of stores openings internationally, as the increasing size of large firms through internationalisation provides dimensional economies in this retail-brand development process.

Fashion firms are the key players in retailing industry since them as been acknowledged as the most international of companies (Moore et al., 2010). However, the intensity and the complexity of structural changes in retailing are creating a particularly turbulent operating context mainly for fashion retailers, which is exacerbating the more general instability in the business environment created by technological change and finance globalization (Dowson, 2001). The result is that the international activity, as shown by mode of entry, choice of country, speed and pattern of development, have to be reviewed in the light of these new conditions as the importance of the internationalization fashion retailers' processes can't be underestimated.

References

Akehurst, G. and Alexander, N. (1996), *The Internationalisation of Retailing*, Frank Cass, London.

Alexander, N. (1995), "Internationalisation: Interpreting the Motives", in *International Retailing: Trends and Strategies*, Financial Times, London, pp. 77-98.

Alexander, N. and Quinn, B. (2002), "International retail divestment", *International Journal of Retail and Distribution Management*, Vol. 30, No. 2, pp. 112-125.

Alexander, NS. and Doherty AM. (2009), *International Retailing*, Oxford University Press, Oxford.

Beck, B. (2004), "Key strategic issues in online apparel retailing" available at http://tc2host.com/techexchange/thelibrary/online_fit.html, (accessed 24th January 2006).

Belussi, F. (1992), "Benetton Italy; beyond Fordism and flexible specialisation: the revolution of the network firm model", in Mitter, *Computer-aided manufacturing and women's employment: the clothing industry in four EC countries*, Springer-Verlag, London, pp. 73-91.

Buzzell, R. (1968), "Can you standardize multinational marketing?", *Harvard Business Review*, Vol. 46, No. 6, pp. 102-113.

Christopher, M. and Peck, H. (1994), "Laura Ashley", in McGoldrick, *Cases in Retail Management*, Pitman, London, pp. 310-327.

Crewe and Lowe (1996), "United colors? Globalisation and localisation tendencies in fashion retailing", in Wrigley and Lowe, *Retailing consumption and capital*, Longman, Harlow, pp. 271-283.

Dawson, J. (1994), "Internationalization of retailing operations", *Journal of Marketing Management*, Vol. 10, No. 4, pp. 267-282.

Doherty, A. M. (1999), "Explaining International Retailers' Market Entry Mode Strategy: Internationalisation Theory, Agency Theory and the Importance of information Asymmetry", *International Review of Retail, Distribution and Consumer Research*, Vol. 9, No. 4, pp. 379-402.

—. (2000), "Factors influencing international market entry mode strategy: qualitative evidence from the UK fashion sector", *Journal of Marketing Management*, Vol. 16, No.1, pp. 223–245.

Fatt, A. (1967), "The Danger of Local International Advertising", *Journal of Marketing*, Vol. 31, No. 1, pp.60-62.

Fernie, J., Hallsworth, A., Moore, C. and Lawrie, A. (1997), "The Place of High Fashion Retailing", *Journal of Product and Brand Management*, Vol. 6, No. 3, pp. 151-163.

Fernie, J., Moore, C.M. and Lawrie, A. (1998), "A tale of two cities: an examination of fashion designer retailing within London and New York", J*ournal of Product & Brand Management*, Vol. 7, No. 5, pp. 366-378.

Gilbert, J. (2012), "Picking an ecommerce platform that is fashion specific", *New Zealand Apparel*, Vol. 45, No. 2, p. 23.

Hines, T. and Bruce, M. (2007), *Fashion Marketing - Contemporary Issues*, Butterworth Heinemann, London.

Hollander, S. (1970), *Multinational Retailing*, Michigan State University, East Lansing, MI.

Hutchinson, K., Alexander, N., Quinn, B. and Doherty, A.M. (2007), "Internationalisation Motives and Facilitating Factors: Qualitative Evidence from Small Specialist Retailers", *Journal of International Marketing*, Vol. 15, No. 3, pp. 96-122.

Keynote (2007), Market Report: Own Brands, Datamonitor.

Kozients, R.V., Sherry, J. F., DeBerry-Spence, Duhachek, A., Nuttavuthisit, K., Storm, D. (2002), "Themed flagship brand stores in the new millennium", *Journal of Retailing*, Vol. 78, No. 1, pp. 17-29.

Laulajainen, R. (1991), "Two retailers go global – the geographical dimension", *International Review of Retail, Distribution and Consumer Research*, Vol. 1, No. 5, pp. 607-626.

—. (1992)," Louis Vuitton Malletier - a truly global retailer", *Annals of the Japan Association of Economic Geographers,* Vol. 38, No. 2, pp. 33-48.

Levitt, T. (1983), "The globalization of markets", *Harvard Business Review*, Vol. 61, No. 3, pp. 92-102.

Lu, Y., Karpova, E. K. and Fiore, A.M. (2011), "A Study of the Factors Influencing Entry Mode Choice in the Fashion Retail Market", *Journal of Fashion Management and Marketing*, Vol.15, No. 1, pp. 58-77.

Mandara, G.(2012), "The internationalisation of fashion retailers: the British and Italian strategy", PhD dissertation, Second University of Naples, unpublished.

Moore, C.M. (1996), "La Mode sans frontiers: the internationalisation of fashion retailing", *Journal of Fashion Marketing and Management*, Vol. 1, No. 4, pp. 345–356.

—. (1997), "L'internationalisation du Prêt a Porter: The case of Kookai & Morgan's entry into the UK Fashion Market", *Journal of Fashion Marketing and Management*, Vol. 2, No. 2, pp. 153-159.

—. (2000), "The internationalisation of Foreign Fashion Retailers into the UK – Identifying the motives, methods and operational challanges", PhD dissertation, University of Stirling, Institute for retail Studies, Scotland.

Moore, C.M. and Burt, S. (2007), "Developing a research agenda for the internationalization of fashion retailing", in Hines and Bruce, *Fashion Marketing: Contemporary Issues*, Butterworth-Heinemann, Oxford, pp.89-106.

Moore, C.M. and Doherty, A.M. (2007), "The International Flagship Stores of Luxury Fashion Retailers", in Hines and Bruce, *Fashion Marketing: Contemporary Issues*, Butterworth-Heinemann, Oxford, pp. 277-295.

Moore, C.M. and Doyle S.A, (2010), "The evolution of a luxury brand: the case of Prada", *International Journal of Retail Distribution Management,* Vol. 38, No. 11/12, pp. 915-927.

Moore, C.M. and Fernie, J. (2004), "Retailing within an International Context", in Bruce, Moore and Birtwistle, *International Retail Marketing; A Case Study Approach*, Elsevier Butterworth Heinemann, Oxford, pp. 3-37.

Moore, C.M. and McColl, J. (2010), An exploration of fashion retailer own brand strategies, *Journal of Fashion Marketing and Management*, Vol. 15, No. 1, pp. 91-107.

Moore, C.M., Fernie, J. and Burt, S. (2000), "Brands without boundaries – the internationalisation of the designer retailer's brand", *European Journal of Marketing*, Vol. 34, No. 8, pp. 919-937.

Ryu, J.S. and Simpson J.J. (2011), "Retail Internationalization: Lessons From 'Big Three' Global Retailers' Failure Cases." *Journal of Business and Retail Management Research,* Vol. 6, No. 1, pp. 1-10.

Salmon, W.J. and Tordjman, A. (1989), "The internationalisation of retailing", *International Journal of Retailing*, Vol. 4, No. 2, pp. 3-16.

Savelli, E. (2011), "Role of Brand Management of the Luxury Fashion Brand in the Global Economic Crisis: A Case Study of Aeffe Group", Journal of Global Fashion Marketing, Vol. 2, No. 3, pp. 170-179.

Schoenbachler, D. and Gordon, G. (2002), "Multichannel Shopping: Understanding What Drives Channel Choice", *The Journal of Consumer Marketing*, Vol. 19, No. 1, pp. 42-54.

Simpson, E.M. and Thorpe, D.I. (1996), "A conceptual model of strategic considerations for international retail expansion", *The Service Industries Journal*, Vol. 15, No. 4, pp. 16-24.

Thrassou, A. and Vrontis, D. (2006), "A small services firm marketing communications model for SME-dominated environments", *Journal of Marketing Communications*, Vol. 12, No. 3, pp. 183-202.

Treadgold, A. (1991), "Dixons and Laura Ashley - different routes to international growth", *International Journal of Retail and Distribution Management*, Vol. 19, No. 4, pp. 13-19.

Verdict (2007), Market View: UK Womenswear Retailing, Datamonitor.

Vrontis, D. (2003), "Integrating Adaptation and Standardisation in International Marketing, The AdaptStand Modelling Process", *Journal of Marketing Management*, Vol. 19, No. 3/4, pp. 283-305.

—. (2005) "The creation of the AdaptStand process in international marketing", *Journal of Innovative Marketing*, Vol. 1, No.2, pp. 7-21.

Vrontis, D., Thrassou, A. and Vignali, C. (2006), "The country-of-origin effect, on the purchase intention of apparel – opportunities and threats for small firms", *International Journal of Entrepreneurship and Small Business*, Vol. 3, No. 3/4, pp. 459-476.

Wigley, S. and Moore, C.M. (2007), "The operationalisation of international fashion retailer success", *Journal of Fashion Marketing and Management*, Vol. 11, No. 2, pp. 281-296.

Yip, G. (1996), "Toward a New Global Strategy", *Chief Executive Journal*, Vol. 110, No. 1, pp. 66-67.

CHAPTER FOURTEEN

GENDER AND CULTURAL IDIOSYNCRASIES OF PERCEIVED ENTREPRENEURIAL PERSONALITY TRAITS: AN EMPIRICAL STUDY IN GREECE

EVANGELOS TSOUKATOS

Introduction

Although the financial crisis the world is currently experiencing has to a large extent been triggered by relentless corporate entrepreneurship, world leaders once again see entrepreneurship as a promising deadlock outlet (Alibaygi and Pouya, 2011). This renewed interest rests upon its proven capacity to contribute to the economy with jobs, goods and services, promoting innovation, increasing productivity and creating wealth (Bogan and Darity Jr, 2008; Fairlie and Holleran, 2012). Although entrepreneurship refers to the entire range of business activity (Ireland et al., 2009), in the current turbulent era it is small entrepreneurship that is looked upon as a job creator capable of providing the necessary means for combating the spiral effects of fiscal austerity, recession, ongoing organizational downsizing and massive staff layoffs on employment and wages (Bogan and Darity Jr, 2008). Promoting entrepreneurship has become uppermost policy priority in the European Union (European Commission) and of major significance to governments around the Globe (Fairlie and Holleran, 2012).

Overall unemployment in the Euro-area has reached unprecedented levels (11.2 % in June 2012) while in deeply affected by the crisis countries like Greece and Spain unemployment has reached 22% and climbing and in the 15-24 age-brackets has sky rocketed to 53% (Eurostat Euro-indicators, 101/2012 - 2 July 2012). As the end of the unemployment tunnel is not anticipated to be visible soon, youth salaried work opportunities are projected to be limited for quite some years to come. For many young job-seekers small entrepreneurial activity might be their only means of untying their personal employment Gordian knots (Ofstad, 2008). As a notion, small entrepreneurship is in many ways equivalent to self-employment encompassing small business start-offs and innovatively restructuring existing small, mostly family, businesses (Islam, 2012). Self-employment in EU-27 (2009 figures) accounts for 32.5 million jobs (including employees) providing more than one in every seven jobs in total. It is even more dominant in southern Europe, e.g. it provides more than 40% of total jobs in Greece (Negreponti-Delivanis, 2012). In addition, self-employment proves quite resistant to the effects of economic crisis. In 2009, lost self-employment jobs were almost half than lost dependent employment jobs (European Employment Observatory Review: Self-employment in Europe 2010).

Contrary to corporate business, in small entrepreneurship the universe spins around the entrepreneur (Antoncic, 2009), a special breed of business-person willing to take on their shoulders the whole risk of a business endeavour. Working individually or in small groups entrepreneurs bear the burdens of both business ownership and management while most often being the only workforce that the business can afford. In return to personally taking advantage of all credit and profits when things turn out right entrepreneurs accept the danger of seeing not only their invested capital vanishing but their jobs lost and, most often than never, their families' reserves and welfare threatened if business goes wrong. Having said all these there are certain questions arising: what are the entrepreneurs' attitudes, personality characteristics and motivation factors; are young people willing to pursue entrepreneurial career; if so, are they aware of what it takes to become an entrepreneur; are schools and other institutions preparing, motivating and supporting young people towards becoming entrepreneurs; are academics and state policy-makers adequately equipped to do this job?

This chapter describes an empirical study that was recently conducted with the objective to answer some of the questions listed above on evidence from a population of undergraduate business students in Greece. The study was undertaken under the dual individual personality and external environment perspectives of examining entrepreneurship (Lee and Peterson, 2000). Under the light of specific sociological characteristics, such as gender and culture, the study aimed at: first, revealing respondent's perceptions of entrepreneurial personality and second, examining the interrelationships between respondents' own personality traits and exposed entrepreneurial personality idiosyncrasies. As of its subject and setting, there certainly is a great deal of topicality associated with the study. Understanding business students' outlook of key entrepreneurial traits and the extent to which students consider themselves as matching what they perceive that the entrepreneurial personality ought to be is critical for government and education policy makers in accordingly constructing/ modifying study curricula and offering appropriate guidance, motivation and support to students (Aghazamani and Roozikhah, 2010). Young people can be motivated towards entrepreneurship through receiving adequate inspiration by their universities (Turker and Selcuk, 2008). The study's findings are equally important to academia. The more is known on entrepreneurial traits, the better entrepreneurship and its variations across social segments, societies and cultures can be understood.

Entrepreneurship and Entrepreneurial Orientation

Generally defined as the *"opportunistic pursuit of economic wealth …within an uncertain environment ..."* (Koe HweeNga and Shamuganathan, 2010: 259) and more specifically as the

> *"…discovery, evaluation, and exploitation of future goods and services … [by] … creation or identification of new ends and means previously undetected or unutilized by market participants"*

(Eckhardt and Shane, 2003: 336), entrepreneurship is long considered as a major driver of economic growth and social development.

Principal ideas underlying entrepreneurship are: *"new entry"* and/or *"new value creation"* (Slevin and Terjesen, 2011: 980). *"New entry"* is about penetrating new or established markets or launching new business ventures through either start-ups or existing firms (Lumpkin and Dess, 1996). *"New value creation"* involves value generation out of improving existing business operations (Slevin and Terjesen, 2011). Related to, but not matching, entrepreneurship is the notion of entrepreneurial orientation denoting the process of acting entrepreneurially (Slevin and Terjesen, 2011) and comprising the means, procedures and policymaking involved in entrepreneurship (Okhomina, 2007). That is, acting lies at the core of entrepreneurship whereas entrepreneurial orientation describes what it takes for entrepreneurship to be undertaken (Lumpkin and Dess, 1996).

Considering entrepreneurship, in particular small entrepreneurship, exclusively under the light of economic theory would certainly lead to methodological error. Economic theory takes for granted the "*rational man*" paradigm (Khurana and Spender, 2012: 14), which by definition neglects idiosyncratic human capabilities and sociocultural influences on the behaviour of individuals (Loasby, 2007). Thus, it ignores variations between individuals in values, norms, skills, experiences and will power (Loasby, 2007; Koe Hwee Nga and Shamuganatha, 2010). Entrepreneurship should better be approached under the individual and/or the environmental/conceptual perspectives (Lee and Peterson, 2000), both attempting to overcome the limitations of the "*rational man*" paradigm (Khurana and Spender, 2012: 14). The former perspective attributes entrepreneurship to the entrepreneur's personal attitudes and character traits. On the other hand, the environmental/conceptual perspective adopts a more macro viewpoint. While not overlooking personality, it considers entrepreneurship as a response to specific socioeconomic conditions either nourishing or hampering entrepreneurship, such as culture, political and economic surroundings etc. (Malecki, 2009). None of the two perspectives, however, is comprehensive enough to fully interpret entrepreneurship. People's attitudes are interwoven with their individual personality characteristics and at the same time affected by surrounding socio-economic conditions, with gender stereotyping and culture being strong links in the chain of complex interrelationships (Pinillos and Reyes, 2011). Thus, an all-round perspective of examining entrepreneurship should encompass both the individual and external environment standpoints and also consider the interconnections between the two.

Attitudes and Personality of Entrepreneurs

At the core of entrepreneurship stands the entrepreneur (Antoncic, 2009); a person whose behaviour and actions are guided by a combination of emotional idiosyncrasies, personality traits, attitudes, and values jointly forming a one dimensional continuum with "*entrepreneurial orientation*" and "*traditional orientation*" at its polar ends (Home, 2011: 295). Entrepreneurial orientation attitudes that have been widely discussed in the literature are: need for achievement (Gartner, 1985; Home, 2011), internal locus of control (Gartner, 1985; Home, 2011), high risk-taking propensity (Gartner, 1985; Home, 2011), tolerance for ambiguity (Home, 2011), high need for autonomy and dominance (Low and MacMillan, 1988), capacity for endurance and innovativeness (Home, 2011), initiative, proactivity and creativity (Hisrich et al., 2005) etc. Entrepreneurs have been found to possess higher scores of tolerance for ambiguity, internal locus of control, proactive personality, self-efficacy and need for achievement compared to non-entrepreneurs (D'Intino et al., 2007).

Although entrepreneurial orientation attitudes are different from personality traits in the narrow sense, there are interconnections between the two that the literature puts emphasis on. Despite early conclusions that it is without merit and should be abandoned (e.g. Gartner, 1988), the entrepreneurial orientation – personality traits paradigm gained momentum in the '90s probably reflecting the escalating support to Costa's and McCrae's (1992) Big Five personality model (Zhao and Seibert, 2006). Recently, the paradigm recurred strongly in the literature (e.g. Zhao et al., 2010) mainly as a result of the economic, financial and social interest once again put on entrepreneurship. The Big Five personality factors are: Openness to Experience (O), reflecting a person's open-mindedness, intellectual curiosity and creativity; Conscientiousness (C), standing for self-control, being-organized, achievement-orientation and dependability; Extraversion (E), signaling a person's energy and enthusiasm and exposed through high degree of cordiality, assertiveness, and talkativeness; Agreeableness, referring to a person's altruism and affection and exhibited through increased helpfulness, cooperativeness, and expressing sympathy towards others; Neuroticism (N), referring to emotional instability, nervousness, aggressiveness and anxiety. Neuroticism is often referred to by its opposite pole, Emotional Stability (Costa and McCrae, 1992). Some findings on proven entrepreneurial orientation–personality traits interconnections are depicted in Table 1 below.

In appraising respondents' personality traits this study has employed the Schein Descriptive Index (SDI) (Schein, 1973. 1975) that was initially introduced to evaluate attitudes towards and gender stereotypes related to male and female managers. Since its introduction in the early '70s it has been widely used to examine perceptions of characteristics and traits attributed to: managers (Brenner et al., 1989; Deal and Stevenson, 1998), accountants (Stivers and Campbell, 1995), college teachers (Kasi and Dugger, 2000) and military leaders (Boyce and Herd, 2003) on evidence drawn from samples of: students (Heilman et al., 1989), teachers (Kasi and Dugger, 2000), cadets (Boyce and Herd, 2003), working executives (Brenner et al., 1989; Duehr and Bono, 2006) etc. both nationally and internationally (Foster, 1994), including cross-cultural comparisons (Schein and Mueller, 1992; Fullagar et al., 2003). The SDI has also been applied for investigating attitudes towards white and nonwhite managers

(Tomkiewicz and Brenner, 1996) and in the frames of entrepreneurship for examining the influence of gender stereotypes on men and women's entrepreneurial orientation (Gupta et al., 2009) and investigating cultural influences on the same (Gupta and Fernandez, 2009). Though developed in US settings (Schein, 1973, 1975), the SDI is still a popular choice in cross-cultural comparative studies since it encompasses a wide range of human attributes and behaviors. This study adopts the SDI to reveal respondents' perceptions of entrepreneurial personality traits and assess gender and cultural idiosyncrasies of the same.

	O	C	E	A	N	
overall entrepreneurial orientation	+		+	+	-	Crane and Crane, 2007; D' Intino et al., 2007; Caliendo and Kritikos, 2008
risk propensity	+	-		-		Ciavarella et al., 2004; Soane and Chmiel, 2005
internal locus of control		+		-	+	Bono and Judge, 2003
need for achievement	+	+			+	Heggestad and Kanfer, 2000; Ciavarella et al., 2004
endurance		+				Ciavarella et al., 2004

Table 1. Interconnections between Fig Five and Attitudes related to EO
Source: Author's review of the literature as indicated above

Gender-role and Cultural Stereotypes in Entrepreneurship

In addition to being examined under the light of personality traits, entrepreneurial orientation is also investigated under a variety of other perspectives among which gender (e.g. Powell et al., 2002; Gupta et al., 2009) and culture (Lee and Peterson, 2000). Despite growing fast (Brush et al., 2006) and contributing significantly to GNP across the world (Allen et al., 2007) women's entrepreneurship is still underestimated. Traditional gender-role stereotyping considers women as lacking in entrepreneurial attitudes such as self-confidence, assertiveness, risk-taking, leadership, etc. and hence being less reliable as business partners. On these grounds women often face all kinds of obstacles and limitations in their entrepreneurial endeavour. Accruing the necessary social, cultural, human, and financial capital, creating for themselves attractive credit histories that will give them admittance to sources of finance, and accessing technical and scientific networks are always far greater challenges for women as compared to men (European Commission, 2008; Gupta et al., 2009). All these affect both the kinds of women start-offs and their ensuing progress (Gupta et al., 2009). Women owned or ran businesses are usually smaller-scale, in terms of turnover and numbers of employees, and thus less aggressive and of limited profitability (Brush et al., 2006). This, in conjunction to a, consistent across-countries, 2 to 1 men vs. women ratio in the number of people becoming entrepreneurs (Gupta et al., 2009) leads to a vicious circle between women entrepreneurship and anti-women in business gender-role stereotyping reinforcing the latter (Carter and Williams, 2003). The consensual idea still is that business and, therefore, entrepreneurship is a man's world and consequently successful entrepreneurs should possess masculine characteristics (Powell et al., 2002). Interesting empirical evidence on entrepreneurial orientation and entrepreneurship related personality differences between male and female respondents is presented in this chapter.

As regards differences in entrepreneurial activity across countries, the general feeling is that the relative stability of variations advocates for other than economic drivers such as demographic, institutional and cultural to be in existence (Grilo and Thurik 2006). Determinants of entrepreneurial activity include the prevalence of culture related push and pull factors nourishing or hampering entrepreneurship (Mueller and Thomas, 2000). Entrepreneurship and entrepreneurial personality are generally thought to reflect the North American cultural model of high Individualism, high Power Distance, low Uncertainty Avoidance, and high Masculinity and to the extent that the cultural distance from this particular model increases entrepreneurial orientation and activity decreases (Lee and Peterson, 2000). The perspective, however, of examining the effects of culture on entrepreneurship and entrepreneurial orientation at the national level suffers at least two limitations: a) seeing culture at the national rather than the individual level and b) considering entrepreneurial orientation on the aggregate not accounting for specific dimensions of the concept that might differ across cultures. Considering culture at the national level usually leads to systematic error, since people are not identical in their cultural orientation even within the barriers of even the most compact national identity (Tsoukatos and Rand, 2007). At the same time, disregarding differences among people across entrepreneurial personality dimensions disputes the whole idea of culture as the software in the mind that distinguishes individuals and groups of individuals from one another

(Hofstede, 1980). This study adopts the perspective of examining the interconnections between culture and entrepreneurial personality at the level of the concepts' dimensions. Furthermore, it considers and measures culture at the level of individuals rather than at the level of nation.

Methodology

Survey Design and Data Collection

Evidence for the study was drawn from the population of business students at a specific public tertiary education institution ion Greece. Data collection was conducted in two stages, 6 weeks apart from each other, with 366 valid responses in total; 193 in stage I and 173 in stage II. The survey was conducted through the school's proprietary Limesurvey electronic platform. An e-tokens system ensured that students could: a) participate to either but not both stages of the survey and b) have questionnaire access only once. Questionnaires were filled in the school's computer labs under the supervision and instruction of teachers on duty. Only fully completed questionnaires could be submitted.

Stage I survey instrument comprised three parts: demographics, Furrer et al's (2000) instrument for assessing respondents' individual cultural profile across Hofstede's (1980, 1997) five dimensions of culture and the SDI (Schein, 1973, 1975). For the Stage II survey the individual cultural profile assessment part was removed and a final question asking students to rate their own entrepreneurial orientation was added. With the exception of demographics, all items were rated in 7 point Likert scales anchored at 1 and 7 as follows: not at all/absolutely characteristic for SDI, absolutely disagree/agree for Furrer et al.s (2000) questionnaire and not at all/absolutely for own entrepreneurial orientation. 7-point Likert scales are more accurate in measuring respondent's real assessments especially in electronically administered questionnaires (Finstad, 2010).

Instructions on the Stage I SDI form were as follows:

> "Your perceptions are sought of the traits of entrepreneurial personality across the following list of 92 items that are used to characterize people in general. Please rate each statement in terms of how characteristic you think it is of entrepreneurs. Choose 7 if you think that the statement in question is absolutely characteristic of entrepreneurs or 1 if you think it is not characteristic at all. If your view is not so adamant choose one of the grades in-between".

62 male and 131 female students provided usable responses. Respondents' ages ranged from 18 to 45, with a median of 22. The sample's male/female ratio adequately reflected the students' population. Management and economics tertiary education in Greece is female dominated in terms of enrolled students.

Stage II instructions on the SDI form were as follows:

> "Your assessment of the traits of your own personality is sought across the following list of 92 items that are used to characterize people in general. Please rate each statement in terms of how characteristic you think it is of you. Choose 7 if you think that the statement in question is absolutely characteristic of you or 1 if you think it is not characteristic at all. If your view is not so adamant choose one of the grades in-between".

56 male and 117 female students provided usable responses. Respondents' ages ranged from 18 to 31, with a median of 21. Again, the sample's male/female ratio adequately reflected the students' population. In effect, the two-stage sample comprised almost half of the entire school's student population.

The survey was conducted in Greek. Research instruments were forth and back translated from/to Greek and English until functional equivalence in the two languages was achieved. Prior to being employed for data collection the instruments were piloted to control samples of 10 respondents each.

Data Analysis

Exploratory Factor Analysis (EFA) was employed, on stage I SDI data, to expose the underlying dimensionality of respondents' perceptions of entrepreneurial personality traits. Prior to the analysis, data was examined for reliability in terms of Cronbach's α (Tabachnick and Fidell, 2001) and refined on the basis of the increase of α if item deleted criterion (Pallant, 2001). The process resulted in a 53 item refined battery of traits with overall $\alpha = 0.956$. EFA was then conducted on the refined battery to produce a four-dimensional 25-item solution explaining 47.5% of total variance. For the analysis, the Maximum Likelihood factor extraction method was used and the rotated solution was produced by Oblimin rotation with Kaiser Normalization. The threshold for meaningful factor loadings was set to 0.5, the threshold between bad (below) and good (over) loadings. (Tabachnick and Fidell, 2001). Prior to the analysis both

KMO (0.909) and Bartlett's Sphericity (Approx. Chi-Square = 6031.443, df = 1378, Sig. = 0.000) tests confirmed sampling adequacy.

The exposed underlying structure (Table 2) depicts respondents' perceptions of entrepreneurial personality across a combination of general attitudes and specific personality traits. Conscientiousness (CONS) (explaining 33.54% of total and 70.60% of explained variance), a psychological personality trait standing for control and constraint (Antoncic, 2009) emerged as the principal factor, followed by Internal Locus of Control (ILC) (explaining 6.23% of total and 13.12% of explained variance). Internal (powerful me) as opposed to External (powerful others) Locus of Control stands for an individual's belief that he/she or others respectively can control the environment and his/her life. Third and fourth dimensions emerged Neuroticism (NEUR) (explaining 4.08% of total and 8.59% of explained variance) and Agreeableness (AGR) (explaining 3.63% of total and 7.64% of explained variance). Neuroticism, stands for negative affectivity and nervousness (Antoncic, 2009) while Agreeableness reflects an individual's tendency towards altruism, affection and generosity (Antoncic, 2009).

In short, respondents perceive entrepreneurs as: thorough, reliable and meticulous (Conscientiousness) and having a strong sense of controlling their lives and the environment (Internal Locus of Control). The negative loadings in Neuroticism indicate that respondents perceive entrepreneurial personality as Emotionally Stable. Emotional Stability is the polar opposite of Neuroticism (Costa and McCrae, 1992). Finally, respondents perceive entrepreneurs as being friendly, empathetic and willing to help (Agreeableness).

Stage I analysis also involved assessing: a) perception differences between male and female respondents across the four dimensions of entrepreneurial personality emerged by EFA and b) links of respondents' cultural profiles across Hofstede's (1980, 1997) dimensions to respondents' perceptions of the dimensions of entrepreneurial personality. For the analysis, the variables CONS, ILC, NEUR and AGR, representing mean item marks of each entrepreneurial personality dimension, were calculated. In addition, the variables PDI, IND, MAS, UAV, LTO representing respondents' propensity towards Hofstede's dimensions: Power Distance, Individualism/Collectivism, Masculinity/Femininity, Uncertainty Avoidance and Long Term Orientation respectively, were calculated as suggested by Furrer et al. (2000).

	CONS	ILC	NEUR	AGR
	33.54% of var $\alpha = 0.85$	6.23% of var $\alpha = 0.77$	4.08% of var $\alpha = 0.77$	3.63% of var $\alpha = 0.83$
Valuing pleasant surroundings	0.677			
Creative	0.657			
Firm	0.620			
Well informed	0.564			
Competent	0.543			
Courteous	0.511			
Consistent	0.506			
Dominant		0.698		
Leadership ability		0.589		
Self-controlled		0.548		
Strong need for achievement		0.546		
Speedily recovering from emotional trauma		0.538		
Self-confident		0.531		
Strong need for security			-0.719	
Interested in own appearance			-0.676	
Talkative			-0.652	
Analytical ability			-0.556	
Desire for friendship			-0.527	
Competitive with people			-0.506	
Tactful				0.713
Generous				0.704
Kind				0.691
Helpful				0.640
Industrious				0.572
Grateful				0.513

Table 2. – Perceived Entrepreneurial Personality Dimensions
Source: SPSS output of Stage I SDI data exploratory factor analysis

Differences in perceptions between male and female respondents were assessed through independent samples t-test comparison of means analysis (Table 3) that revealed no statistically significant differences (95%) between mean values of male and female respondents across the CONS, ILC, NEUR and AGR variables. However, although non-significant at the 95% level, there is evidence of differentiation between sexes as per the ILC and AGR variables with the males' ILC and AGR mean values exceeding and lagging the females' values respectively. Should a 90% confidence interval had been chosen for the analysis both t-values would have been statistically significant, an indication of that *t-test* results concerning the specific variables could well have been sample specific and must be further researched.

	t	df	Sig. (2-tailed)	Mean Dif.	Std. Error Dif.
CONS	-0.752	191	0.453	-0.09473	0.12590
ILC	1.729	191	0.085	0.24713	0.14290
NEUR	-0.105	191	0.917	-0.01451	0.13858
AGR	-1.902	191	0.059	-0.30389	0.15977
Levene's test indicated equal variance across sub-samples.					

Table 3. Independent Samples t-test
Source: SPSS output

Effects of cultural values were appraised by bivariate correlation analysis of the variables CONS, ILC, NEUR and AGR, PDI, IND, MAS, UAV, LTO (Table 4). The analysis revealed no effect of Collectivism/Individualism and Uncertainty Avoidance on the dimensions of Entrepreneurial Personality. High Power Distance was found to inversely affect Internal Locus of Control ($r = -0.150$, sig. 0.05) while Long Term Orientation was positively related to the same ($r = 0.235$, sig. 0.01). On the other hand, high Masculinity inversely affected Conscientiousness ($r = -0.154$, sig. 0.05), Internal Locus of Control ($r = -0.191$, sig. 0.01) and Agreeableness ($r = -0.167$, sig. 0.05).

The analysis went on examining similarities between characteristics attributed to entrepreneurs (Stage I) and own attributed characteristics by male and female respondents (Stage II). It involved computing intraclass correlation coefficients (r') representing agreements between two or more raters or evaluation methods on the same set of subjects (classes). For the analysis the CONS, ILC, NEUR and AGR variables were set as classes and the mean variable ratings as scores across classes. Table 5 illustrates the analyses conducted and the corresponding r' values. Under the assumption that scores comprise a random sample from a larger population the two-way random effects model was used. Large r' values denote high similarity of observations across classes under examination (Brenner et al., 1989).

	CONS	ILC	NEUR	AGR
PDI	-0.032	-0.150*	-0.053	0.001
IND	-0.005	-0.063	-0.044	-0.069
MAS	-0.154*	-0.191**	0.025	-0.167
UAV	0.119	0.136	0.096	0.129
LTO	0.049	0.235**	-0.036	-0.002

*. Correlation is significant at the 0.05 level (2-tailed)
**. Correlation is significant at the 0.01 level (2-tailed)

Table 4: Bivariate Correlation Analysis
Source: SPSS output

Results in Table 5 depict that no statistically significant r' values were produced, an indication that no substantial similarity exists between own attributed personality characteristics by both males and females in Stage II and characteristics attributed: a) to entrepreneurs in general in Stage I and b) to entrepreneurs in Stage I by males and females respectively. Stage II men identify themselves as closer to entrepreneurs in general (r'=0.257) as compared to women (r'=0.249). However, Stage II men identify themselves less to the personalities attributed to entrepreneurs by Stage I men (r'=0.117) than stage II women to the personalities attributed to entrepreneurs by Stage I women (r'=0.356).

Analysis	r'
Men (Stage II) vs. Entrepreneurs in General (Stage I)	0.257
Women (Stage II) vs. Entrepreneurs in General (Stage I)	0.249
Men (Stage II) vs. Entrepreneurs as perceived by Men (Stage I)	0.117
Women (Stage II) vs. Entrepreneurs as perceived by Women (Stage I)	0.356

Table 5. Intraclass Coefficients
Source: SPSS output

Last but not least, Stage II analysis included comparison of mean scores provided by male and female respondents as regards their individual entrepreneurial orientation, measured in terms of a seven point Likert scale. Although men's mean score (4.95) was higher than that of women (4.58), independent samples t-test analysis revealed no significant statistical difference between the two (t = 1.525, df = 171, sig = 0.129).

Discussion of Results

Personality Traits Attributed to Entrepreneurs

The description of entrepreneurial personality in terms of Conscientiousness (as principal factor), Internal Locus of Control, Emotional Stability (inverse Neuroticism) and Agreeableness, offers support to numerous findings of previous research. All emerged dimensions have been extensively discussed in the entrepreneurship literature e.g. Conscientiousness: Heggestad and Kanfer, (2000); Bono and Judge, (2003); Ciavarella et al., (2004) etc., Internal Locus of Control: Gartner, (1985); Low and MacMillan, (1988); Home, (2011) etc., Emotional Stability (inverse Neuroticism) and Agreeableness: Crane and Crane, (2007); D' Intino et al., (2007); Caliendo and Kritikos, (2008).

However, the elements that the literature discusses as lying at the core of entrepreneurial personality: High Risk-Taking Propensity (Gartner, 1985; Hisrich et al., 2005; Home, 2011) and Tolerance for Ambiguity (Home, 2011), are not present in respondents' perceptions of the same. This may be attributed to that respondents are students, mostly not having any real-life working experience, as opposed to previously conducted studies on samples of actual entrepreneurs and/or managers. This certainly refers to the need, discussed earlier, of providing adequate training and insight to students as regards what entrepreneurship is about; more so in tertiary business education where entrepreneurship and entrepreneurial orientation courses should be built in study curricula.

As regards differences of entrepreneurial personality perceptions across genders, findings of this study support Gupta's et al.'s (2009) proposal that perceptions of men and women do not differ. No statistically significant differences between male and female respondents across perceived Entrepreneurial Personality dimensions were revealed. However, higher Internal Locus of Control and lower Agreeableness mean values of men as compared to women provide directional, but not statistically significant, support to the general idea that business in general and, thus, entrepreneurship is a "man's world" and thus masculine rather than feminine personality characteristics should be anticipated for entrepreneurs (Powell et al., 2002). Internal Locus of Control is supposed to be masculine (e.g. Lee and Peterson, 2000) whereas Agreeableness tends to be considered as feminine (e.g. Lippa, 1995; Marusic and Bratko, 1998; Envick and Langford, 2003) personality characteristics. In view of the weakness of evidence, though, further research on this particular subject is required.

Previous research on the interconnections between Hofstede's cultural dimensions on entrepreneurial personality in general correlates the latter with high Individualism, high Power Distance, low Uncertainty Avoidance, and high Masculinity (Lee and Peterson, 2000). As regards the relationships between Hofstede's dimensions and specific dimensions of Entrepreneurial Personality existing evidence is not so clear and to some extent contradicting. In this respect this study's findings provide interesting input to the ongoing debates:

Femininity/Masculinity: Contradicting evidence exists in the literature on the relationship between Femininity/Masculinity and Conscientiousness. There are researchers linking Conscientiousness to Masculinity (e.g. Marusic and Bratko, 1998) while others (e.g. Lippa, 1995) maintaining that conscientiousness is linked to Femininity and a third group (e.g. Envick and Langford, 2003) reporting no such connection whatsoever. Support to the notion is, hereby, provided that as regards people's perceptions of entrepreneurial personality traits, Masculinity is inversely linked to Conscientiousness. On the other hand, findings of this study are in line with the consensual notion linking Femininity to Agreeableness (e.g. Lippa, 1995; Marusic and Bratko, 1998; Envick and Langford, 2003). Bivariate correlation analysis of the interconnection between Femininity/Masculinity and the Locus of Control dimension of perceived entrepreneurial personality challenges previous results of both this study and pre-existing research. Although the difference is non-significant at the 95% but only at the 90% level, the mean Internal Locus of Control value of male respondents exceeded that of females (Table 3) while Masculinity, a predominantly male cultural value, was found negatively related to the same. One might argue that a paradox exists here and most probably it does. In this respect, Gupta et al. (2009: 398) argue that in relation to entrepreneurship it is preferable to examine differences between men and women through the "*lens of gender*", that is in relation to what people "*do*", rather than the "*lens of sex*", that is in relation to what people are born as. The exposed inverse relationship between Masculinity and Internal Locus of Control is inconsistent to the findings of previous studies examining the relationships between national culture and entrepreneurship (e.g. Lee and Peterson, 2000) but consistent to findings of other studies measuring cultural values at the individual rather than the national level. In this regard, Chelariou et al., (2008) found a positive relationship between Masculinity and the "powerful others" dimension of Locus of Control, expressing negative Internal Locus of Control. In any case, a motivating research question presents itself here: why male respondents scored higher on the Internal Locus of Control dimension of perceived entrepreneurial personality when Internal Locus of Control was subsequently found to be negatively linked to Masculinity? Further research is certainly needed here.

Power Distance: The inverse relationship between power distance and Internal Locus of Control is consistent to previous findings of Chelariu et al., (2008) who maintained that Power Distance is negatively related to the internal dimension of Locus of Control while positively related to the Powerful others dimension of the same. Power Distance affects differently individuals perceiving themselves as weak or powerful. While powerful individuals scoring high in Power Distance tend to consider themselves as capable of controlling the environment, thus presenting high scores on Internal Locus of Control, weak individuals with high Power Distance scores tend to consider themselves as unimportant and the higher their Power Distance score, the more they cherish the powerful others rather than the internal dimension of Locus of Control (Tsoukatos and Rand, 2007). The sample of respondents in this study was one of students expected to consider themselves as relatively weak.

Time Orientation: The exposed positive relationship between the Internal Locus of Control dimension of perceived entrepreneurial personality and Long Term Orientation is consistent with previous research findings linking Internal Locus of Control to long-time perspective (e.g. Macintosh, 2006).

Own Attributed vs. Perceived Personality Characteristics

Despite consensual agreement that entrepreneurship is a predominantly male domain and that the personality of entrepreneurs exhibit male characteristics (Powel et al., 2002) this is only weakly supported by the findings of this study. No statistically significant intraclass coefficients (**r'**) were produced in any of the analyses conducted. Neither men nor women respondents identify their own personalities to perceived entrepreneurial personality. Although the "Men (Stage II) vs. Entrepreneurs in General (Stage I)" analysis produced a slightly higher **r'** (0.257) than the one produced by the "Women (Stage II) vs. Entrepreneurs in General (Stage I)" analysis (0.249), indicating higher identification of men to Entrepreneurs than women, this is just a directional indication that can provide no solid attitudinal evidence. On the other hand, Women identify themselves to Entrepreneurs as perceived by women more closely (r'=0.356) than Men identify themselves to Entrepreneurs as perceived by men (r'=0.117). Again, since both r' values are non-significant no statistically significant attitudinal difference between men and women respondents can be inferred.

Entrepreneurial orientation of Men and Women

Comparison of entrepreneurial orientation between men and women provided no significant difference between the two means (t = 1.525, df = 171, sig = 0.129) although the mean men's' score (4.95) is higher than that of women (4.58) thus providing weak directional evidence on men's higher propensity to entrepreneurship. In 1 to 5 Likert scales, Stivers and Campbell (1995) recommended mean rating of 4 or higher to consider an item as characteristic of the target population. By analogy and since individual entrepreneurial orientation was measured in this study in terms of a seven point Likert scale, the corresponding to men and women scores of 4.95 and 4.58 cannot be considered as indicating high entrepreneurial orientation.

Implications, Limitations and Further Research Directions

This study's findings yield important implications to both academia and policy making. In relation to academia the study adds to the literature on expressing entrepreneurial personality in terms of both attitudes and psychological personality traits. It also contributes to the debates on: a) differences among genders as regards entrepreneurial personality perceptions and b) interconnections between respondents' individual cultural profiles and perceived dimensions of entrepreneurial personality. Due to inconclusive evidence, however, findings call for thorough further research in similar or different settings.

Of particular interest, though, are the implications of the study's findings to policy making, especially in view of the current and anticipated future scenery of high unemployment and shortage of available salaried jobs. The sample respondents, notably tertiary education business students, appeared to disregard the risk taking propensity (Gartner, 1985; Hisrich et al., 2005; Home, 2011) and Tolerance for Ambiguity, and uncertainty tolerance (Home, 2011) elements that are widely discussed in the literature as predominant in entrepreneurial personality. Students of both genders also appeared to not only having relatively low entrepreneurial orientation but also not identifying themselves with previously perceived entrepreneurial personality. These are serious defects in students' ability to cope with real world conditions in view of that almost all respondents were about to graduate and enter production where salaried job engagement is not easy.

State policy-makers should see to that entrepreneurship is promoted, especially among young people about to graduate, as a promising alternative to salaried employment in view of the unemployment deadlock that most graduates are expected to face. Academic policy-makers should see to: a) integrating entrepreneurship modules in study curricula of all business schools and b) adding an entrepreneurial perspective to most modules taught. The bottom line is that, as of the findings of this study, a nation-wide action to promote entrepreneurship and explain to young people what it takes to become an entrepreneur should be undertaken by all available means in view of the current situation in the Country. Increasing entrepreneurial awareness of young graduates is critical. On the other hand, perceptions of entrepreneurial personality proved to be culturally influenced and this must be seriously taken into account both by state and academic policy makers. Planting horizontal programs of promoting entrepreneurship from abroad would certainly lead to failure as so often has been the case in the past. There is a great deal of cultural variation among students that should be taken into account. A custom made, for the targeted cultural environment, programme needs to be devised from starters.

Limitations of this study are certainly related to: a) drawing evidence from a single business school and b) surveying through the internet. However, the sample size in relation to the students' population and the due care taken to design data collection so that sampling bias is excluded ensures that the study did not suffer significant defects.

Further research is certainly needed so that the dimensions of entrepreneurial orientation are better understood and their interconnections with the dimensions of culture are better explained. Moreover, the paradox of higher ILC values of males as compared to women while ILC was found to be inversely related to Masculinity should certainly be further researched. Although the situational variables in Greece may differ from those in other countries, the study's methodological framework can be adapted to apply to every research setting especially in settings in Southern Europe where the situation, if it is not similar already, certainly tends to approach the one in Greece. Since the issue of entrepreneurship is vital under the current socio-economic climate, the better academics and policy-makers are equipped to understand entrepreneurial personality and its interactions and effects the better they can provide young people in their respective countries with the ability to take advantage of chances to get a job that are there but to be exploited need more than filling in job applications and submitting CVs for salaried jobs.

References

Aghazamani, A. and Roozikhah E (2010), "Entrepreneurial Characteristics among University Students: A Comparative Study between Iranian and Swedish University Students", *European Journal of Social Sciences*, Vol. 18, No. 2, pp. 304-310.

Alibaygi, A. and Pouya, M. (2011), "Socio-demographic determinants of entrepreneurial intentions: A case from Iran", *African Journal of Business Management*, Vol. 5, No. 34, pp. 13316-13321.

Allen, E., Elam, E., Langowitz, N. and Dean, M. (2007), *The GEM women's report*, Wellesley, MA: Centre for Women's Leadership, Babson College.

Antoncic, B. (2009), "The Entrepreneur's General Personality Traits and Technological Developments", *World Academy of Science, Engineering and Technology*, Vol. 53, Vol. 3, pp. 236-241.

Bogan, V. and Darity (Jr), W. (2008), "Culture and entrepreneurship? African American and immigrant self-employment in the United States", *The Journal of Socio-Economics*, Vol. 37, No. 5, pp. 1999-2019.

Bono, J.E. and Judge, T.A. (2003), "Core Self-Evaluations: A Review of the Trait and its Role in Job Satisfaction and Job Performance", *European Journal of Personality*, Vol. 17, No. 1, pp. 5-18.

Boyce, L.A. and Herd, A.M. (2003), "The Relationship between Gender Role Stereotypes and Requisite Military Leadership Characteristics", *Sex Roles*, Vol. 32, No. 4, pp. 457-474.

Brenner, O.C., Tomkiewicz, J. and Schein, V.E. (1989), "The relationship between sex role stereotypes and requisite management characteristics revisited", *Academy of Management Journal*, Vol. 32, No. 3, pp. 662–669.

Brush, C.G., Carter, N.M., Gatewood, E.J., Greene, P.G. and Hart, M.M. (2006), "Introduction: The Diana Project International", in Brush, C., Carter, N.M., Gatewood, E.J., Greene, P.G. and Hart, M.M. (eds) *Growth-oriented women entrepreneurs and their businesses*, Edward Elgar, Cheltenham and Northampton, pp. 3–22.

Caliendo, M. and Kritikos, A.S (2008), "Is Entrepreneurial Success Predictable? An Ex-Ante Analysis of the Character-Based Approach", *Kyklos*, Vol. 61, No. 2, pp. 189-214.

Carter, N.M. and Williams, M.L. (2003), "Comparing social feminism and liberal feminism: The case of new firm growth", in Butler J. (Ed.), *New perspectives on women entrepreneurs* (pp 25–50). Information Age Publishing, Charlotte, NC, USA.

Chelariu, C., Brashear, T.G., Osmonbekov, T. and Zait, A. (2008), "Entrepreneurial propensity in a transition economy: exploring micro-level and meso-level cultural antecedents", *Journal of Business and Industrial Marketing*, Vol. 23 No. 6, pp. 405 – 415.

Ciavarella, M.A., Buchholtz. A.K., Riordan, C.M., Gatewood, R.D. and Stokes, G.S. (2004), "The Big Five and venture survival: Is there a linkage?", *Journal of Business Venturing*, Vol. 19, No. 4, pp. 465-483 .

Costa, P. T. (Jr) and McCrae, R.R. (1992), "Four ways five factors are basic", *Personality and Individual Differences*, Vol. 13, No. 6, pp. 653-665.

Crane, F.G. and Crane, E.C. (2007), "Dispositional optimism and entrepreneurial success", *The Psychologist-Manager Journal*, Vol. 10, No. 1, pp. 13-25.

D'Intino, R.S., Goldsby, M.G., Houghton, J.D. and Neck, C.P. (2007), "Self-leadership: A process for entrepreneurial success", *Journal of Leadership and Organizational Studies*, Vol. 13, No. 4, pp. 105-120.

Deal, J.J. and Stevenson, M.A. (1998), "Perceptions of female and male managers in the 1990s: Plus ca change", *Sex Roles*, Vol. 38, No. ¾, pp. 287-300.

Duehr, E.E. and Bono, J.E. (2006), "Men, women and managers: Are stereotypes finally changing?", *Personnel Psychology*, Vol. 59, No. 4, pp. 815–846.

Eckhardt J.T. and Shane S.A. (2003), "Opportunities and entrepreneurship", *Journal of Management*, Vol. 29, No. 3, pp. 333–349.
Envick, B.R. and Langford, M. (2003), "The Big-Five Personality Model: comparing male and female entrepreneurs", *Academy of Entrepreneurship Journal*, Vol. 9, No. ½, pp. 1-10.
European Commission (2008), Evaluation on Policy: Promotion of Women Innovators and Entrepreneurship, Final Report submitted by the EEC within the framework of ENTR/04/093-FC-Lot 1, DG Enterprise and Industry, available at: http://ec.europa.eu/enterprise/newsroom/cf/_getdocument.cfm?doc_id =3815 (accessed 30 July 2012)
European Commission, Enterprise and Industry Policies, SMEs, Promoting Entrepreneurship, available at: http://ec.europa.eu/enterprise/policies/sme/promoting-ntrepreneurship/index_en.htm, (accessed 30 July 2012).
European Employment Observatory Review: Self-employment in Europe 2010.
Fagenson, E.A. and Marcus, E.C. (1991), "Perceptions of the sex-role stereotypic characteristics of entrepreneurs: Women's evaluations", *Entrepreneurship Theory and Practice*, Vol. 15, No. 4, pp. 33–47.
Fairlie, R.W. and Holleran, W. (2012), "Entrepreneurship training, risk aversion and other personality traits: Evidence from a random experiment", *Journal of Economic Psychology*, Vol. 33, No. 2, pp. 366-378.
Finstad, K. (2010), "Response Interpolation and Scale Sensitivity: Evidence against 5-Point Scales", *Journal of Usability Studies*, Vol. 5, No. 3, pp. 104-110.
Foster, F. (1994), "Managerial sex role stereotyping among academic staff within UK business schools", *Women in Management Review*, Vol. 9, No. 3, pp. 17-22.
Furrer, O., Shaw-Ching Liu, B. and Sudharshan, D. (2000), "The relationships between culture and service quality perceptions: Basis for cross-cultural market segmentation and resource allocation", *Journal of Service Research*, Vol. 2, No. 4, pp. 355-371.
Gartner, W.B. (1985), "A conceptual framework for describing the phenomenon of new venture creation", *Academy of Management Review*, Vol. 10, No. 4, pp. 696-706.
—. (1988), "Who is an entrepreneur?' is the wrong question", *American Journal of Small Business*, Vol. 12 No. 4, pp. 11-32.

Grilo, I. and Thurik, A. R. (2006), "Entrepreneurship in the old and the new Europe", in Santarelli, E. (ed.), *Entrepreneurship, growth and innovation*, Springer, Berlin, pp. 75-103.

Gupta, V. and Fernandez, C. (2009), "Cross-Cultural Similarities and Differences in Characteristics Attributed to Entrepreneurs: A Three-Nation Study", *Journal of Leadership and Organizational Studies*, Vol. 15, No. 3, pp. 304-318.

Gupta, V.K., Turban, D.B., Wasti, S.A. and Sikdar, A. (2009), "The Role of Gender Stereotypes in Perceptions of Entrepreneurs and Intentions to Become an Entrepreneur", *Entrepreneurship Theory and Practice*, Vol. 33, No. 2, pp. 397-417.

Heggestad, E.D. and Kanfer, R. (2000), "Individual differences in trait motivation: Development of the motivational trait questionnaire", *International Journal of Educational Research*, Vol. 33, No. 7/8, pp. 751–776.

Heilman, M.E., Block, C.J., Martell, R.F. and Simon, M.C. (1989), "Has anything changed? Current characterizations of men, women and managers", *Journal of Applied Psychology*, Vol. 74, No. 6, pp. 935–942.

Hisrich, R.D., Peters, M.P. and Shepherd, D.A. (2005), *Entrepreneurship*, McGraw-Hill/Irwin, New York.

Hofstede, G. (1980), *Culture's Consequences: International Differences in Work-Related Values*, (abridged version), Sage Publications, Beverly Hills, CA.

—. (1997), *Cultures and organizations: software of the mind*, Mc Graw Hill, London.

Home, N. (2011), "Entrepreneurial orientation of grocery retailers in Finland", *Journal of Retailing and Consumer Services*, Vol. 18, No. 4, pp. 293-301.

Ireland, R.D., Covin, J.G. and Kuratko, D.F. (2009), "Conceptualizing Corporate Entrepreneurship Strategy", *Entrepreneurship Theory and Practice*, Vol. 33, No. 1, pp. 19-46.

Islam, S. (2012), "Pull and push factors towards small entrepreneurship development in Bangladesh", *Journal of Research in International Business Management*, Vol. 2, No. 3, pp. 65-72.

Kasi, B. and Dugger, J. C. (2000), "Gender equity in industrial technology: The challenge and recommendations", *Journal of Industrial Technology*, Vol. 16, No. 4, pp. 1-9.

Khurana, R. and Spender, J.C. (2012), "Herbert A. Simon on What Ails Business Schools: More than a Problem in Organization Design", *Journal of Management Studies,* Vol. 49, No. 3, pp. 619-639.

Koe Hwee Nga, J. and Shamuganathan, G. (2010), "The Influence of Personality Traits and Demographic Factors on Social Entrepreneurship Start Up Intentions", *Journal of Business Ethics*, Vol. 95, No. 2, pp. 259-282.

Lee, S.M. and Peterson, S.J. (2000), "Culture, entrepreneurial orientation and global competitiveness", *Journal of World Business*, Vol. 35, No. 4, pp. 401-416.

Lippa, R.A. (1995), "Gender-related individual differences and psychological adjustment in terms of the Big Five and circumplex models", *Journal of Personality and Social Psychology*, Vol. 69, No. 6, pp. 1184-1202.

Loasby, B.J. (2007), "A Cognitive Perspective on Entrepreneurship and the Firm", *Journal of Management Studies*, Vol. 44, No. 7, pp. 1078-1106.

Low, M.B. and MacMillan, I.C. (1988), "Entrepreneurship: Past research and future challenges", *Journal of Management*, Vol. 14, No. 2, pp. 139-161.; .

Lumpkin, G.T. and Dess, G.G. (1996), "Clarifying the entrepreneurial orientation construct and linking it to performance", *Academy of Management Review*, Vol. 21 No. 1, pp. 135-172.

Macintosh, G. (2006), "Personality and Relational Time Perspective in Selling", *Journal of Selling and Major Account Management*, Vol. 6, No. 2, pp. 19-33.

Malecki, E.J. (2009), "Geographical environments for entrepreneurship", *International Journal of Entrepreneurship and Small Business*, Vol. 7, No. 2, pp. 175-190.

Marusic, I. and Bratko, D. (1998), "Relations of Masculinity and Femininity with Personality Dimensions of the Five-Factor Model", *Sex Roles*, Vol. 38, No ½, pp. 29-44.

Mueller, S.L. and Thomas, A.S. (2000), "Culture and Entrepreneurial Potential: A Nine Country Study of Locus of Control and Innovativeness", *Swede Journal of Business Venturing*, Vol. 16, No. 1, pp. 51–75

Negreponti-Delivanis, M. (2012), "Open letter by Maria Negreponti-Delivanis to Mrs. Christine Lagarde, Head of the IMF (in relation to her statement that "Greeks do not pay taxes")", *Romanian Distribution Committee Magazine*, Vol. 3, No. 2, pp. 8-9.

Ofstad, D. (2008), "Competency Testing Methods for Education and Training of Entrepreneurs outside Formal Education", in Diesberg, C. and Fessas, Y. (eds.), *Developing Practices and Infrastructures for Entrepreneurship Education and Training in Europe*, Rostocker

Arbeitspapiere zu Wirtschaftsentwicklung und Human Resource Development, No. 29, Rostock 2008, pp. 15-23.

Okhomina, D. (2007), "Does level of education influence psychological traits? Evidence from used car entrepreneurs", *Journal of Management and Marketing Research*, Vol. 3, No. 1, pp. 1-14.

Pallant, J. (2001), *The SPSS survival manual: A step-by-step guide to data analysis using SPSS for Windows (version 10)*, Allen and Unwin, St Leonards, NSW.

Pinillos, M-J. and Reyes, L. (2011), "Relationship between individualist – collectivist culture and entrepreneurial activity: evidence from Global Entrepreneurship Monitor data", *Small Business Economics*, Vol. 37, No. 1, pp. 23-37.

Powell, G.N., Butterfield, D.A. and Parent, J.D. (2002), "Gender and managerial stereotypes: Have the times changed?", *Journal of Management*, Vol. 28, No. 2, pp. 177–193.

Schein, V.E. (1973), "The relationship between sex role stereotypes and requisite management characteristics", *Journal of Applied Psychology*, Vol. 57, No. 2, pp. 95–100.

—. (1975), "The relationship between sex role stereotypes and requisite management characteristics among female managers", *Journal of Applied Psychology*, Vol. 60, No. 3, pp. 340–344.

Schein, V.E. and Mueller, R. (1992), "Sex role stereotyping and requisite management characteristics: A cross cultural look", *Journal of Organizational Behavior*, Vol. 13, No. 5, pp. 439–447.

Slevin, D.P. and Terjesen, S.A. (2011), "Entrepreneurial Orientation: Reviewing Three Papers and Implications for Further Theoretical and Methodological Development", *Entrepreneurship Theory and Practice*, Vol. 35, No. 5, pp. 973-987.

Soane, E. and Chmiel, N. (2005), "Are risk preferences consistent? The influence of decision domain and personality", *Personality and Individual Differences*, Vol. 38, No. 8, pp. 1781-1791.

Stivers, B.P. and Campbell, J.E. (1995), "Characterizing accounting consultants: Gender does make a difference", *Journal of Organizational Change*, Vol. 8, No. 1, pp. 23-31.

Tabachnick, B. G. and Fidell, L. S. (2001), *Using multivariate statistics*, Alyn and Bacon, MA, USA:

Tomkiewicz, J. and Brenner, O.C. (1996), "The Relationship between Race (Hispanic) Stereotypes and Requisite Management Characteristics", *Journal of Social Behavior and Personality*, Vol. 11, No. 3, pp. 511-520.

Tsoukatos, E. and Rand, G.K. (2007), "Cultural Influences on Service Quality and Customer Satisfaction: Evidence from Greek Insurance", *Managing Service Quality*, Vol. 17, No. 4, pp. 467-485.

Turker, D. and Selcuk, S. (2008), "Which factors affect entrepreneurial intention of University students?", *Journal of European Industrial Training*, Vol. 33 No. 2, pp. 142-159.

Zhao, H., Seibert, S.E. and Lumpkin, G.T. (2010), "The relationship of personality to entrepreneurial intentions and performance: A meta-analytic review", *Journal of Management*, Vol. 36, No. 2, pp. 381-404.

CHAPTER FIFTEEN

MOBILE MARKETING:
A NEW DIRECT MARKETING
PROMOTIONAL CHANNEL

MONALIZ AMIRKHANPOUR
AND DEMETRIS VRONTIS

Introduction

The main purpose of this chapter is to introduce and highlight the importance of marketing through the mobile channel. Mobile marketing is one of the latest direct marketing promotional channels and is getting quite popular among marketers and business owners because of the various benefits that it offers to the potential customers as well as to businesses. Therefore, this chapter follows a top-down approach starting with briefly elaborating on the most general and at the same time relevant concepts associated with mobile marketing and then narrowing down to the specific issues and concepts related to marketing through the mobile channel.

In its simplest form and as stated by the Chartered Institute of Marketing (CIM, 2009), "marketing is the management process responsible for identifying, anticipating, and satisfying customer requirements profitably." Although there are various definitions of marketing, all of them point to satisfying the 'needs' and 'wants' of the customers in the appropriate time. In other terms, Brassington et al., (2003) states that all the definitions of marketing emphasize the fact that marketing is a management process, it identifies customer requirements, fulfills them profitably and exchanges ideas, goods and services. The marketing concept suggests that the concentration of marketing should be on identifying the customers' needs and wants rather than on finding ways to produce and sell products that the customers may or may not want (Moriarty et al., 2009). In order to accomplish the process of satisfying the needs and wants of the customers within the appropriate timeframe, special attention has to be made on the different elements of the marketing mix. Marketing mix is a set of marketing tools and a combination of marketing elements that are extensively used by the enterprises to implement their marketing strategies and to identify their objectives in a specific target market (Vranesevic et al., 2006). Traditionally, marketing mix is composed of four elements which are denoted as the '4 Ps of marketing'. These elements are *product, price, place*, and *promotion*. With the expansion of marketing scope, three other elements: *people, process*, and *physical evidence* were added to the marketing mix and thus is now known as the '7 Ps of marketing' (Kotler et al., 2009).

This chapter will center on the promotional aspect of the marketing mix with a focus on direct marketing and mobile marketing. Promotion is the process of making a product or service widely known and successful (Law, 2009). Vranesevic et al. (2006: 315) indicates that "the basic intention of promotion is to inform and persuade, and thus influence the customer's decisions." In other terms, promotion is a means to describe all the marketing communication activities performed by a company to promote its products or services (Marketing Teacher, 2012). As a result, promotion has to be carefully integrated within the business communication activities through the Integrated Marketing Communication (IMC) (Moriarty et al., 2009). The IMC incorporates the marketing communications in which all the elements of the promotional mix are systematically coordinated with each other. The promotional mix elements encompass a company's entire promotional endeavors including advertising, sales promotion, public relations, publicity, point-of-sale activities, trade fairs and exhibitions, sponsorship, packaging, word-of-mouth and direct marketing (Brassington et al., 2003).

As a significant element of the promotional mix, direct marketing is a basic form of marketing that occurs directly between the manufacturers and customers without the presence of an intermediary (Turban et al., 2009). The emergence of Internet and Communication Technologies (ICT) has reshaped direct marketing into what is known today as online or digital marketing which uses the Internet to communicate with the potential customers (Kotler et al., 2009). Using the Internet as an online marketing channel links the potential customers with the sellers electronically. Moreover, Blythe (2006) suggests that "direct marketing relies on having good, up-to-date information about the individuals it seeks to approach." This is further supported by Groucutt et al. (2004: 346), who argues that "the key to successful direct marketing is in its targeting, although this can also be its weakness. The ability of direct marketers to find the right audience for the product at the right time is crucial to success." Direct marketing uses various types of channels to address the target customers. Some of these channels include: direct/personal selling, direct mail, telemarketing, telemedia, TV marketing, catalogue marketing, digital coupons, E-mail marketing, social media marketing, and mobile marketing. It should be noted that permission-based marketing is particularly influential on E-mail marketing, social media marketing and mobile marketing (Mobile Marketing Association, 2011). In this chapter the emphasis will be on the most recent direct marketing channel and its associated concepts: mobile marketing.

This chapter continues with permission-based marketing, which is one of the underlying concepts of mobile marketing. It is then directed towards defining mobile marketing, followed by the various communication tools used through the mobile channel.

Varnali et al., (2011: 59) states that "explicit permission results in perceived user control which increases the likelihood of positive feelings and confidence about the outcome of engaging in any kind of marketing activity" that may be in the form of E-mails, social media and mobile marketing which is the focal point of this chapter. As a result, these marketing activities are influenced by permission in order to guarantee their success within the target audience (Carroll et al., 2007). Permission-based marketing, or permission marketing, introduced first by marketing consultant Seth Godin in 1999, is defined by Kotler et al., (2009: 129) as "a type of marketing which seeks permission in advance from consumers before they are sent marketing communications where such communications may be distributed through E-mails, mobile phones, and interactive digital television." Moreover, Brey et al., (2007: 1408) indicates that "permission marketing is a broad term covering all kinds of permission seeking; consumers provide interested marketers with information about the types of communication they would like to receive and this information enables marketing managers to target marketing communication to interested consumers." As pointed out by Lancaster et al., (2004: 366), "in many cases having too many commercial messages becomes rather annoying to many people and instead of paying attention to the message people either ignore them or do something to try and avoid them." Godin (1999) emphasizes the fact that "permission marketing turns strangers into friends and friends into loyal customers." Consequently, permission marketing guarantees the fact that consumers will pay more attention to the specific marketing message as compared with the traditional and unsolicited direct marketing approaches. This is further supported by the Mobile Marketing Association (2011) which states that "permission marketing aims to change the advertising paradigm from interruption to communication because it enables the brands to move from a broadcast monologue to a dialogue that offers to continue a deep engagement with the loyal customers." According to Gilbreath (2010), the permission marketing approach directs the businesses to treat their target customers respectfully by asking for their consent either by E-mail or by phone before sending them marketing messages.

Mobile Marketing Definition

The latest direct marketing channel is known as mobile marketing which is highly influenced by permission-based marketing. Mobile marketing is defined by the Mobile Marketing Association (MMA) as "a set of practices that enable organizations to communicate and engage with their audience in an interactive and relevant manner through any mobile device or network" (Mobile Marketing Association, 2009). From the viewpoint of Dushinski (2009: 3), "mobile marketing connects businesses and each of their customers through their mobile devices at the right time and at the right place with the right message and requires the customer's explicit permission and/or active interaction." In simpler terms, mobile marketing has to be implemented with the definite permission and consent of the end-users in order to succeed and if done correctly it could quickly become deeply intertwined into people's daily lives.

As mentioned by the Mobile Marketing Association (2011), "permission-based mobile marketing is the practice of gaining consent from consumers in advance of a continuing marketing dialogue taking place on mobile devices and in return for some kind of value exchange." Additionally, the emergence of mobile as a desired promotional channel for many consumers has enabled the marketers to upgrade the level of permission-based marketing. The MMA (2011) emphasizes that the mobile channel is the best medium for permission-based marketing because it allows the brands to deal with each target customer as an individual. Varnali et al., (2011: 58) points out that "a mobile phone is an intimate object that is part of an individual's personal sphere. Uninvited messages may be viewed as intrusions into the personal sphere." Therefore, factors that may moderate and alleviate intrusiveness include permission, message relevance, and inclusion of incentives (Krishnamurthy, 2001). Moreover, as stated by Varnali et al., (2011: 59), "explicit consumer permission is not only necessary for ethical reasons but is also crucial for the acceptance and success of mobile marketing." Similarly, Gilbreath (2010) believes that mobile devices are becoming an integral part of the daily life of people and points out that "the technology will only continue to improve over the next few years since the mobile devices will be the primary tool for connection to the Internet for most people in the world by the year 2020." As a result, the concept of 'value exchange' becomes the focal point of effective and successful permission-based mobile marketing because according to the Mobile Marketing Association (2011), "consumers exchange their consent, and sometimes personal demographic and preference information in advance for a product, service, or offer that they deem of interest, of relevance, or of worth to them."

Mobile Marketing Penetration in the Business

Moto Message (2012) states that "mobile marketing is quickly becoming one of the 'go to' marketing strategies for businesses both small and large as it is one of the most innovative ways to market a specific product or service to new and potential customers." As stated by the MMA (2011), "consumers are eager to use their mobile phones to keep connected with the brands they love and to receive communications that enhance their lifestyles." This clearly implies that mobile will become an essential part of the promotional mix (Krum, 2010). Furthermore, mobile marketing covers an extensive set of applications, i.e. mobile apps which have essentially revolutionized the way that modern enterprises conduct their day-to-day business activities. According to Frangold (2012), "the popularity of mobile marketing has steadily increased over the past few years with both businesses and consumers. With more consumers using smartphones and tablet PCs to research and purchase goods and services online, small business owners have to constantly adapt to meet this increasing need for consumer convenience."

Mobile marketing enables the relevant information to be distributed on a personalized and interactive basis to online customers. As a result, this new marketing trend is becoming even more striking and attractive as the mobile devices and mobile web browsing technologies gain noticeable popularity among consumers (Hopkins et al., 2012). Mobile devices such as smartphones and tablet PCs are extensively used for web browsing, social networking, photo/video sharing, and online shopping, in addition to making phone calls or sending text messages (Krum, 2010). However, the Mobile Marketing Association (2011) points out that "much of today's permission-based mobile marketing is delivered through the messaging channel; as smartphones and tablet PCs become the predominant mobile devices, the transition towards using mobile apps, the mobile web, and other mobile functionalities will lead to increased interactivity." Obviously, this requires an appropriate framework which will incorporate value exchange via mobile network operators as well as brands either by 'opting in' to receive marketing communications or by agreeing upon receiving updates from the mobile network operators. Additionally, Gilbreath (2010: 250) argues that "the only way to win in a mobile marketing campaign is to add value to consumers' lives by providing useful services and fun tools."

Tsirulnik et al., (2010) states that "companies should promote their mobile offerings via every channel possible; just as some companies have for example a Facebook or Twitter icon on their home pages to make it easy for visitors to connect with them via social media, there should be information on the home pages about how to connect with the specific company via SMS and there should be an image of the company's website on a mobile device." According to Marketing Sherpa (2011), "having an effective mobile strategy takes more than just making the website of a company mobile-friendly; going mobile calls for an integrated approach." As mobile marketing is getting more attractive and popular, many marketers are, or soon will be dealing with this promotional channel for the first time. Additionally, Moto Message (2012) states that "marketing in the mobile channel provides a much higher read rate, redemption rate, and Return on Investment (ROI) compared to direct mail, TV marketing, and other forms of direct marketing." This is essentially due to the fact that most of the customers always carry their mobile phones with them and regardless of where they are they will read their messages (i.e. SMS) instantly.

Furthermore, Dam (2012) points out that "mobile marketing is still in its infancy and many consumers as well as businesses do not know what opportunities are behind the smartphones and tablet PCs." In simpler terms, lack of consumer education about mobile marketing is one of the main reasons why growth in this new marketing channel is relatively slow. Additionally, Tode (2012) believes that "despite all the advances in mobile marketing, there are still a large number of marketers doing very little or nothing in the channel. Since this has nothing to do with the need for better technology or analytics, mobile marketing is likely to not make another big advance until marketers make it a bigger priority." Kats (2012) argues that "entering the mobile space requires a well thought-out strategy and many times marketers dive into the medium without fully thinking about their goals. It is suggested that marketers should include specific strategies for different devices as behaviors can vary widely." For instance, smartphones are mainly used to satisfy an immediate need such as finding directions whereas tablet PCs are used for web browsing and generating conversions. Therefore, marketers should know what mobile devices their target consumers are reaching them from and what type of content they use on those devices in order to guarantee that they are delivering the best experience at all times. Moreover, Kats (2012) indicates that "mobile is still new and changing rapidly and it needs continuous maintenance in order to be truly successful."

The most important step that has to be taken in any mobile marketing strategy is having a web presence (Snyder, 2011). According to Dam (2011), "even though mobile marketing is still a relatively young industry, there are two important aspects that should be considered when creating a mobile website: (1) mobile users are looking for information on-the-go and (2) they want it fast." The mobile web presence can be classified into four main types: (a) mobile versions of traditional websites, (b) mobile landing pages, (c) dedicated mobile websites, and (d) plug-in-based mobile websites. Traditional websites were initially designed to be accessed from desktop computers, but they can be redirected into mobile devices. The mobile landing pages are basically single-page entities that can be designed and created in a short period of time in order to add a mobile web presence to the specific mobile marketing campaign. On the other hand, dedicated mobile websites are stand-alone and multi-page entities which are not the same as traditional websites; instead, they have their own design and coding strategies in order to fully satisfy their mobile customers' needs. Finally, plug-in-based mobile websites are very similar to the mobile versions of traditional websites with the difference that they can also use free open-source plug-ins to format the website for mobile accessibility purposes (Krum, 2010; Dushinski, 2009).

According to Bellamkonda (2012), "there is a large gap between the rapidly increasing mobile search volumes and the majority of small businesses lagging behind in mobile search strategy; this is mainly because the small businesses currently do not have a mobile search strategy and are missing out on consumers who try to find them via a smartphone or a tablet PC." Snyder (2011) points out that "mobile marketing does not succeed as an isolated channel; it works best when integrated with other channels and tactics to form a cross-platform strategy." As mentioned by Moto Message (2012), "mobile marketing is still growing in acceptance and marketing penetration; however, the number one reason for failure in mobile marketing is failure to aggressively promote it." Sankaran (2011) argues that "the research on mobile marketing is quite nascent and has not kept pace with the evolution of the mobile technology." Furthermore, Hof (2012) believes that "the problem with going mobile is that marketers have been relatively slow to move to mobile marketing." Marketers also need to realize that the utilization of mobile devices such as smartphones and tablet PCs varies; for instance, around 80 percent of traffic from tablet PCs takes place after working hours while watching TV whereas the traffic generated from smartphones mostly belongs to the working hours and while people are more on-the-go. This clearly indicates that a built-for-mobile path for the tablet PCs and a built-for-mobile path for the smartphones are strongly required mainly because the mobile marketing activities tailored for smartphone users will not prove useful for the tablet PC users and vice versa.

Mobile Marketing Benefits

Mobile marketing and mobile advertising are the next big challenges in the marketing community. This is mainly because of the latest technological advancements which brought about a totally new era in the mobile world. As stated by Bober (2011: 33), "mobile technology provides new ways for the advertisers and marketers to communicate with target markets." Furthermore, marketers are always searching for innovative, cost-effective, and highly influential methods in order to increase revenue; however, considering today's shrinking economy small businesses as well as marketers look for ways to increase customer response rates by designing targeted marketing campaigns. Additionally, they need to carefully monitor the outcomes of every campaign in order to boost the ROI. Mobile marketing is the most appropriate medium to achieve these goals particularly because of the several benefits that it offers to the businesses and marketers as listed below (Strategic Growth, 2009):

- **Affordability:** Mobile marketing offers a better value because the postage and printing costs of using traditional marketing channels are eliminated and therefore prices are very reasonable.

- **Distribution:** By using mobile marketing techniques, marketers can reach people all over the world because the delivery of marketing messages is almost always guaranteed, unlike the use of other forms of unsolicited direct marketing channels.
- **Immediacy:** Mobile marketing campaigns are simplified, flexible, and easy to execute because they are delivered to the potential recipients within seconds.
- **Interactivity:** Mobile marketing enables the marketers to reach potential customers 'on-the-go' by creating an interactive and highly effective two-way communication.
- **Marketing Campaign Integration:** Due to the flexibility of mobile marketing, it is very easy to integrate new and innovative forms of promotional tools with existing ones in order to boost their effectiveness and interactivity. For instance, the integration of mobile marketing with social media marketing results in an innovative form of marketing which is known as mobile social media marketing.
- **Mobility:** As its name indicates, marketing through the mobile channel has high reachability because most people have their mobile phones 80% of the time within their personal reach (Strategic Growth, 2009).
- **Quantifiable and Measurable:** The outcomes of mobile marketing campaigns are measurable because they can be monitored through customer opt-ins, page visits and downloads.
- **Targeted:** The mobile marketing content is personal and tailored on the basis of the preferences of those customers who have opted-in to receive them. In simpler terms, the customers who have explicitly expressed their permission to receive marketing messages will get targeted forms of marketing content directly on their mobile phones.
- **Viral Potential:** The mobile marketing messages can be easily shared by the customers who have already received them with other people. This obviously increases the potential of reaching new customers at no cost.
- **WOW Factor:** Since mobile marketing is a relatively new marketing medium, it can give marketers as well as businesses the opportunity to establish themselves as leaders in their own sector and guarantee that marketing messages will reach the potential customers with higher impact.

The next section first introduces the various mobile marketing communication tools and then explores each tool with further details. Some of these communication tools are specifically used by the smartphones and tablet PCs because they cannot be implemented on ordinary mobile phones.

Mobile Marketing Communication Tools

Arnold (2011) believes that "the time for mobile marketing is now and by using the various channels designed specifically for mobile marketing." There are several methods provided by the mobile network operators to reach the mobile users. It is essential to incorporate all the available mobile communication options into mobile marketing activities (Krum, 2010). These mobile marketing channels include: Short Message Service (SMS)/Multimedia Message Service (MMS), mobile applications, Quick Response (QR) codes, mobile social media, mobile E-mail, proximity (location-based) marketing, and mobile advertising.

According to Krum (2010: 105), "one of the best opportunities in mobile marketing is the capability to build brand awareness and goodwill with the target market. Mobile promotions help customers feel appreciated and more loyal to a particular brand." Moreover, Krum (2010) believes that loyalty programs can be customized based on consumers' preferences in order to create a closer relationship between the customers and the specific brand. The most common mobile promotions start with SMS, MMS, proximity marketing, mobile coupons and discounts that are sent directly to the customers' mobile phones provided that they have expressed their permission to receive marketing communication messages via their mobile devices.

SMS/MMS Marketing

SMS is extensively used by most of the businesses to send text-based messages to customers with links to call a phone number or visit a website in order to gain further information related to the specific advertisement, promotion, etc. According to Moto Message (2010), "SMS is a very effective way to deliver a marketing message to a wide, yet targeted group of people because it has a huge potential reach compared with other mobile technologies like mobile applications or the mobile web which rely on smartphones." Additionally, many retailers take advantage of the instant nature of SMS marketing in order to push timely sales offers via text-based mobile coupons and vouchers.

Due to its significant low cost for marketers and high return rate that is crucial in today's shrinking economy, an SMS marketing campaign can be set up and implemented easily, and is thus a great way to enter mobile marketing. SMS marketing is also permission-based since the customers have given their permission to be contacted via SMS. Furthermore, customers that express their consent to receive information are more likely to purchase in comparison with customers who receive a direct mail or other forms of unsolicited direct marketing offers. As stated by Moto Message (2010), "multi-channel campaigns are increasingly effective with so many consumers interacting via mobile; this is mainly due to the importance of a multi-channel approach to mobile marketing which has been realized by many outstanding brand advertisers such as Marks & Spencer and KFC who effectively use SMS marketing alongside other mobile and non-mobile marketing channels."

Kats (2011) believes that "even with all of the information available on SMS marketing, it is still a relatively new mobile marketing medium and with quick adaptation from businesses, mistakes do happen." As a result, the Mobile Marketing Association (MMA) suggests that marketers should take into consideration some aspects that directly affect an SMS marketing campaign. These aspects include: making the call-to-action ubiquitous, avoid running a mobile marketing campaign based on price, avoid using SMS as a one-off feature, and making the SMS have a personal tone and feeling because it leads to building relationships with the target customers (Mobile Marketing Association, 2011).

Similar to the SMS is the MMS that supports multimedia files such as images and audio/video (Marketing Sherpa, 2011). As a result, MMS provides marketers with extra tools for promoting a specific brand, product, or service. Moreover, MMS has reshaped mobile communication by making it more targeted, versatile, and expressive as compared to the SMS (Hsu et al., 2006).

Mobile Applications

Mobile applications, mostly known as mobile apps are computer programs specifically designed and created for smartphones and tablet PCs which are gaining popularity among mobile users (Hughes, 2011). A mobile operating system, also known as mobile OS, is a system that is specifically designed to run on mobile devices such as smartphones and tablet PCs. In simpler terms, it is the software platform where other programs known as mobile apps can run on the mobile device. Some of the most significant mobile operating systems are Apple iOS, Google Android, Blackberry RIM, Nokia Symbian, Samsung Bada and others. According to Stat Counter (2012), Google Android and Apple iOS are the dominant mobile operating systems based on their market shares.

Android is a relatively new mobile operating system which is based on the Linux platform. It is an open-source operating system specifically designed for portable devices such as smartphones and tablet PCs (Speckmann, 2008). Additionally, it delivers a complete set of software for mobile devices by acting as middleware and accommodating key mobile applications (mobile apps). The open-source characteristic of Android clearly indicates that the underlying source code is openly available to and freely customizable by third-party software developers. There are a number of different versions for the Android operating system where each newly released version offers enhanced features of the previous one.

On the other hand, the iOS, previously known as the iPhone OS, is the mobile operating system of Apple Inc. which was initially released in June 2007. As its previous name indicates, this operating system was first developed for the iPhone, but due to the variance in Apple mobile devices it was expanded further to support the iPad, iPod Touch, and the Apple TV. The iOS is not licensed to be installed and configured on non-Apple mobile devices (Apple.com, 2012). The operating system; however, contains several system applications such as Phone, Mail, Safari Browser, and many others that provide standard system services to the end-user (iOS Technology Overview, 2011).

Price is a key differentiator between Android and iOS because most of the Android-powered mobile devices have feasible, economical, and in some cases competitive prices which attract lots of potential buyers. On the other hand, most of the iOS-powered mobile devices are often more expensive than their Android-powered counterparts (Hughes, 2011; Hughes, 2012). It should also be noted that Android and iOS will remain as 'rivals' to each other due to their brand name levels, popularity among people, competitive market shares, innovative development and management teams, targeting the latest mobile communication technologies and trends, enhanced features and services embedded into their various platform versions and many other factors that make it noticeably difficult to decide which mobile OS of the two is the best in today's smartphone and tablet PC market.

According to Hopkins et al., (2012: 50), "with the population of smartphone users ever growing, and the capabilities of mobile devices daily increasing, apps offer unlimited possibilities in terms of expanding business opportunities and improving personal productivity." Moreover, Krum (2010: 324) defines mobile apps as "small programs that can be downloaded and added to a mobile phone to customize it for the user specific needs and wants." On the other hand, Hopkins et al., (2012: 51) states that "the key to successful application is customer values. If the mobile app is not compelling and useful to the customers, it will be quickly forgotten, or even ignored, among the much more interesting competition."

QR Code Marketing

Quick-Response (QR) codes, generally known as the 2-Dimesnion (2D) codes, are mobile barcodes that enable the camera of a smartphone or a tablet PC to act as a scanner (Hopkins et al., 2012). Krum (2010, p. 113) defines QR codes as "small square dot matrix barcodes that can be captured by the camera of a mobile phone and then decoded by software on the phone known as QR code reader to execute specific tasks." These tasks could be: opening a website, placing a call, sending a text message, viewing an online video, donating a pre-nominated amount to a charity, linking to a special promotion, or even 'Like' a Facebook page (Tranter, 2012). According to Dam (2011), "the beauty of a QR code is that it delivers information to the reader/decoder on the smartphone or the tablet PC and with one or two simple on-screen instructions, the user is delivered a wealth of information."

As a result, QR code marketing is one of the simplest mobile marketing channels to connect businesses with consumers mainly because marketers can send the target consumers to a plethora of information stored online which are related specifically to a particular business (Dam, 2011). Moreover, Dam (2012) believes that "QR code marketing is a good place to start with mobile marketing as many companies still use print media for their marketing activities." It is of great significance to educate both the businesses and the consumers to know what a QR code is, how to interact with it, and what the consumer expectations are once it has been scanned

(Dushinski, 2009). Figure 1 shows a sample QR code and its anatomy which explains in detail what each section of the code does.

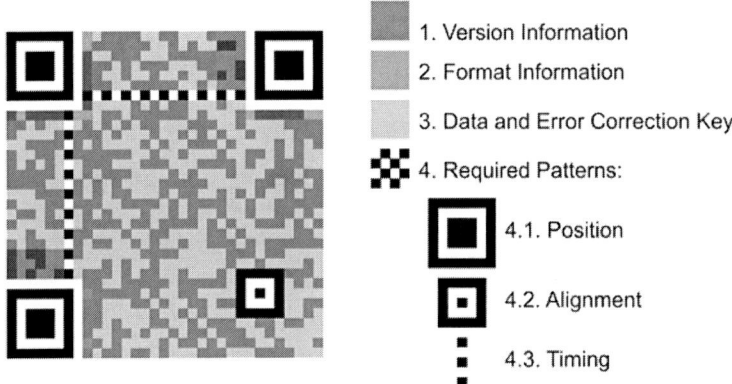

Figure 1: Sample QR Code[1]

Furthermore, Viveiros (2012) suggests that "marketers need to realize that there are '4 Ms' to make QR codes a successful part of a marketing initiative which are: (a) motivate, (b) mobilize, (c) monitor, and (d) monetize." In the motivation phase, the consumers need to scan the specific QR code using a QR code reader/decoder application which can be downloaded for free into the smartphone or tablet PC. Then, in the mobilization phase the destination of the QR code has to be suitable for the smartphones and tablet PCs; it needs to be relevant at the specific timeframe, i.e. when the consumers scan the QR code. Moreover, marketers need to understand the promotion outcomes and differentiate results from various channels and offers using monitoring systems; this is done in the monitoring phase. Finally, the companies need to know how the QR code generates ROI for the specific marketing initiative during the final phase of monetization.

One of the most outstanding QR code campaigns of the first quarter (Q1) of 2012 is that of Starbucks. According to Kats (2012), "when it came to promote its new coffee roasts, Starbucks used QR codes which allowed the consumers to vote for their favorite roast and watch a video to learn

---

[1] *QR Code Examples* (2011) [Online Image] Available from:
<http://www.urbanmediainc.com/qr-codes/> qr-code-anatomy.png [Accessed 29 June 2012]

more about the company's coffee." According to the Economist Newspaper (2012), "for marketers QR codes bridge the gap between offline and online worlds. Customers who use them are asking to be told more about the company and as a result, the success of a campaign is easy to measure by the number of scans." This is further supported by the QR Code Press (2012) which states that "QR codes have proven themselves to be the most valuable tool in a marketer's arsenal and the use of them continues to grow." As a result, there are some advantages associated with using QR codes such as no printing costs, fast response, and enhanced customer excitement. Bober (2011: 58) indicates that "QR codes can also be used to conduct surveys and obtain customer feedback about products and/or services. Even though QR codes are still fairly new, consumers already recognize and use them in magazines, brochures, and in retail stores."

Mobile Social Media Marketing

As its name indicates, mobile social media marketing is combining the two recent direct marketing approaches: social media marketing and mobile marketing. As a result, it is essential to have sufficient knowledge and understanding of the concepts related to social media marketing prior to combining it with the mobile channel. This section first introduces social media marketing and then proceeds with more depth on mobile social media marketing.

Social media marketing is the process of gaining traffic or attention through social media tools such as the social networks. Social media refers to the online platforms and tools which are extensively used by people to share experiences and resources such as photos, videos, music, and perceptions with each other (Turban et al., 2010). The networked structures of these social platforms in addition to the user-generated content enable massive communication and collaboration among social media users. Social networks are made up of nodes of individuals, groups, and enterprises which are connected to each other by types of interdependency. In simpler terms, a social network is a 'social' structure where users create their own web space and write blogs, post photos/videos/music, exchange ideas, and link to other web locations. Therefore, social media marketing can be defined as the process of gaining traffic or attention through social media tools and applications which primarily include the social networks such as Facebook, Twitter,

LinkedIn, YouTube, Pinterest, Google Plus and several other social networking websites.

According to Tode (2012), "mobile is a great activation channel that complements marketers' other social media efforts because there is a great synergy between mobile and social media as well as the benefits of combining these two together, i.e. mobile social media." Moreover, Gregg (2012) points out that "although social media growth has been exponential through most of the last decade, the incorporation of mobile social media has been like pouring gasoline on the flame mainly because it played an important role in the growth of smartphone and tablet PC usage."

The simplicity expected by users is the most important difference between mobile social media and traditional social media. As stated by Segreto (2010), "whereas users are fairly tolerant of cluttered pages on their home computers, they expect sites, pages, and apps on their mobile devices to be especially well-organized, user-friendly, and easy to navigate." Mobile social media can take various forms, but the primary forms are: mobile social networks, social gaming, content sharing and streaming, location-based check-in services, and content sharing via social sites (Berkowitz, 2010). According to Gregg (2012), "the beauty of social media is that it engages the customer and communicates with them. Mobile social media is the more intimate extension of this relationship where users have continuous access to their mobile devices and can communicate with the businesses." One successful example of using mobile social media is Dunkin' Donuts. Johnson (2012) points out that "Dunkin' Donuts took their already successful social media campaign to a new level with their implementation of the 'Dunkin' Coffee Customizer' application which is based on Facebook's mobile platform and allows customers to build their own custom drinks from scratch, place an order for the drink, and post it on their wall to share with friends, all from their mobile device." It should be noted that almost all the significant social networks have mobile applications that can be downloaded for free into the smartphone or the tablet PC.

Mobile E-mail Marketing

Mobile E-mail marketing is basically integrating E-mail marketing with the mobile channel. In simpler terms, the concepts associated with E-mail marketing are also applicable and valid when implemented in the mobile channel. As a result, this section introduces E-mail marketing in detail and then relates it to mobile E-mail marketing.

E-mail marketing, as its name indicates, is the sending of promotional messages and alerts to potential customers via E-mail services. It is considered feasible and easy to design, test, and implement by most marketers (Georgieva, 2012). According to Lancaster et al. (2004, p. 370), "E-mail is an inexpensive way of reaching an existing database of customers who have visited and registered on a website." Furthermore, Brassington et al. (2003: 1076) argues that "E-mail has emerged as a powerful means of communication that marketers are increasingly adopting as part of their promotional activities mainly because they are attracted to the potential of E-mail marketing as a communication tool that can target individuals rather than using mass media approaches." There are six different types of E-mail marketing: (a) E-mail newsletters, (b) E-mail digests, (c) dedicated E-mail, (d) lead nurturing, (e) sponsorship E-mails, and (f) transactional E-mails.

E-mail newsletters are useful for marketing to potential customers as well as keeping in touch with the existing customers and updating them with the latest news and product or service announcements of the specific company (Georgieva, 2012). E-mail digests are very similar to E-mail newsletters; they provide links and lists of available information within a specific time-frame, e.g. within a month. E-mail digests focus on the most significant pieces of content that the readers will be attracted to such as receiving an E-mail digest from Amazon listing the top books of the month. Dedicated E-mail is defined by Georgieva (2012: 30) as "E-mail containing information about only one offer. Dedicated E-mails help setting up the context to introduce the main call-to-action." On the other hand, lead nurturing is a new marketing tactic which is primarily based on identifying the potential customers who are interested in a specific product or service and finding the right timing to connect with them (NurtureHQ, 2009). Lead nurturing enables the marketers to automatically intertwine a series of E-mails to a specific activity and send them to the potential customers in the time that they need to know about the product or service.
Sponsorship E-mail campaigns are linked to a paid media strategy which consists of display advertising, Pay-Per-Clicks (PPCs), and mobile advertising. The main feature of sponsorship E-mails is to pay for including the specific products or services in another vendor's newsletter. Using sponsorship E-mails, marketers can be specific in defining the

segment(s) that they plan to reach, such as, 20 to 30 year-old European females.

Finally, there are transactional E-mails. These are messages sent to customers in response to a monitored action they had completed. Messages sent by E-Commerce websites like Amazon or eBay thanking the customers for completing an order with them are examples of transactional E-mails.

As pointed out by Brassington et al. (2003: 1077), "carefully designed E-mail marketing can help to create initial contact as well as helping to develop an online relationship once transactions have taken place." From a marketing standpoint, the aim of E-mail marketing is to encourage the E-mail recipients to look at a specific website and give 'permission' to the marketer to send them more information (Krum, 2010).

Proximity (Location-Based) Marketing

Proximity marketing is the dissemination of marketing content related to a particular place. Varnali et al. (2011: 32) indicates that "a unique feature of the mobile medium is that it allows the mobile marketer to know the current position of the target user with great precision and therefore, adapt the marketing impulse accordingly." As stated by Krum (2010: 115), "Location-Based Services (LBS) are digital systems that broadcast digital messages to enabled devices within a specific proximity." Dushinski (2009: 175) states that "proximity marketing can be done by a business that is accessing a person's location through its mobile device's built-in Global Positioning System (GPS) or by determining its position by the nearest cell phone tower, wireless access point, or other near-field communication technique such as Bluetooth." Additionally, there are several benefits associated with considering proximity marketing as a part of the mobile marketing plan. These benefits are: (a) development of one-to-one relationship marketing, (b) captured target customers, (c) enhanced ROI, (d) building brand recognition and loyalty (Krum, 2010).

The most important technologies for implementing location-based marketing campaigns include Bluetooth, Wi-Fi, Radio Frequency Identification (RFID), Near-Field Communication (NFC), Infrared (IR), and Ultra-Wide Band (UWB). Marketers, retailers, and independent advertisers usually use one of these technologies for their proximity marketing purposes (Varnali et al., 2011).

Mobile Advertising

As pointed out by Young (2010), "mobile advertising is the platform for next generation of advertising. With increasing numbers of consumers turning to mobile devices capable of full wireless connectivity, mobile networks, and web browsers becoming progressively refined, industry analysts predict that a boom in mobile advertising is not far off." Loehnis (2012) indicates that "integration of other media around mobile helps to create a level of engagement that has always been lacking, letting consumers move effortlessly from online-to-offline-to-online." In other terms, mobile should not be seen as an independent platform but rather as a complement to the other online/offline advertising platforms in order to influence the buying decisions of the target customers (Digital Market, 2012). According to Arnold (2011), "mobile advertising involves pulling customers to the advertising campaign by placing ads on external mobile sites such as the mobile versions of the newspapers, blogs, and other content-based sites in addition to pushing out the advertising campaign by including ads in the E-mails, SMS, mobile content, and branded apps." Moreover, Young (2010) states that "advances in mobile technology and online usability also permit advertising on a more interactive and personalized level than was previously possible."

The Convergence of Social, Local, and Mobile Marketing (SoLoMo Marketing)

The last section of this chapter introduces and highlights the importance of adopting a multi-channel marketing approach by marketers and business owners, resulting in what is known as SoLoMo marketing. The term 'SoLoMo' refers to the very latest online marketing trend. Essentially, it involves the integration of social media, location-based services, and the mobile channel. According to OIC (2012), "SoLoMo marketing is a novel concept of providing smartphone users access to locally-focused promotions and store offerings through mobile search based on their current location." Furthermore, Turner (2012) explains that the 'social' part of SoLoMo is simply related to the social media tools such as Facebook, Twitter, Google Plus and others that enable potential customers to have a dialogue with a specific business of their interest and share their opinions and comments with others. The 'local' part of SoLoMo is based on geo-targeting which allows businesses to target their marketing messages to potential customers in a specific geographic location. Geo-targeting, as pointed out by Turner (2012), "can be accomplished when customers provide their address or more commonly, when they let a company know their location based on their smartphone or tablet PC use." This clearly indicates that SoLoMo marketing is also a form of permission-based marketing. Finally, the 'mobile' part of SoLoMo highlights the fact that in addition to being able to use the social media and location-based services from the desktop PCs, they can also be used on the smartphones and tablet PCs by simply downloading their mobile app into the mobile device.

This new marketing concept enables businesses to promote their offers easily mainly because potential customers can receive highly relevant search results specific to their current location. For instance, suppose that a potential customer is looking for an Italian restaurant while walking in town. SoLoMo-based mobile apps like Foursquare, Path, and Facebook Places can provide instant search results and locations of restaurants with Italian cuisine in the customer's vicinity in addition to showing if the specific restaurant has special offers or if friends are available at the same location. This is a very innovative method of targeting potential customers in a personalized and location-centric fashion.

According to Reed (2011: 4), "the fundamental driver of SoLoMo is smartphone adoption. By 2015, the number of people accessing the Internet from smartphones and tablet PCs will surpass the number of users connecting from a desktop PC as stated by market analyst firm IDC." This clearly implies that mobile plays an important role in the Internet traffic because in the foreseeable future most online users will access the Internet without owning a desktop PC; hence the post-PC era which is sometimes denoted as the emergence of SoLoMo era. Moreover, Reed (2011) indicates that SoLoMo services dominate customer attention mainly because of their social nature.

Finally, it is essential to highlight a few points before using SoLoMo as a marketing tool. Turner (2012) states that "SoLoMo is not right for every business" and stresses that businesses should decide if this category of marketing tool is appropriate for them by following the SoLoMo matrix shown in Figure 2.

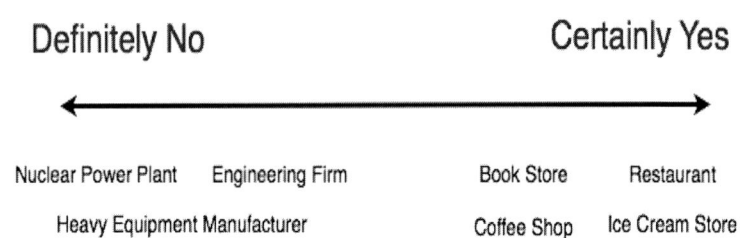

Figure 2: SoLoMo Matrix[2]

As seen in Figure 2, SoLoMo is not the right marketing choice for manufacturing businesses. SoLoMo, however, is an optimum marketing choice for most retail businesses particularly because it is easier for them to target potential customers on a personalized and targeted basis. Thus, retail businesses should register themselves with location-based services such as Foursquare, Yelp, Path, WHERE, or Facebook Places which are the best-known services for proximity marketing and enable the potential customers to 'check-in' as soon as the specific business is registered. Additionally, location-based services such as Groupon, Living Social, and Google Offers ask the specific business to provide a special 'deal-of-the-day' discount to the potential customers using their services. It is therefore suggested to create promotions that are attractive and appealing to the target customers. Figure 3 illustrates an example promotion created on WHERE which highlights the importance of having a call-to-action and a deadline incorporated within the special offer in order to make it attractive and profitable.

---

[2] *SoLoMo Matrix* (2012) [Online Image] Available from: < http://www.socialmediaexaminer.com/is-social-local-mobile-right-for-your-business/#more-18556 > jt-is-solomo-right.jpg [Accessed 2 September 2012]

Figure 3: Sample Promotion on WHERE with 'Call-to-Action' and 'Sense of Urgency' Elements[3]

Finally, it should be pointed out that SoLoMo marketing provides businesses especially those in the retail sector with a number of advantages such as increased ROI, higher redemption rates, and enhanced customer reach on a personalized and targeted basis which can leverage the entire performance of the businesses.

Conclusion

Every day more businesses are incorporating mobile marketing options into their marketing plan in order to communicate effectively and efficiently with their customers. The main purpose of mobile marketing is to increase the awareness level of the businesses by assisting them in gathering relevant information about the needs and preferences of their target customers in a timely and profitable manner. Moreover, mobile marketing plays a significant role in enhancing the interaction between the potential customers and their favorite brands. This is particularly due to the specific characteristics that marketing through the mobile channel has: intimacy, immediacy, intelligence, and innovation. The popularity of personal mobile devices such as smartphones and tablet PCs has introduced a new form of marketing to businesses that can target a large number of people anywhere in the world. As a result, integrating mobile into the marketing plan should become a priority for businesses that want to stay ahead in their relevant industries and enhance their profitability. As

---

[3] *Sample WHERE Promotion* (2012) [Online Image] Available from: <http://www.socialmediaexaminer.com/is-social-local-mobile-right-for-your-business/#more-18556> jt-buy-now-call-to-action.png [Accessed 2 September 2012]

mobile technology continues to rapidly evolve, marketing through the mobile channel will become pervasive and not negligible in the upcoming years. Therefore, to entirely monetize the channel marketers are required to evolve along with it. Otherwise, they will gradually lose a large number of customers who are mobile. Having a mobile website is the first step to consider in any mobile marketing campaign. Business enterprises should develop a website that is mobile user-friendly, has simplified user interface for the mobile screen, and loads quickly. If these requirements are not satisfied, a business may run the risk of turning loyal customers away from its mobile website and reducing sales because consumers will be attracted to the more mobile-savvy competitors.

Furthermore, the increased potential of having the marketing messages delivered to the right person at the right time and in the right place by using the mobile channel will result in converting interactions into purchases. This clearly implies increased ROI and guaranteed profitability. In order for a business to connect with its target market successfully, innovative forms of marketing and advertising have to be deployed in conjunction with traditional marketing methods. Mobile marketing is an important promotional channel to be considered by businesses to reach out to their target customers using an effective technique. For instance, mobile marketing is more effective in comparison to E-mail marketing and other new forms of advertising in that there are higher chances that customers will read an SMS/MMS, scan a QR code or click through an advertisement on a mobile website than reading an E-mail promoting specific products or services. Therefore, marketing through the mobile channel is beneficial for businesses both small and large as well as the potential customers because it allows a two-way communication between businesses and customers (i.e. B2C) which leads to a sharing of their opinions and perceptions. SoLoMo marketing thus also allows businesses to target potential customers on the basis of their social attitudes and location relevance all by taking advantage of the power and intelligence of smartphones and tablet PCs.

Considering today's competitive business world and the global economic crisis, business owners and more specifically marketing managers should choose the most efficient, cost-effective strategies in order to be successful and profitable. Customers are somehow addicted to mobile phones and use them for online shopping, social networking, reading books, and several other things in addition to making phone calls. It should be taken into account that mobile marketing opens new horizons for businesses and marketing managers which will ultimately result in increasing sales and leads, driving offline sales up by incorporating location-based search strategies, and building customer loyalty and trust by asking for their permission prior to initiating a marketing dialogue with them. Connecting with mobile customers helps businesses keep them informed and updated about various issues such as launching new products or services, special offers, sales periods, special promotions and several other issues in addition to gaining more credibility in comparison with their competitors.

References

Apple, Inc. (2012), iOS [Internet]. Apple, Inc. Available from: http://www.apple.com/ios [Accessed 15 March 2012].

Arnold, K. (2011), Apple Releases iPhone SDK, Demos Spore, Instant Messaging [Internet]. Mac Rumors Available from: http://www.macrumors.com [Accessed 17 March 2012].

Bellamkonda, S. (2012), "Study finds 84% of small business see business increase through mobile marketing" [Internet] Washington Business Journal Available from:
http://www.bizjournals.com/washington/blog/2012/05/ [Accessed 10 May 2012].

Berkowitz, D. (2010), "Social Gaming" [Internet] SlideShare Available from: http://dawngregg.com/smedia/?tag=social-media-strategy [Accessed 25 April 2012].

Blythe, J. (2006), *Essentials of Marketing Communications*, 3rd Edition, Harlow: Prentice Hall Financial Times.

Bober, B. (2011), *Mobile Marketing for Local Businesses*, 1st Edition, UK

Brassington, F. and Pettitt, S. (2003), *Principles of Marketing*, 3rd Edition, Harlow: Financial Times

Brey, E. T., So, S. I. A., Kim, D. Y., and Morrison, A. M. (2007), "Web-based permission marketing: segmentation for the lodging industry", *Tourism Management*, Vol. 28, pp. 1408-1416.

Carroll, A., Barnes, S. J., Scornavacca, E., and Fletcher, K. (2007), "Consumer perceptions and attitudes towards SMS advertising: recent evidence from New Zealand", *International Journal of Advertising*, Vol. 26, No. 1, pp. 79-98.

Chartered Institute of Marketing (CIM) (2009), "Definition of Marketing", [Internet] Chartered Institute of Marketing. Available from: http://www.cim.co.uk/resources/understandingmarket/definitionmkting.aspx [Accessed 14 March 2012].

Dam, K. (2011), "Mobile Marketing for 2012 and beyond" [Internet] Mobile Marketing, Media & Technology | Mobile Media Marketing Available from: http://www.mobilemediamarketing.com.au/mobile-marketing/ [Accessed 15 May 2012].

—. (2012), "One Small Step for Marketers, One Giant Leap for Mobile Marketing" [Internet] E-Web Marketing Available from: http://www.ewebmarketing.com.au/blog/ [Accessed 15 May 2012].

Digital Market (2012), "Bridging the Gap with Mobile" [Internet] Digital Market Available from: http://www.digitalmarket.asia/2012/04/bridging-the-gap-with-mobile/ [Accessed 1 May 2012].

Dushinski, K. (2009), *The Mobile Marketing Handbook*, New Jersey: Information Today, Inc.

Economist Newspaper (2012), "Mobile Marketing Square Deal" [Internet] The Economist Available from: http://www.economist.com/node/21556993 [Accessed 5 May 2012].

Frangold, C. (2012), "AT & T's New Mobile Features: This Is Just The Beginning" [Internet] Seeking Alpha. Available from: http://seekingalpha.com/article/563811-at-t-s-new-mobile-features-this-is-just-the-beginning/ [Accessed 7 May 2012].

Georgieva, M. (2012), *An Introduction to Email Marketing*, E-Book Edition.

Gilbreath, B. (2010), *The Next Evolution of Marketing: Connect with your Customers by Marketing with Meaning*, New York: McGraw-Hill.

Godin, S. (1999), *Permission Marketing: Turning Strangers into Friends and Friends into Customers*, New York: Simon & Schuster.

Gregg, D. (2012), "The Role of Mobile in Social Media" [Internet] Business School, University of Colorado Available from: http://dawngregg.com/smedia/?p=1824/ [Accessed 10 May 2012].

Groucutt, J., Leadley, P., and Forsyth, P. (2004), *Marketing: Essential Principles, New Realities*, London: Kogan Page.

Hof, R. (2012), "Google to Marketers: Go Mobile or Go Home" [Internet] Forbes. Available from: http://www.forbes.com/sites/roberthof/2012/04/25/ [Accessed 27 April 2012].

Hopkins, J. and Turner, J. (2012), *Go Mobile*, New Jersey: John Wiley and Sons, Inc.

Hsu, C. L., Lu, H. P., and Hsu, H. H. (2006), "Adoption of the Mobile Internet: An Empirical Study of Multimedia Message Service (MMS)", *The International Journal of Management Science*, pp. 1-5.

Hughes, J. (2011), *Android Apps Marketing*, Indianapolis: QUE

Hughes, J. (2012), *iPhone & iPad Apps Marketing*, 2nd Edition, Indianapolis: QUE.

iOS Developer Library (2012), iOS Overview [Internet]. iOS Developer Library Available from: http://developer.apple.com [Accessed 13 March 2012].

Johnson, L. (2012), Mobile Marketer – Dunkin' Donuts Connects Social Media Buzz via Interactive Mobile Campaign.

Kats, R. (2011), "Top 10 QR code campaigns of Q1" [Internet] Mobile Marketer: the news leader in mobile marketing, media and commerce Available from: http://www.mobilemarketer.com/cms/news/software-technology/12604/ [Accessed 20 April 2012].

—. (2012), "Mobile minefields – and how to avoid them" [Internet] Mobile Marketer: the news leader in mobile marketing, media and commerce Available from: http://www.mobilemarketer.com/cms/news/strategy/12815/ [Accessed 15 May 2012].

Kokkinaki, A. I., Mylonas, S., Thrassou, A., Economon, L., Kountouris, I., and Panayiotou, P. (2008), "Local E-Government in Cyprus: A Comparison of Perceptions between Citizens and Decision Makers", *ICIS 2008 Proceedings*, Paper 48, Available from: http://aisel.aisnet.org/icis2008/48.

Kokkinaki, A. I. and Thrassou, A. (2008), "A Usability Study of E-Government Initiatives in Cyprus", *Proceedings of Interfaces and Human Computer Interaction,* Amsterdam, the Netherlands, 25-27 July, 2008, pp. 212-217.

Kotler, P., Keller, K. L., Brady, M., Goodman, M., and Hansen, T. (2009), *Marketing Management*, Harlow: Prentice Hall.

Krishnamurthy, S. (2001), "A comprehensive analysis of permission marketing", *Journal of Computer Mediated Communication*, Vol. 6, No. 2, p. 4.

Krum, C. (2010), *Mobile Marketing: Finding Your Customers No Matter Where They Are*, Indianapolis: Pearson Education Inc.

Lancaster, G. and Reynolds, P. (2004), *Marketing*, New York: Palgrave Macmillan.

Law, J. (2009), *Oxford Dictionary of Business and Management*, 5th Edition, Oxford: Oxford University Press.

Loehnis, B. (2012), "Bridging the gap with mobile" [Internet] Digital Market Available from: http://www.digitalmarket.asia/2012/ [Accessed 1 May 2012].

Marketing Sherpa (2011), *Top 5 Mobile Marketing Case Studies & How To's*, Marketing Sherpa LLC, Warren: USA.

Marketing Teacher (2012), "Sales Promotion" [Internet] Marketing Teacher Available from: http://www.marketingteacher.com/lesson-store/lesson-sales-promotion.html [Accessed 2 April 2012].

Mobile Marketing Association (MMA) (2009), "Definition of Mobile Marketing" [Internet] Mobile Marketing Association Available from: http://www.mmaglobal.com/news/mma-updates-definition-mobile-marketing [Accessed 7 April 2012].

—. (2011), *An Introduction to Permission-Based Mobile Marketing*, London: Mobile Marketing Association.

Moriarty, S., Mitchell, N., and Wells, W. (2009), *Advertising Principles & Practice*, 8th Edition, New Jersey: Pearson Prentice Hall.

Moto Message (2010), "What is the future of SMS marketing?" [Internet] Moto Message – Text Message Marketing Available from: http://www.motomessage.com/future-sms-marketing/ [Accessed 6 April 2012].

—. (2012), "Reasons why businesses engage in mobile marketing" [Internet] Moto Message – Text Message Marketing Available from: http://www.motomessage.com/reasons-businesses-engage-mobile-marketing/ [Accessed 5 April 2012].

NurtureHQ (2009), "Why Lead Nurturing?" [Internet] SlideShare Available from: http://www.slideshare.net/neilbetter/an-introduction-to-lead-nurturing-what-is-lead-nurturing [Accessed 15 March 2012].

OIC (2012), "What's This SoLoMo Marketing All About?" [Internet] Increase Your Rank Available from: http://www.increaseyourrank.com/what-solomo-marketing-is-all-about.html [Accessed 2 September 2012].

QR Code Press (2012), "Survey shows QR codes are the most popular mobile marketing tool" [Internet] Mobile Commerce Press Available from: http://www.qrcodepress.com/survey-shows-qr-codes-are-the-most-popular-mobile-marketing-tool/859624/ [Accessed 5 June 2012].

Reed, R. (2011), *The SoLoMo Manifesto*, Whitepaper Edition, Moment Feed.

Sankaran, G. (2011), "Mobile Marketing Strategy – Exploring the Race for the Tiny Space" [Internet], Unaccented Thoughts Available from: http://gopi.5qadvisors.com/2011/08/24/ [Accessed 6 May 2012].

Segreto, P. (2010), Simplifying Social Media for Optimum Results, *International Franchising Association*.

Snyder, M. (2011), "Get Started in Mobile Marketing: 4 Insights to Guide your Strategy", Marketing Sherpa's Top 5 Mobile Marketing Case Studies and How To's [Internet]. Marketing Sherpa LLC Available from: http://www.sherpastore.com [Accessed 4 March 2012].

Speckmann, B. (2008), *The Android Mobile Platform*, Eastern Michigan University.
Stat Counter-Mobile OS (2012) [Online Image] Available from: http://gs.statcounter.com/#mobile_os-ww-monthly-201201-201208-bar StatCounter-mobile_os-ww-monthly-201201-201208-bar.png [Accessed 27 August 2012].
Strategic Growth (2009), "11 Benefits of Using Mobile Marketing to Grow Your Business" [Internet] Strategic Growth Available from: http://strategicmktgconcepts.wordpress.com/2009/06/23 [Accessed 27 August 2012].
Thrassou, A. and Lijo, P. R. (2007), "Customer Perceptions Regarding Usage of Mobile Banking Services - The Case of Kuwait", *World Journal of Business Management*, Vol. 1, No. 1, pp. 3-16.
Thrassou, A. and Lijo, P. R. (2008), "Motivators and Critical factors in Mobile Banking Communications - The Case of Kuwait", *Journal for Global Business Advancement*, Vol. 1, No. 4, pp. 327-349.
Thrassou, A. and Vrontis, D. (2006), "A Small Services Firm Marketing Communications Model for SME-Dominated Environments", *Journal of Marketing Communications*, Vol. 12, No. 3, pp. 183-202.
Thrassou, A. and Vrontis, D. (2009), "A New Consumer Relationship Model: The Marketing Communications Application", *Journal of Promotion Management*, Vol. 15, No. 4, pp. 499-521.
Thrassou, A., Vrontis, D., Chebbi, H. and Yahiaoui, D. (2012), "Transcending Innovativeness towards Strategic Reflexivity", *Qualitative Market Research: An International Journal,* Vol. 15, No. 4.
Thrassou, A., Vrontis, D. and Kotabe, M. (2011), "Towards a Marketing Communications Model for Small Political Parties - A Primary Principles Strategic Perspective for Developed Countries", *Cross Cultural Management: An International Journal*, Vol. 17, No. 3, pp. 263-292.
Thrassou, A., Vrontis, D. and McDonald, M. (2009) "A Marketing Communications Framework for Small Political Parties in Developed Countries", *Marketing Intelligence and Planning*, Vol. 27, Issue 2, pp. 268-292.
Tode, C. (2012), "Four mobile marketing strategies that are working right now" [Internet] Mobile Marketer: the news leader in mobile marketing, media and commerce Available from: http://www.mobilemarketer.com/cms/news/advertising/12382/ [Accessed 27 March 2012].
Tranter, K. (2012), "Social Media Marketing – QR Codes" [Internet] UTICAOD.com Available from:

http://www.uticaod.com/blogs/x1965984658/Social-Media-Marketing-QR-Codes/ [Accessed 27 April 2012].

Tsirulnik, G. (2010), "Companies need to promote their mobile offerings more aggressively: study" [Internet] Mobile Marketer: the news leader in mobile marketing, media and commerce Available from: http://wwww.mobilemarketer.com/cms/news/research/8490 [Accessed 1 September 2012].

Turban, E., King, D., and Lang, J. (2009), *Introduction to Electronic Commerce*, 2nd Edition, New Jersey: Pearson Education Inc.

Turban, E., Volonino, L., McLean, E., and Wetherbe, J. (2010), *Information Technology for Management*, 7th Edition, New Jersey: John Wiley & Sons.

Turner, J. (2012), "3 Steps to Determine if Social Local Mobile is Right for Your Business" [Internet] Social Media Examiner Available from: http://www.socialmediaexaminer.com/is-social-local-mobile-right-for-your-business/ [Accessed 2 September 2012].

Varnali, K., Toker, A., and Yilmaz, C. (2011), *Mobile Marketing Fundamentals and Strategy*, 1st Edition, New York: McGraw-Hill

Viveiros, B. N. (2012), "Incorporating QR Codes into Multichannel Campaigns" [Internet] Chief Marketer Available from: http://chiefmarketer.com/print/mobile-marketing/ [Accessed 10 May 2012].

Vranesevic, T., Vignali, C., and Vrontis, D. (2006), *Marketing and Retailing Strategy*, Zagreb: Accent.

Vrontis, D. and Thrassou, A. (2007), "A new conceptual framework for business-consumer relationships", *Marketing Intelligence & Planning*, Vol. 25, Issue 7, pp. 789-806.

Vrontis, D., Thrassou, A. and Ching-Wei, H. (2008), "The Marketing Implications of the 'Undesired Self' – the case of Chinese Y-Generation", *Journal for Global Business Advancement*, Vol. 1, No. 4, pp. 390-408.

Vrontis, D., Thrassou, A. and Lamprianou, I. (2009), "International Marketing Adaptation versus Standardization of Multinational Companies", *International Marketing Review*, Vol. 26, No. 4 and 5, pp. 477-500.

Young, A. (2010), "Mobile Advertising Set to Skyrocket" [Internet] E-Web Marketing Available from: http://www.ewebmarketing.com.au/blog/mobile-advertising-set-to-skyrocket/ [Accessed 15 May 2012].

CHAPTER SIXTEEN

GLOBAL SUSTAINABLE TOURISM CRITERIA: AN INTERNATIONAL PERSPECTIVE ON RESTAURANT SUSTAINABILITY MODEL DEVELOPMENT

IAN JENKINS AND ROBERT S. BRISTOW

Introduction

Restaurants are at the forefront of the hospitality and tourism industry and it therefore seems contingent that in these times of sustainable development and the spectre of climate change, they will also be developing new innovative business models to ensure their success.

The apparent abundance of food in developed western countries means that the idea of food shortages is something of an anomaly. This has not always been the case; some 50 to 100 years ago food shortages were common and significant numbers of the population were employed within agriculture. The last 50 years have seen massive changes in food production in developed countries, to the extent that food production now has fewer employees in this sector of the economy. It is posited that developed countries are now service economies containing most of a nation's employment including the hospitality and tourism industries. Tourism and hospitality are also, on average, strong contributors to a country's GDP with figures ranging from averages of 5% to 10% (VisitBritain, 2003) and international tourism receipts have exceeded one trillion USD in 2011 (UN World Tourism Organization 2012). When this figure is compared to agriculture and food production, it is clear to see the decline of employment in this sector, which has been replaced by an increase in technology and the mechanisation of food production; on average agriculture has about 3 to 5 % of a developed country's employment

(EuroStat, 2007). It is therefore suggested that food is not as important as the new service economies that dominate the global economy.

The prediction of climate change threatens world food production and when this is coupled with a predicted peak oil crisis (reduced oil production) the outlook for agriculture is uncertain. Both climate change and oil shortages will inevitably affect restaurants and their food sourcing policies. Consequently, it is purported that sustainability will be a necessary policy instrument for business survival and in particular the food business. It is asserted that restaurants and restaurant policies will have to include food sourcing and ethical employment policies for future success and businesses that do so now could be regarded as innovative.

It is also evident that the sustainability paradigm is here to stay and that businesses will have to incorporate its principles into their plans and structures if they are to remain competitive and sustainable (economically). It is suggested that competitiveness and sustainability are not necessary oxymora, but are new innovative ways to do business. Even global corporations and multinationals have recognized the need to appear green and sustainable; BP, Exxon, Shell, Virgin are examples of transformations of companies to 'green corporations'. However, these conglomerates seem to be at odds with what the Brundtland Report (WCED, 1987), suggested as our sustainable future. From a UK perspective, BP and Virgin Atlantic are seen to be carriers not only of their national flag but also the flag of sustainability. A quick review of their websites demonstrates the importance of sustainability (BP 2012; Virgin 2012). In addition, nationally focused businesses, such as the UK's famous Marks & Spencer's retail store, have wholeheartedly embraced sustainability.

Restaurants are an important part of the tourism and hospitality industry and one would have expected this sector to be at the vanguard of sustainability, especially due to their closeness to food production. That said, the number of hospitality companies having sustainable policies is more difficult to locate. However there are moves to embrace this new paradigm with novel and innovative associations emerging. In the UK there is the SRA (Sustainable Restaurant Association, 2012), which has approximately 500 members. The SRA provides advice and assessment of sustainable restaurant products for its members. They state

> "[t]he SRA is here to offer practical help. Our team includes former chefs and restaurateurs, so we know the challenges you face daily... Whether it's sourcing produce, equipment or non-food consumables, we can help you

find the most sustainable choice that's right for your business." (SRA 2012).

In the US there is the National Restaurant Association (NRA) which states that:

> "today's restaurant industry is growing rapidly. It employs 12.9 million Americans in 970,000 locations — and 2012 sales are expected to reach $632 billion." (NRS 2012).

The NRA too, has a section on sustainability and the importance this has to the USA industry, again supporting the supposition of the growing importance of sustainability to restaurant success (NRA 2012). However, one must also question to what extent sustainability concepts permeate the industry and it is interesting to note that some key educational texts, used in hospitality schools, are still devoid of sustainable principles and measures (Davis et al., 2008). Given the longevity of the concept this appears to be somewhat worrying.

A restaurant's visibility and ubiquitous nature make it well positioned to make a high-quality impact upon the customer, possibly influencing and changing consumer attitudes towards sustainable products. Perhaps one of the biggest challenges and innovations for restaurants is to *change consumer attitudes* towards food rather than the consumer dictating changes.

Restaurant Developments

It is posited that food is a cultural tenet and an anthropological symbol of a country. In many ways it stereotypes the country and emits a certain presence in terms of its tourism and hospitality products. In many respects restaurants are the *tip* of a country's cultural iceberg and perhaps a semiotic symbol of its tourism product. As mentioned earlier, restaurants are also one of the main elements that a country's tourism product is based upon. Any visit to a country usually includes a number of visits to restaurants.

Banqueting and feasting have been part of human history since time immemorial. Certainly *fast food* can be traced back to Roman times as many citizens of Rome had limited cooking facilities and were used to buying their meals from street vendors. Not surprisingly then the current range of food outlets is immense, ranging from the humble café, which is a necessary part of any working man's lunch time break, to a top Michelin starred restaurant. However, both require the same functions and business acumen, which should currently include sustainable measures.

The food industry has been innovative and a number of movements have emerged over the years, such as 'Slow Food' gathering momentum towards the end of the twentieth century, possibly reflecting environmental concerns and closely linked to the Organic Food Movement, both perhaps a presage to sustainability. However, to state that these movements have affected restaurants in general, would be too broad an assertion; certainly they would have had an effect but to what extent is questionable. *Fast food* has also changed and there is clearly a move towards a healthier and perhaps sustainable business practice by these restaurants and companies. This is possibly best illustrated by McDonald's which clearly has a new marketing campaign towards 'Green Issues' (McDonald's 2010). To what extent this is a real move towards sustainable practices or simply a response to a market change remains to be seen. But, whichever way this is interpreted it certainly supports the move towards restaurants demonstrating sustainable measures.

Restaurants require a number of key attributes to function and all of these can be incorporated into the paradigm of sustainability. Table 1 summarizes a restaurant's role in sustainable management.

It is perhaps axiomatic that the diversity of restaurants is immense, and a quick review of a city's 'eating place list' confirms this assertion. Given the eminence of sustainability in today's media agenda one would also expect this to be reflected in the marketing and details of restaurants, but this is often far from clear.

Table 1* Restaurant Sustainable Management Areas

FUNCTION AREA	SUSTAINABLE ELEMENTS
Environment & Buildings:	Energy efficiency, insulation, use of natural resources (grass roof), carbon neutral materials, carbon offsetting,
Employment and Service attributes	Appropriate wages & conditions, appropriate training, Pensions, employment health & safety, fair employment to local labour, brainstorming, employee rewards for innovation
Management strategies and control	Further training, employee discussions, appropriate communication channels, attendance at courses, community sharing and communications
Food sourcing and preparations	Local sourcing, CO_2 reduction, sustainable transport,
Energy supplies	Sustainable energy supply, reduced CO_2 output, transport reduction and control.
Waste disposal	Recycling of all waste, verification of disposal, reuse of materials
Creativity	Incorporating sustainable measures in menu and other areas of business

*Source: Davis et al., 2008 ; SRA 2012

Innovation

Restaurants like all other businesses are affected by change and especially new technology. Innovation is really about creating new and better products. "Better" is one of those words that is elusive and transitory and perhaps there is a need to define it in terms of efficiency and effectiveness. It also, perhaps, has a variety of meanings depending upon the stakeholders: to the customer it may mean a more creative menu or faster booking systems; for the business the *raison d'être* is usually more profit orientated. So where might sustainability fit into these objectives? With the augur of climate change ever present and the current world recession still deepening in many countries, profits are hard to come by. This puts pressure on restaurants to embrace new and innovative ideas, which could well include a move towards the use of more sustainable resources if this can be linked to profits.

That said it is argued that in fact sustainability, as defined by the Brundtland Report, is to an extent innovative. It is clearly a new way of thinking and requires a change of management culture. It is asserted that the restaurant which embraces sustainability can be seen as an innovator and perhaps ahead of the competition and this, as we know, means in many cases business success. As noted earlier the SRA has only 500 restaurants which compared to all restaurants in the UK is a very small proportion indeed (SRA, 2012). It is asserted that businesses that enter the market first with new products are usually those that gain the greatest profits. Perhaps this could be so with sustainable restaurants where competition is limited and in the current market sector considered to be a niche market, which can be linked to reduced competition and increased profits (Jenkins, 2007).

The importance of innovation is really measured by its effect upon the customer and to what extent it increases business. A customer who does not appreciate new innovations is a customer who is unlikely to pay the increased cost that perhaps specialised markets might offer. Sustainable food sourcing and the use of appropriate local labour could add money to the products offered and hence would mean a more expensive service and meal. This may well affect certain sections of the market especially those who are *price elastic*. However, it is evident that when talking about restaurants 'per se', the market is vast and consumers, especially on a global scale, would have different cultural tenets which could affect restaurants offering sustainable products. Perhaps there is a need to divide the restaurant market into different categories and to then evaluate sustainable techniques in each sector. It is suggested that this would be a new approach (perhaps innovative). This could then be linked to the new bench marking criteria for tourism (Global Sustainable Tourism Criteria, 2012) which appears to have been designed to apply to all sectors of the tourism market including hospitality and restaurants.

Perhaps the major debate at the moment is about food sourcing and whether local is best (Darlin 2010). Especially with the climate change debate now more or less accepted, the notion of CO_2 reduction is a top priority for many governments. Transporting (mainly flying) goods around the world seems not to be a sensible solution to the sourcing of food. That said the question remains: how much does the consumer actually care about CO_2 reduction?

It seems axiomatic that many restaurants do seem to have an emphasis on local food sourcing especially when the menu is closely examined; but when it comes to beverages, with the exception of microbreweries, to what extent should one restrict these to being supplied only from local sources? Perhaps one can dispense with bottled water from other countries and look for water sources closer to home; however where wines are concerned would it seem sensible to restrict wines only to those that are home produced? What about countries that have little or no wine production?

Perhaps another salient argument is the aspect of seasonality. Is it good business to restrict food to only seasonal goods? To what extent would the consumer be happy with a restriction on when certain products can be purchased? In some countries this is considered the norm (France for instance and to some extent Switzerland) but other markets such as Britain and the US seem to expect food availability for the whole 12 months. Both approaches (seasonal/non-seasonal) it could be argued have an impact on sustainability and climate change. Limiting global food exchange means that countries that supply food will have their GDP much reduced. In many cases these are developing countries badly in need of hard currency and limiting their ability to supply food would affect employment and may reduce their sustainability (Desrochers and Shimizu, 2012). Also the notion of growing locally can be challenged in a number of ways (Desrochers and Shimizu, 2012).

Firstly, restaurants that have sourced local food can find that local suppliers have a monopoly of this market and raise prices, judging that they can control the food source for the area. This makes the food presented at the restaurant so expensive that is not worth serving to the customer. Secondly, many local food producers are connected to the export market and frequently restaurants cannot buy direct, but have to purchase it in the new destination where it has been exported to. In the UK this is what happens with shellfish which are exported to France and Spain and then have to be re-purchased by British restaurants. This doubles transport costs and is not a sustainable business method. So, although the theory of local growing seems acceptable the practical realties are plagued with problems. It is also purported that food exports may be of a higher quality and can command a higher price, further limiting the local purchase.

Perhaps local restaurants should consider an alternative, which is a co-operative of local producers, either owned by or contracted to supply local restaurants first, at reasonable prices, and where super-profits are not the only motive. This approach to supply locally is not particularly innovative but it does have some potential to address the sustainability of restaurant food. There are examples of this: the Taste of Wales has managed to encourage producers to be linked to outlets through Welsh restaurants and these campaigns are also connected to supermarket outlets where local products are clearly marketed to consumers. (Jenkins and Jones, 2002).

Perhaps what is needed is ideas on how to develop innovative ideas using sustainability. As can be seen above, there are associations that are calling for more sustainable restaurants and the UK has some 500 members who seem committed to sustainability (SRA, 2012). But how can sustainability be made innovative? There is clearly a need for new business models to be developed based upon the balance of profits and sustainable measures. It is posited that further research is needed to explore the links between profitability and sustainability. As mentioned earlier, evidence suggests that consumers do not seem exceedingly worried about sustainability and in many cases they appear to pay *lip service* to it, rather than embracing it fully, especially where higher prices are concerned. It is perspicacious to suggest that restaurants are reticent to embrace sustainable measures especially if they affect profit or perhaps the quality of the product itself.

Sustainability

Even today, sustainability is somewhat of an elusive term. Born out of the Environmental Movement of the 1960s and '70s, sustainable is often labelled as a "green approach". But as Hall and Lew (1998) have noted the definition is often not understood by the public and if that is the case, industry must also be struggling with the concept. Early green approaches attacked problems of waste reduction, recycling and the re-use of resources. But other than composting, food is not something that can be recycled or re-used. One needs to look at food as a resource for (human) consumption in a holistic or geographic setting.

Within a region, the term "foodshed" (Getz 1991) is critical given that the geography of the ecosystem is often limited. One goal is to describe a food system within an area that is based on high quality, sustainability and social justice (see for example Yurtseven and Kaya 2011). Given worldwide population growth, an exploration of the management acceptance of sustainable practices of food provision is warranted.

Sustainable tourism is frequently identified as a fundamental tool for economic development (Sharpley, 2000). A significant economic impact occurs when one considers travel and lodging expenses with food and drink making up to one third of typical total tourist expenditure (Torres 2002; Meler and Cerović 2003). Yet despite this apparently large economic impact, Belisle (1983) found that food imports for tourist consumption for restaurants, reduced the real local economic impact and use of local food items.

Growing awareness of these and several other food industry challenges characterize the food-system, creating a powerful demand for food that is "good, clean and fair" (Petrini, 2007). The interest in eating locally and regionally sourced food has emerged as a response to this. Eating local food is believed to potentially reduce energy consumption by shortening supply lines, protect unique agricultural and culinary traditions, preserve scenic agricultural landscapes and agro-biodiversity, and to provide just compensation for producers and laborers (Kloppenburg et al. 1996; Nabhan 2002; Pollan 2007; Sims 2009). These goals dovetail with tourist interests in experiencing the uniqueness of places and regions.

Locally sourced food is an important element used to promote economic development in a region. Feenstra (1997) notes long-term health of a community's food system promotes sustainability. For example, the planned tourist development in Cancun, Mexico has stressed the importance of locally sourced food as an economic development strategy in the State of Quintana Roo, Mexico (Torres, 2002). Building these local linkages is encouraged to promote a market advantage, minimize risk and boost staff morale, amongst other reasons (Ashley et al., 2006). It should be clear that bringing the consumer closer to the food producer is an important element of food tourism (Everett, 2012).

Global Sustainable Tourism Criteria (GSTC)

Numerous models of sustainability have been proposed over the decades. Many build on the need for resource protection (e.g. clean water), promotion of economic development (jobs), long term benefits (social discounting) and protecting local values (culture). These are all important goals of a sustainability model.

A useful bench mark for sustainability in tourism and hospitality is the Global Sustainable Tourism Criteria (GSTC) formulated in 2008 by

Rainforest Alliance, the United Nations Environment Programme (UNEP), the United Nations Foundation and the United Nations World Tourism Organization (UNWTO). These criteria are designed to be the minimum practices to ensure sustainability for a business as well as to protect natural and cultural resources. In addition, the 37 voluntary standards, within the criteria, are to be instruments to alleviate poverty (Global Sustainable Tourism Criteria, 2012).

The criteria were developed by sustainability experts and the tourism industry and based on more than 60 existing models of sustainable tourism certification already deployed around the world. The GSTC model is founded on the desire to create baseline guidelines for businesses, both large and small, to become more sustainable and to serve as a starting point for the more specific needs of governments, NGO's and the private sector. Since deployment in late 2008, the criteria are starting to be critiqued at business level.

GSTC also has a number of purposes that prove useful. It serves as basic guidelines for businesses of all sizes to become more sustainable and helps them choose sustainable tourism programs that fulfil these global criteria; it seems to have very adaptable elements which reduce the prescribed aspects of other sustainable guides.

It also serves as the minimum guidelines for the industry to cooperate. Having a common thread to base management decisions on, the GSTC could also be used for other sectors of the tourism industry allowing a number of measurement and assessment methods that could be applied to other areas.

Furthermore, it tries to help consumers "act green" which from a restaurant customer's point of view, could be very useful, as it also places pressure on restaurants to demonstrate what sustainable measures they are using. It is posited that very few customers would actually know whether a restaurant is acting in a sustainable way, therefore using this benchmark could be a useful guide to a restaurant's sustainability index.

Once again the attempt is to try to standardise the meaning of sustainability, so that there is a unifying bond of evaluation, making assessment clear for everyone in terms of whether a restaurant is or is not sustainable. Hence, the GSTC 'serves as a common denominator for information media to recognize sustainable tourism providers' (GSTC,

2012). Finally, GSTC can provide 'basic guidelines for education and training bodies, such as hotel schools and universities' (GSTC, 2012) who are the educators of the next generation of business and tourism developers.

The overall axioms of the GSTC produce a measurement system that can be used to reflect the founding principles of sustainable development as illustrated in four main concepts:

- Reducing Negative Impacts on the Environment
- Maximizing Social and Economic Benefits
- Effective Sustainability Planning
- Enhancing Cultural Heritages

As has been evidenced earlier in this chapter, it is proposed that most food producers and those that provide food at restaurants would be fully aware of the need for sustainable principles not only given the GSTC criteria but also the length of time that consumers and the public have been exposed to green issues and sustainability. The evidence suggests that the environmental movement appears to have developed around the time of the Second World War, initially beginning with a need to protect the agricultural resource (USDA-NRCS, 2012) together with a more refined practice of agricultural production (Soil Association, 2011). Combined, these movements have evolved into "Conservation Agriculture" (Hobbs, 2007). These movements have become relevant for the farm manager, which essentially is the protection of the soil through ensuring that there is no till and mulching that reduces soil loss.

Although, as already mentioned, there is also the premise that even though sustainability should be embedded within all types of business, the reality is somewhat different, to the extent that 'Green Washing' (paying lip service to sustainability) is prevalent. There is certainly anecdotal evidence to support the view that consumers may not be interested in sustainability as a primary motivation factor, but rather on the more immediate aspects of cost and good experiences at restaurants. However, management seeking to meet the needs of consumers, as well as balance costs, may view sustainability issues more importantly.

Model Development

Todorov and Marinora (2009a) suggest a model of sustainability that is evolving over time, based on the role of humans as "guardians". The definition is founded on an historical background from the earliest days of environmental awareness to a contemporary one where human dimensions are integrated into the model. Combining the social, environmental and economic elements in sustainability is critical and serves as the foundation of the GSTC. Therefore Todorov and Marinora (2009b) have described the science that studies models and measures sustainable development, providing a theoretical basis for the GSTC.

Useful for this study is the practical and realistic needs of the food service industry in a highly competitive market. Numerous studies have examined the rise and fall of food services (Parsa et al., 2005; Dube et al., 1994), yet those restaurants that cater to the seasonal fluctuations of tourists and local needs are especially challenging.

Case Study Evidence

In order to support some of the previous assertions the authors have been involved in primary research dealing with the idea of restaurant sustainability. The authors have designed a survey to solicit information from restaurant management and sought to identify the particular cuisine offered, size of operation in terms of seats and staff and sources of food products offered. For food, additional questions enquired about production practices (e.g., organic, grass fed, free range and so on). Lastly a series of statements prepared by the GSTC was evaluated by restaurant management. These criteria are designed to assess the social and economic wellbeing as well as employment value.

The survey was pre-tested and minor editorial changes were needed. The questionnaire was then administered in four locations: the Turks and Caicos Islands during the summer of 2011, Western Massachusetts in the US in the Fall of 2011, Switzerland, Spring 2012, and Wales in the UK, Summer 2012. The survey was managed in person, self-collected, or via an online survey software program (Survey Monkey). All in all 78 complete surveys were collected, yielding an approximate 20-30% response rate across the four locations. Due to the nature of social science data collection the response rate is approximate since the absolute total population varied for each geographical area and is not exactly known.

Restaurants were closed or the staff may have been on vacation during the sampling period. For these reasons, our results are descriptive at best. Excluded from the sample were chain and fast food restaurants. Table 2 provides the sample sizes for the four countries.

A variety of restaurants were surveyed and the size ranged from 6 to 340 seats with an average of 88 seats and 15 full time and 14 part time staff. Also, a variety of cuisines was offered with the most common being American (n=29), British (n=10), Caribbean (n=15), Italian (n=17), Seafood (n=17), Vegetarian (n=16), with a smattering of European, Latin American, and Asian styles. It must be noted that since most restaurants offered more than one type of food on the menu, the percentages reflect that overlap.

Table 2. Sample Size in Sustainable Restaurant Study

Country	Sample Size	Percent
Switzerland	11	14.3
Turks and Caicos	22	28.6
United Kingdom	13	16.9
United States	31	40.3
Total	77	100.0

The next section of the survey solicited information about the sources of food offered. "Local" was defined as the total travelling distance from producer to consumer of less than 2 hours transport time. Managers were asked to identify sources of food on a 1 to 4 scale with 1 being all food of this type is local, 2 most of the food is local, 3 some of the food is local, to 4 where none of the food is local. For the sample, baked goods tended to be locally sourced with most of the food being local (mean equals 2.07), while some meats and poultry were found to be locally sourced (mean value 3.01 each). Table 3 summarizes the sources of food.

Consumers often desire particular characteristics of their food. Besides vegetarian, gluten free and vegan menus, customers want organic food, free range chickens and eggs, grass fed beef and so on. Managers are sensitive to these requests but they also desire high quality, reasonably priced food that is readily available and uniform in size, shape and color. Table 4 highlights the importance of these items on a five point scale, with 1 being most important, and 5 being not very important.

As might be expected quality, price, availability and uniformity were most important to restaurant managers. Next, in order of importance was fish sourced from certifiable stocks, chemical free, GMO free, Integrate Pest Management, free range, organic, and then grass-fed. Also note the standard deviations tended to be the least for price, uniformity, availability and quality, inferring the overall and consistent high ranking importance of these practices to the managers. Cost influences the purchase of organic and other production practices, so the rating probably reflects this element. Price and availability are typically important to consumers. Research has found this to be the case in the EU where half of European shoppers will purchase more ethical food and drink (Institute of Grocery Distribution, 2010).

Table 3. How Local is the Food Procured by Restaurants?

Food	N	Min	Max	Mean	SD
Meats	73	1	4	2.7397	1.0933
Poultry	72	1	5	2.7778	1.1287
Seafood	72	1	5	2.5000	1.3531
Dairy	74	1	4	2.5541	1.2402
Produce	72	1	5	2.2778	1.0240
Baked Goods	75	1	5	1.9200	1.2494
Beverages	73	1	5	2.6986	1.1016

Table 4. Importance of Food Production Practices

Factor	N	Min	Max	Mean	SD
Quality	74	1	3	1.0946	0.3380
Availability	74	1	4	1.4595	0.6660
Price	75	1	4	1.5600	0.7396
Uniformity	72	1	5	1.8056	0.9290
Fish sourced from certified sustainable stocks	71	1	5	2.2254	1.1489
Chemical free	73	1	5	2.4247	1.0791
GMO free	71	1	5	2.5352	1.1191

Next, managers were asked to assess the importance of the GSTC. Ten of the criteria were selected for this study and addressed the environmental impacts of restaurant management as well as one criterion directed to wages offered to employees. Table 5 highlights the aggregate responses.

All the criteria were found to be important in our study of restaurants in four countries. "The international or national legal protection of employees is respected, and employees are paid a living wage" was the most important criteria to management (mean=1.50), followed by "The use of harmful substances, including pesticides, paints, swimming pool disinfectants, and cleaning materials, is minimized; substituted, when available, by innocuous products; and all chemical use is properly managed" (mean = 1.73) and "The purchase of disposable and consumable goods is measured, and the business actively seeks ways to reduce their use" (mean = 1.93). It was found that managers were indifferent to the criterion "Greenhouse gas emissions from all sources controlled by the business are measured, and procedures are implemented to reduce and offset them as a way to achieve climate neutrality" (mean = 2.51) perhaps reflecting businesses' surrendering on this important environmental concern.

It should be noted that the more important the criteria ranked by restaurant management, the more agreement we find in the results. That is, a smaller standard deviation is typically found for the GSTC that are ranked important. Greater variation for acceptance of the criteria is found with "Wastewater, including gray water, is treated effectively and reused where possible". This possibly reflects the varying demand and costs of water and energy usage among the sample. For example both water and energy are extremely expensive on the Caribbean islands and are in high demand.

In summary, most of the restaurants surveyed seemed to be in agreement with the main criteria of the GSTC. This was a very pleasing result. The areas of concern identified within the literature were also being addressed by the restaurants. In particular, the notion of locally sourced food and quality/price seems to be clearly an agenda item of customers and restaurants. Restaurants were also clearly aware of the more socially specific characteristics of the criteria, such as appropriate wages and conditions for the employees. It seems evident that this sector is working towards acceptance and delivery for sustainable development, with some exceptions (perhaps carbon emissions of local businesses and grey water usage)

Table 5. Restaurant Management Importance of Global Sustainable Tourism Criteria

Criteria	N	Min	Max	Mean	SD
The international or national legal protection of employees is respected, and employees are paid a living wage.	74	1	4	1.5000	0.6672
The use of harmful substances, including pesticides, paints, swimming pool disinfectants, and cleaning materials, is minimized; substituted, when available, by innocuous products; and all chemical use is properly managed.	71	1	4	1.7324	0.8274
The purchase of disposable and consumable goods is measured, and the business actively seeks ways to reduce their use.	76	1	4	1.9342	0.8380
A solid waste management plan is implemented, with quantitative goals to minimize waste that is not reused or recycled.	75	1	5	1.9467	0.9711
Energy consumption should be measured, sources indicated, and measures to decrease overall consumption should be adopted, while encouraging the use of renewable energy.	76	1	5	2.0263	0.9930
Purchasing policy favors environmentally friendly products for building materials, capital goods, food, and consumables.	74	1	5	2.0541	0.9636
Water consumption should be measured, sources indicated, and measures to decrease overall consumption should be adopted.	76	1	5	2.1184	0.9794
Wastewater, including gray water, is treated effectively and reused where possible.	74	1	4	2.1486	1.0686
The business implements practices to reduce pollution from noise, light, runoff, erosion, ozone-depleting compounds, and air and soil contaminants.	74	1	5	2.2568	0.9801
Greenhouse gas emissions from all sources controlled by the business are measured, and procedures are implemented to reduce and offset them as a way to achieve climate neutrality.	75	1	5	2.5067	1.0184

Conclusion

It should be expected that in the highly competitive market of food service, restaurants that remain in business have balanced the costs of operations with meeting the needs of the customer. In the long run, customer patronage and loyalty determine which restaurants stay open. For example, organics may be valued by the consumer, yet cost may limit the quantity purchased (Vermeir and Verbecke, 2004). So managers need to consider their clientele in deciding what food to offer as well as the kind of restaurant is in demand.

The decision to seek non-local food products in this study can be attributed to several factors. Local restaurateurs are concerned with the variety and quality of locally produced foods. Availability, cost, price and uniformity remain a challenge. A restaurant needs a dependable source of food products. Cost of food is critical in the industry since it contributes to the overall cost of the business with labour being another major outgoing. And uniformity is desired by the consumer since they have come to expect a dish to be consistent in taste and appearance.

Research by Buller and Morris (2004) and Torres and Momsen (2004) found for example that a tourist's desire for local foods can create opportunities to develop sustainable agriculture and help the local economy. Larger internationally owned businesses can buy food in bulk at a considerable saving, compared to local businesses (Timms, 2006). Timms recommends that the producer, that is local farmers, strengthen community organizations and focus on long term capacity building to link the farmers with the demand of the tourism industry.

Smaller locally owned tourism operations purchase more local food than larger foreign owned operations as a percentage of their purchases (Momsen 1998). While price remains an important aspect in the food service industry, current research by Schubert et al., (2010) suggests consumers are willing to pay more for "green" practices in restaurants. Broader communication and partnerships between consumers, the restaurant and the farm will improve the likelihood of sustainable food. Feenstra (2002) concludes that public participation, partnerships and principles does not mean the consumer must work on the farm, but should meet on some common ground.

There exist multiple challenges in the restaurant industry. While cost in the short run is critical for the success of the business, it should become clear that sustainable practices may have long term and thus more sustainable benefits in the long run. Energy savings, by employing CFL lighting increases the initial purchase price, yet will save in energy use in the long term. Consequently, restaurants should try and follow the following precepts:

- Reducing Negative Impacts on the Environment
- Maximizing Social and Economic Benefits
- Effective Sustainability Planning
- Enhancing Cultural Heritages

If the goals of sustainable management practices are to be successful, restaurants must reduce their environmental footprint, acknowledge and support local citizens by buying local products and pay living wages, promote proactive planning to consider future needs, and support local societal organizations, rather than try to modify them.

References

Ashley, C. Goodwin, H., McNab, D. Scott, M., and Chaves, L. (2006), "Making Tourism Count for the local economy in the Caribbean. Pro-Poor Tourism Partnership and the Caribbean Tourism Organisation", available at: www.propoortourism.org.uk/Caribbean (accessed 17 May 2012).

Belisle, F. (1983), "Tourism and Food Production in the Caribbean", *Annals of Tourism Research* Vol. 10, pp. 497-513.

Buller, H., and Morris, C. (2004), "Growing goods: The market, state and sustainable food production". *Environment and Planning, A*, Vol. 36, pp. 1065–1084.

BP (British Petroleum), (2012), Environment & Society, available at: http://www.bp.com/genericsection.do?categoryId=4004120&contentId =7016335, (accessed 3 September 2012).

Darlin D. (2012), "A Balance Between the Factory and the Local Farm", *New York Times, Business*, available at: http://www.nytimes.com/2010/02/14/business/14every.html?_r=3, (accessed 3/9/2012).

Davis, D. Lockwood, A. Pantelidis I. and Alcott P. (2008), *Food and Beverage Management*, Butterworth Heinemann, London.

Desrochers P. and Shimizu H. (2012), "Point of view", *Geographical*, July, pp.77, Geographical Magazine Ltd, Brentford.

Dube, L., Renaghan, L., and Miller, J. (1994), "Measuring customer satisfaction for strategic management", *Cornell Hotel and Restaurant Administration Quarterly*. Vol. 35, No. 1, pp. 39-47.

Everett, S. (in press) "Production Places or Consumption Spaces? The place making Agency of Food Tourism in Ireland and Scotland", *Tourism Geographies*, DOI: 10.1080/14616688.2012.647321.

Eurostat. (2007), "EuroStat Pocket Book, Agriculture Statistics Data 1995-2005", *Office for Official Publications of the European Communities*, Luxembourg, available at: http://epp.eurostat.ec.europa.eu/cache/ITY_OFFPUB/KS-ED-07-001/EN/KS-ED-07-001-EN.PDF, (accessed 3 September 2012)

Feenstra, G. (1997), "Local food systems and sustainable communities", *American Journal of Alternative Agriculture*, Vol. 12, No. 1, pp. 28-36.

—. (2002), "Creating space for sustainable food systems: Lessons from the field", *Agriculture and Human Values,* Vol. 19, pp. 99-106.

Frasman J. (2012), "A Taste of History", *Intelligent Life*, July/August, pp.115-119, *The Econo*mist Newspaper Ltd, London.

Getz, A. (1991), "Urban Foodsheds", *Permaculture Activist*, Vol. 7, No. 3, pp. 26-27.

Global Sustainable Tourism Criteria, (2012), "Global Sustainable Tourism Criteria", available at: http://new.gstcouncil.org/ (accessed 1 June 2012).

Harris R., Griffin T., and Williams P. (2002), *Sustainable Tourism, A Global Perspective*, Butterworth Heinemann, London.

Henson, R. (2008), *Climate Change The symptom, The Science, The Solutions*, Rough Guides Ltd London.

Institute of Grocery Distribution. (2010), "Half of European shoppers will buy more ethical food and drink in the future". Press Release. available at http://www.igd.com/index.asp?id=1&fid=6&sid=25&tid=90&cid=1623 (accessed 1 Sept 2012)

Jenkins, I.S. (2007), *Postmodern Tourist Niches*, PhD Thesis, University of Wales Swansea.

Jones, A and Jenkins, I. (2002), "A Taste of Wales- Blas Ar Gymru: Institutional malaise in promoting Welsh food tourism Products", in G Richards & Anne- Mette Hjalager (eds) Tourism and Gastronomy, Ch7: pp. 115-132, Routledge.

Kim, H., Zheng, G. (2003), "Risk-adjusted performance: A Sector Analysis of Restaurant Firms", *Journal of Hospitality & Tourism Research*, Vol. 27, No. 2, pp. 200-216.
Todorov, V.I. and Marinova. D. (2009), "Models of Sustainability", 18th World IMACS / MODSIM Congress, Cairns, Australia 13-17 July, available at: http://www.mssanz.org.au/modsim09, (accessed: 24 July 2012).
McDonald's (2010), "McDonald's Europe Best of Green", available at: http://www.bestofgreenmcdonaldseurope.com/downloads/Anti_litterin g_all_case_studies.pdf, (accessed 33 September 2012).
NRA (National Restaurant Association) (2012), "About us", available at: http://www.restaurant.org/aboutus/, (accessed 3 September 2012).
—. (2012), "Sustainability & Social Responsibility", Available at: http://www.restaurant.org/sustainability/, (accessed: 3 September 2012).
Parsa, H., Self, J., Njite, D., King, T. (2005). "Why Restaurants Fail", *Cornell Hotel and Restaurant Administration Quarterly,* Vol. 46, No. 3, pp. 304-322.
SRA (Sustainable Restaurant Association). (2012). "Some Good Things", available at: http://www.thesra.org/, (accessed 17 August 2012).
Todorov, V.I. and Marinova. D. (2009a), "Models of Sustainability", 18th World IMACS / MODSIM Congress, Cairns, Australia 13-17 July, available at: http://www.mssanz.org.au/modsim09, (accessed 24 July 2012).
Todorov, V.I. and Marinova. D. (2009b), "Sustainometrics: Measuring sustainability", 18th World IMACS / MODSIM Congress, Cairns, Australia 13-17 July, Available at: http://www.mssanz.org.au/modsim09, (accessed 24 July 2012).
United Nations, World Tourism Organization. (2012), "International tourism receipts surpass US$1 trillion in 2011", Press Release 12027, available at http://media.unwto.org/en/press-release/2012-05-07/intern ational-tourism-receipts-surpass-us-1-trillion-2011, (accessed 3 September 2012)
UNCTAD (2010), "Trade and Environment Review, Promoting Poles of Clean Growth to Foster the Transition to a More Sustainable Economy", United Nations, Geneva.
Virgin (2012), "Virgin Group's Corporate Responsibility and Sustainable Development Report 2010", available at: http://www.virgin.com/people-and-planet/blog/virgin-group-s-corporate-responsibility-and-sustainable-development-report-2010, (accessed 3 September 2012).

VisitBritain (2003), "Employment Generated by Tourism in Britain", Available at: http://www.visitbritain.org/Images/Employment%20gatefold%20PDF_tcm29-15224.pdf, (accessed 3 September 2012).

Willard, B. (2012), "3 Sustainability Models, Building the Next Sustainable Wave", available at: http://sustainabilityadvantage.com/products/index.html, (accessed 24 July 2012).

World Commission on Environment and Development (WCED) (1987), "Our Common Future", Oxford University Press, New York NY.

CONTRIBUTORS

Editors

Professor Demetris Vrontis is a Professor of Marketing and a Dean and Director at the University of Nicosia, Cyprus. Dr Vrontis is the Editor-in-Chief of the EuroMed Journal of Business and the President of the EuroMed Research Business Institute. His prime research interests are in strategic marketing planning, branding, marketing communications and wine marketing; areas in which he has widely published in about 100 refereed journals and 18 books *and* gave numerous presentations in conferences around the globe. Professor Vrontis is a Fellow Member and certified Chartered Marketer of the Chartered Institute of Marketing and a Chartered Business and Chartered Marketing Consultant certified by the Chartered Association of Business Administrators. Professor Vrontis also serves as a consultant and member of Board of Directors to a number of international companies.

Academic journal publications include the Journal of Business Research, the Journal of Marketing Management, the International Marketing Review, the European Business Review, the Journal of General Management, the Journal of Marketing Communications, the Journal of Business and Industrial Marketing, the Cross Cultural Management: An Inter. Journal, the Marketing Intelligence and Planning, the Journal of Product and Brand Management, the Journal of Brand Management, the Marketing Review, the International Journal of Business Studies, the Global Business and Economics Review, the Journal of Textile Institute, the British Food Journal, the World Review of Entrepreneurship, Management and Sustainable Development and many more.

Further information regarding Professor Vrontis can be found at http://unic.academia.edu/DemetrisVrontis

Dr Alkis Thrassou is an Associate Professor at the School of Business, University of Nicosia in Cyprus (EU). He holds a PhD in Strategic Marketing Management from the University of Leeds (UK) and is also a Chartered Marketer (CIM, UK), a Chartered Builder (CIOB, UK) and a Research Fellow of the EuroMed Research Business Institute (EMRBI). In the 1990s he worked as a business and project manager for a consulting firm in Cyprus, leading teams of professionals through many projects of varying size and nature. Dr Thrassou subsequently joined the Marketing Department of the University of Nicosia, involving himself in various scholarly activities, lecturing on marketing-related subjects at all levels, and undertaking extensive research in the fields of strategic marketing, services and consumer behaviour. He served as the Head of the Marketing Department and was also a member of the University Council. His work has been published in dozens of prominent scientific journals, books and conference proceedings. Dr Thrassou continues to retain strong ties with the industry, acting also as a consultant to companies across many economic sectors.

Contributors (alphabetic order)

Monaliz Amirkhanpour (PhD Candidate, University of Gloucestershire, UK). Her research is focused on the application of mobile marketing as a promotional channel within the retail industry. She holds an MBA (with Distinction) from the University of Nicosia (Cyprus) and a BSc in Computer Science from the University of Indianapolis (USA).

Professor Kip Becker Is the Chairman, Department of Administrative Sciences. With over sixty publications, he is editor of Journal of Transnational Management, co-editor of the Journal of Euromarketing and on seven editorial review boards. Experiences include: TDX systems, Cable and Wireless Ltd.; U.S. Department of Justice; Presidential task force and army helicopter pilot. www.bu.edu/GoGlobaL

Dr Stefano Bresciani is a Researcher in Business Management at the University of Turin, Italy. His prime research interests are in innovation and business management. He is the Editor-in-Chief of *Management* and of *Global Perspective on Engineering Management*, the Country Director for Italy of the EuroMed Research Business Institute (EMRBI), and Chairman of the EMRBI Research Group on "Multinational R&D, embeddedness, and innovation".

Professor Robert S. Bristow is Professor and Chair in the Department of Geography and Regional Planning at Westfield State University, Massachusetts, USA. His current research focus is in sustainable tourism. Examples of journal articles authored by Prof. Bristow include Tourism Review, Journal of Geography in Higher Education, Tourism Geographies, and Geografiska Annaler.

Professor Bernd Britzelmaier is a professor for finance and accounting at Pforzheim University. He has written and edited a dozen books for publishing houses like Pearson and Springer and a number of articles in the fields of Finance, Accounting and Controlling. He is the associate editor of the World Review of Entrepreneurship, Management and Sustainable Development and is a member of several editorial boards.

Dr Hela Chebbi is a Professor of Strategic Management and the Director of the Observatory and Research Center in Entrepreneurship at EDC-Paris. Her research interests are focused on Innovation/Corporate Entrepreneurship and Transnational Management. She has published several book chapters and articles in numerous refereed journals (Qualitative Market Research, World Review of Entrepreneurship, Management and Entrepreneurship),

Professor John C. Crotts is a Professor of Hospitality and Tourism Management at the College of Charleston, USA. Prior to this position, he lectured on tourism subjects at Otago University, NZ and was Director of the University of Florida's Center for Tourism Research and Development. His research encompasses the areas of economic psychology.

Dr Carrie Foster is a Visiting Lecturer at Chester University Business School, and Organization Development practitioner who specializes in the facilitation of Organization and People Development interventions that deliver added value and a measurable ROI to bottom line performance.

Thoukis Georgiou is a PhD candidate at the University of Gloucestershire Business School in the UK. The foundation of his research interest is a conceptual framework towards succession effectiveness in the family wineries of Cyprus. At this basis, he presented three papers to conferences on a European and global basis.

Dr Ian Jenkins has worked in the tourism/ leisure industries for the last twenty four years as a director of research, lecturer, and consultant. This work has resulted in numerous academic and industry publications and his research and consultancy expertise encompasses niche tourism through to safety management of tourism products.

Dr Saroj Kumar Datta is Senior Professor and Dean, VIT Business School, VIT University, India; He has over 25 years of industry experience (in USA and India) and more than 15 years of academic experience in management area. He has also authored several books and his scholarly research papers published extensively in different national and international journals.

Sukanya Kundu is an Assistant Professor in Operations Management at the Alliance School of Business, Alliance University. She worked as Assistant Professor in MITS, Rajasthan and IMT, Ghaziabad. She has a Master of Computer Application and Post Graduate Diploma in Business Management and is presently pursuing her Ph D. Sukanya has 6 years of experience in IT industry. Her research papers have been published in national and international journals of repute.

Dr Gabriella Mandara in Assistant Professor in Business Strategy at Second University of Naples. She got a PhD in Entrepreneurship and Innovation. During her PhD visiting at the Glasgow Caledonian University, she wrote a doctoral dissertation on the Internationalisation of fashion retailers. She wrote on entrepreneurship and technology transfer.

Professor Christopher M. Moore is Chair in Marketing / Associate Dean at Glasgow Caledonian University. His research area is fashion and luxury brand internationalisation. He has published in the European Journal of Marketing and other important journals. He currently consults to Marks & Spencer, Top Shop and Miss Selfridge.

Dr Neil Moore has a PhD and is a Senior Lecturer at the University of Chester. He lectures, tutors and consults in a range of areas. These include international business, management development, contemporary management issues in small and medium sized enterprises and sport management. He is also an Associate Editor of the International Journal of Organizational Analysis.

Professor Angelo Nicolaides joined Vaal University of Technology in 2008. He is a member of the IIPE and Ethics South Africa, as well as a member of the SAIMS and a Master HR Practitioner of the SABPP and a mentor to industry and government. His major interest area is Ethics.

Dr Helena Nobre is a Ph.D. in Management Science. She is an Assistant Professor of Marketing at University of Minho (Portugal), an Adjunt Assistant Professor at Boston University, has numerous publications and is on the editorial board of Journal of Transnational Management. Helena

Nobre's research was financed by national funds through Foundation for Science and Technology.

Carola Normann was awarded the degree of Master of Controlling, Finance and Accounting from Pforzheim University in 2011. She is now a part-time student in a PhD programme at the University of Chester (UK). She is working in the controlling department of a German company in the household appliance industry.

Professor Bernard Paranque is professor at Euromed Management/Kedge Business School. He holds the AG2R LA MONDIALE Chair in "Finance Reconsidered: Investment, Solidarities and Responsibility". His research focuses on the "Commons", and social and solidarity economy with a particular specialisation in the specific organisations known as "cooperatives". Publications available at www.ssrn.com.

Anastasia Paul was born in Russia. After having finished her degree in education she moved to Germany to study Controlling, Finance and Accounting at Pforzheim University. Since 2011 she is working in the controlling department of Bosch Austria where she is responsible for the "Gear pump and Components" area.

Dr Constantinos-Vasilios Priporas is Senior Lecturer in Marketing at Middlesex University Business School. He has published in various international journals and conferences such as Tourism Management, Qualitative Market Research, Journal of Brand Management, Marketing Intelligence & Planning. He is an ad hoc reviewer of academic journals, and conferences papers.

Dr Ruth Rios-Morales is Deputy Director of Research at Les Roches–Gruyère, University of Applied Sciences, Switzerland. Ruth is also Country Director for Switzerland of the EuroMed Research Business Institute. Prior to this position, Ruth taught international business in Trinity College Dublin. Ruth has conducted advanced research in international business and finance.

Dr Matteo Rossi is an Assistant Professor of Corporate Finance at the University of Sannio, Italy. His main publications are Italian Wine Firms: Strategic Branding and Wine Performance, Financing innovation: venture capital investments in biotechnology firms and Mergers and Acquisitions In The Hightech Industry: A Literature Review

Dr Max Schweizer heads the Center for Foreign Affairs and Applied Diplomacy at the University of Zurich for Applied Sciences (ZHAW). Max served as a Swiss Diplomat until May 2012 in Africa, Asia and Europe. He studied Geography, History and Political Science at the University of Zurich, where he wrote his doctoral thesis.

Professor Peter Stokes, Deputy Dean Faculty of Business Enterprise and Lifelong Learning at the University of Chester, is Editor-in-Chief of the *International Journal of Organizational Analysis*, EMRBI UK Country Director and UK Ambassador for the *Association de Gestion des Resources Humaines*.

Constantinos Theodoridis is a Lecturer in Retail Management in Lancashire Business School. He holds an MBA from the Nottingham Trent University, and an MRes from the Manchester Metropolitan University. His research focuses on retail strategy. He is an active researcher and his work has appeared in various conferences and journals.

Dr Alkis Thrassou is an Associate Professor at the School of Business, University of Nicosia (Cyprus). He holds a PhD from the University of Leeds (UK) and is a Chartered Marketer, a Chartered Builder and an EMRBI Research Fellow. He published dozens of prominent scientific works and retains strong industry ties.

Dr Evangelos Tsoukatos is Assistant Professor, Management, at the Technological Educational Institute of Crete, Greece. He has earned his Ph.D. from Lancaster University - Management School and is currently Director for Operations and Development of EMRBI. Dr Tsoukatos's full resume with experience, awards and publications is accessible at http://teicrete.academia.edu/EvangelosTsoukatos

Professor Demetris Vrontis, Professor of Marketing and Dean and Director at the University of Nicosia (Cyprus). Dr Vrontis is the Editor-in-Chief of the EuroMed Journal of Business and the President of the EuroMed Research Business Institute. His prime research interests are in strategic marketing planning, branding, marketing communications and wine marketing, areas in which he has widely published and consulted.

Further information regarding Professor Vrontis can be found at http://unic.academia.edu/DemetrisVrontis

Dr Dorra Yahiaoui is a Professor of Human Resource Management and a chair of the "Cross-cultural Management" research group at Normandy Business School. Her research area is focused on International Transfer of HRM practices and Transnational Management. She has published several book chapters and articles in different academic journals (World Review of Entrepreneurship, Journal of Transnational Management, Qualitative Market Research).